LEISURE AND AGING
ULYSSEAN LIVING IN LATER LIFE

THIRD EDITION

FRANCIS A. McGUIRE

ROSANGELA K. BOYD

RAYMOND E. TEDRICK

SAGAMORE PUBLISHING
Champaign, IL

Interior and Cover Design: K. Jeffrey Higgerson

ISBN: 1-57167-552-3
Library of Congress Card Number: 2003099219

www.SagamorePub.com

Printed in the United States

CONTENTS

ACKNOWLEDGMENTS

Just as in the first and second editions of this book, we are indebted to all our students who helped form and solidify many of our ideas. We would be remiss if we did not acknowledge colleagues from our academic departments who have offered encouragement and advice not only for this book but also throughout our careers. We also thank our spouses who willingly gave us the unobligated hours required to finish a task of this magnitude. David Dillard, a librarian to Temple University, was crucial in finding many of the resources cited in Chapter 8. Finally, and most importantly, we thank our parents, our first, and best, teachers.

INTRODUCTION

We are in the midst of the graying of America. There are more people over the age of 65 than there have ever been, and this trend will continue well into the future. This cadre of older individuals is unlike any seen before. They are generally healthier, more financially secure, and more independent than previous cohorts. In addition, they are probably more visible and vocal than previous groups of older individuals. In fact, it is impossible to watch the news, walk into a grocery store, or board an airplane without coming into contact with older individuals.

However, the increasing presence of elderly people in our society has not necessarily resulted in a deeper understanding of this group. Certainly, the work of gerontologists has cleared up many misconceptions of older people and the aging process. We know more about the mechanisms of aging, physical as well as social, than at any time in history. Our knowledge base is expanding every year. Unfortunately, many have not received these messages. An archaic view of aging still is firmly entrenched in our society. It is viewed as a time of loss and decline with little hope for the future. In fact, to speak about the future and old age together will strike many as ludicrous. What is the future in aging within this perspective? At best, stability for as long as possible; at worst, death after confinement to a long-term care facility. Unfortunately, our misguided images often interfere with our ability to effectively work with this population.

Several years ago, there was a popular book entitled *All I Really Need to Know I Learned in Kindergarten,* which purported to identify life's most important lessons. The author's thesis was that many of these lessons were learned early in life. A similar compartmentalizing of life into periods of appropriateness appears to extend into other areas. There is a time to learn and a time to earn, a time to grow and a time to fade away. The result of this perspective has been the placing of limits on the later years. Individuals who break out of this mold are viewed as media marvels meriting special attention. For example, June inevitably brings stories of septuagenarians graduating from college, December stories typically include pieces on extremely active older volunteers, and in April the media celebrates individuals who have achieved athletic milestones later in life. The focus of these stories is the remarkable ability to accomplish these things in spite of being old. We view this perspective as inappropriate.

People do not do things in spite of being old. Rather, they achieve success because of who they are. Being old should not be viewed as a handicap to accomplishing anything. In fact, the most difficult thing many people face in reaching their goals is a resistant society that places obstacles in the way of many older people and prohibits them from reaching their potential.

A major concern of gerontologists is the quality of life of older individuals. The role of activities in enhancing later life is often examined as part of this concern. The use of leisure, simply defined as freely chosen activities, to fill time and replace what has been lost through retirement appears to be an important element in the quality of life. However, this perspective on activities fails to acknowledge the powerful force they can be. Rather than being merely a substitute for what has been lost, leisure can provide new pathways to growth and development. People who select this approach are not unusual or overachievers. They are instead individuals dedicated to living. We have adopted the term "Ulyssean" from McLeish (1976) to describe this approach. The Ulyssean approach varies. It does not imply anything about the quantity of activities. It does, however, require a willingness to be open to new ideas and opportunities. The perspective is built upon the belief that each year of life provides occasions for renewal as well as growth. Trained professionals who are able to assist older individuals in using leisure to contribute to the quality of life can enhance these opportunities.

This book is designed to help identify ways leisure can contribute to later life. It links the aging process and leisure to Ulyssean living. This is accomplished in three ways. First, basic information about aging and the aging process is provided. The first five chapters are devoted to helping develop an understanding of what happens as people age. The focus is on social, biological, cognitive, and psychological factors related to aging. The relationship of these factors to Ulyssean living is explored throughout this section. The second part of the book explores leisure and its role in later life. Chapters 6 through 9 are designed to increase knowledge of the place of leisure in the later years, with particular attention paid to the Ulyssean approach. The final section of the book examines the environments where aging occurs. Community as well as institutional settings are discussed as we detail the relationship of the environment to the quality of life.

Since the publication of the first edition of this book there have been changes in the aging population in America and the emergence of a changing perspective on this population. Data (National Institute of Health, 2001) indicate that from 1982 to 1999 the percentage of older Americans with disabilities declined from 26.2 percent to 19.7 percent. This has occurred in conjunction with a 30 percent increase in the 55 and over population during that same time span. These data point dramatically toward a reality of aging, a growing population healthier than at any time in our country's history. Perhaps more important than these changes has been the emergence of a perspective that focuses on successful aging. The work of individuals including Rowe and Kahn (1998), described later in this book, has been adopted by other gerontologists and is becoming an increasingly acceptable paradigm for examining the aging process.

George Valliant (2002) identified the contradictory messages we receive about aging: longer life, high-achieving older individuals, abused elders in long-term care facilities, economically deprived people forced by financial need to eat dog food. All are accurate images of aging, none are accurate images of aging. Valliant mused, "Some may argue that the term *successful aging* is an oxymoron. For is *aging* inextricably associated with loss decline, and approaching death? Is not success inextricably associated with gain, winning, and a zestful life?" (p. 5). This book provides a framework for understanding successful aging, Ulyssean living. Within this framework what matters in later life is not what happens to people as they age, but rather what individuals do as they age. We know there will be decline and loss as people reach their later years. However, we also know that growth and development can occur at any age.

One caution is needed at this point. The assumption in many parks and recreation curricula seems to be that aging is the purview of therapeutic recreation programs. Students who are interested in working with older individuals are seen as needing a therapeutic recreation emphasis to be effective professionals. The authors of this book do not share that perspective. Certainly, there are subgroups within the aging population who do need therapeutic intervention. There are older adults with mental health problems, developmental disabilities, and cognitive and physical impairments. Although this book includes material related to these groups, the focus is not on these special populations. Rather, the intent is to provide an overview of the aging process and its relationship to leisure. Further study is clearly needed if the reader's interest is in working with subgroups of elderly.

ONE

THE AGING JOURNEY

This book is about two misunderstood concepts: aging and leisure. Aging is typically viewed as a largely undesirable period of life during which a series of physical, cognitive, social, and emotional declines occur. Leisure is often seen as somewhat frivolous and certainly secondary to the more serious business of life. The authors of this book disagree with both perspectives, and in fact, view aging as a natural part of the life cycle, accompanied by advantages as well as losses. Leisure is a primary realm of behavior during which great personal growth and development can occur. This book is about the joining of these two forces.

As a culture, we have tended to perceive old age as a time set apart from the rest of life. To many it has been seen as a problem, and older individuals are sometimes viewed as part of the problem. They may be viewed as individuals whose time has come and gone and who have now moved to the fringe of society.

This perception of social uselessness has frequently been accompanied by personal hopelessness. Decisions are made for people solely on the basis of age. Some believe that the life of the individual ends at 65, when a period of less than full life begins. This attitude is manifested in recreation programs that are designed to help the elderly fill their empty hours and keep them busy until death. Time is viewed as the enemy, and activities are viewed as a weapon to fight it. Fortunately, this outdated perception is changing.

As a result of the growth of gerontology, the study of old age, and an increased awareness of aging, we have come to realize that old age is not a period of problems, unhappiness, and decline. In fact, we now know there is really no such thing as a well-defined period of life that is appropriately labeled "old age." The reality is that later life is a time of opportunity, growth, and happiness for many. Therefore, individuals involved in service delivery to this group must understand aging, the aging process, and leisure from a broad, non-stereotypic perspective. As in all cases of ignorance and prejudice, education is the tool of the informed. There is a responsibility to learn to help older individuals be all they can be.

Most older individuals are not daring or heroic. Rather, they lead simple lives marked by success and failure, continuity and change. There is no such thing as the typical older person. As you read this book, look around you. You may be surrounded by other students. You share at least one characteristic with them: you are all students. Nevertheless, you would probably be unhappy if someone you did not know came along and claimed to know everything she needed to know about you because you are a student. You would even be more unhappy if this person then produced a list of the recreation activities you could participate in and identified them as "appropriate" student activities.

Of course, this would never occur, since we all know students are unique. Similarly, it is not right to label certain activities "senior citizen activities" and base an activity program on them. The purpose of this book is to provide you with accurate information about aging and the aging process. This information should start with the conviction that all individuals, regardless of age, are unique. Increasing age does not eliminate that uniqueness. In fact, it magnifies it.

We are gradually coming to view the advantages of aging as being as real as the disadvantages. One of the advantages that has received little attention is the increase in the amount of unobligated time many individuals have. The authors of this text have conducted many pre-retirement seminars for individuals facing retirement. Inevitably, these programs include sessions on financial planning, health, retirement benefits, and leisure. Just as inevitably, leisure is given the shortest length of time on the program. While each of the other areas may consume a half day or even several days, the session on leisure receives one or two hours on the agenda. This occurs for at least two reasons.

The first is that leisure is not seen as that important. People need fiscal and physical well-being in retirement. Leisure is viewed as secondary to these twin pillars of happiness. The second reason is a perception that leisure will take care of itself. How hard can it be to find something to do with that additional 30 hours per week?

This attitude also appears to pervade the gerontology literature. Relatively little appears in journals such as *The Gerontologist* and *The Journal of Gerontology* pertaining to leisure. In fact, Alexander Comfort's (1976) view of leisure would probably find many supporters today. He wrote, "Leisure is a con." He continued that people "don't need the Coney Island-Retirement Village package which makes them into permanent children; this is good for an afternoon, not for a life-style" (p. 124).

Unfortunately, many leisure professionals have provided unwitting support for Comfort's uncomfortable perspective on leisure. This has resulted from an acceptance of an outdated perspective of old age as a time of loss and decline and a stereotypic view of leisure programs for older people. This text will approach aging from a different perspective and use that perspective to show that leisure is not a con perpetrated upon the elderly, but rather is a potentially powerful force in helping make the later years positive and exhilarating.

A POSITIVE PERSPECTIVE ON AGING

Rowe and Kahn's (1998) groundbreaking book, *Successful Aging*, discusses the failure of gerontologists to incorporate a new, positive view of aging. They wrote, "The progress of gerontology began to stall in the mid-1980s . . . There was a persistent preoccupation with disability, disease, and chronological age, rather than the positive aspects of aging" (p. xi).

They believed a conceptual foundation was required to understand aging and all its components. We agree and have provided such a foundation, or unifying concept. Old age is viewed throughout this text as a stage in the lifecourse. It does not stand alone, apart from all that has come before. It is a time of continued growth and development marked by continuity with the past. The model followed in this book views aging as a journey, or series of journeys, rather than as an arrival at a terminal point in the life span. Within this perspective, the increased unobligated time that many individuals experience is not considered a problem but an opportunity. It is an instrument for growth and development.

John McLeish (1976) coined the term "Ulyssean Adult" to identify individuals who continue to seek new adventures and opportunities in their later years. The prototype for such an individual comes from Ulysses, who was more than 50 years of age when the adventures described in the Odyssey began and close to 70 when he began his last voyage.

According to McLeish, only death can end the journeys of such an individual. The Ulyssean lifestyle should not be limited to the select few blessed with an extraordinary personality. McLeish wrote, "The Ulyssean life is on some term, in small or large arenas, potentially accessible to all men and women" (p. 31). Indeed, McLeish stated:

> To gain entry to the country and company of the Ulyssean people no passport is required. No restrictions exist as to race, class, religion, political ideology, or education—just the reverse. The Ulyssean country is an open commonwealth of older adults of every racial group under the sun; its membership includes every degree of wealth and non-wealth, every level of education, every form of belief and non-belief. Membership has nothing to do with whether one is physically well or dogged by ill-health, whether one is personable or plain, well-travelled or confined to a limited area . . . . It is a process, not a state; a process of *becoming*, and great practitioners of the Ulyssean way would certainly describe themselves as voyagers, not inhabitants (p. 285).

Although McLeish was using the Ulyssean concept to explain creativity in later life, it also provides a conceptual framework for understanding the potential of leisure in late adulthood. To be Ulyssean is to seek out opportunities for growth. Leisure can provide the arena for development. It can also provide a mechanism for developing the skills needed to approach life with the zest and confidence necessary to Ulyssean living.

A Ulyssean life is possible not only in the later years but may be easier to achieve during that period than at any other point in life. McLeish believes a "Ulyssean life is possible, and the Ulyssean way is accessible and free, because in many ways the conditions required for the creative life are *more available* in the later years of adulthood than earlier in life (p. 246). Many older Americans have the time, experience, and freedom needed to enter the Ulyssean world. They are released from many roles, such as work- and family-related, which restrict behavior and limit the opportunity to enter new worlds. Concurrently, many years of experiences provide a plethora of potential paths for Ulyssean journeys.

Dangott and Kalish (1979) supported this belief in the potential for Ulyssean living in the later years. They wrote "the old concept of aging was a downhill path, beginning at age 60 or 50 or even 40 or 30; it implied slow deterioration, accelerating with time. The new concept of aging dispels these grim inaccuracies. Instead of a single downhill path, there can be a network of paths, many going uphill; instead of accelerating deterioration, there can be opportunity for extensive personal growth" (p. 1). Their words are as true today as when they were written. Unfortunately, they have not yet become part of the "conventional wisdom," guiding the delivery of leisure services. Although Dangott and Kalish's belief that aging should be viewed as an opportunity for growth rather than as a period of deterioration was stated approximately 20 years ago, the "old concept" of aging prevails. Rowe and Kahn (1998), directors of the MacArthur Foundation Study of Successful Aging, indicate that the aged are viewed as "sick, demented, frail, weak, disabled, powerless, sexless, passive, alone, unhappy, and unable to learn—in short, a rapidly growing mass of irreversibly ill, irretrievable old Americans" (p. 12).

Calls for a new perspective on aging have been part of the gerontological literature for many years. For example, Prado (1986) called for a perspective change in how aging is viewed. Prado's central thesis is that we retain a view of aging from the era when few people lived past their fifties. This antiquated view of aging sees "the aged as a homogeneous group marked by above-average dependency on others, special economic needs, health problems, and a general decline of competency and productivity" (p. 3).

Prado's perspective is based on the belief that accumulating data on aging pointing toward the revelations it makes about the positive aspects of aging is not enough to change concepts of later life. A shift, or in Prado's words "a new conceptual matrix," in perspective may be needed to bring about a realization of the richness and diversity of aging. The change requires realization that "certain changes that seem real enough in aging are better thought of as a function of what we do than of what we become." Recent evidence indicates that much of what had been seen as part of aging is actually the result of disease, disability, inactivity, and lack of exercise.

An emphasis on old age as a time of decline will result in leisure programs based on stereotypic attitudes of what is appropriate for older people and will result in a limited approach to activity provision. Anything that will help pass the time will do.

Activities that are work-like in nature may be helpful, since they are more palatable to retirees than other activities. Nothing too challenging, strenuous, or new should be attempted, and those individuals who break the mold are seen as media marvels. However, if the positive nature of aging and the role leisure can play in personal growth and development are recognized, programs cannot be constricted by ageistic notions of "appropriate" leisure.

Leisure activities are vehicles. They can be ships upon which individuals embark on Ulyssean journeys. Rather than deciding what activities are best suited for people who share a chronological age, leisure service providers must realize that any activity is a useful vehicle for the journey if the participant so decides. The emphasis shifts from the activity to the individual. As a result, the function of the leisure service provider shifts from activity provider to enabler, guide, facilitator. The individual involved in providing leisure services to older people becomes a member of the crew on the Ulyssean journey. The older individual is in control of the ship. Such a perspective is necessary if leisure is to become one of the uphill paths conceptualized by Dangott and Kalish and not a con foisted upon the elderly.

It is important to look at aging realistically. There are losses, primarily physiological, that are concomitants of the aging process. These declines (see Chapter 3) are a natural part of the aging process. However, they are not the entire story. There are many positive aspects that are necessary to understand if aging is to be realistically perceived. It is necessary to separate the myth of aging from the reality. Much of what we "know" about old age is based on long-standing myths and stereotypes. Two aspects of aging, social and demographic, provide an excellent starting point for what will come later in this book. They provide basic information for a context for viewing aging.

SOCIAL ASPECTS OF AGING

Aging is a multi-faceted process. Later chapters of this book will focus on biological, cognitive and psychological factors in aging. However, the social forces impacting aging may be the most important influences on the aging process. When examining the aging process, it is important to consider both individual and environmental factors, since behavior is a consequence of the interaction of a person with his or her physical and social environment. The following sections will address social factors influencing successful aging. Initially, the changes in social roles will be addressed. Secondly, societal responses to aging will be covered. The focus will be on how professionals working with older adults can assist them in coping with negative changes and maintain a sense of well-being during their Ulyssean journey.

CHANGES IN SOCIAL ROLES

In order to understand social roles, it is necessary to recognize that every individual lives in a social context that influences his or her behavior. The process of "socialization," that is, the process through which we absorb values, beliefs, and knowledge that guide our behavior as a member of a social group, is a lifelong one. From a very young age we are directly or indirectly instructed to behave in ways that conform to the norms created within our social group. We learn to conform as a result of reinforcement or punishment encountered as we interact with other members of the group.

This process also teaches us to assume certain roles. We may carry out a variety of roles, each related to a particular position we occupy in society. For instance, in a family context, we may be parents, siblings, or partners; at work we may be the employee, employer, or co-worker; in the community, we may be a civic leader, a neighbor, or a volunteer. The list varies according to the tasks we carry out. The roles we play are filled with social expectations; it is through a general consistency in behaviors associated with such roles that we are able to establish relationship patterns with one another.

How do social norms and roles change as we age? After conducting a review of literature, MacNeil and Teague (1992) concluded that "there are few norms pertaining to specific behaviors of the elderly, and that the few norms that do exist are primarily extensions of middle adulthood norms" (p. 53). Given the fact that there are no specific norms associated with old age, individuals have more flexibility to choose to behave in ways that have been successful for them in the past. Having no set norms may be perceived as negative if norms are directly associated with having social value; however, when norms are seen as constraints to creativity and choice, their absence may be interpreted as a reward for those individuals who spent much of their life conforming to social demands.

Cox (1998) paints a positive picture of the opportunities future cohorts of older individuals will have. The post-industrial society will see the emergence of recreation, leisure, and education as "legitimate means of enriching the quality of one's life" (p. 54). As a result, old age will be marked by an expanded range of socially acceptable roles. An increased focus of quality of life, concomitant with a decreased focus on the importance of productivity, will place leisure and leisure service providers in the forefront of meeting the needs of individuals in later life.

SOCIAL RESPONSES TO AGING

What do you see when you first meet someone? According to Cuddy and Fiske (2002) age is one of the first characteristics we notice and it drives a great deal of the interaction. We make decisions about how to address the individual, decisions about competence, physical ability and knowledge, as well as draw inferences about political and social beliefs. These decisions are crucial in our treatment of others. How then do we evaluate older individuals upon first meeting them? To a great extent this evaluation may be based on social forces impacting seniors; ageism, myths and stereotypes. Ultimately, however, professionals working with seniors must avoid decision making based on these contrivances. A first step in that direction is recognizing the power of these forces in shaping attitudes and beliefs about older individuals.

The examination of social responses of younger generations toward the elderly is especially relevant if we consider that the percentage of older people in the U.S. population is growing steadily, leaving today's younger cohorts with the responsibility of caring for the welfare of the elderly in the near future. Many of these young individuals will be expected to perform some role that will directly or indirectly affect the well-being of older adults; examples of such roles are: caregivers, service providers, volunteers, and policy makers. Besides the potential to affect service delivery, attitudes may also affect opportunities for social interaction and active involvement available to the older individual. Another rationale presented for the study of social responses toward the elderly is that self-image and consequent behaviors are affected by conceptions of the elderly currently held by society members.

One response to aging is the development of stereotypes, untruths or oversimplifications about a group of people. There are many stereotypes, positive as well as negative, about older individuals. Cuddy and Fiske (2002) proposed that there are two primary dimensions of stereotypes, competence and warmth. Competence relates to issues of independence, skill, and ability, whereas warmth entails trustworthiness, sincerity and friendship. They conducted a series of surveys to examine how a variety of social groups were arranged across the two-dimensional model. A few groups, such as whites, the middle class and Christian women were rated as high on both dimensions and a few, homeless people, poor people, recipients of welfare, were negatively rated on both dimensions. Generally, groups were viewed as high on one of the dimensions and low on the other. Asians, Jews and the wealthy were viewed as competent but cold, whereas older people, along with people with disabilities, were viewed as warm but incompetent. It is interesting to note that many of the negative stereotypes about older people fit the incompetent dimension and the positive stereotypes tend to fit a perception of warmth.

Some authors stress the existence of negative stereotypes about old age (Birchenall & Streight, 1993). Other researchers, like Schonfield (1982), blame methodological inaccuracies for the general assumption that such stereotypes exist. Reviewing the body of research, we may be led to believe that both positions have some merit but cannot stand alone.

After many years researching the topic of social responses toward the elderly, Palmore (1990) summarized the stereotypes, attitudes, and types of discriminant behavior uncovered by his and other investigators' studies. He classifies each concept as negative or positive. More recent evidence continues to document that stereotypes about aging are positive as well as negative and positive associations may be as likely as negative ones (Chasteen, Schwarz, & Park, 2002).

NEGATIVE STEREOTYPES

1. Most older persons are sick or disabled.
2. Most older persons have no sexual activity or desire.
3. Old persons are ugly.
4. Mental abilities start to decline after middle age.
5. Most old persons are "senile."
6. Old workers are not as effective as younger ones.
7. The majority of older persons are socially isolated and lonely.
8. Most older persons live in poverty.
9. Older persons feel miserable (cranky, depressed).

POSITIVE STEREOTYPES

1. Older persons are kind and warm.
2. Most older persons have great wisdom.
3. Older persons are more dependable.
4. Older persons are well off financially.
5. Older persons are a powerful political force.
6. Older persons are free to do whatever they want.
7. It is possible to slow down the aging process.
8. Old age is full of peace and serenity.

NEGATIVE ATTITUDES

1. Very few people perceive the sixties or seventies as the best years of one's life.
2. Most people choose the sixties and seventies as the worst years of a person's life.
3. The older years are the worst because of bad health or physical decline, loneliness, and financial problems.
4. Children prefer being with younger adults rather than older adults.
5. Most people have a mixture of negative and positive attitudes toward the elderly, but few have predominantly positive attitudes.

POSITIVE ATTITUDES

1. Some people look forward to retirement as the "golden years."
2. Society holds pseudopositive attitudes about the elderly, offering compliments even when performance does not meet standards held for younger members of society.

NEGATIVE DISCRIMINATION

1. Employment practices are still discriminatory (e.g., early retirement packages).
2. Governmental agencies providing services to the elderly are found to discriminate, particularly against the oldest age groups.
3. Families discriminate by deferential treatment of the elderly.
4. Housing segregation occurs, with the elderly becoming concentrated in certain areas.
5. Health care practices are still inadequate to cover the needs of older persons.

POSITIVE DISCRIMINATION

1. Tax benefits, discounts, and employment benefits are available.
2. In the political arena, the elderly fare better as candidates for office and enjoy legislative benefits.

3. Medicare is available only for the elderly.
4. Some families see the elderly as matriarchs or patriarchs.
5. Governmental programs support public housing for the elderly, and retirement communities cater exclusively to them.

Rowe and Kahn (1998) reviewed myths about aging and were able to identify the six most common. They were able to debunk each based on the scientific literature in the gerontological field. The myths included:

1. **To be old is to be sick.** The evidence clearly contradicts this belief. People are living longer and healthier than ever. The number of older individuals with disabilities is declining, fewer older individuals are experiencing severe limitations in activities of daily living, and there is agreement that aging and disease are not synonymous. Chapter 3 provides strong evidence for the fallacy of the belief that old is the equivalent of sick.

2. **You can't teach an old dog new tricks.** The evidence (see Chapter 4) indicates learning is a lifelong process. There is no chronological age at which individuals are no longer able to learn.

3. **The horse is out of the barn.** This myth is based on the belief that a lifetime of bad habits cannot be reversed. Smoking, high blood pressure, being overweight, and poor physical fitness all have deleterious effects on the body. However, the belief that there is a point in life at which changes in these behaviors would not be beneficial is untrue. Evidence strongly supports the value of making positive lifestyle changes in old age.

4. **The secret to successful aging is to choose your parents wisely.** Although heredity is related to longevity, there is ample evidence that various environmental factors contribute to physical aging (see Chapter 3 for further details). People are not prisoners of their genes. Lifestyle choices impact the aging process more dramatically than heredity.

5. **The lights may be on but the voltage is low.** This myth relates primarily to sexual activity in later life. While there may be a decrease in sexual activity by some older individuals, many continue to be sexually active. In fact, "Many older people enjoy an active sex life that often is better than their sex life in early adulthood. The idea that your sexual drive dissolves sometime after middle age is nonsense" (Mayo Clinic Health Letter, 1998).

6. **The elderly don't pull their own weight.** Most older individuals are not burdens to society. About 12% were in the labor force in 1997, many more are contributing to society through volunteer efforts, and most are vital members of their communities.

Haim Hazan (2000a) discussed stereotypes in the later years. He claimed that the ambiguity of the information we receive about older people allows the stereotypes to override "our perception of them [the elderly] even in face-to-face interactions" (2000a, p. 15). As a result, stereotypes, rather than accurate perceptions of characteristics, shape our behavior toward older people. Among the stereotypes identified by Hazan are a view of older people as conservative, inflexible and resistant to change, asexual, senile, wise beyond the wisdom of younger individuals, powerless and dependent, stuck in the past, prefer to socialize with others of their age, depressed, unhappy and leading aimless lives. Hazan successfully refutes these with evidence to the contrary. However he also views the existence of stereotypes as a trap distorting self-perception (2000b) among older individuals.

Evidence about the impact on older individuals of myths and stereotypes is mixed. Recent evidence provided by Levy, Slade, Kunkel and Kasl (2002) supported the danger of accepting stereotypic views of old age. They wrote, "Internalized old age stereotypes contribute to the formation of their self-perceptions of aging, which, in turn, can have a physiological outcome" (p. 261). They view aging stereotypes as particularly deleterious because they're acquired by individuals years before they become old, and so they are accepted without questioning their validity. As a result, "When individuals reach old age and the stereotypes become self-relevant, they have already internalized these stereotypes" (p. 261). There is a danger that older individuals accept stereotypic notions of the later years with deleterious effects. The authors of the study examined self-perceptions of aging with a five-item scale: things keep getting worse as I get older; I have as much pep as I did last year; as I get older, I am less useful; I am as happy now as when I was younger; and, as I get older, things are (better, worse, about the same) as I thought they would be. The authors also examined length of life and found that the "median survival of those in the more positive self-perceptions of aging group was 7.6 years longer than the median survival of those in the more negative aging self-stereotype group" (p. 265). In fact, the authors found that self-perceptions of aging have greater impacts on survival than gender, socioeconomic status, functional health and loneliness. Clearly myths and stereotypes impact older individuals in dramatic ways.

The Levy et al. study provides good news as well as bad news. The good news is that positive perceptions of aging can actually increase longevity, while the bad news is that negative messages decrease longevity. As a result, two approaches to addressing the issue of myths and stereotypes are suggested. First, "One approach would emphasize positive stereotypes of aging among the young by such means as promoting positive intergenerational activities" (p. 268). The other approach is to de-emphasize negative stereotypes by engaging older individuals in processes of "self-awareness" designed to examine negative stereotypes and their impacts in later life. Both approaches facilitate Ulyssean living by removing stereotypes as barriers to growth and development.

How can stereotypes be combated? Hazan (2000b) stated that society's images of aging are confirmed when older individuals adopt the images by changing their behavior to conform to the images. The result is a "vicious cycle wherein the behaviour adopted by the elderly reinforces the negative images attached to them" (p. 19). However Hazan also allowed for the possibility that older people have at their disposal various strategies allowing them to negate the consequences of stereotypic images of aging. These include: conformity to expectations when in the company of strangers, but exploration of new self images and social identity when with peers; withdrawal and detachment from a hostile society; rebellion; and, exerting control over symbols, situations and people in order to avoid negative images of aging, for example moving into retirement communities.

Golub, Filipowicz and Langer (2002) suggested that "mindful" engagement may be effective in diminishing stereotypes. Mindfulness involves "actively drawing novel distinctions, questioning new information and its implications, and considering new information from multiple perspectives" (p. 277). They contrast this with mindlessness, "relying on distinctions that have already been drawn and accepting preestablished categories as immutable" (p. 9). Individuals working with older people should be mindful of individuals rather than operating on stereotypes. Golub et al. provide some suggestions of how service providers might be mindful of aging, aging stereotypes and their impacts. Awareness is crucial. Be aware of individual differences rather than broad characteristics of old age. Examine the basis for judging and classifying individuals. Be aware of how stereotypes may result in treatment that supports stereotypes. Be aware of creating environments designed to support stereotypic perspectives rather than Ulyssean living.

Ragan and Bowen (2001) noted the success of accurate information about aging and reinforcement of that information over time in improving perceptions of aging. Myths and stereotypes will yield to reality if planned interventions are put into place. Leisure professionals working with older individuals should incorporate such efforts into their programming.

The existence of myths and stereotypes about aging has implications at the social, as well as the individual, level. Society is deprived of the potential contributions the elderly can make, while the individual may be deprived of opportunities for Ulyssean living.

In addition to stereotypes, some individuals are guilty of ageism, the "biased conception of someone based on his or her chronological age" (Cox, 1993, p. 18). If you have ever been told that you were "too young" to do something, then you have been a victim of ageism. Palmore (2001) identified ageism as "the ultimate prejudice, the last discrimination, the cruelest rejection. I believe it is the third great 'ism' in our society, after racism and sexism" (p. 572). However, Palmore (2001) and Levy and Banaji (2002) agree it is different from the other "isms" since it is frequently unconscious, anyone may become a target of it, and it occurs without intention to harm others. We are typically not aware of our ageism and there are not presently social sanctions against the expression of ageism. While many are hesitant to express racist or sexist attitudes, no similar hesitancy occurs in expressing agonistic attitudes. To find support for that, you only need to visit the greeting card section of a store. It will not be difficult to find greeting cards containing ageistic messages. It is much less likely you will find cards expressing the other "isms." A recent issue of *Sports Illustrated* (June 16, 2003) inadvertently captured the essence of ageism. The following blurb appeared in the "This week's sign of the apocalypse" section:

> "Police in Norway stopped a 94-year-old runner because they thought she had escaped from a nursing home."

The police had an image of what older individuals did, and that did not include jogging. It is doubtful whether their reaction to a 45-year-old runner would have been similar. Older people live in nursing homes and the only logical interpretation of fast movement is that an escape is in progress!

Ageism is pervasive in our society. Palmore (2001) found that 77% of the individuals he studied had experienced at least one incident of ageism. What follows is a partial list of ageistic behaviors Palmore used in conducting his research. It provides an excellent illustration of the components of ageism.

1. I was told a joke that pokes fun at older people.
2. I was sent a birthday card that pokes fun at old people.
3. I was ignored or not taken seriously because of my age.
4. I was called an insulting name related to age.
5. I was patronized or "talked down to" because of my age.
6. I was refused rental housing because of my age.
7. I had difficulty getting a loan because of my age.
8. I was denied a position of leadership because of my age.
9. I was treated with less dignity and respect because of my age.
10. A waiter or waitress ignored me because of my age.
11. A doctor or nurse assumed my ailments were caused by aging.
12. I was denied employment because of my age.
13. Someone assumed I could not hear well because of my age.
14. Someone assumed I could not understand because of my age.
15. Someone told me, "You're too old for that."

Pasupathi and Lockenhoff (2002) examined the behavioral consequences of ageism and identified three patterns of age-differentiated behavior. The first was behaviors effectively distancing, excluding, or marginalizing older individuals compared to younger people. Examples of this behavior include spending less time with older patients by physicians, failing to reinforce dependent behaviors in long-tem care residents and failing to include the concerns of older people in the planning process. This was the most pervasive of the behavioral patterns. Pasupathi and Lockenhof's second behavioral type entailed those beneficial, positive, compassionate and protective of older individuals. Deferential treatment and protecting residents of long-term care facilities would be examples of this type of behavior. The final behavioral category is behaviors that are negative or harmful, and the most clearly ageistic of the three behaviors. Denial of access to services, negative depictions of older people in the media, and use of baby talk when interacting with seniors are examples of this type of behavior. Levy (2001) indicated that ageism not only influences the behavior of caregivers toward older individuals but also directly impacts the behavior of older individuals. For example, her research has documented that performance on memory tasks by seniors is related to exposure to aging stereotypes. Clearly ageism is an insidious "ism" affecting treatment of and behavior of elders.

Ageism is not only pervasive but also difficult to eliminate. Levy and Banji (2002) indicated that even contrary evidence does not reduce an implicit stereotype, those operating below our level of awareness. In fact, evidence of behavior that does not fit a stereotype is viewed as an exception to the rule rather than a reason to change the rule. They provide the example of John Glenn whose successful aging could be dismissed as an anomaly rather than an accurate representation of aging.

The question of how to reduce ageism is important to leisure service providers on several levels. First, we must deal with our own ageism. Awareness that we stereotype older individuals is a first step. However, it is also important to recognize that older individuals themselves may believe in ageistic stereotypes, and there is a danger this may limit their opportunities for Ulyssean living. One of the authors recalls working at a camp for seniors. All participants were in their later years. It was common for people to respond, "I am too old for that" when offered the opportunity to participate in activities such as horseback riding or softball. The solution was to get individuals to try the activity and realize their actual experiences disconfirmed their perceptions. Once an individual tried an activity and succeeded, the concept of being too old was overridden by the enjoyment of the activity.

An affective way of reducing negative perceptions about the elderly is through programs bringing old and young individuals together. The benefits of intergenerational programs have been widely noted (Scannell & Roberts, 1994; Newman, Ward, Smith, Wilsson, McCrea, Calhoun & Kingson, 1997; McGuire & Hawkins, 1999) and should therefore be encouraged in most recreation centers as a means to foster changes in perceptions and create increased opportunities for social interaction and exchange. Not only should younger adults be put in the positions of helpers to the elderly, but they should also have the opportunity to learn from the elderly. Contact is not enough to change attitudes; the quality of the interaction is crucial.

Another factor observed in the literature is that experience working with older adults becomes more effective when combined with instruction. Therefore, a combination of intellectual and effective components should be included when developing intergenerational experiences. We only value what we appreciate; if we want older persons to be valued, we need to create avenues for them to present themselves in a positive light, and for younger generations to learn to appreciate them as individuals, not simply members of a stereotypical group.

The importance of having an accurate knowledge of aging cannot be overstated. The leisure service provider lacking such knowledge risks treating the individuals served in such a way that stereotypical beliefs are supported. Forgetfulness will be interpreted as senility, any interest in sexuality will support a "dirty old person" image, conservative opinions will signify rigidity, time spent alone will be viewed as a time of isolation and loneliness, a decision to not become involved in activities will be blamed on depression and fear, and automobile accidents will prove it is time to revoke drivers' licenses.

If older individuals are to be viewed as the unique, varied individuals they are, it is necessary to erase the false pictures that have developed in many of us. Whether our function is to facilitate leisure involvement or deal with aging parents, the first step is to gather factual, accurate knowledge of the aging process and the forces experienced by the aging person.

DEMOGRAPHY OF AGING

Prior to examining the forces shaping leisure in later life, it is important to understand the general characteristics of the aging population in America. Demographics provide a composite picture of this group. However, demographics do not provide information about any given individual. Knowing the percentage of individuals residing in urban areas or the proportion of people who are college graduates does not increase knowledge about the individuals behind the statistics. Nevertheless, demographics provide a necessary starting point to understanding the forces resulting in the social phenomenon of aging.

LIFE EXPECTANCY

More people are living longer than ever before. Life expectancy at birth in 1900 was 47.3 years, in 1996 it was 76.1 years and by 2000 had risen to 76.9 years. Recent increases in life expectancy are increasingly due to decreases in mortality among individuals who are middle aged or above. This is in contrast to earlier in the century when increases in life expectancy were attributable primarily to decreased death rates in the young. As a result, life expectancy at age 65 has increased dramatically. Since it is unaffected by infant mortality rates, life expectancy once individuals reach age 65 is a more accurate indicator of later life longevity. In 1900 an individual who was 65 could expect to live an additional 11.9 years. By 1996 this had increased to 17.7 years. By the year 2000 an individual aged 65 could expect to live an additional 17.9 years (Administration on Aging, 1997; 2002). Clearly life does not end at 65!

However, life expectancy varies based on gender and race. There has been a gender gap in life expectancy, with women experiencing greater increases in life expectancy than men. A female born in 1997 had a life expectancy of 79.4 years, whereas a male had a life expectancy of 73.6 years. A woman reaching age 65 in 1997 had a life expectancy of an additional 19.2 years, whereas a similarly aged man could expect to live an additional 15.9 years. In addition to gender differences in life expectancy, there are racial differences. White males born in 1995 had a life expectancy of 73.6 years compared to 64.8 for black males and 74.9 for Hispanic males. The comparable figures for females were 80.1 years, 74.5 years, and 82.2 years. Similar racial differences exist once people reach their 65th birthdays. White females have an average life expectancy of 19.4 years after age 65. Black females have a life expectancy of 17.6 years at age 65, and Hispanic females have an average of 21.8 additional years. The 15.7 years of additional life expectancy at age 65 experienced by white males compares to the 13.6 years for black males and 18.5 years for Hispanic males (Administration on Aging, 1997b; Federal Interagency Forum on Aging-Related Statistics, 2000).

Projections for the year 2010 indicate that 65-year-old men will have a life expectancy of 16.2 years and women can expect 21 additional years of life at age 65. Obviously, life does not end at 65 or some other arbitrarily defined benchmark. Many more years are available for growth, developments, and change.

AGE COMPOSITION

The American population is growing older. In 1900, fewer than four percent of the population was 65 or over. By 2000 this had increased to 12.4 percent. This represents approximately 35 million individuals. Every day approximately 5,570 individuals celebrate their 65th birthday, and the net increase in the 65 and over population is 650 every day! The projections for the future indicate this aging trend will continue. The Census Bureau's "middle series" projections have the over 65 population doubling by the year 2050 to 80 million. The aging of the baby boom could result in one in five Americans being over the age of 65 by 2050 or earlier (U.S. Census Bureau, 1997; Federal Interagency Forum on Aging-Related Statistics, 2000).

The increase in the population of individuals 85 years of age or over, frequently labeled "the oldest old," has been dramatic. In fact, they are the fastest growing age group. There was a 274 percent increase in the number of people 85 or over between 1960 and 1994, and they now compose 10 percent of the entire elderly population. By the year 2050, the oldest old will make up 24 percent of the 65 and over population and five percent of the total population of this country (U.S. Census Bureau, 1997; Administration on Aging, 2002).

RACE AND ETHNICITY

The proportion of the white population over the age of 65 is greater than the proportion of either the black or Hispanic population. Approximately 15 percent of the white population is 65 or over. This compares to 8.2 percent of the non-Hispanic black population, 4.9 percent of the Hispanic population, and 7.8 percent of the American Indians and Native Alaskans, and 7.8 percent of the Asians and Pacific Islanders (Administration on Aging, 2002).

The proportion of the older population composed of minorities is increasing. According to the Administration on Aging (2002), 16.4 percent of the elderly population in the United States is other than non-Hispanic white. This will increase to approximately 33 percent by 2050.

RESIDENTIAL DISTRIBUTION

Fifty-two percent of all individuals 65 years of age or over resided in nine states: California, Florida, New York, Pennsylvania, Texas, Illinois, Ohio, Michigan, and New Jersey. Each of these states had more than one million residents aged at least 65. In 2000 Florida had the highest proportion of residents 65 or over, 18.1 percent. It was followed by Pennsylvania (15.6 percent), West Virginia (15.6 percent), Iowa (15.2 percent) and North Dakota (15.0 percent). The states with the smallest proportion of older residents were Alaska (5.8 percent), Utah (9.2 percent), Georgia (9.9 percent), California (10.4 percent), and Texas (10.4 percent). Fourteen states had an increase of more than 20 percent in the 65 or over population between 1990 and 2000. The states with the greatest increase were Nevada (71.5 percent), Alaska (59.6 percent), Arizona (39 percent), New Mexico (30.1 percent), Hawaii (28.5 percent) Utah (26.9 percent), Colorado (26.3 percent), and Delaware (26.0 percent) (Administration on Aging, 2002, Federal Interagency Forum on Aging-Related Statistics, 2000).

In 2000, most older people lived in family settings. The most common living arrangement was with one's spouse. Seventy-three percent of all males and 41 percent of females aged 65 or above lived with their spouse (Administration on Aging, 2002). On the other hand, 17 percent of men and 40 percent of women lived alone. The number of elderly living alone increases with advancing age. In 1997 more than half (57 percent) of all women and 32 percent of men over 85 live alone (U.S. Census Bureau, 1997; Administration on Aging, 2002; Federal Interagency Forum on Aging-Related Statistics, 2000).

Few older individuals reside in nursing homes. In 2000, only 4.5 percent of the over-65 population were in a long-term care facility. However, 18.2 percent of those 85 or over were living in this setting (Administration on Aging, 2002).

GENDER

Women outlive men, and as a result there are more women than men in the elderly population. For every two males aged 65 or over there are approximately three females. With increasing age there is an increasing disparity in the number of men and women. The ratio of women to men in the 65 to 69 population is six to five. However, the discrepancy between the number of women and the number of men increases to five women for every two men in the 85 and over population (U.S. Census Bureau, 1997; Administration on Aging, 2002).

MARITAL STATUS

One result of the longer life expectancy of women is a likelihood they will outlive their husbands. In fact, 73 percent of noninstitutionalized older men were married and living with their spouses in 2001, while only 41 percent of the older women were living with their spouses.

Approximately 46 percent of all older women were widows, a percentage that increases to 77 percent of women 85 or older. Among men aged 85 or older, 42 percent are widowed (Administration on Aging, 2002; Federal Interagency Forum on Aging Related Statistics, 2000).

ECONOMIC CHARACTERISTICS

The older population is poorer than the general population. However, there is great variation in the financial status of the elderly. The Administration on Aging (2002) reports that in 2001 the median income of older individuals was $19,688 for males and $11,313 for females. For households headed by individuals 65 years of age or over median income was $33,938. Families where the head was white had a median income of $34,661, whereas the median income for African-Americans was $26,610 and for Hispanics was $24,287 (Administration on Aging, 2002).

Large numbers of older individuals live below the poverty level, 10.1 percent. However, an additional 6.5 percent of all individuals 65 and over were classified as "near-poor." These people had incomes within 125 percent of the poverty level. The poverty rate was higher among blacks (21.9 percent) and Hispanics (21.8 percent) than among whites (8.9 percent). Older women (12.4 percent) had higher poverty rates than men (7.0 percent) and older persons living alone (19.7 percent) were more likely to be in poverty than those living with family (5.5 percent) (Administration on Aging, 2002).

The meaning of limited income is dramatic in the later years. According to Harris (1978), "Income is the crucial determinant of how the aged live. The level, adequacy and maintenance of income directly affect other aspects of the lives of the elderly" (p. 36).

HEALTH CHARACTERISTICS

In addition to reporting incomes below those of younger people, aging individuals also experience poor health. In 2000, 27 percent of all individuals aged 65 or over rated their own health as fair or poor whereas only nine percent of all adults rated their health at that level. More than 41 percent of older African Americans and 35 percent of older Hispanics rated their heath as fair or poor, compared to 26 percent of older whites. Poor health impacted the daily lives of older individuals. More than 26 percent of individuals aged 65 to 74 reported limitations in activities because of health reasons. Among those at least 75 years of age, 45 percent reported activity limitations because of chronic conditions (Administration on Aging, 2002).

The leading cause of death among older individuals is heart disease followed by cancer and stroke. The rate of death from both heart disease and stroke has decreased by approximately one third since 1980. However, there has been a large increase in deaths from diabetes (32 percent) and chronic pulmonary diseases (57 percent) during that same period of time (Federal Interagency Forum on Aging Related Statistics, 2000).

CONCLUSION

The data reported above provide a macro-level perspective of the aging population in the United States. They form a starting point from which to build an understanding of this age group. However, the reader should not lose sight of the individuals making up the statistics. As people age, they become increasingly unique. Therefore, it is impossible to make predictions about the behavior of older people based on the above information. According to Kalish (1975):

> Highly accurate predictions can be made about newborns based only on knowing their ages and that they are basically normal. As people become older, our ability to predict behavior simply from knowing a person's chronological age diminishes . . . In brief, older adults vary more in biological and behavioral functioning than do younger adults (p. 4).

As Myers (1990) indicated, "Traditionally we have distinguished between aging as an individual phenomenon and aging as an aggregative process through which population structure is modified" (p. 21). Generally, individuals providing leisure services will be more concerned with aging at the individual level rather than at the structural level. Services should be based on the needs of each individual. Nevertheless, an understanding of aging in the aggregate is significant for the development of policy related to leisure services.

An equally important approach is to examine subgroups of the aging population. For example, the oldest old, those 85 years of age and over, are receiving increased attention. They can be defined by their specialized needs and by the level of services needed. Later chapters of this book will examine several subpopulations of the elderly.

The perspective we take toward aging will influence the services we provide. If the later years are viewed as a time of decline, lost hope, and ultimately death, services will be based on maintaining functioning to as great a degree as possible while placing minimal demands and expectations on the individual.

An alternative perspective, and the one to be pursued in this book, is what Kalish identified as a Personal Growth Model of Aging over 15 years ago (1979). As a result of role loss (viewed as an opportunity, not a problem), the reduced need to be constrained by social convention, increased discretionary time, and motivation growing out of knowledge that time is finite, older individuals have the opportunity to enter a new stage of development marked by growth and expansion. The Ulyssean lifestyle described in this chapter is harmonious with the personal growth model.

Although there are losses that accompany the aging process—some biological and necessary but many social and contrived—these do not negate the opportunity for growth. All periods of the life cycle are marked by events and situations that are potentially confining.

The high school student without money, the individual committed to caring for children and unable to attend law school, the 48-year-old executive unable to quit her job and become an artist because she fears an uncertain future—all are operating under constraints. They are no less burdened than the 70-year-old with arthritis.

These individuals have the potential to change their situations, or at least accept them and begin a Ulyssean journey. The help of a trained professional may be needed. This book is the start of your Ulyssean journey toward becoming a trained professional prepared to deliver leisure services. As you examine the information to be presented, remember the later years can be one of the freest, most fulfilling periods of life. Many individuals will have more unobligated time than ever. Older people are people first and only incidentally "old" as a result of the labeling process experienced by all groups. It does not mean infirm, disabled, or used up. It identifies an individual who has successfully negotiated at least 65 years of life, nothing more and nothing less. If we allow ageism, myths and stereotypes to shape our view of older people and drive the program planning process, we will deprive people of the opportunity for Ulyssean living.

TWO

THEORETICAL PERSPECTIVES ON AGING

By Bryan McCormick and Francis McGuire

Approaches to studying aging face some difficulty, as there is disagreement over what is meant by the very term "aging." After all, the process of aging in its most comprehensive sense begins at birth and ends with death. We are all currently in the process of aging. An improvement might be to substitute the term "old age" in order to specify a particular period in a lifetime of aging. Yet even the term "old age" presents some ambiguity. When does one become "old"? While I may be considered "old" by my elementary school-aged children, I am still considered "young" by my 80-year-old grandparents. Much effort has gone into attempting to understand the aging process, often at the theoretical level. This chapter explores these attempts to address the particular experiences of people in later life and to identify how it is qualitatively different from younger age periods.

THEORETICAL PERSPECTIVES ON AGING

Early approaches to theories of aging examined the experience of aging from one of two perspectives. Either they focused on the personal experience of aging as related to change and adaptation in later life, or they focused on social factors that shape the experiences of later life. More recently, theories of aging have tried to incorporate both individual experiences and social factors into explanations of later life experience. This chapter presents an overview of eleven major theories related to aging and later life. These theories were selected to be representative of general perspectives on the experience of aging. However, readers should be aware that a number of other theories of aging have been proposed.

PERSONAL EXPERIENCE OF LATER LIFE

Theories such as disengagement theory (Cumming & Henry, 1961), activity theory (Lemon, Bengston, & Peterson, 1972; Longino & Kart, 1982), and continuity theory (Atchley, 1977; Neugarten, Havighurst, & Tobin, 1968), have all presented ideas about the experience of becoming older. In particular, these theories have tended to use the concept of "successful aging" as an indication of personal experience in later life. While the three theories share a focus on aging successfully, they are based on different general social-psychological theories and, as a result, characterize the process and outcomes of aging differently. The early theories presented below continue to have a presence in the literature. In addition, they provide a commonsense view of aging. Each reflects popular conceptualizations of aging and each has some merits, providing insight into potential mechanisms for successful aging. Therefore, they are a starting place for looking at theoretical perspectives on aging. A brief presentation of each of these theories, in terms of characteristic processes and outcomes, follows.

DISENGAGEMENT THEORY

Disengagement theory was one of the first theories on aging to be explicitly stated. The theory was developed by Cumming and Henry (1961) based on data collected from 279 white adults between the ages of 50 and 80 years old residing in Kansas City. According to disengagement theory, aging in later life is a process characterized by gradual social disconnection (Cumming & Henry, 1961). This disconnection takes place through the severing of relationships and through a change in the nature of remaining relationships. Further, according to disengagement theory, this process of social disconnection is beneficial both to the individual and society.

PROCESS OF DISENGAGEMENT

The first aspect of disengagement theory is that there is a severing of relationships. According to the theory, the process of disconnection can be seen in the reduction in individuals' role counts (the number and variety of interactions with others), interactions (the density or amount of time spent in interaction with others), and social life space (the number of interactions engaged in during the past month). Overall, "The aging person sees fewer kinds of people, less often, and for decreasing periods of time as he grows older" (Cumming & Henry, 1961, p. 51). However, not all relationships are disengaged from equally. Kin relationships, particularly relationships with children, tend to be the most enduring.

In addition, disengagement theory argues that not only are social ties severed, but those relationships that are retained change in nature. These changes entail a shift in the quality and goal orientation of remaining relationships. As people age and disengage, they are less likely to seek love and approval from those with whom they retain social ties. The implication of this aspect of disengagement theory is that as people age they become less concerned with others' approval and more likely to act on egocentric interest. That is, not only does aging include a disengagement from social relations in terms of the number of social ties, it also entails a disengagement from social expectations of relationships.

OUTCOMES OF DISENGAGEMENT

One of the basic beliefs of disengagement theory is that this process of disengagement is one of mutual satisfaction between the individual and society. In the view of disengagement theory, older people want to gradually separate themselves from society in anticipation of final disengagement (death), and society needs them to disengage in order to make room for younger generations.

While Cumming and Henry (1961) identified this process as one of mutual satisfaction for both the individual and society, they also note that there are a number of variants in terms of general disengagement. Cumming and Henry (1961) noted the following variants:

> When both the individual and society are ready for disengagement, completed disengagement results. When neither is ready, continuing engagement results. When the individual is ready and society is not, a disjunction between the expectations of the individual and of the members of his social systems results, but usually engagement continues. When society is ready and the individual is not, the result of the disjunction is usually disengagement (p. 214).

They further noted that in the last case, lowered morale can follow. That is, people who are socially pressured to disengage when they are not ready for disengagement would demonstrate patterns of "unsuccessful aging."

However, while disengagement theory characterized most disconnection from society as mutually satisfying for the individual and society, it did identify some difficulties related to disengagement. "Because the abandonment of life's central roles—work for men, marriage and family for women—results in a dramatically reduced social life space, it will result in a crisis and loss of morale unless different roles, appropriate to the disengaged state are available" (Cumming & Henry, 1961, p. 215).

According to the authors, these losses entail for men a lack of instrumental tasks and the loss of status identity. In addition, they noted that resolution to these problems comes through changes in the ego that lead to a preoccupation with inner states. For women, upon death of spouse, losses entail the loss of an emotional social relationship, loss of status derived from their spouse's occupation, and a shift from obligatory (based on husband's social obligations) to voluntary relationships (based on personal interests).

Overall, the characteristic process of aging according to disengagement theory is one of gradual separation of social ties, changes in the character of remaining social ties, increasing constriction of life space, and increasing egocentricity. The outcomes of disengagement are satisfactory to both the individual and society in that there are fewer demands placed on the energies of older people, they can begin to prepare for final disengagement, and through disengagement they "make room" in society for younger generations.

CRITIQUE OF DISENGAGEMENT THEORY

While evidence does suggest that some disengagement occurs in involvements in later life (e.g., Gordon & Gaitz, 1976; McGuire & Dottavio, 1986), these disengagements tend to be most prevalent among the oldest segments of society who reduce involvement in physically demanding engagements. Another consideration is that the sample from which disengagement theory was principally derived was an urban sample. One theory of aging that is presented later argues that in societies based on industrial systems of production, the status of older people declines. The findings of disengagement may be more a function of an urban setting that affords fewer opportunities for meaningful engagement than the results of a "natural" process.

ACTIVITY THEORY

While disengagement theory was one of the first explicitly stated theories of aging, much of the work in social gerontology prior to the 1960s was implicitly based on what was later to be identified as activity theory (Breystpraak, 1984; Lemon, Bengston, & Peterson, 1972; Longino & Kart, 1982). In addition, the formal statement of disengagement theory by Cumming and Henry (1961) gave impetus to the development of a formal statement of activity theory (Breystpraak, 1984). While Havighurst and Albrecht (1953) first identified the principle on which activity theory is based, it was not until 1972 that Lemon et al. (1972) presented a formal statement of activity theory.

PROCESSES OF ACTIVITY

In almost direct opposition to disengagement theory, activity theory maintained that successful aging depended on one's ability to maintain social activity, not disengage from it.

Activity theory has taken much of its foundation from a sociological perspective termed "role theory." Role theory argues that people's identities are largely created through the roles they assume in their lives. People play a number of different roles over their lives. One may assume such roles as "mother or father," "son or daughter," "college student," "professor," or "business executive" just to name a few. We create these roles in our lives through action. However, over the course of our lives, opportunities for acting out certain roles are lost or change significantly.

Activity theory argued that successful aging was dependent on maintenance and enactment of roles through participation in activity. From the perspective of activity theory, the severing of relationships without the creation of new relationships would result in diminished opportunities for role performance.

OUTCOMES OF ACTIVITY

According to activity theory, one's sense of self (self-concept) is strongly dependent on role occupancy. The self-concept is dependent on role occupancy because through the occupation of a role and the interaction with others associated with the role, one's identity is validated by others' responses. This validation of one's self-concept by others is termed "role support."

Activity theory stated that intimate interpersonal activities elicit the greatest role supports, followed by relatively impersonal formal activities, and solitary activities elicit the weakest role supports since others can only provide imagined role support (Lemon et al., 1972). Studies of older people have found that informal social activity is positively related to life satisfaction. (Lemon et al., 1972; Longino & Kart, 1982). Older people who reported the greatest frequencies of social activity also demonstrated the highest levels of life satisfaction. In addition, research has found that solitary activity has little relationship, positive or negative, to life satisfaction (Longino & Kart, 1982).

The loss of roles results in the loss of arenas of role performance and hence a loss of role supports. The loss of role supports equates to a loss of identity, or sense of who one is. At the heart of activity theory is the belief that the loss of activity, without replacing those activities, results in a decrease in life satisfaction (Lemon et al., 1972). That is, according to activity theory, disengagement would constitute unsuccessful aging.

CRITIQUE OF ACTIVITY THEORY

While activity theory has been explicitly stated and empirically tested with some consistency in the findings, there are a number of grounds on which it can be criticized. First, while it has been applied in the area of social gerontology, the principles of the theory are based in role theory. In the formal statements of activity theory, there are no reasons why it is a theory of aging as opposed to a general theory of adaptation and life satisfaction. It is only truly a theory of aging if the underlying belief is that old age is characterized by role loss and/or role change more so than younger ages. To the extent that old age is characterized by role loss, activity theory would come close to disengagement theory.

Another difficulty with activity theory is that the direction of causality is difficult to determine. Are high activity levels cause for high levels of life satisfaction, or are high levels of life satisfaction cause for high levels of activity? Finally, Longino and Kart (1982) note one of the difficulties of this theory. That is, activities provide a context for role performance, and it is the relationship between the actor and the audience that would appear to be more determinative of role support, positive self-concept, and higher life satisfaction than the activity itself.

Activity theory continues to appear in the literature and the link between active engagement and research continues to provide some support for the activity theory. For example, Menec (2003) studied the link between leisure engagement and successful aging, based on a six-year longitudinal study. She found activity level was related to happiness, reduced mortality and better functioning.

CONTINUITY THEORY

A third perspective on aging that developed in gerontological literature was that of continuity theory (Neugarten, Havighurst, & Tobin, 1968; Atchley, 1977). The initial orientation of continuity theory was to link adaptation and adjustment to personality types (Breystpraak, 1984).

Continuity theory held that neither society (in the form of social expectations of disengagement) nor personal action (in the form of high levels of activity) were determinative of successful aging. Instead, the relative degree of success in aging was a function of personal style of adaptation and adjustment that had been developed over the course of one's life.

Neugarten et al. (1968) argued that while there may be older people who disengage and are satisfied with their lives, it is also possible that some people who maintain high activity involvement in later life are also satisfied with their lives. In addition, they also noted that some people may be dissatisfied with disengagement, while others may be dissatisfied with continued high levels of activity involvement.

One basic difference between continuity theory and the other personal experience theories of aging is that while activity and continuity theories sought to characterize the experience of aging as a single pattern, continuity theory sought to identify a variety of patterns of aging.

PROCESS OF CONTINUITY

Atchley (1991) identified that continuity theory was not to be considered as psychologically determinative. That is, while lifestyles are predispositions to continuity, continuity itself is a function of predispositions and situational opportunities. While people may develop characteristic styles of adaptation, these styles can only be enacted if their life situations permit. In terms of life styles, Neugarten, Havighurst, and Tobin (1968) identified eight patterns of aging. These patterns were developed based on (a) personality styles, (b) level of role activity, and (c) life satisfaction.

The first three patterns are grouped under the "integrated" personality type. People with an integrated personality are those who have a complex mental life, intact cognitive abilities, and a positive self-concept.

The pattern for those of the "re-organizer" type is one in which lost opportunities for role activity are substituted with new role activity. These people maintain high levels of role activity.

The second pattern is termed "focused." People exhibiting this pattern of aging demonstrate a narrowing in the variety of roles they play but expansion in the amount of time devoted to those roles.

The third pattern of aging is termed "disengaged." This pattern is representative of disengagement theory. Neugarten et al. (1968) noted that these people disengage as a result of personal preference, not as a result of losses in social opportunities or physical abilities.

The second group of patterns of aging are grouped under the "armored-defended" personality type. People with this personality type are achievement oriented and exhibit high defenses against anxiety. In addition, these people demonstrate a need to "maintain tight control over impulse life" (Neugarten et al., 1968, pp. 175-176).

One pattern of aging exhibited among people with this personality type is that of "holding on." People with this pattern show a need to maintain roles of middle age well into later life. For these people, aging constitutes a threat (Neugarten et al., 1968). The second pattern within the armored-defended personality type are people who exhibit a pattern of "constricted" aging. For this pattern, there is a preoccupation with losses and deficits associated with aging. People demonstrating the "constricted" pattern of aging deal with these threats and losses through limiting their social interactions and expenditure of energies.

The third group of patterns are representative of people demonstrating a "passive-dependent" personality type. People with this personality type show little initiative or energy, and tend to rely heavily on others. One pattern within this personality type is that of "succorance-seeking." These people have high needs for responsiveness from others and adapt to aging through reliance on one or two other people. They seek people from whom they can receive assistance in meeting both material and emotional needs.

The second pattern within the passive-dependent personality type is the "apathetic" pattern. For these people, passivity is "a striking feature of their personality" (Neugarten et al. 1968, p. 176). They exhibit a pattern in which losses resulting from aging tend to reinforce lifelong patterns of apathy and passivity.

The final personality type has only one pattern of aging. Within the "unintegrated" personality type is the pattern of "disorganized" aging. People exhibiting this personality type demonstrate defects in psychological functioning, poor emotional control, and deteriorated cognitive processes. People presenting a "disorganized" pattern show only limited role activity.

OUTCOMES OF CONTINUITY

The outcomes of continuity are dependent on the personal styles of adaptation that older people have developed and used over the course of their lives.

For people with an integrated personality, outcomes of continuity are positive. Essentially, for these people, the degree of role activity has little impact on life satisfaction or successful aging.

For those patterns characteristic of people with armored-defended personality types, life satisfaction tends to be high to medium. For people with this personality type, successful aging is related to their abilities to maintain either high numbers of roles, or maintain a few important roles.

The outcomes of aging for people with passive-dependent personality styles tend to be less positive than the previous two personality styles. Aging among people with passive-dependent personality styles tends to involve both medium to low role activity and life satisfaction.

Finally, people with an unintegrated personality style show poor overall functioning, and, as a result, the experience of aging tends to result in low life satisfaction.

In summary, continuity theory posits that aging in old age is a function of one's adaptational style developed over one's life. Implicit in continuity theory is a view of the individual as seeking to maintain continuity. Thus, continuity is to some extent negotiated based on personal style and situational opportunities.

CRITIQUE OF CONTINUITY THEORY

In general, the personal experience of "successful aging" according to continuity theory is dependent upon people's competence in adapting to change, which has been developed throughout their lives. However, as it is presented, there is no particular reason that continuity theory pertains to the personal experience of later life. To state that people develop styles of adaptation during their lifetimes and that these styles continue into later life says nothing about the qualities of later life. For example, if the theory is truly one of continuity, one would assume that people demonstrating a "constricted" pattern of aging have always had few role activities and medium to low life satisfaction. However, continuity theory does make implicit statements about the quality of aging.

As noted above, activity theory pertains particularly to later life. One assumption is that later life is characterized by role loss more than previous age periods. Continuity theory makes a similar assumption in that unless later life is more characterized by adaptation than earlier periods of life, it ceases to be a theory particularly pertaining to later life.

SUMMARY OF PERSONAL EXPERIENCE THEORIES OF LATER LIFE

Personal experience theories of aging locate the meanings of aging within aging people. Through the severing of social ties, the maintenance of activity, or continuous patterns of adaptation, negotiation of later life is seen. All of the above theories make certain assumptions about later life if they are to be considered characteristic of this part of life. These assumptions are that later life is characterized by severing of social ties, loss of social opportunities, or greater demands for adaptation.

SOCIAL FACTORS SHAPING THE EXPERIENCE OF LATER LIFE

While the above theories of later life have focused on personal experiences, other theories have presented later life in terms of its social context. These theories consider processes of socialization, processes of stratification, and social system-level change as influential on the experience of later life. This section will present factors of socialization, stratification, and systemic social change in terms of their actions and outcomes on the context of later life.

The three theories considered in this section share a common basis in that they consider aging as being influenced by the characteristic processes and structures existing in societies. The processes and structures considered include how people enter and exit various roles how certain roles are distributed based on age, and finally, the process of "modernization" is considered as a number of interacting changes occurring within a society, which create changes in the status of "old age."

SOCIALIZATION TO OLD AGE

Irving Rosow (1974) argued that later life implies a social position. That is, later life is qualitatively different from earlier age periods because the position people in later life occupy in society is different from social positions occupied by people in younger age periods. In order to understand the social position of later life, one has to grasp the transition from one social position to another and the alterations in social identity and relationships that accompany such transitions.

Rosow uses a life-stage approach characterized by successive stages with associated, normatively guided age-sex roles. These stages and their defining roles have distinctive patterns of activity, responsibility, authority, and privilege. Rosow characterized the transition from one stage to the next as "status sequences" and noted that these changes frequently entail rites of passage, social gains, and role continuity.

PROCESS OF SOCIALIZATION TO OLD AGE

As with activity theory, the theory of socialization to old age draws from role theory. However, while activity theory considers the relationship between role occupation and successful aging, socialization to old age considers how people learn and adopt the social role of "old age." Learning and adopting social roles is the process known as socialization. Through the process of socialization, novices in social roles learn new norms, behavior patterns, and self-images and, as a result, are integrated into society. Implicitly, Rosow identified that social integration is the basis for a high quality of life.

Rosow identified three basic conditions for socialization. First, the actor must have knowledge of expected actions based on norms of the new role. Second, the actor must have the ability to perform these actions adequately. Finally, the actor must have sufficient motivation to adopt the new role and associated behaviors.

One difficulty in terms of socialization for older people is the implicitness of the norms applicable to old-age roles. Rosow argued that the only consistently identified norms for older people deal with intergenerational family ties. These norms essentially proscribe forms of relation with family (independence as long as possible, and maintenance of family relations). This absence of norms regarding old age results in a lack of expectations to effectively structure an older person's activities and general life outside of the realm of familial relationships. Rosow (1974) noted "in this sense, an old person's life is basically 'roleless,' unstructured by the society, and conspicuously lacking in norms, especially for nonfamilial relationships" (p. 69).

The second condition for socialization is that the actor must have the ability to perform role-associated actions with some degree of proficiency. What this means is that when engaged in the actions of a particular role, the individual must receive some form of positive feedback that the performance is in keeping with the norms of the role. As noted above, there are few norms to structure old age roles. In the absence of clear norms, or socialization criteria, role performance cannot be defined as either conformist or deviant. Performance, hence, is not available for reward or punishment.

The third condition for effective socialization is that the individual must have sufficient motivation to adopt the new role. That is, the person to be socialized into new roles must want to adopt this new role. According to Rosow (1975) this is problematic for older people in an industrialized society. A number of institutional forces operate in American society to limit and curtail the status of old age.

One change is that rapid developments in science and technology have created a society in which "strategic knowledge" (knowledge that is socially valued) is rapidly replaced. As a result, socially valued knowledge is no longer located in older people but in formal education.

Changes have also occurred in the workforce, such that the greatest labor demands exist in high-technology jobs. Unless older people can keep pace with rapid changes in technical knowledge, their abilities to compete for these jobs is limited. Another factor in the limitation on the status of old age has been the increasing individuation and self-sufficiency associated with industrialization. That is, interdependence has increasingly given way to independence, such that the extent to which younger generations rely on older generations has diminished.

Finally, in a society dedicated to progress, the heritage carried on by present generations is relatively small, and hence, older people as symbols of continuity and tradition have limited social power. Given the effect of these institutional forces, there is little motivation to adopt old-age roles due to their relatively low social status.

OUTCOMES OF SOCIALIZATION TO OLD AGE

People in transition to old age face a different form of change from passages experienced earlier in life stages. While they possess the necessary ability for socialization to old age, they lack the knowledge (since norms and roles are vague) and motivation for this socialization, given the socially devalued status of old age. Given that the outcome of socialization is social integration, the question for older people becomes how effectively they are socially integrated through old-age roles.

Rosow noted that three factors are relevant in analyzing the social integration of older individuals. First, in terms of social values, older individuals show no significant differences from younger people in social values as a function of aging. As a result, at least in terms of social values, the elderly are essentially integrated in society. Second, social roles, particularly central life roles such as employee and spouse, are lost as a function of aging, resulting in reduced integration. Third, social integration involves group memberships. Given the loss of social roles, Rosow argued that group memberships decline with increasing age, resulting in reduced integration.

In summary, becoming old presents a devalued position with ambiguous norms and role losses. In addition, there is little motivation to be socialized into these roles. As a result, old age becomes a "roleless role," and older people are poorly integrated into society.

AGE STRATIFICATION THEORY

Another social factor in later life concerns the nature and process of one's location and change in the age structure of society. This perspective has been identified as "age stratification theory" (Riley, 1971, 1985). Basic to this perspective is the view that society is conceived of as "an age stratification system within which important roles are age-graded and particular individuals and successive cohorts of individuals are continually aging" (Riley, 1985, p. 370).

Streib (1985) noted that stratification generally is considered the "process dealing with the distribution of valued things" (p. 339). As with socialization approaches to "old age," the distribution of roles according to age is of particular relevance to age stratification theory. Riley (1985) argued that changes in the age structures of a society and associated age-graded roles influence individual aging.

PROCESSES OF AGE STRATIFICATION

The boundaries of age strata are socially defined and vary from societies in which there may be few age strata to those in which there may be many (Riley, 1985). Age strata are groupings, based on age, that are recognized within a society. For example, in U.S. society, we tend to recognize age strata of childhood, adolescence, young adulthood, middle age, and old age. The age strata within a society vary in terms of size and composition. In addition, age-related characteristics and capacities are related to various age strata in a society. That is, age strata differ in the "contributions they can make to the activities and processes of the groups and the society to which they belong" (Riley, 1985, p. 378).

Roles, on the other hand, are stratified through criteria that open or close certain roles to certain age strata. For example, roles can be tied formally to chronological age such as voting rights. However, criteria are just as likely to be age-related physical concomitants (the role of "parenthood" is limited by development of secondary sex characteristics) or social norms (the role of "retiree" is only available to adult strata). Finally, age affects how people are expected to perform in roles and the rewards and sanctions related to role performance.

Riley (1985) argued that at the heart of age stratification theory is an attempt to understand both how changes in the age structure of society and the process of individual aging come about. Riley (1985) noted that aging of the individual is biological, physical, and social, and that as a cohort ages, its members "move forward across time and upward through age strata" (p. 371). Tied to this movement through age strata are movements through a sequence of age-structured roles.

According to Quadgno and Reid (1999) age stratification theory evolved into the political economy of aging perspective. McMullin (2000) views this perspective as shifting focus when examining problems of the aging population from the individual and his or her declining capacities to social structures. Quadagno and Reid (1999) stated that the political economy approach views public policy as an "outcome of the social struggles and dominant power relations of the era, which are not merely components of private sector relationships but also are adjudicated within the state" (p. 348). Factors such as social policy and the social structure are explanations for the problems faced by older individuals. For example, decisions about medical care, retirement benefits, transportation and food stamps programs are based on political ideology and these decisions impact older individuals. The focus of the political economy perspective shifts from the individual's ability to change and adapt over time, as seen in selective compensation with optimization or socioemotional selectivity, to an examination of how institutions impact well-being in the later years (Quadagno & Reid, 1999). As Quadagno and Reid wrote, political economy "emphasizes that the analysis of social policy must not only consider political, social, and economic consequences of policy provisions but also the underlying processes that create structural barriers to equality" (p. 355).

OUTCOMES OF AGE STRATIFICATION

While successive cohorts are born and move upward through the succession of age-graded roles together, society can be seen as made up of people occupying a variety of age strata. The particular makeup of the society, in terms of age strata, is constantly changing. Riley (1985) noted that "each cohort experiences a unique era of history" (p. 371).

Overall, age stratification theory is based on a view of society in which aging individuals are constantly changing as they age, and the society within which they are aging is changing over time as well. Riley (1985) states that "because of social change, different cohorts cannot grow up and grow old in precisely the same way. . . Persons in the older age strata today are very different from older persons in the past or in the future" (p. 371).

MODERNIZATION THEORY

The third theory of aging that considers social factors influencing later life is that of modernization theory (Cowgill, 1974). Modernization theory largely grew out of a comparative perspective on aging across cultures (Cowgill, 1974). The premise of modernization theory, simply stated, is that the status of older people declines with increasing modernization. However, this begs the question, just what constitutes modernization?

PROCESS OF MODERNIZATION

Cowgill (1974) stated the following definition of modernization:

> Modernization is the transformation of a total society from a relatively rural way of life based on animate power, limited technology, relatively undifferentiated institutions, parochial and traditional outlook and values, toward a predominantly urban way of life based on inanimate sources of power, highly developed scientific technology, highly differentiated institutions matched by segmented individual roles, and a cosmopolitan outlook that emphasizes efficiency and progress (p. 127).

Cowgill (1974) noted two key elements in this process. First, modernization is the transformation of a total society; there are no aspects or pockets of the society left untouched. Second, the process is unidirectional. It always moves from predominantly rural to predominantly urban.

Cowgill (1974) specified four general changes accompanying modernization that impact on the status of older people. These four changes are (a) technological advances in health, (b) the application of scientific technology to economic production and distribution, (c) urbanization, and (d) literacy and mass education.

The effects of technological advances in health (including public health, nutritional, and medical advances) on social change tend to change the age structure of societies (Cowgill, 1974). Initially, the change is such that they tend to reduce infant mortality rates, thus bringing about a "younging" of the society. In addition, these changes tend to extend longevity among the population. Cowgill (1974) identifies, however, that the long-run effects of the changes in health technologies is a reduction of birth rates, which, coupled with extended longevity, leads to an aging of the society.

The second area of modernization change associated with a changing status for older people is that of economic modernization. While the changes associated with modernization in economic production are pervasive, Cowgill (1974) cited the emergence of new and specialized occupations as most relevant to changes in the status of the old people of a society. As the means of economic production for a society are increasingly modernized, changes occur in the knowledge and skills required for participation in many areas of the labor force. Since these occupations are new and specialized, the knowledge and skills needed tend to be acquired more through education than through experience. As a result, younger workers tend to have the advantage over older workers.

Urbanization presents another major aspect of modernization that affects aging. Cowgill (1974) noted that while urbanization is closely related to changes in economic production, it has significance to facets beyond those of changes in economic production. Two principal effects of urbanization were noted by Cowgill (1974). First, urbanization is associated with an increasing separation of work from the home. Second, urbanization tends to produce a separation of "youthful urban migrants from their parental home" (Cowgill, 1974, p. 132).

The fourth aspect of modernization that is salient to aging is literacy and mass education. Pre-modern societies were dependent on an oral tradition for knowledge beyond that of personal experience. In this type of society, older people held a valued status since their personal experiences were more extensive than those of younger people.

In a society without written language or with few literate members, knowledge is inherently tied to people. Cowgill (1974) identified that efforts to promote literacy are usually undertaken early in the process of modernization. Along with efforts to promote literacy are programs to improve the educational level of the members of a society. According to Cowgill (1974), these efforts and programs are particularly targeted to the young.

OUTCOMES OF MODERNIZATION

Cowgill (1974) asserted that with changes in modernization of a society, the long-term effects are the creation of an aging society. This aging of a society, in turn, leads to an increased competition between generations for jobs or roles as a result of a greater proportion of older generations living longer. Cowgill (1974) argued that out of this competition, in a modernizing society with changing occupations (due to science in economic production) and valuing youth, the old will be "eventually pushed out of the labor market" (Cowgill, 1974, p. 130).

The second outcome of the process of modernization results from the development of new and specialized occupations. The emergence of these new occupations are relevant because they tend to develop in urban areas, tend to accrue greater monetary rewards, and they tend to be assumed by younger, more mobile members of the society. Cowgill (1974) argued that this adoption of higher status roles by younger members of the society creates a status inversion in which children achieve higher status than their parents, as opposed to moving up to the status of their parents. Interestingly enough, this very phenomenon is one conceptualization of "progress" in modern societies, that is, to want one's children to "do better" in life than one's self. In addition, the emergence of new professions tends to deprive older people of the traditional role of vocational tutor.

The third outcome of modernization is a result of changes in patterns of residence associated with urbanization. As noted above, urbanization tends to separate work from the home and younger generations from older ones. According to Cowgill (1974), the result of these two effects of urbanization is to weaken the bonds of the extended family, increase the spatial separation between generations, and to establish the nuclear family as the norm.

All of these effects tend to create a social ethic of independence among generations, replacing an ethic of interdependence. However, given the potential for status inversions and devalued status in the labor market noted above, independence tends to translate to dependence for older people whose children have achieved greater social status and rewards.

The final outcome of modernization is a result of increased literacy and mass education, which are primarily targeted toward younger generations. The effect is that "once a society is launched into the process of modernization, no matter what its stage of development, adult children are always more highly educated than their parents" (Cowgill, 1974, p. 135).

Additionally, once the process of modernization begins, the rate of social change continually accelerates (Cowgill, 1974). With rapid social change, the young are increasingly socialized for a future that is unknown. When knowledge is independent of people, and the past and present experiences of the old are not thought to be relevant to the future of the young, the status of old people in the society declines.

SUMMARY OF SOCIAL FACTORS AFFECTING LATER LIFE

The three theories presented above have characterized later life as related to social roles that are both age and status stratified. In addition, the process through which these roles are created, distributed, and entered into is influenced by the degree of differentiation and specialization of roles within the society. In general, the above theories characterize later life in industrialized societies as ambiguous and normless, with available roles that hold relatively low social status, and the experience of aging is ever changing such that it tends to be cohort-specific. With the exception of age stratification theory, the presentation of later life according to these theories is relatively bleak.

THE NEGOTIATION OF LATER LIFE

Increasingly in the study of aging, there has been a shift from research methods that attempt to describe the nature of aging to the description of the process of aging. This can be seen in calls for the use of longitudinal research methods, in which people are studied over many years (or even a lifetime!). The theories that have grown out of this change are relatively recent (mid 1980s-present) and approach aging as neither solely personal nor socially determined experience. Instead, theories of this sort have recognized that the personal experience of aging both influences, and is influenced by, social expectations and opportunities. As a result, these theories attempt to explain how people negotiate the process of aging.

LIFE COURSE PERSPECTIVE

Although the life course perspective is included in this chapter, there is some debate whether or not it constitutes a "theory" (Bengston, Burgess, & Parrott, 1997). However, there appears to be some consistency in the way gerontologists employ the concept. In essence, the life course perspective assumes that people's histories influence personality and attitudes, that the modern life course has been institutionalized with "accepted" stages (school, work, marriage, child rearing, retirement, etc.), and that the outcomes of earlier life experiences can persist and influence later life experience (George, 1996).

PRINCIPLES OF LIFE COURSE PERSPECTIVES

The first principle is that the life course perspective examines how social and historical factors interact with individual experience. Along these lines, life course perspectives typically examine socially recognized sequences, differentiated by age, that characterize the life of the individual. According to George (1996), a key assumption of this interaction of history and biography is that heterogeneity exists. In other words, within a single cohort, the pattern of life course transitions and the impact of these transitions is not assumed to be singular. Instead, variability is assumed to exist both within and across cohorts (Dannefer, 1988).

A second principle is that the life course can be understood by examination of transitions and trajectories (Elder, 1985). George (1996) stated that "transitions refer to changes in status (most often role transitions) that are discrete and relatively bounded in duration, although their consequences may be observed over long time periods" (p. 250). In comparison, the concept of trajectory implies that in the long term, patterns of stability and change can be seen in the lives of aging people. Along this line, some theorists have used the metaphor of a "career" (e.g., Elder, 1985; Marshall, 1979) to explain later life trajectories.

IMPLICATIONS OF LIFE COURSE PERSPECTIVES

Unlike other theories of aging, life course perspectives on aging tend not to offer descriptions of the experience of later life. Instead, the perspective offered is that the experience of later life can only be understood in terms of what has gone before. The nature and sequence of transitions individuals experience over their lives may continue into later life, or changes in the trajectories may occur. In a sense, the life course perspective has certain similarities to continuity theory. However, unlike continuity theory, life course perspectives also include the possibility for fairly radical changes in trajectories at any stage in life, including later life. In addition, the negotiation of later life is not unidimensional. There are multiple trajectories, and later life is just as heterogeneous in its patterns as earlier life stages. Although life course perspectives have attempted to explain the interaction of the individual and society, they have also been criticized as being deterministic. Marshall (1995) argued that life course perspectives that have cited the agent of change as culture or one's social system have minimized the agency of the individual. In other words, life course analyses that simply focus on the impact of transitions into and out of highly socialized roles on aging individuals do not give adequate attention to the power of the individual to negotiate these transitions.

GERODYNAMICS

Another theoretical perspective that has been proposed to explain the experience of aging is that of gerodynamics (Schroots, 1995a, 1995b). As noted above in the life course perspective, one of the challenges of theories of aging is the issue of heterogeneity or variability with age. The premise of gerodynamics is that with increasing age comes increasing variability. Schroots (1995b) termed this "differential aging." The theory of gerodynamics was proposed as the process that drives differential aging and, hence, the increasing variability seen as people age.

PRINCIPLES OF GERODYNAMICS

Based on laws of physics related to systems, Schroots (1996) proposed that the increasing variability of life experience could be explained through two concepts. First, one characteristic of systems is that over time, they tend to move from energetic and orderly to dissipating and disorderly. This physical law (the second law of thermodynamics) is referred to in physics as "entropy." For the human system this process ultimately results in the death.

However, entropy alone seems inadequate to explain living systems. According to Schroots (1995b), this is due to assumptions of equilibrium in the second law of thermodynamics. According to laws of physics, systems work to restore equilibrium or steady states. However, living systems continue to function in far-from-equilibrium states and may redefine what constitutes "equilibrium." In other words, living systems, including individuals, may reorganize in order to adapt to increasing disorder. For example, as was seen in the theory of gerotranscendence, people may redefine their existence in the face of increasing physical decline (disorder). As a result, the second main concept of gerodynamics drew from "chaos" theory. In general, chaos theory proposed that entropy was not inherently related to decline. Instead "under nonequilibrium conditions certain systems run down, while other systems simultaneously evolve and grow more coherent at a higher level of organization" (Schroots, 1995b, p. 57).

Overall, Schroots (1995b) defined the process as follows, "In terms of nonlinear dynamics (chaos theory) aging can now be defined as the process of increasing entropy with age in individuals, from which disorder and order emerge" (p. 57). The result is a "branching" of the life course in which fluctuations and challenges may cause the individual to respond in higher- or lower-order structures. Higher-order structures correspond to more integrated functioning, whereas lower-order structures correspond to declines in functioning (Schroots, 1995a; 1995b). However, living systems are constrained by biological factors. Inevitably, there is an increasing trend toward disorder (entropy) over time, ultimately resulting in the death of the individual.

IMPLICATIONS OF GERODYNAMICS

According to the theory of gerodynamics, the outcomes of aging are difficult to specify. Schroots (1996) stated that "There is a wide range of individual differences in the rate and manner of aging at all levels of analysis—biological, psychological, and social" (p. 748). Thus gerodyamics is more descriptive of the process of aging than its outcomes. However, the theory does propose that over time, there is a preponderance of branches in one's life experiences in which lower-order structures occur. Ultimately the individual experiences overwhelming disorder that results in his or her death. Yet one of the important implications of this theory is that events that exist at branching points are not necessarily negative. For example, although it would seem that the death of a spouse would be a negative experience, for some people this experience may in fact be liberating. Another important concept brought to light by this theory is that the process of aging is not unidimensional. In other words, although at the biological level an individual may experience a branching point that results in a lower-order structure, or functioning, this same branching point may not affect other aspects (e.g., social, psychological, cognitive) of functioning. Finally, as noted at the beginning of this section, the process of gerodynamics assumes variability in the process of aging. As a result, there is no assumption that the experience of aging is identical for everyone.

Two theories (see McGuire and Norman, forthcoming, for a further description of these theories and their relationship to leisure), selective optimization with compensation (further discussed in chapter 5) and socioemotional selectivity theory, are built on the notion that successful aging springs from what Baltes and Carstensen (1999) identify as a "redistribution of resources" by older people. Both acknowledge loses as concomitants of aging but also acknowledge the importance of older individuals reacting to these losses and not "bullied" by them. They provide a unique perspective on losses of aging by viewing losses as counteracted by gains.

SELECTIVE OPTIMIZATION WITH COMPENSATION

The selective optimization with compensation theory (SOC) has been developed by Baltes (Baltes & Carstensen, 1996; Freund & Baltes, 1998; Freund & Baltes, 2002) to reflect a process that is crucial for continued growth in the later years. Within the SOC perspective, individuals seek to simultaneously maximize gains while minimizing losses over time and successful aging is defined as the minimization of loss and the maximization of gains. This is accomplished through the interplay of three mechanisms: selection, optimization and compensation. SOC is based on the assumption that the three processes underlie behavior and that "In their orchestration, they generate and regulate development and aging." (p. 218) Selection is the process of narrowing the range of possible activities to a smaller set and the "restriction of life domains as a consequence or in anticipation of changes in personal and environmental resources." (Baltes & Carstensen, 1996). Lang, Rieckmann and Baltes (2002) view selection as the process of reducing the number of domains, goals or activities in which one is engaged in order to allow an increased focus on the things most important to one's life. They illustrate selection using a leisure example: "we argue that in the context of aging, selection relates to reducing the diversity of activities (e.g., playing tennis or jogging) by excluding other activities within a domain of goal-relevant leisure activities (e. g., physical activity" (p. 502). Selection may be as comprehensive as avoidance of an entire realm of behavior and as restricted as tasks within a single domain (Baltes & Carstensen, 1999). The result is the individual is able to focus energy and effort on fewer activities. Optimization follows selection by allowing an individual to optimize engagement in a more limited activity set through utilizing remaining abilities at the highest level possible. Optimization may include focusing attention, persisting in movement toward a goal, practicing of skills, acquiring new resources or skills, and devoting more time or effort to a specific activity. Finally, compensation is the process of adapting activities and skills in order to shape them to meet goals. Compensation can occur through use of external aids, increased effort or use of prosthetic devices. It involves using alternative ways to reach desired goals once losses are experienced. Individuals with many resources are more able to successfully compensate for loss (Lang, et al., 2002) and effectively reach desired goals. Baltes and Baltes (1998) provide an example of SOC in their discussion of pianist Arthur Rubenstein. Rubenstein was asked how he was able to remain such a good concert pianist in his ninth decade of life. He responded that he played fewer pieces and practiced more. In addition he used "variations and contrasts in speed to generate the impression of faster play. Rubenstein was reflecting selection (reducing the number of pieces he played), optimization (allowing more practice time on those pieces) and compensation (using an alternative approach to compensate for the loss of finger agility and psychomotor coordination). Baltes and Baltes (1998) summarized, "By careful selection, optimization, and compensation we are able to minimize the negative consequences from losses that occur with old age and to work on aspects of growth and new peaks of success, albeit in a more restricted range." (p. 18)

OUTCOMES OF SELECTIVE OPTIMIZATION WITH COMPENSATION

SOC implies that older individuals make choices in order to maximize opportunities for Ulyssean living in later life. As Baltes and Smith (1999) wrote, "In late adulthood, because of the basic architecture of the life course, selection and especially compensation become increasingly important to maintain adequate levels of functioning and permit advances in select domains of functioning" (p. 162). Within the SOC perspective there would be choices made about losses. Some would be accepted as inevitable, irreversible and non-negotiable. For example, failing eyesight and reaction time might render driving impossible. Inability to drive may cause restrictions in the freedom to come and go as one pleases. However, an SOC approach would indicate the possibility of riding with a friend, but doing so on a limited basis in order to not overdo it. Rather than seeking ways to retain the status quo, the SOC model requires seeking maximization of a progressively shrinking life space. Baltes and Baltes concluded: "Making smaller territories of life larger and more beautiful is at the core of *savoir vivre* in old age." (p. 19) There is evidence (Freund & Baltes, 1998) that using selection, optimization and compensation may become more difficult in advanced old age since SOC-related behaviors require resources, including efforts, skills and organizational metastrategies that may be lost with increasing age. At this point, assisting in negotiating limits imposed by concomitants of aging may become the focus of interventions.

SOCIOEMOTIONAL SELECTIVITY THEORY

The socioemotional selectivity theory focuses on social interaction and its decrease with increasing aging. According to Baltes and Carstensen (1999) the "reduction in the breadth of older people's social networks and social participation reflects, in part, a motivated redistribution of resources by the elderly person, in which engagement in a selected range of social functions and a focus on close emotional relationships gives rise to meaningful emotional experience" (p. 215). A process similar to that identified in the selective optimization with compensation theory occurs within socioemotional selectivity, limited to social relationships. The focus in social relationships becomes emotional support and more peripheral relationships not providing this support are curtailed. The theory views reduction in social circles as an efficacious approach to successful aging, or as Carstensen (1993) wrote, "As I pursued a line of research initially aimed at identifying the psychopathological concomitants of social inactivity in the very old, I became increasingly convinced of the adaptive value of reduced social activity" (p. 210). She describes socioemotional selectivity as a choice by older individuals, rather than as an imposition by society, to narrow one's social environment by reducing social contacts. According to Carstensen (1993) social contact becomes less important to many older individuals for three reasons. First, there is a decreasing need for the transmission of knowledge and information through social interaction with increasing age. This occurs because the amount of information an individual has increases with age, and therefore "information rich" contacts are less likely to occur. In addition, individuals acquire skills needed to acquire information through other means such as reading. However, the need for knowledge increases in novel situations, such as moving to new communities, and in those cases the hypothesized decrease in social interaction will not occur. The second reason older individuals may seek fewer social interactions is that they have decreasing need to develop a sense of self, a process requiring exposure to a wide circle of individuals, and an increased focus on maintaining the already established sense of self, requiring more selectivity in partners since affirmation and support is necessary. As a result the focus shifts from seeking the widest variety of social contacts possible to seeking affirmation from a smaller circle of intimates. The final reason for socioemotional selectivity is that older individuals increasingly seek social contacts because of their affective quality. That is, the importance of emotions in social interactions increases with age. As a result there is a preference for contact with people already known rather than seeking novel interaction. The outcome of all this is a reduction of social interaction accompanied by increases in interaction with close friends and loved ones since they are more likely to provide what is needed from social interaction. Carstensen (1993) concluded, "It may well be that old age, more than any other period in life, liberates people from the need to pursue social contacts devoid of emotional rewards, in which complex emotions dominate the affective sphere and a final integration of meaning and purpose in life can be achieved" (p. 244).

OUTCOMES OF SOCIOEMOTIONAL SELECTIVITY

Baltes and Carstensen (1999) hinted at the relationship of socioemotional selectivity to Ulyssean living. They wrote, "By molding social environments, constructing them in a way that maximizes the potential for positive effect and minimizes the potential for negative effect, older people increase the odds that they will regulate the emotional climate, which, at the end of life, may represent the supreme social goal" (p. 216). The ultimate outcome of socioemotional selectivity is a decrease in the size of an individual's social circle. New friendships are less likely than earlier in life, although the friendships that exist will provide strong emotional support. Socioemotional selectivity will allow older individuals to use their remaining resources to seek Ulyssean living within the comfort of a circle of supportive friends.

GEROTRANSCENDENCE

A different view of aging is provided by a theory called gerotranscendence (Tornstam, 1992; Jonson & Magnusson, 2001; Lewin, 2001) Gerotranscendence posits a redefinition of the self as individuals age, and according to Jonson and Magnusson (2001), was developed by Tornstam based on a belief that gerontological theorizing reflected a perspective that activity was good and inactivity bad. He viewed this as a Western bias that productivity was valued, whereas weakness and dependency were to be avoided. According to Jonson and Magnusson, "Tornstam set out to outline an alternative and phenomenologically inspired theory of aging where performance-oriented human qualities of the productive sphere were replaced by alternative qualities such as rest, relaxation, comfortable laziness, play, creativity and 'wisdom'" (p. 318). The process of gerotranscendence is marked by a shift in perspective from a material one to a more cosmic and transcendent one. The transcendent individual sees the world with a new lens, marked by decreased occupation with the self and material things. The link with earlier generations is strengthened. However, general social interactions may lose importance. Solitude increases in importance, as does altruism. Material things may also lose importance, with this loss counterbalanced by an understanding of the freedom of asceticism. The changing worldview experienced as gerotranscendence frees the individual from traditional ways of viewing life.

IMPLICATIONS OF GEROTRANSCENDENCE

An individual reflecting a gerotranscendent approach to later life will focus on the self. The Ulyssean journey may be a journey into understanding one's role in the world and concern about the well-being of future generations. Introspection, meditation, and opportunities for solitude and reflection may assist in the Ulyssean journey, although the scope and amount of engagement in leisure activities may decrease as the individual's life becomes internally oriented.

Intergenerational efforts may also be the path chosen toward a gerotranscedent life. The desire to support, educate and nurture future generations through sharing the wisdom accrued over a lifetime can be met through activities designed to assist older individuals in developing meaningful roles in the lives of younger individuals.

SUMMARY OF THE NEGOTIATION OF LATER LIFE

The theories presented in this section make two assumptions. First, in order to understand aging, one must follow aging individuals over time. The life course perspective, gerodynamics, SOC, socioemotional selectivity, and gerotranscendence make the assumption that in order to understand how people experience later life, one must understand their history. In other words, these theories imply a need to use longitudinal methods for studying aging. To an extent, earlier theories, such as continuity theory, made a similar assumption that aging in later life was often consistent with patterns in earlier life stages. A second major assumption that differentiates these theories from either the personal experience or social forces theories is the explicit assumption that aging is a heterogeneous process. One of the major reasons for this heterogeneity is that later life is seen as a process of negotiating challenges and experiences. This differs considerably from theories such as disengagement theory, which makes a broad assumption about the experience of later life. Overall, the theories presented in this section are the most recent. They have developed, to some extent, as a response to earlier theory that has not adequately captured the variety of experience in later life.

CONCLUSION

This chapter has presented 11 theoretical perspectives on aging. These perspectives are not the only existing theories. However, they were chosen to provide an overview of the attempts to explain the experience of growing old. The theories view aging as a life period in which one is faced with potential changes. These changes may result from changing personal expectations and abilities, from changes in social structure and social expectations, or a combination of both. The quality of late life is defined by how effectively the individual manages these changes.

As noted in the beginning of the chapter, the term "aging" presents difficulty in definition. However, when one considers the experience of old age, two factors should be examined. First, aging is a process, and each individual experiences it differently. Second, society also structures the experience of aging. There are social norms, expectations, and systemic forces that impact the experience of aging. Ulyssean adults successfully develop their own styles to negotiate the social factors that shape the aging experience.

THREE

BIOLOGICAL PROCESSES

When Butch Cassidy told the Sundance Kid, "Every day you grow older, that is the law," he addressed two important realities of life. The first reality is that growing older is an inevitable part of living; it is a law common to all species. Related to this same concept, there is the assumption that aging is a progressive process that does not occur suddenly. Contrary to what some seem to believe, individuals do not wake up on their 65th birthdays to realize they have become old overnight. Aging is an entire package of changes occurring throughout the lifespan and senescence is the deterioration of body functions over time. At some point, and some may argue that is at birth, while others view it beginning later in life, the slow degenerative process of aging begins (National Institute on Aging, 2002a).

Although the process of biological aging is an unavoidable "law," it allows for both variability and generalization. The great variability in aging is one of the main reasons why a definition of old age based on chronological age is inappropriate. Aging is a highly variable process that occurs at different rates for different individuals and at different rates within an individual.

While some will experience the effects of biological changes in their 60s, others will not feel their impact until the age of 80 or older. In addition to differences in rate of decline, variability is also observed in the types of changes that happen to each person. For example, although some hearing loss is considered a quite common aspect of old age, many older people do not have significant problems with their hearing.

Such variability may be explained by at least three reasons. Although members of the same species share some genetic characteristics, individual genetic makeup may account for differences among human beings. Also, the path of aging is expected to be altered by environmental and lifestyle factors, such as pollution, diet, and amount of exercise. Another explanation to consider is the interaction between biological aging and social and psychological aging in determining the makeup of the aging individual; therefore, changes in biological functions may be aggravated or minimized by such factors as social support, personal attitudes, and opportunities to exercise control.

Certain aspects of senescence, however, may be generalized because they are shared by all. Timiras and Hudson (1993) identify these shared characteristics as: universality, intrinsical irreversibility, deleteriousness, and progressiveness. The potential limitations imposed by biological aging must be recognized if effective preventive and/or rehabilitation programs are to be developed.

Organ reserve capacity may be defined as "the level of excess energy stored in various bodily organs beyond what is required for immediate functional needs" (MacNeil & Teague, 1992, p. 74). All individuals are born with excess organ reserve that is used to restore "homeostasis"—balance and regulation of all bodily functions—anytime the body is placed under physiological stress. As individuals age, reserve capacity decreases and, consequently, so does the body's ability to restore equilibrium. Therefore, one of the effects of biological aging is the general slowdown in the ability of all bodily systems to return to pre-stress levels. As stated by Timiras and Hudson (1993), "Decrements become apparent only in response to increased demands and stress. When the aging organism is challenged by environmental changes, the efficiency of maintaining homeostasis is decreased compared with younger ages" (p. 32).

In studying the aging process, there is a risk of either seeing it with rose-colored glasses or with pessimistic eyes; both of these positions represent extremes that may prevent older adults from receiving the adequate support needed to maintain a Ulyssean approach to later life.

The potential role of physical decline in later life should not be overestimated. The gradual nature of the aging process allows most individuals ample opportunity to cope and adapt to the changes their bodies undergo. Senescence is not synonymous with illness and disability. Most older adults are able to lead full, unencumbered lives until well into old age. Many individuals are able to adapt and compensate for losses (Crandall, 1980; Hooyman & Kiyak, 1993). As Whitbourne (2002) wrote, "The human body is remarkable in its ability to make many physiological changes in its functioning and integrity over time. Rather than simply progressing downward until the end of life, the body actively attempts to integrate the deleterious change in its tissues into new levels of organization to preserve life and functioning for as long as possible" (p. 75).

Nevertheless, such declines cannot be ignored. For example, more than 80 percent of individuals over 65 years old have some type of chronic condition with approximately 19 percent experiencing total limitations in activities of daily living and 3.5 percent categorized as severely disabled (U.S. Senate Special Committee on Aging et al., 1991; Administration on Aging, 1997b). In fact Ebersole and Hess (2001) view chronic illness as a major area of health care concern and view it as "the hallmark of aging" (p. 343). The primary types of chronic illness are arthritis (58 percent of individuals aged 70 or over had arthritis in 1995), diabetes (12 percent), cancer (19.4 percent), stroke (8.9 percent), hypertension (45 percent), and heart disease (21.4 percent) (Federal Interagency Forum on Aging-Related Statistics, 2000).

By being able to realistically appraise the impact of changes in biological processes, service providers will be better prepared to identify techniques that will assist in keeping functional losses minimal. The role of service providers may be better understood by examining the concepts of "primary aging" and "secondary aging."

PRIMARY AND SECONDARY AGING

Primary aging, or genotypical aging, is the deteriorative, degenerative process experienced by all species. It is universal, inevitable, naturally occurring, gradual, and variable. It cannot be reversed, retarded, or postponed. It could be conceptualized as "pure" biological aging, without the intervention of external forces. According to Helender (1978), this form of aging is theoretically optimal, since the only factor limiting further development is the biochemical structure of the genetic code.

Secondary aging, or phenotypical aging, however, goes beyond primary aging. It is the speeding up of the genetically determined aging process. It can be more clearly represented by those factors that accelerate natural decline, such as stress, poor nutrition, radiation, untreated disease, and unhealthy lifestyle habits like smoking and lack of physical activity. Many of these factors may be altered through intervention. In fact, the likelihood that a Ulyssean lifestyle will be maintained in later years will be enhanced to the degree the older individuals and service providers take an active role in cleaning the path of primary aging from as much secondary aging debris as possible.

The figure below (Figure 3.1) summarizes the goal of service providers working with individuals growing old. Line A traces the path of primary aging by showing the gradual decline in functioning experienced with increasing age. It is what Helender (1978) referred to as "optimal aging." If no environmental influences interfered with the aging process, this line would suffice to depict the path of aging. Yet no individual leads a life totally devoid of environmental influences; that is why line B, representing secondary aging, is also needed. As the graphical representation indicates, the line for secondary aging shows a faster decline in functioning as age increases.

The gap between lines A and B can thus be viewed as the premature functional loss caused by environmental interference in the genetically determined aging path. At this point in history, there are no interventions known to alter genetic programs; consequently, primary aging does not seem amenable to change.

Although it may be naive to expect that deleterious environmental factors can be eradicated, it is realistic to believe that the gap between the two lines may be narrowed through appropriate interventions. This position is illustrated in Figure 3.2 by the dotted line (B0), falling between lines A and B. This new line represents the desired path of aging, one in which the negative effects of secondary aging have been met with planned intervention. Line B0 shows how service providers may help shape everyday existence in such a way that the path of secondary aging is brought closer to that of optimum or primary aging.

It is important to keep in mind, though, that all the above lines are imaginary ones. It is not possible yet to determine the exact extent to which both genetic and environmental influences shape the aging process.

Figure 3.1

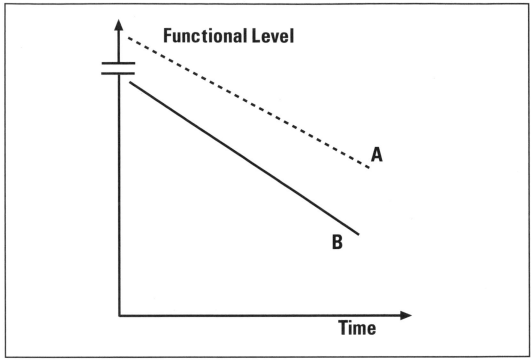

(J. Helender, 1978)

Figure 3.2

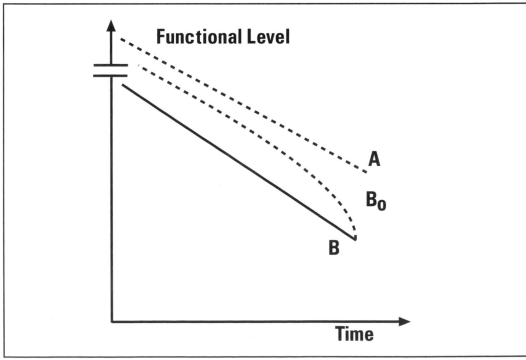

(J. Helender, 1978)

Scientists have been successful in identifying many of the factors responsible for accelerating the aging process. As a result, they have been able to identify several strategies for enhancing later life. For example, there is ample evidence that exercise "can prevent or reverse about half of the physical decline normally associated with aging" (CIGNA HealthCare of Colorado, 1995). The benefits of strength training in reversing or slowing the loss of muscle strength have also been well established. Other factors such as nutrition, stress reduction, and smoking cessation are also effective in maximizing the likelihood of a long and healthy life.

The MacArthur Foundation Study of Successful Aging has focused to a large extent on the issue of improving the physical and mental abilities of older Americans (Rowe & Kahn, 1998). The concept of successful aging, as defined in the study, is based on a belief that the absence of disease and disability is only part of successful aging. Low risk of disease and disease-related disability, high physical and mental functioning, and active engagement with life are the components of successful aging. They come together to provide optimum aging. Achieving successful aging, therefore, requires an active approach marked by awareness of risk factors and the motivation to address those factors. The good news from this research is that people can take responsibility for their own aging. It is not something that befalls an individual, rather it is something the individual has a role in creating. Lifestyle is more important than genetics in determining the path aging will take.

WHY DO WE AGE?

For years, scientists have been contemplating the question, "Why do people age and eventually die?" The search for answers has led to the development of various theories of aging. According to Cox (1993) although a variety of theories exist to explain the biological aging process, none has "yet convinced the scientific community of its validity" (p. 85). Recent advances, however, have some researchers convinced we are on the right path to answer this question. According to the National Institute on Aging (2002a) we know that aging "is viewed as many processes, interactive and interdependent, that determine lifespan and health" (p. 5) A brief examination of the variety of explanations for physical aging follows.

The multitude of biological theories precludes examining them all in this text. However, a brief description of some of the more common perspectives will provide a picture of historic and current beliefs. (For additional information, see Campanelli 1990; Ebersole & Hess, 1998; Timiras & Hudson, 1993; Wold, 1993; Bowles, 1998; National Institute on Aging (2002a). According to the National Institute on Aging (2002a), biological theories fall into two groups. Programmed theories view aging as following a timetable, and change occurs according to that timetable. Damage or error theories hypothesize that aging results from "environmental assaults" to the system that gradually cause things to go wrong.

PROGRAMMED THEORIES

Programmed longevity—A sequential switching on and off of specific genes causes aging. Senescence begins when age-associated deficits start to occur.

Endocrine theory—Hormones, driven by the "biological clock", control the aging process.

Immunological theory—A decline in the immune system functions results in increased vulnerability to infectious disease and ultimately aging and death.

ERROR THEORIES

Wear and tear theory—Aging is viewed as a preprogrammed process that sets off a biological clock. Humans are viewed as gradually wearing out as age increases, and ultimately the wear and tear progresses to a point where the life span is "used up." This process occurs at the cellular and tissue level.

Crosslinking Theory—Accumulated crosslinked proteins slow down the body's processes by damaging cells and tissues.

Rate of living theory—Lifespan is related to an organism's rate of oxygen basal metabolism.

Free radical theory—Free radicals are highly reactive chemical compounds possessing an unimpaired electron. Produced normally by the use of oxygen within the cell, they interact with other cell molecules and may cause DNA mutations, cross-linking of connective tissue, changes in protein behavior, and other damage (Hooyman & Kiyak, 1993, p. 90). Antioxidants, such as vitamin E and beta carotene, have been identified as potential inhibitors of damage from free radicals and are currently the focus of popular antiaging remedies.

Somatic DNA damage—As time passes, genetic mutations occur and accumulate, ultimately causing cells to deteriorate and malfunction.

A recent perspective views aging as resulting from the gradual decline in the cells' ability to replicate. Cells can divide a limited number of times, a phenomenon referred to as the "Hayflick limit," and once this limit has been reached, cells no longer reproduce. One theory for why cells appear to have a clock that keeps track of cell divisions is the telomere hypothesis. Telomeres are responsible for maintaining the structure of DNA and genes. They shrink each time DNA replicates, and it appears shortened telomeres may not be able to facilitate DNA replication, and at that point cells cease dividing (American Museum of Natural History, 1998; Johnson, Marciniak, & Guarente, 1998). This hypothesis holds great promise but awaits further research.

Despite significant strides in understanding the biological mechanism that triggers senescence, there is still no unified theory of aging. However, it is known that genetics clearly have a role in how we age. In fact, it is estimated that 7,000 genes are involved in the aging process (Columbia/HCA, undated). It is also known that a variety of environmental and personal forces also shape physiological aging. Such a view seems to best fit the notion of primary and secondary aging examined in the last section. In order to align it with Ulyssean thinking, it would be helpful to add the idea of environmental impact not always constituting an insult to the individual, but rather contributing to the maintenance of optimal aging.

The following section will examine the biological aspects of aging as they relate not only to potential loss, but as they also represent opportunities for the older adult and service provider to develop creative approaches to maximize functioning.

SPECIFIC CHANGES IN BIOLOGICAL SYSTEMS

The aging process, whatever its cause, results in specific, identifiable changes in bodily function. However, prior to examining these changes, it is important to put them in perspective. The declines, *per se*, are not as relevant as their meaning to the older adult and the degree to which they may be combated by intervention. According to Kalish (1982), the meaning of particular changes can be ascertained by focusing on the following questions:

1. Does it matter? Do these changes have an impact on the lives of the people affected?
2. Does it imply other changes of a more serious nature?
3. Will an intervention alter the path of decrement? Will a surgical procedure, or any health treatment, serve to lessen or eliminate the problem? Will improved social relationships, the re-establishment of feelings of personal meaningfulness, an increase in sensory stimulation, or other interventions, make a difference?
4. Is there any mechanical device that can help? Eyeglasses, hearing aid, etc.?
5. How is the individual coping with his losses? How can she be helped to cope more effectively? (pp. 21–22)

By examining the losses of aging within this framework, it is possible to identify those that are inevitable and cannot be helped, those that cannot be altered but may require supportive services to prevent them from becoming obstacles to growth, those that may be helped but do not require immediate attention, and those that may be altered and require prompt action.

The next section of this chapter will explore some specific changes that accompany the aging process in some of the major bodily systems and interventions that may ameliorate the losses experienced by individuals. The active approach required for Ulyssean living is embodied in these interventions. In addition to the references accompanying each section, a variety of resources provides extensive information on physical aspects of aging (Birchenall & Streight, 1993; Ebersole & Hess, 1998; Ferri & Fretwell, 1992; Lewis, 1990; Ryan, 1993; Schneider & Rowe, 1990; Wold, 1993; National Institute on Aging Age Page, 1995a, 1995b, 1995c, 1995d, 1996a, 1996b, 1996c; National Institute on Aging, 1998; 2000a, 2000b, 2000c, 2002b, 2002c, 2002d, 2002e, 2002f, 2002g, 2002h, 2002i, 2002j; Ebersole and Hess, 2001; Whitbourne, 2002).

PHYSICAL APPEARANCE

If asked about how most older persons look, a large number of Americans would probably mention wrinkled or sagging skin and graying or receding hair. Changes in the layers of the skin combined with reduced activity of sebaceous glands account for dryer and less rigid skin. Although both baldness and gray hair are genetically determined, some loss of pigment and thinning of the hair are expected changes.

These changes, although variable among older adults, do occur to some degree to all human beings as they age. More than having a functional significance, they primarily have social implications. Depending on how individuals utilize social standards for self-evaluation, they may also have some impact on self-image and self-concept. Uneasiness about physical appearance may result in reluctance to participate in activities where these badges of aging are exposed. Aside from the mere cosmetic functions, the skin also is responsible for regulating body temperature and sensory perception (which will be discussed under "touch").

Of special importance to those individuals who are no longer ambulatory is the tendency of the skin to develop pressure sores (also known as decubitus ulcers) when under prolonged pressure on bony areas. Sitting or lying for long periods of time on rough seats or wet clothes as well as poor nutrition may precipitate skin breakdown.

One health factor commonly ignored though is nail care. With age, nails become rougher and, if not properly cared for, may cause infections. Discomfort brought about by nail problems may lead to locomotion problems, reducing independence (Saxon & Ettel, 1987).

Teeth are another area that have both cosmetic and functional meaning. Due to changes such as decrease of enamel and simple attrition caused by continued usage, older adults may have problems with their teeth. If proper care is not given, both teeth and gums will show decay. Not only are teeth important for social interaction (speech, smiles, social meals), but they also are needed for chewing food and reducing it to pieces manageable by the digestive process.

There are also changes in the shape and size of the body with increasing age. Lean body mass decreases and fat is increasingly deposited toward the center of the body. In addition, height decreases as a result of changes in joints, muscles, and bones. Changes in body size and shape may result in difficulties with balance, gait, and mobility.

ULYSSEAN APPROACHES

Concerns with physical appearance should be respected, although older adults should also be encouraged to discuss their options before they seek major interventions such as plastic surgery. Education programs that prepare individuals for age-related changes and society's reactions to them may decrease feelings of inadequacy, helping older adults decide what changes are acceptable and which ones they would like to "correct."

Such educational programs should also concentrate on changes that will more directly affect functioning. Discussion groups, led by wellness specialists, may be helpful in generating awareness regarding issues such as dental care and foot care. They may also assist older adults in identifying strategies to cope with losses and learn to live with "older equipment" in their Ulyssean journey.

Sunlight is the major cause of skin changes we associate with aging (National Institute on Aging, 2000a), and so one intervention is to stay out of the sun or dress appropriately when in the sun. In addition to sun exposure, cigarette smoking causes wrinkles, and not smoking may be an effective deterrent to wrinkled, dry skin.

For individuals who use wheelchairs or need prolonged periods of bed rest, it is important that either they or their caregivers are taught how to shift weight, adjust positions at regular intervals, avoid rough bedding or seats, watch their diets, and apply medication when even minor abrasions are detected.

MUSCULOSKELETAL SYSTEM CHANGES

Two specific age-related changes are loss of muscle mass and decrease in muscle elasticity. With muscle mass loss, individuals usually experience decreased strength and endurance. Muscle strength peaks between the ages of 20 and 30 and gradually declines thereafter; however, significant decline does not occur until individuals reach their late 60s or 70s (MacNeil & Teague, 1992).

Decrease in the number and bulk of muscle fibers may eventually result in "atrophy." Muscular atrophy is closely related to physical inactivity. Deterioration in muscle mass may also contribute to muscular fatigue and difficulty in establishing prompt homeostasis after exposure to intense muscle activity. Reduced elasticity will often result in decreased flexibility that, when combined with skeletal changes, may result in stiffness and mobility problems (Saxon & Ettel, 1987; HealthAnswers, 1997a). Changes in muscle structure may also lead to coordination problems. Impaired muscular coordination may contribute to an increased accident rate in old age.

With increasing age, many people undergo decreases in bone mass. A consequence of bone loss is increased porosity and brittleness. If bone degeneration is extreme, it is called "osteoporosis." Several factors have been identified as contributors to this condition: family history, lack of calcium throughout life, early menopause, surgery to remove the ovaries, extended bed rest, small body frame, use of certain medications for an extended period, and alcohol and smoking. (National Institute on Aging, 2002b; Whitbourne, 2002). It is estimated that osteoporosis-related fractures occur in 12.5 percent of older males and 50 percent of older females (National Institute on Aging Age Page, 1996c; 2002b). Osteoporosis places individuals at great danger of bone fractures, particularly in the hip, and a concomitant loss of functioning. One of the visible manifestations of osteoporosis is curvature of spine and consequent loss of height; as much as three inches of reduction in stature may be observed in old age (Atchley, 1991).

Spinal problems such as scoliosis are also potential complications of this condition. Lack of spinal alignment may create the need to adopt a new form of gait as an attempt to regain balance.

The joints, including the knee, elbow, and ankle, tend to stiffen with age; as a result, movement can often be painful and restricted. Although arthritis is a disease of all ages, it is prevalent in later years, affecting half of all individuals 65 or over (National Institute on Aging Age Page, 1996b; 2002c). It is the leading chronic condition limiting general activities in this age group, second only to heart conditions when limitation in major activities is considered. There are more than 100 different forms of arthritis. The two most common, osteoarthritis (non-inflammatory disorder characterized by degeneration of connecting cartilage) and rheumatoid arthritis (a disease of connective tissue marked by joint inflammation, redness, swelling, and tenderness), involve pain and may reduce activity. Arthritis may also limit functioning through its effect on the ability to grasp and manipulate objects. The degree of affliction varies throughout time, and a crisis may be precipitated by factors such as stress and extreme changes in temperature. Evidence (National Academy on an Aging Society, 2000a) indicates individuals with arthritis, compared to individuals without arthritis, are more likely to have physical limitations, have more financial problems, have more occupational limitations, be less optimistic about the future and less satisfied with their current circumstances. Clearly arthritis can be a barrier to successful aging.

The poor posture, diminished height, and gait changes that often accompany changes in bones and joints may increase the likelihood of older adults having accidents. Persons 65 and older have the highest accidental death rate in the United States. Accidents are the seventh-leading cause of death in individuals 65 years of age and over (Brock, Guralink, & Brody, 1990).

Many older individuals have problems with their feet. Years of use as well as factors such as poor-fitting shoes and poor circulation can limit mobility as a result of foot damage. Foot-related problems can range from fungal and bacterial conditions such as athlete's foot to corns and calluses to calcium growths (bone spurs) on the foot (National Institute on Aging, 2000b).

The complications resulting from muscular and skeletal changes may block the path to Ulyssean journeys, as they reduce the older adult's ability to achieve desired goals. Several suggestions to address the challenges created by changes in the musculoskeletal system will be discussed below.

ULYSSEAN APPROACHES

The ideal form of Ulyssean intervention is prevention, followed by early detection. Health education programs focusing on proper nutrition will assist the older adult in selecting the types of food needed to avoid problems such as osteoporosis.

Educational programs may also create awareness regarding risk factors and warning signs for some conditions. For instance, arthritis sometimes goes undetected because stiffness is not uncommon to the elderly. If the older adult is educated about other symptoms, she or he will be more likely to seek medical assistance.

By learning what aggravates the condition, the individual may be able to avoid much of the discomfort that interferes with a Ulyssean lifestyle. The early identification of some of these conditions may also result in elimination or reduction of secondary effects, such as loss of independence and social interaction. If leisure service providers interpret their roles as that of facilitators who assist people in being all they can be, then the inclusion of health-related programs such as health screenings with other traditional recreation programs makes sense.

One programmatic intervention that seems appropriate for a variety of purposes, ranging from prevention to rehabilitation, is exercise. Research indicates that vigorous physical conditioning brings about significant improvement in several areas including musculature and body composition, musculoskeletal flexibility, and increased bone mass (Goldberg & Hagberg, 1990; Lakatta, 1990: Dinsmoor, 1993; National Institute on Aging Age Page, 1995b; National Institute on Aging, 2002b). Researchers at Tufts University have conducted studies with nursing home residents between 86 and 96 years of age. The results of their studies debunked older myths about older persons not benefiting as much from high-intensity weight training. Despite the presence of severe frailty and chronic illnesses, participants in the muscle training program doubled their muscle strength and increased the size of their leg muscles significantly. In addition, they also experienced an improvement in balance and gait (Mazzeo, Cavanaugh, Evans, Fiatarone Singh, Hagberg, McAuley & Startzell, 1998). Evidence that balance can be improved through exercise was also obtained (Jones, Robinchaux, Williams, & Rikli, 1992). Ambulatory females between 57 and 93 years old were assigned to exercise and control groups. Participants in the exercise program (consisting of strength, endurance, flexibility and balance exercises) showed a significant increase in dynamic balance scores from pre- to post-test while no improvement was noticeable for the control group.

Other studies have pointed to the benefits of exercise for healthy joints and bone density. A study conducted at Stanford University compared 538 older members of a running club to 423 individuals who did not exercise. The two groups were followed for eight years to determine signs and progression of osteoporosis. Only five percent of the runners had pain and disability by the time the study was concluded; however 20 percent of the non-exercisers reported such symptoms. An additional finding of the study was the fact that runners had greater bone density and less mineral loss than non-runners (Kovacevic, 1995; BBC News, 2002). Increase in bone mineral density of the hip and spine was also observed in post-menopausal women who engaged in strength training and fitness exercise program. Gains in bone density were even higher for the strength training group than the fitness group (American Federation for Aging Research, 2003).

Thirty minutes of moderate activity every day is recommended. A complete exercise program will include aerobic or endurance activities, strength activities, and stretching activities. Such activities as walking, jogging, and swimming would be most beneficial. Swimming is also one of the recommended forms of exercise for individuals undergoing treatment for joint problems since it allows for range of motion training. Recently, more and more types of "water exercise" programs are catering to older adults. Weight training has become recognized as one of the most beneficial forms of exercise. Even if participation in exercise intended at improving fitness is not possible, older adults should engage in lower intensity activities (e.g. yardwork, climbing stairs, walking) that increase daily energy expenditure and maintain muscular strength (DiPietro, 2001).

A word of caution about exercise: It must fit the needs and limitations of older persons. An overly enthusiastic recreation specialist, hearing about all the benefits of aerobic exercise, may decide to introduce aerobic classes into her program. Although aerobic activity is indeed very beneficial, some of the motions used in regular aerobic classes may not be appropriate for persons suffering from skeletal problems such as arthritis. In this case, exercise could do more harm than good. However, the fear of causing injury should not stop service providers from instituting exercise programs, since the dangers of not exercising outweigh those of exercising. A less experienced professional may want to rely on exercise programs that have been especially developed for use with older adults.

In programming for older adults, it is important to take physiological changes into consideration. For example, sitting activities should have stretch breaks, since prolonged periods of sitting may result in stiffness. Also, planned breaks are needed in physical activities. Because of the increased time it takes for homeostasis to be restored, older persons may need more frequent breaks to recuperate from exertion.

It is also a good practice to allow each individual to find an appropriate pace in order to avoid unnecessary stress. For those working with persons with arthritis, it is helpful to understand precipitating factors such as extreme temperature changes to prevent them from blocking the older adult's active lifestyle.

Diet and nutrition are also important interventions when seeking a Ulyssean lifestyle in the later years. For example, losing weight may reduce the stress on an individual's joints and therefore reduce the impact of arthritis. The importance of getting enough calcium in building strong bones has been well documented. Nutrition education programs are important tools in maximizing opportunities for healthy living.

Older individuals are at risk of falling and suffering injury as a result of predisposing risk factors and situational risk factors. Predisposing factors include the use of medication, disability to lower extremities, gait and balance difficulties, cognitive impairment, poor vision, foot problems, and sensory changes. Situational factors include stairs, snow, and unseen or loose objects on the floor or stairs (Simoneau & Leibowitz, 1996). Saxon and Ettel (1987) provide several suggestions for decreasing the likelihood of falls. The first concerns the type of furniture used; preferably, protruding legs on chairs and tables should be avoided, and solid chairs with arms should be used to provide support and decrease the amount of strain put on joints when sitting. Other things to avoid are rugs, waxed floors, or any other type of slippery surfaces. Because accidents with older adults are also related to poor vision, other suggestions for safety will be discussed when "vision" is examined. Ebersole and Hess (2001) and the National Institute on Aging (1998) add additional items individuals should consider when developing a falling prevention intervention: get tested for hearing and vision, be aware of medications that might affect balance and coordination, limit alcohol consumption, rise slowly from bed or a sitting position, wear appropriate footwear (preferably rubber soled and low heeled), be aware of body temperature since being too hot or too cold can make one dizzy, exercise regularly, avoid taking chances such as walking on a freshly washed floor, make sure rugs are firmly attached and have a rough texture, have light switches at the top and bottom of stairs, use nightlights, place electrical cords away from walking areas, and use assertive devices such as canes, handrails, or walkers as needed.

CARDIOVASCULAR SYSTEM

According to Whitbourne (2002) the sole purpose of the heart is to pump blood throughout the circulatory system to nourish the body's cells. Aging negatively impacts this function and a variety of changes occurs. With increasing age, the following changes in the cardiovascular system occur (Rockstein & Sussman, 1979; Saxon & Ettel, 1987; Ryan, 1993; HealthAnswers, 1997b; Ebersole & Hess, 2001; Whitbourne, 2002):

1. Heart valves increase in thickness and rigidity; this loss of elasticity decreases efficiency and may produce heart murmurs.
2. The heart muscle weakens and heart rate decreases; the heart becomes less effective as a pump, showing reduced cardiac output and resulting in decreased endurance.
3. The amount of fatty tissue in the heart increases, and deposits of fatty tissues are also present in the veins and artery walls.
4. Blood vessel walls, particularly arterial walls, become thicker and harder. It is estimated that maximum blood flow through the coronary artery is 35 percent lower at age 60 than at age 30.
5. Arterial walls lose elasticity; with increased arterial resistance, blood pressure also increases.
6. The heart muscle takes longer to recover after each beat; this may diminish the heart's capability to compensate for stress when it is forced to beat faster.

Two conditions known to be associated with cardiovascular disease are arteriosclerosis and atherosclerosis. Arteriosclerosis refers to the thickening and loss of elasticity of arterial walls, popularly known as "hardening of the arteries." It results from calcification in the lining of vessels and from atherosclerosis. Atherosclerosis is the deposit of pasty, fatty materials in the arteries, eventually blocking blood flow.

Cardiovascular disease is the major cause of death in later years. Even when not fatal, it disrupts daily routines; heart conditions head the list of chronic conditions causing major disabilities in the elderly in the U.S. Among the three top causes of mortality among the elderly in the U.S., two pathological conditions associated with cardiopulmonary deficiencies appear. They are myocardial infarction (known as heart attack) and cerebrovascular accidents (known as strokes). They result from shortage of oxygen to the heart muscle and to the brain, respectively. In both cases, the arteries through which blood is carried are either blocked by clots or burst.

The three major causes of interruption in oxygen supply are: thrombosis, embolisms, and hemorrhages. Thrombosis is the obstruction of the blood vessel by large clots (or thrombi); embolism is the occlusion of the vessel by a free-floating clot (or embolus) that was formed somewhere else in the body and traveled to the artery, blocking blood flow; hemorrhages occur when a weakened arterial wall ruptures, allowing the blood to flow to adjacent tissues, increasing pressure on them (MacNeil & Teague, 1992).

Another cardiovascular-related disease is hypertension, commonly known as high blood pressure. Approximately 48 percent of women aged 70 or over and 41 percent of men had hypertension in 1995 (Federal Interagency Forum on Aging-Related Statistics, 2000). However, the prevalence of hypertension is significantly higher among older women and blacks (National Academy on an Aging Society, 2000b).

There is evidence that interventions have reduced the effect of cardiovascular disease. Between 1980 and 1997, death rates from heart disease and stroke declined by approximately 33% (Federal Interagency Forum on Aging-Related Statistics, 2000).

ULYSSEAN APPROACHES

Programs designed to increase cardiovascular fitness are particularly important, as are those designed to identify and eliminate risk factors. Diet, excessive weight, cigarette smoking, internalization of emotions and exercise should be discussed (Ebersole & Hess, 2001). Stress has also been identified as a risk factor, therefore, training programs that teach individuals to handle stress may be beneficial as well. Programs such as meditation, yoga, Tai Chi, and biofeedback may be of interest to people seeking to reduce stress. Lifestyle management should be introduced in rehabilitation programs geared toward individuals who have already experienced heart attacks.

The National Institute on Aging (2002d) details "healthy habits" effective in keeping blood pressure under control: keep a healthy weight, exercise every day, eat more fruits, vegetables, low-fat dairy foods and whole grains, reduce salt intake, drink less alcohol, and take blood pressure medications as directed by a physician. These should be incorporated into a Ulyssean lifestyle.

It seems clear at this point that a crucial part of programs should be encouraging the older person to engage in physical activity. Research has consistently shown that vigorous physical conditioning brings about improvement in cardiovascular fitness, lowers blood pressure, increases ability to relax, and reduces body fat, lessening the impact of factors related to heart disease. One particular study in cardiac rehabilitation showed that a much higher number of men had heart complications while engaged in aerobic exercise than during resistance training. Although more studies are needed to confirm such results, the trend seems to point to the greater safety and equal effectiveness of resistance training in relation to aerobic exercise (American Federation for Aging Research, 2003). It is important to keep in mind that an older individual's endurance is lower than that of younger individuals. As with the muscular system, the cardiovascular system of older adults takes longer to return to equilibrium.

Diet and proper nutrition are also crucial to cardiovascular health. In addition programs in cardiopulmonary resuscitation should be instituted in community centers and other places.

RESPIRATORY SYSTEM

The following are age-related changes specific to the respiratory system (Rockstein & Sussman, 1979; Saxon & Ettel, 1987; MacNeil & Teague, 1992):

1. Skeletal changes in the rib cage limit capacity for extension, which limits the amount of air that may be taken into the lungs.
2. Lungs lose elasticity and muscles may become weakened and atrophied; increased energy is needed to sustain adequate ventilation. It is estimated that voluntary breathing capacity at age 85 is only half of what it was at age 25.
3. The amount of air that can be expelled after each inspiration decreases and residual air volume increases within the lungs, limiting the amount of air available for oxygenation; residues not expelled by lungs may lead to viral and respiratory infection.
4. The total respiratory functional surface is reduced; the ability of the lungs to exchange air with the blood system decreases and each breath becomes less effective. The ability of the lungs to oxygenate blood decreases about 50 percent from age 20 to age 75.
5. With less oxygen being available to the cells, the respiratory system becomes limited in reserve capacity; feelings of fatigue and shortness of breath are not uncommon when the body is exposed to demanding physical activity.

Declines in the respiratory system rarely produce disability in most older adults, however, when compounded with environmental factors, they may create problems for Ulyssean living. Rockstein and Sussman (1979) and Hooyman and Kiyak (1993) warn about the deleterious impacts of environmental insults, such as pollution and smoking, on the respiratory system. Also, the cardiovascular and the pulmonary systems are closely related. Cardiovascular problems may lead to secondary pulmonary abnormalities.

Chronic Obstructive Pulmonary Disease (COPD) is a major problem for some older people. COPD includes emphysema, chronic bronchitis, and asthma and is responsible for seven deaths per 1,000 people age 65 or over and is primarily caused by smoking. (Ebersole & Hess, 2001).

ULYSSEAN APPROACHES

Most of the recommendations for the cardiovascular system also apply here. Again, education about environmental and lifestyle factors is desirable. Simple activities such as coughing to expel secretions and proper swallowing to prevent aspiration of foreign substances by the lungs may be crucial, considering that older adults may be more susceptible to contracting diseases such as pneumonia. In addition, smoking cessation programs should be instituted since smoking is a primary cause of pulmonary disease.

As mentioned above, major limitations due to age-related respiratory declines are expected in some older individuals. The most important point to remember about such changes is that physical exertion may be especially stressful on the lungs; consequently, pacing activities is important to allow the person proper air exchange and maintenance of homeostasis.

GASTROINTESTINAL SYSTEM

Old age is marked by a decreased efficiency in the gastrointestinal system. Some of the age-related changes are listed below (Rockstein & Sussman, 1979; Crandall, 1980; Saxon & Ettel, 1987; Ryan, 1993; Texas Agricultural Extension Service, 1995a):

1. Less saliva is secreted as a result of atrophy of the salivary glands, impacting not only chewing ability, but also producing dryness and proliferation of bacteria in the mouth.
2. The number of taste buds in the mouth decreases.
3. Loss of teeth occurs, affecting the ability to chew.
4. The peristaltic movements of the esophagus decline, increasing the time it takes for food to reach the stomach.
5. Loss of muscle tone in the stomach may result in reduced gastric motility; this combined with reduced secretion of digestive enzymes that break down food contents may delay digestion.
6. Shrinkage of intestinal lining and decrease in the number of absorbing cells, diminish the efficiency of the small intestine to absorb nutrients.
7. Decreased muscle tone in the intestinal muscle may also limit peristalsis once food residues reach the large intestine.
8. Loss of elasticity in abdominal muscles makes constipation more likely to occur.
9. Inefficiency in the production of bile may increase the risk for gallbladder disease.

The aforementioned changes do not typically have a significant limiting impact on the lifestyles of older adults. Ebersole and Hess (2001) report "the primary function of digestion and absorption by the digestive system handles age-related changes better than most systems of the body" (p. 97). However, it is possible that when associated with other lifestyle factors, gastrointestinal changes will affect proper nutrition. For example, loss of teeth and digestive problems may be accompanied by factors such as low income, lack of knowledge regarding nutritional diets, depression, medication aftertaste, physical restrictions affecting meal preparation and shopping, as well as the lack of motivation to cook and eat alone. A cycle may be formed since inadequate nutrition will also induce tooth decay and aggravate digestive problems and possibly constipation.

ULYSSEAN APPROACHES

There is a need for nutrition education programs. Such programs should be designed to increase knowledge of proper nutrition and encourage the effort to eat nutritious meals. Best food buys, both economically and nutritionally, as well as meal preparation, should be discussed. The availability of programs such as meals on wheels or nutrition sites could be brought to the participant's attention. Pot luck suppers and similar efforts to share meals might be organized for those to whom eating has social meaning. According to the National Institute on Aging (2002e) a good diet includes six to 11 servings of grains per day, three to five servings of vegetables, two to four servings of fruits, two to three servings of milk, yogurt and cheese, and two to three servings of meat, poultry, fish, dry beans, eggs and nuts. In addition it is recommended that individuals drink eight eight-ounce glasses of water every day. Individuals should combine nutrition with exercise for maximum effect. According to Rosenberg (1993), "The bottom line: Our research shows, without a doubt, that good nutrition coupled with a regular program of aerobicizing exercises can have a beneficial effect on the health of almost all older people—and is the best way we know to retard and even reverse the process of aging" (p. 3).

In addition to proper nutrition, programs to enhance oral health are also important (National Institute on Aging, 2002f). Proper techniques for brushing and flossing, as well as denture care, are useful interventions. In addition, some older individuals may have decreased saliva, possibly caused by medications or other medical treatments. Recommendations to lessen "dry mouth" include drinking extra water, cutting back on sugary snacks and drinks with alcohol or caffeine, reducing tobacco use, and using artificial saliva available at drug stores.

URINARY SYSTEM

Although changes in this system have very little impact on functional ability for most people, they may interfere with continued involvement in certain activities. Some of changes to be considered are (Saxon & Ettel, 1987; Ryan, 1993):

1. Blood flow in the kidneys decreases; the amount of blood circulating through the kidneys at age 80 is about half of what it was at age 20. With less blood available to transport nutrients and waste products, the body becomes less efficient in its purification processes.
2. The numbers of nephrons (responsible for eliminating chemical waste products from the blood) drops as individuals age; consequently, filtration rate decreases

(approximately 50 percent from age 30 to 75), and the body has increased difficulty in absorbing filtered substances and expelling toxic ones.

3. Loss of muscle tone and elasticity in the urinary structures leads to inability to completely empty the bladder; residues not excreted may produce renal infections.

4. Bladder capacity (the amount of urine the bladder is able to hold) decreases about 50 percent as individuals reach old age. This, combined with the inability of the bladder to eliminate all its contents, makes for the need to urinate more frequently. With age, the signal given by one's body indicating it's time to urinate may be delayed until the bladder is almost full; this may intensify feelings of urgency.

A problem experienced by at least 10 percent of individuals 65 years of age or over is urinary incontinence (National Institute on Aging, 2002g). Ranging from mild leakage to uncontrolled wetting, it can be a major cause of activity curtailment. However, most cases can be either cured or controlled when proper treatment, including bladder control training, medicines, implants, surgery or absorbent underclothing, is received (National Institute on Aging 2002g). Urinary incontinence is not caused by aging. Rather, it results from factors such as disease or drugs, weak or overactive bladder muscles, blockage caused by an enlarged prostate, damage to the nerves controlling the bladder, or diseases, including arthritis that may make walking slow and painful (National Institute on Aging Age Page, 1996a, National Institute on Aging, 2002g). Whatever the cause, social interactions and selfesteem may be affected by the inability to control one's body fully.

ULYSSEAN APPROACHES

For those persons experiencing problems with bladder control, physical exercise focusing on muscle tone may be helpful. Sensitivity to the need to urinate more frequently is an important aspect in providing pleasant experiences to older adults. Making frequent stops during longer community trips or asking a nursing home resident if he or she needs to use the restroom before being taken to a particularly lengthy activity may reduce the chances of humiliation and allow the person to relax and enjoy the activity more completely.

ENDOCRINE SYSTEM

Although some structural changes may be observed in different glands, they rarely have any impact on normal functioning in old age. Perhaps the most relevant change in this system is related to the pancreas. A decrease in insulin secretion is noted with advancing age; this may account for a reduced glucose tolerance in some older adults. Although diabetes mellitus (the adult form of diabetes) is known to manifest itself as early as age 40 and is not considered an age-related disease, it is impossible to disregard the fact that it occurs about seven times as often among those 65 years of age or older (National Institute on Aging Age Page, 1991).

Diabetes is among the 10 top chronic conditions affecting major activities of older adults, affecting approximately 12 percent of the older population (U.S. Senate Special Committee on Aging et al., 1991; Federal Interagency Forum on Aging Related Statistics, 2000), and is a leading cause of death among individuals aged 65 or over (Federal Interagency Forum on Aging-Related Statistics, 2000). In addition, it may have secondary complications, such as blindness, heart disease, and kidney disease, and may cause difficulty in healing infections, leading to amputations.

ULYSSEAN APPROACHES

In dealing with older adults in health education programs, it may be helpful to discuss the symptoms associated with diabetes (thirst, constant urination, unexplained fatigue, visual difficulties, ulceration, etc.). Early detection may prevent further complications. Also, discussing dietary needs and suggesting flavor full alternatives to prohibited food items may heighten the older person's sense of control and increase compliance.

In dealing with individuals already exhibiting diabetes, service providers should be attentive to possible indications of insulin insufficiency, be aware of possible medication secondary effects, and be ready to adapt activities to accommodate some of the classic symptoms listed above.

In addition to a proper diet and drugs, exercise is an important component of intervention into diabetes. Exercise helps burn off excess glucose and improves blood glucose levels. Individuals with diabetes also need education about proper foot care, skin care and care of teeth and gums (National Institute on Aging, 2000c).

REPRODUCTIVE SYSTEM

Changes in both the male and female reproductive system occur with age. The basic changes for both sexes are described below (Saxon & Ettel, 1987; National Institute on Aging Age Page, 1995d; National Institute on Aging, 2002h):

FEMALES

1. As women reach menopause, fertility terminates.
2. The vagina wall contracts and loses elasticity.
3. The Barthlin gland, which lubricates the vagina, becomes less effective; a longer period of stimulation is required before appropriate lubrication occurs.
4. As a result of reduced circulating hormones, the vulva becomes more susceptible to infection and inflammation.
5. As a result of the loss of subcutaneous fat and elasticity, external genitalia, such as the clitoris slightly shrink.
6. A combination of muscle tone loss, replacement of glandular tissue by fat, and reduction in skin elasticity produces less firm breasts.
7. The vagina shortens and narrows.

MALES

1. The number of sperm decreases.
2. The level of testosterone drops; testes diminish in size.
3. The prostate, bulbo-urethal glands and seminal vesicles show regressive changes, resulting in a reduction in volume of seminal fluid; ejaculatory force diminishes.
4. Enlargement of the prostate may put pressure on the urethra, interfering with the flow of urine.
5. Changes in the veins and arteries and the erectile tissue of the penis may increase the time required to achieve erection; erection is lost faster after ejaculation; however, erection may be sustained for a longer period of time before ejaculation occurs.
6. The refractory period (time between ejaculation and ability to respond again to sexual stimulation) is longer.

The important question to be asked about the above changes is, "Do they matter?" In spite of structural and functional changes, older adults remain capable of experiencing sexuality. The reason why some may not is most likely related to factors such as social pressure, lack of information, lack of suitable partners, or other physical reasons.

Safe sex is as important in the later years as at any other time during life. Older people can and do get sexually transmitted diseases. In fact, one out of every 10 individuals with AIDS is over 50 years of age (National Institute on Aging, 2002h).

ULYSSEAN APPROACHES

Sexuality and sensuality are important aspects of everyone's lives; they are filled with emotional components. Sexual identity is part of an individual's overall identity. To increase the opportunities for a comprehensive style of Ulyssean living, it is important to facilitate sexual satisfaction in later years if so desired by the older person. Facilitation may include discussing society's taboos, recommending counseling or medical services when problems are present, and respecting privacy needs (particularly when communal living is the case).

NERVOUS SYSTEM

Even though some structural changes do occur in the aging brain, they do not appear to greatly impact the ability of most individuals to function. The most significant change in the brain is related to the slowdown of the central nervous system. Reaction time, that is, that time elapsed from stimulus to response, increases with advancing age. Such changes in reaction time are proportional to the level of task complexity and may be affected by factors such as previous experience with the given task and motivation to perform it.

Because the central nervous system regulates the overall level of functioning of the human organism, it is natural to expect that this slower pattern of response will be common to many activities performed by the older person; nevertheless, the slowdown is usually minimal, having little impact on the ability of the individual to lead a Ulyssean lifestyle.

ULYSSEAN APPROACHES

In a society that thrives on its fast pace, any indication of slowness may be devalued. Allowing older adults enough time to respond may be the best way to assist them in maintaining their Ulyssean pattern of growth. By believing in the ability of older adults to learn and perform different tasks, service providers are responsible for creating optimum opportunities for learning. They also need to become aware of making activities meaningful in order to build up motivational levels. Last, they must develop tolerance for individual differences and learn that, "The good things in life are worth waiting for."

SENSES

The senses provide individuals with windows through which the world is perceived. Vision, hearing, touch, smell, and taste permit contact with the environment and awareness of the world. As with other physiological systems, the senses decline with age.

Because losses are gradual, the individual usually has enough time to adjust, sometimes not even realizing that changes have occurred. It is not unusual for older persons to compensate for losses in one sense modality by making more efficient use of other unimpaired sense organs. This does not mean that the other senses improve to make up for impaired ones; it simply means that the individual is maximizing the use of certain senses to adjust to losses in others. Changes in each sense modality will be discussed next (Rockstein & Sussman, 1979; Atchley, 1991; Saxon & Ettel, 1987; Schneider & Rowe, 1990; Ryan, 1993; Braus, 1995; National Institute on Aging Age Page, 1995a, 1995c; Texas Agricultural Extension Service, 1995a, 1995b, 1995c; HealthAnswers, 1997c; National Institute on Aging, 2002i, 2002j).

VISION

One of most certain concomitants of aging is decreased visual acuity. In fact, nearly everyone over the age of 60 needs glasses at least part of the time, and visual impairments are third on the list of chronic conditions limiting activities in old age. About one percent of adults younger than 55 years have vision impairments. The percentage increases to 21 percent for those 75 to 86 years old, reaching 42 percent for those over 86 years of age (Smith, 1999). However, fewer than 20 percent of the elderly have vision poor enough to impair driving, only five percent become unable to read, and many elderly people will retain good vision into their ninth decade of life. The following are agerelated changes in sight:

1 . Loss of transparency in the lenses, accompanied by reduction in pupil size, results in decreased acuity, the ability to see small objects clearly. The decline begins at age 40;

by age 65, about 60 percent of the women and 40 percent of the men will have less than 20/70 vision and will need corrective aids such as magnifying glasses to counter acuity loss.

2. As the lenses of the eyes become more rigid and eye muscles lose tone, the ability to shift from far to near vision (accommodation) declines; a visual deficiency known as presbyopia (presby = old, opia = sight), characterized by decreased ability to see close images sharply, is not uncommon. One sign of presbyopia is the need to hold reading materials away from the eyes in order to focus. It is usually first noted between ages 40–55, when the greater declines take place.

3. Changes in the retina result in a decrease in dark and light adaptation and vice versa; in other words, as people age, they take longer adapting to changes in light intensity. Difficulty in adjusting to the glare may create reluctance about driving at night when oncoming headlights may seem too bright. Also, waking up at night to use the restroom may require turning on a night light since it will take some time to adjust to the darkness in the room.

4. Visual threshold (the minimum amount of light needed to stimulate the visual receptors and allow the brain to recognize visual information) increases with age; greater illumination is needed to register information.

5. The lens in the eye gradually becomes more yellow, affecting color discrimination. By age 70, older adults have great difficulty in discriminating shorter light waves of the color spectrum (colors in the blue-green-violet range). They are better able to discriminate longer light waves, thus differentiating reds, yellows, and oranges more effectively.

6. Changes in the fluid in the eyes may cause "floaters" or small particles in one's vision. They may be noticed on bright days or in well-lit rooms. They are normal and do not typically reduce vision.

7. Many older individuals experience dry eyes as a result of the decreased production of tears. Dry eyes may result in itching, burning, and possibly loss of vision. Special eyedrops can relieve the condition.

8. There may be a reduction in peripheral vision with increasing age. The visual field may therefore be reduced.

Although not common to all older persons, cataracts, glaucoma, macular degeneration, and diabetic retinopathy are related to aging. These diseases can permanently damage the eyes if medical attention is not sought.

Cataracts result from changes in the chemical makeup of the lens, which produces a clouding effect. They usually develop gradually, and the most common symptoms are: (a) blurred vision, (b) excessive tearing or discharge, (c) double vision, (d) halos around lights, and (e) changes in the color of the normally black pupil.

Cataracts are present in about half of the population in their 80s. However, cataracts can be treated successfully by surgery in many cases (Braus, 1995; National Institute on Aging, 2002i).

Glaucoma is a consequence of increased pressure in the eyes due to an inefficient drainage of eye fluids. The fluid pressure damages the optic nerve and causes vision loss. It occurs more frequently after age 30 and is difficult to detect because there are hardly any symptoms until irreversible damage occurs and vision loss is felt. Some may experience nausea or headaches but misinterpret them as sinus infections. Checkups with an ophthalmologist may prevent more serious consequences. Treatment usually includes eyedrops, pills, laser treatments, and surgery.

Macular degeneration develops more frequently among persons 65 or older, representing the leading cause of severe visual loss in the elderly. It is caused by damage to the macula, a small portion in the retina, which is responsible for fine, acute, straight-ahead vision. Loss of central vision will interfere with tasks such as reading and driving. There is no known cure for this condition. In some cases, if detected early, laser treatments may help. Peripheral vision is left intact, allowing individuals to rely on partial vision to function.

Diabetic retinopathy results from damage to the small blood vessels. Sometimes the weakened blood vessels swell, leak into the retina, causing blurred vision. Newly formed vessels may burst and bleed into the center of the eye and form scar tissue, producing severe vision loss. Approximately 40 percent of all diabetics have some degree of this disease. As with macular degeneration, this condition is best detected through eye examination. If diagnosed early, laser treatment may be used to lower risks of losing sight.

HEARING

Hearing impairment is one of the most chronic conditions among the elderly (fourth on the list of conditions affecting general activities); however, it does not always translate into restriction of major activities (10th on the list). Among Americans with hearing impairments, 60 percent are 55 years or older. Men seem to be affected more than women. Between the ages of 70 and 79, 55 percent of women have hearing loss (more than 25 decibels) compared to 83 percent of men. For those age 80 or older, the percentages are 86 percent for women and 97 percent for men (Smith, 1999).

Certain behaviors are good indicators of decreased hearing ability. For instance, when an individual constantly accuses others of mumbling, he or she may be showing difficulty in distinguishing sounds. Other signs are the need to turn up the volume on radio or television, having to roll up the window when in heavy traffic to be able to hear someone else's voice, failing to hear the doorbell or the phone, or having to keep the ear close to the phone to follow the conversation.

The medical term used to describe age-related hearing loss is presbycusis. It is caused by nerve cell degeneration; therefore, it is permanent. It is more common among men, affects both ears, and progressively worsens with advancing age. The use of a hearing aid can help the individual partially increase hearing ability.

One of the common problems experienced due to presbycusis is difficulty in understanding high-frequency and pitch sounds such as higher-pitched voices of children and females, high-frequency consonants such as *s, z, f, g,* and *t,* or other sounds such as whistles and bells.

Other functional abnormalities in hearing include impaired sound localization, diminished sound sensitivity, and reduced loudness perception. The effects of aging on hearing may be compounded by prolonged exposure to environmental sound pollution throughout life.

A common hearing problem in older individuals in tinnitus, roaring, ringing, or other sounds heard inside the ear. Ear wax, ear infection, nerve disorder, or excessive use of aspirin or other antibiotics may cause tinnitus. Other causes for hearing problems are conductive hearing loss and sensorineural hearing loss. Conductive hearing loss occurs when sounds from the eardrum to the inner ear are blocked. Ear wax, infection, fluid, or abnormal bone growth are possible causes. Damage to the inner ear or auditory nerve can cause sensorineural loss (National Institute on Aging Age Page, 1995a).

TOUCH

There appear to be several changes in the sense of touch with increasing age, although it is uncertain whether these changes are age related or the result of disease and disorders. Three areas show functional changes. The first, touch sensitivity or the ability to perceive objects brought in contact with the hands, seems to decline with age. Also, pain sensitivity appears to decline; older individuals seem less sensitive to both the sensations of pain and pressure. Pain is usually a natural sign given by the body to alert individuals that something is wrong; therefore, losses in this adaptive device may result in unnecessary harm to the person.

With aging, people also show a lessened ability to resist cold and heat, to adjust to temperature changes, and to maintain homeostasis even in unchanging environments. Cold and heat sensitivity are also important because they affect the level of comfort experienced by an individual.

Although not considered part of the sense of touch, balance will be included since it is related to sensitivity. Proprioception, or the perception of one's position in and relatedness to time and space, is impaired with increasing age. Dizziness also becomes an increasing problem with advancing age. With gradual losses occurring in the vestibular senses, balance and equilibrium become impaired.

TASTE

The data on age-related changes in taste are conflicting. Age itself may not be related to losses in taste. Rather, environmental factors may be responsible. Nevertheless, there is a decrease in the number of taste buds with age. Sweet and salty tastes are typically lost first, followed by bitter and sour tastes. Losses in taste may be related to decreases in the number of taste buds, and they may be affected by eating habits, medication intake, or cigarette smoking. It is not uncommon to hear older persons complain about tasteless food or to see them putting extra salt in the food, which is unhealthy, since it may lead to hypertension. Increased intake of sugar may also be observed. In addition, declines in taste may be accompanied by decreased interest in food and eating. The result may be poor nutrition and excessive weight loss.

SMELL

Recent studies have confirmed the belief that smell decreases with age. Odor identification abilities diminish, and odor thresholds increase. The reduction in odor sensations may be associated with what is interpreted as decreases in taste, since both senses are so closely related. A variety of factors may contribute to smell and taste disorders; they include: (a) upper respiratory track infections, (b) polyps in the nasal or sinus cavities, (c) dental problems, (d) prolonged exposure to chemicals such as pesticides and medication, (e) continued smoking, (f) hormonal disturbances, and (g) head injuries (Division of Aging and Seniors, 1997). Changes in smell become significant if the notion of safety is raised; both the odor of smoke and rotten food, when not detected, may become hazardous to the older person.

As previously stated, changes in the senses usually occur gradually and can often be compensated for. Decrements in sensorial sharpness may interfere with Ulyssean living if they prevent the individual from enjoying pleasurable experiences or limit social exchange. Individuals may place self-imposed limits on their behavior, as in the example presented below:

> Irma, with great reluctance, began to talk about her failing eyesight. Because of her pride and fear of becoming dependent on others, she decided to stay home in familiar surroundings and not come to the center any longer. She confessed she was afraid of crossing streets alone, yet was reluctant to ask someone to help her. She was embarrassed to eat meals with friends because occasionally she spilled food or knocked over cups of coffee. She could not see the numbers on the playing cards so she had to give up bridge. These were just a few of the problems Irma described that were forcing her into isolation and depression (Robertson & Welcher, 1978, p. 19).

When losses are coupled with environmental dullness, sensory deprivation may occur. Individuals undergoing physical and mental deterioration are particularly vulnerable to sensory deprivation. With lack of appropriate stimulation, the person may become confused, have difficulty focusing on a given topic, and lose parameters for reality orientation. When deprivation is extreme, hallucinations and delusions may occur (MacKenzie, 1980). This may generate a destructive cycle for psychological well-being, since individuals labeled as "disoriented" may experience little social contact and stimulation.

ULYSSEAN APPROACHES

Combined with vision loss, hearing loss has been found to be the most predictive of loss of independence of older adults. Investigators at UCLA followed a group of 5,444 elderly persons for 10 years, finding that even for those who age well, vision and hearing losses are common. Although some decline is to be expected, many of the pathological conditions that result in loss can be prevented (Smith, 1999). Even when some sensory loss is detected, procedures and medication can be used for correction and devices prescribed to minimize the negative effects.

Sensory retraining programs are useful in reversing or compensating for sensory decline. Practice at using the senses may increase their effectiveness. Sensory retraining programs, designed to provide older individuals with differentiated stimuli to improve perception of and response to physical and human environments, can result in an increased ability to adapt to sensory losses. In such programs, individuals are given opportunities to exercise their senses. Stimuli useful in this process include mirrors and colorful objects (sight); sharp and acrid substances compared with other sweet, pleasant-smelling ones (smell); music, records of sounds, humming (hearing); soft, smooth, and rough items (touch); candy, pickles, spices (taste).

Other suggestions to maximize the ability of older adults to use their senses and are listed below. They apply to those designing environments for the elderly and also to those who teach older individuals how to make their own homes more conducive to Ulyssean living (Shore, 1976; Saxon & Ettel, 1987; Texas Agricultural Extension Service, 1995b, 1995c; HealthAnswers, 1997c; National Institute on Aging Age Page, 1995a; National Institute on Aging, 2002i, 2002j).

VISION

Regarding lighting

1. Allow for an even distribution of light in the room. Instead of one 200-watt bulb, use four 60-watt bulbs in different points of the room.
2. Use dimmer switches or three-way lamps to control the degree of light in the room.
3. Use blinds or shades on windows to reduce brightness during the day, and keep a ceiling light on to balance incoming light.
4. If bright light is needed, use fluorescent light or ceiling fixtures.
5. Keep a night light on all night to help adjust to dark/light changes.
6. For watching television, use floor lamps to avoid glare.
7. Use gooseneck lamps or battery-lighted magnifiers when there is a need to focus on small objects.

8. Have lamps and light switches in places where they can be easily accessed when entering the room.

9. Use motion lights that automatically turn on when someone enters a room.

Regarding color contrast

1. Contrast the color of food, kitchen utensils, dishes, and tablecloths; avoid transparent glass cups and dishes that seem to disappear against the background.

2. Draw colored lines on measuring cups or pans if it is hard to see water level;

3. Paint walls a light color and hang light-colored drapes if the room seems too dark.

4. Paint cupboards or cover with contact paper to help see doors.

5. Make use of yellow, orange, and red as background color; avoid blue, green, and violet.

6. To help identify different keys, stick different colored tape around the top of each one.

7. Use contrasting colors of yellow, orange, and red to identify areas and objects.

8. Avoid using subtle color contrasts such as pink on red or light brown and dark brown. The easiest contrast to see is black on white. In addition, leave white space on documents rather than filling pages with print (Braus, 1995).

9. Use dark colored electrical outlets and switches that can be easily seen.

Regarding safety

1. Increase lighting on steps or stairways.

2. Avoid waxed floors (to avoid glare) or cover them with non-slippery coverings.

3. Paint doorsills a bright color to avoid tripping over them.

4. To help see borders of tubs, drape dark bathmats over their side.

5. Use different colors for bottom and top steps; paint handrail with bright color.

6. To avoid leaving stove on, paint a small colored dot on the "off" point of stove knobs.

7. Use different textures to indicate changes.

8. Emergency numbers should be written in large print and kept close to the phone.

9. Low objects such as footstools or magazine racks should be kept out of the way to prevent tripping.

10. Be aware of fast-moving beings such as cats and children.

11. Use a color-coded system to distinguish among different medications.

12. Provide transportation to evening programs.

13. Keep windows and mirrors in vehicles clean.

14. Put colored tape on the edges of steps to avoid falls.

1. Order talking books from the National Library Service for the Blind for those individuals having trouble reading print; have magnifying lenses available for those who require enlargement.

2. Use or provide adaptive devices such as telescopic glasses, lenses that filter light, magnifying glasses, software that enlarges text on computer screens, large-print clocks/ watches, large-print telephones, large-print playing cards, bingo cards, or other games available though special catalogs.

3. In making signs, use large print and big surfaces; contrast colors to enhance discrimination; avoid using unnecessary words that only take up space.

4. In developing printed materials, use large, well-spaced lettering; use comfortable line lengths, from five to six inches.

5. Make use of symbols to mark areas such as restrooms, dangerous places, or individual rooms in community residences.

6. If visual presentations are given (or films shown), arrange chairs to accommodate constriction of peripheral or central vision.

7. Position objects consistently.

8. Position objects in a person's visual field.

9. Use auditory as well as visual cues.

10. Write with black felt-tipped markers.

HEARING

1. Do not shout; instead, enunciate words clearly and speak in well-paced manner; avoid high pitches in voice tone.

2. Look directly at the person when talking to him or her.

3. In a group situation, to attract someone's attention, call the person by name before addressing any questions or comments to them; if near the person, touching may also be appropriate.

4. Use gestures, and signs and facial expressions as cues.

5. Be objective and organize information well; give most relevant information first; elaborate on details later.

6. Check for understanding. Stay patient. Repeat information if necessary; be ready to ask questions in different ways when you suspect a person is reluctant to admit to not hearing it.

7. Do not cover mouth or chew while speaking.

8. Avoid background noise and distractions.

9. If communication through speech seems inefficient, write message down.

10. Avoid microphones when speaking to persons with hearing aids.

11. Make use of special devices designed for persons with hearing impairment, such as lights connected to doorbells or TTY telephones.

12. Use short sentences.

13. Ask how you can help.

TOUCH AND BALANCE

1. Avoid uneven or slippery floor surfaces that may cause falls; fasten rugs firmly to the floor.

2. Keep floor clean of debris.

3. Avoid pedestal tables that tip easily; use four-legged tables instead.

4. Encourage people to make use of supportive devices, such as canes, railings on walls, and arms of sturdy chairs to keep balance or to come to standing position.

5. Warn individuals about the risk of dizziness with abrupt movements such as getting out of bed too fast.

6. For individuals lacking stimulation, enhance touch sensations through rubbing different textured objects against the skin.

7. Carefully monitor and adjust hot water temperature.

TASTE AND SMELL

1. Create awareness of the risks of not recognizing certain odors; teach individuals to be careful about foods that have been stored for long periods of time and to check if gas has been properly turned off.

2. Teach about different spices and how to make foods more flavorful without the need to add salt or sugar.

3. Enhance environmental smells, and encourage people to take time to smell different aromas.

One general rule in using the senses to their fullest is to adopt a multisensorial approach. To maximize the capacity to compensate, make use of as many sources of stimulation as possible; when communicating, use both verbal and visual cues; combine taste and smell for more pleasurable experiences. By understanding changes and seeking creative alternatives to help individuals adjust to them, service providers enable older individuals to maintain independence and self-respect as they proceed in their Ulyssean journey.

TECHNOLOGY SOLUTIONS

One area that is receiving increased attention is that of assistive technology. Professionals working with older adults need to keep up with technological advances that help compensate for functional losses, allowing them to retain independence and control. The Assisitive Technology Act of 1988 (PL 100-407) defined assistive technology devices as any device, piece of equipment, or product system that is used to increase, maintain or improve functional capabilities of individuals with disabilities. It also emphasized the importance of services to assist consumers in the selection, acquisition, or use of assistive technology devices (Wallace, Flippo, Barcus, & Behrmann, 1995; Bryen & Goldman, 2002). Examples of devices are provided below.

- Daily living: Built up handles for cooking tools and utensils, reachers, key and knob turners, lifter seats, swivel cushions, plate guards, non-skidding placemats, carton and soda bottle handles, box and jar openers, long-handled brooms and dust pans.
- Self-care: Button hooks, cuff extenders, zipper pulls, velcro clothing and shoes, suction scrub brushes, nailclipper boards, toothpaste squeezers, handheld shower sprayers, bath chairs, pantyhose aids, elastic shoelaces.
- Mobility aids: Canes, crutches, walkers, wheelchairs, scooters, adapted vans.
- Vision and Hearing aids: Tape-recorded materials, screen readers, scanners with voice synthesizers, assistive listening devices, phone amplifiers, captioning, audio description.
- Communication: Low-tech communication boards, electronic augmentative communication devices, access devices such as switches, head pointers, infrared and scanning systems.
- Environmental controls: Switches and remote control units that control doors, lighting, appliances, electronics.
- Work and education: Adapted hardware, specialized software (such as voice-operated pencil and pen holders), phone holders.
- Leisure: Magnifier glasses or lenses, needle and yarn threaders, large button phones and remote controls, large or Braille playing cards, card holders and card shufflers, page turners, hand-powered bikes, computer software and games, fishing rod holders, adapted golf clubs, built-up gardening tools.

A quick examination of the abbreviated list of categories and devices provided above may lead to several conclusions. It is easy to see how devices may help individuals function in various life domains. The same reacher that helps grab a box from a kitchen cabinet lets someone reach for items on a top shelf of a supermarket or at work and may allow independent access to clothing items. The other possible observation is the diverse nature of devices. Some are very low-tech (e.g., pencil holder) while other are more complex and costly (e.g., communication device). Many of the devices listed are no longer only available through specialized catalogs. They can be found in generic stores, which shows that technology is becoming more extensive component of daily life.

The concept of universal design is gaining visibility as the concept of accessibility has expanded to encompass more than accommodations for people with disabilities (Bergman & Johnson, 1995). The Center for Universal Design (Mace, 1997) defines this term as "the design of products and environments to be usable by all people, to the great extent possible, without the need for adaptation or specialized design." As the word "universal" implies, the emphasis is on designing for everyone, recognizing that good design should aim to fit the broadest range of user abilities possible. As a consequence of well-planned design, many individuals benefit. As advances in telecommunications, electronics and cybernetics have had beneficial implications for individuals with disabilities, work in the field of disabilities has produced devices and systems that increase overall convenience and access for all. This constant cross-over will continue to enhance quality of life for older adults in years to come.

However, older adults tend to be more technophobic. Persons aged 60 or older have less high-tech products in their homes and tend to be reluctant to embrace assistive technology. Aside from the fact that most have had little exposure to technology throughout their lives, older adults tend to associate assistive technology with disability. The desire to avoid the disability label often leads to rejection of technological solutions that may enable them to continue carrying out activities of daily living, working, and participating in family and community life (Scherer, 2002; Cavanaugh & Emerman, 2003). For instance, only 30 percent of those who could benefit from hearing aids wear them (Smith, 1999). The fact that more and more devices are now available for the general public is encouraging. The more technology becomes a natural part of our lives, the less older adults will avoid it for fear of being stigmatized. More public education is needed to show assistive technology in a positive light and to remove the fear associated with it.

CONCLUSIONS

As people grow older they will face inevitable declines in physiological functioning. However, the evidence clearly indicates that the rate of decline is influenced by a variety of lifestyle factors, such as exercise and nutrition. The realization that biological aging is amenable to intervention has resulted in increased programmatic efforts to slow the aging process. The results of these effort are being seen in the daily lives of older people. A recent report from the National Institutes on Health (1997) cited data from the National Long Term Care Surveys indicating that disability rates among older Americans are falling dramatically and the rate of reduction is accelerating. The result of increased well-being and higher functional levels is increased opportunities for Ulyssean living.

It is helpful to examine the physical losses of aging by placing them in the context of the groups of individuals that service providers encounter in their daily practices. Because of the immense variability among older individuals, it should be expected that different levels of ability and disability will be seen. In a recent position paper (undated) Kelly calls attention to the fact that aging may be viewed as a continuum, a path along which different types of individuals travel. Not all older adults may be classified as either healthy and active or disabled and dependent. In fact, the space between these two extreme cases is often filled by "in-betweeners," as Kelly indicates. This perspective is also illustrated by Atchley's (1991) health continuum, which ranges from a holistic sense of well-being to death (see Table 3.1).

Table 3.1
Stages of the Health Continuum

Good Health				Poor Health			
Absence of disease or impairment	Presence of a condition	Seeks treatment	Restricted activity	Restricted in major activity	Unable to engage in major activity	Institution-alized	Death

(Atchley, 1991. Reprinted by permission of Wadsworth Publishing.)

Depending on the setting in which older adults are served, different stages of the above model will be encountered more frequently. For instance, in an age-integrated recreation center, consumers may fall within the two first stages, while in a senior center, they may range from stages three to six. Adult day care agencies and nursing homes, however, will probably see larger number of individuals in the last stages of the continuum. It becomes clear that the meaning of losses to individuals and the types of interventions needed to foster Ulyssean living patterns will depend heavily on each person's overall status concerning the aging process. While prevention will still be realistic for some, for others the major goal may be to minimize the secondary effects of particular conditions already present. Therefore, while some services may be supportive in nature, others may assume more clinical characters.

This chapter has provided an extensive description of the biological processes accompanying aging. Although many of the changes described in this chapter are inevitable, they need not be obstacles to Ulyssean living if trained professionals are able to effectively intervene.

FOUR

COGNITIVE PROCESSES

Wold (1993) indicated that "cognitive perceptual health pattern deals with the ways people gain information from the environment and the way they interpret and use this information" (p. 251). Perception involves collecting, interpreting, and recognizing stimuli, whereas cognition involves memory, intelligence, language, and decision making. Willis (1992) viewed cognition, along with physical health, as having a major role in maintaining independence in later life, particularly as it relates to everyday competencies. These include: managing finances, taking medication, shopping, using the phone, carrying out housekeeping chores, transporting one's self, and preparing meals (p. 80). Clearly, these factors relate to Ulyssean living.

In this chapter, the focus will be on the areas of intelligence, learning, memory, and creativity as they relate to the aging process. As with the previous chapter, the emphasis will not be on the magnitude of losses, but on the factors that may inhibit or contribute to Ulyssean living.

Rowe and Kahn (1998) address the question of whether cognitive losses are an inevitable part of aging. The answer, as with many such questions, is yes and no. There are losses in some mental processes but not all. Many of the losses, although real, are exaggerated. Other losses are still not sufficiently researched to be completely understood. It is important to keep in mind that the patterns of age-related changes detected in human cognition do not imply a deficit in functioning. As with the biological processes, losses are gradual and variable among different individuals; most are not noted until late old age. Furthermore, research has indicated that some of the changes observed may be delayed or even ameliorated with proper interventions. Even when losses are experienced, individuals have the capacity to cope with them by optimizing performance and relying on environmental support.

Once again, the questions raised in the previous chapter regarding the meaning of the losses to the individual are pertinent. Except for pathological conditions, which affect only a small percentage of older adults, losses typically are too minimal to have any significant impact on quality of life.

SPECIFIC CHANGES

INTELLIGENCE

The concept of intelligence is not an easy one to define. A construct used in psychology, it has been the topic of much debate because of its complex nature. Since it cannot be directly observed, intellectual abilities are inferred from actions and behaviors exhibited by individuals; in other words, competence is evaluated through performance.

A common procedure used in the measurement of intelligence is the administration of standardized tests, such as the WAIS (Wechsler Adult Intelligence Scale). The WAIS is divided into two domains: verbal and performance. Categories under the verbal domain include categories such as vocabulary, comprehension, and arithmetic, while performance encompasses picture completion, block design, and digit symbol.

Studies have shown that when this instrument is used to compare older adults to younger adults, differences are much more evident in the performance section of the test than on the verbal one, with verbal scores showing much stability over time (Botwinick, 1967).

Such differences in performance may be explained by viewing verbal tasks as related to crystallized intelligence (intelligence reflecting acculturation and general knowledge; Birren & Fisher, 1991) whereas performance tasks rely more heavily on fluid intelligence (the ability to reason, categorize, and sort information; Birren & Fisher, 1991). Fluid intelligence declines with age, whereas crystallized intelligence grows with age. Also, responses to performance tasks may involve speed; considering the discussion regarding slower reaction times among the elderly, it is understandable that they may be at a disadvantage in relation to such tasks. However, there is evidence that fluid intelligence can be improved through training in problem-solving strategies and cognitive skills (U. S. Department of Health and Human Services, 1999).

Intelligence tests such as the WAIS have been the focus of much criticism. Ebersole and Hess (1998) have identified a variety of reasons why older people's performance may be unfairly represented by such tests. These include:

1. Test content may not be relevant to older people.
2. Older people may not be in the habit of being tested.
3. Older individuals may not have developed test wisdom.
4. Text anxiety may make concentration difficult.
5. Factors such as nutrition may influence test scores.
6. Older people may respond more slowly than their younger counterparts.
7. Older individuals may be less likely to guess at answers than younger individuals.

Schaie (1996) reviewed results from the Seattle Longitudinal Study, a project measuring age changes and age differences in primary mental abilities. The study examined several abilities including: verbal meaning, space, reasoning, and number and word fluency. In addition, measures of inductive reasoning, spatial orientation, perceptual speed, numeric and verbal ability, and verbal memory were also taken. The results indicated there is generally a gain in these areas until the late 30s or early 40s followed by stability until the mid-50s to early to late 60s. At that point decrements are noted, although they are small, until the mid-70s. While all individuals experienced declines in at least one of the five areas of mental abilities, none of the study participants had declines in all five and fewer than half had significant declines in more than two areas. Furthermore, changes were more likely to occur in areas less central to an individual's daily life. The losses that occurred were more significant in situations that were highly challenging, stressful, or complex. Normal, familiar, practiced behaviors were less likely to be impacted by these losses.

An interesting concept with application to Ulyssean living is practical intelligence (Stemberg & Wagner, 1986). It holds promise as a more useful way of examining intelligence than the traditional testing methods. According to Schaie (1990), "There is an aspect of intelligence that is not measured by conventional processing or psychometric approaches because it involves the pragmatics of applying intellectual skills to everyday activities, and further, that the activities involved therein may differ across the life course" (pp. 300-301). Sternberg and Lubart (2001) view practical intelligence as relying upon tacit knowledge, a form of "knowing how" rather than "knowing that" (p. 506). They provide an example of having to deliver bad news to employees but waiting until after Christmas vacation to do so. It is practical intelligence and tacit knowledge, which evolves from experience, that leads an individual to the decision to withhold the bad news in order to not ruin the Christmas season. Willis (1996) discussed this movement away from measuring cognitive aging in the laboratory and toward measuring it within the context of problem solving in everyday life. This approach provides a more realistic appraisal of the ability to think when presented with typical situations. While Willis indicated there are age-related differences in approaches to problem solving, factors other than age may be responsible. Further examination of this concept should cast new light onto the significance of intellectual decline to the routine demands faced by older adults.

Cross sectional and longitudinal studies. In measuring age-related changes in intelligence, different types of methodology have been employed. Cross-sectional studies compare different cohorts at one point in time in attempting to uncover differences in intelligence between younger and older adults. Cross-sectional studies usually show that intelligence increases until early adulthood, remains on a plateau until the fourth decade, and declines from the fifth decade on.

Such declines, however, may or may not be due to age, since generational effects may confound the results. Because of the experiences typical to different cohorts, it is possible that differences found reflect changes in the educational system or cultural values rather than actual losses in intellectual ability by older adults.

Longitudinal studies follow groups of individuals over periods of time, measuring them at different time intervals. These studies show only slight declines in some areas of intelligence, accompanied by improvements in other areas; they also indicate that such declines occur much later in life than was previously thought (MacNeil & Teague, 1992).

Like cross-sectional studies, longitudinal ones have drawbacks regarding internal validity. Repeated testing and survival of the most fit may contribute to more favorable findings associated with such studies. The combination of both methods through sequential developmental techniques seems to be a better alternative. Studies utilizing this type of methodology seem to indicate the existence of age-related declines in intellectual functioning; however, they clearly show that such changes are not pervasive and that they are not noticeable until relatively late in the life course.

The optimization of cognitive functioning. According to Schaie (1996), individuals tend to preserve levels of performance achieved at earlier ages by optimizing their intellectual functioning in adjusting to biological declines and environmental insults. This statement is based on a number of sequential studies of adult intelligence conducted by Schaie and associates (Schaie & Hertzog, 1986; Schaie, 1996).

Their findings seem to confirm the ability of older adults to maintain intellectual functioning levels by optimizing their abilities. The fact that declines were not consistent across all areas and that different areas showed decrements for different individuals also points to the need to look for factors that may explain the selectivity in maintenance or decline by different individuals throughout life.

Baltes, Smith, and Staudinger (1991) view this selective optimization with compensation model (see Chapter 5 for a more thorough discussion) as a "strategy of mastery that permits effective management of one's aging, despite age-associated losses in mental and physical reserves" (p. 152). This coping strategy requires individuals to focus on their strengths, practice and use remaining abilities, and find compensatory mechanisms when necessary. This model suggests that the impact of intellectual declines will be minimized through careful selection of the arenas for intellectual challenge as well as through practice in intellectual endeavors.

By reviewing the literature, Schaie (1990, 1996) has pointed to the following as possible variables mediating the maintenance of cognitive functioning: (a) absence of pathological health conditions, particularly cardiovascular disease, (b) speed of performance, (c) demographic characteristics such as education and occupational status, (d) stimulating environments, (e) flexibility in personality, and (f) self-efficacy. A recent report from the Surgeon General (U. S. Department of Health and Human Services, 1999) identified four variables as crucial for high cognitive functioning: (a) education, (b) strenuous activity at home, (c) peak pulmonary flow rate, and (d) self efficacy, the belief that one is able to execute the actions necessary to deal with the future.

MacKenzie (1980) has also suggested that social conditions may play an important role in maintaining mental abilities. "Older people who remain in the mainstream of life, who continue to pursue and initiate normal social contacts, and who remain personally involved with others are far less likely to experience intellectual decline than are elderly individuals who are cut off from others and endure long periods of social isolation" (pp. 66-67).

ULYSSEAN APPROACHES

From examining the information presented above, it seems clear that significant deficits are more the exception than the norm among older adults. For the most part, declines are not noted until later in life and are small and not specific enough to constitute major barriers to Ulyssean living. Furthermore, a number of studies have shown that cognitive training results in gains for older adults (Willis, 1987). This trend has been observed even for those who had already shown declines, with gains sometimes returning subjects to levels of functioning demonstrated more than a decade ago (Willis & Schaie, 1986). Intellectual abilities such as concept formation, figural relations, and inductive reasoning are some of the examples cited in literature (Schooler, 1990).

If the factors mediating cognitive functioning are taken into consideration, some logical conclusions can be drawn. If speed of performance seems to interfere with effective functioning, individuals should be allowed enough time to consider their options in problem solving and decision making. Also the prevention of damaging health conditions such as cardiovascular disease should prove helpful in ensuring continued cognitive effectiveness. Considering the negative self-evaluations that may result in self-fulfilling prophesies, it is important to eradicate myths regarding age-related declines in intelligence. It is also important to manipulate the environment to eliminate threatening characteristics and to make it increasingly supportive.

Part of this task lies in providing positive stimulation. Continuous involvement in stimulating activities does to the mind what exercise does to the body. Environmental support should not be limited to the physical aspect, though. Human conditions such as social interaction should also be facilitated to enhance the Ulyssean experience.

LEARNING AND MEMORY

One of the greatest fears of many older individuals is Alzheimer's disease and the concomitant loss of independence. As a result, memory lapses are accompanied by anxiety and dread. It is crucial that service providers be aware of the normal changes in memory with age and be prepared to address issues relating to memory. In addition, service providers must base their programs on a realistic perspective of memory and learning in the later years. The old adage "You can't teach an old dog new tricks" seems to reflect society's views regarding learning and old age. As a result, a number of the programs offered for older adults are based on set routines. A belief in the ability of the old to learn new activities would demand the incorporation of more challenging and thought-provoking activities in programs.

Learning and memory are closely related. Memory involves the ability to retrieve information stored in the brain. Learning is the process of encoding information into memory. Both are crucial to Ulyssean living.

Hooyman and Kiyak (2002) indicated there are three types of memory—sensory, primary, and secondary. Sensory memory involves receiving information and briefly holding it. Sensory memory includes visual information such as colors, signs or words (iconic memory) and auditory input such as sounds. This information is quickly lost if it is not processed at a deeper level. For example, as you read this page, you are being bombarded with visual and auditory input. The sights and sounds around you are part of your sensory memory. However, most of this information will have been forgotten by the time you reach the end of this sentence.

However, some of the information is passed to primary memory. At this stage, the information has been processed, labeled, and prepared to be sent to secondary memory. Usually, it remains stored in short-term memory for only a short period of time, until capacity is reached with the input of new stimuli. If the information is not used or given further meaning, it is most likely to be displaced. If rehearsal takes place, the information may be retained longer under conscious attention. For example, if asked, you might be able to repeat what you just read in this paragraph. However, this memory will soon fade unless you actively seek to retain it.

To store information more permanently, some form of encoding must occur. Through encoding, information is manipulated as to be given meaning and is organized in a conceptual way that allows for prolonged retention under secondary memory. When needed, information stored in long-term memory is sent back to short-term memory to be activated in the form of a verbal or motor response. This retrieval process is not always successful; when information previously stored is not accessible for retrieval, it is considered to be forgotten. Your secondary memory for this material, for example, may be tested during an examination. You will be required to retrieve stored information and display this knowledge on demand.

Research on age-related changes in memory shows that age differences in primary memory are negligible, provided that the individual has fully perceived the items to be remembered and that reorganization is not required. The data indicate, however, that older individuals do not perform as well as younger ones when secondary memory is involved. Even when primary memory is intact, declines in secondary memory are observable (Hooyman & Kiyak, 2002).

Another component of memory, known as remote memory (also called old memory or tertiary memory), is related to the ability to recall events from a distant past. Traditionally, it was thought that this type of memory remained quite stable with age. Anecdotal evidence of this belief is often provided from the number of war stories and family histories told by older adults. However, data obtained from laboratory tests show that older adults' performance at recalling events from the past is poorer than that of younger people.

Findings related to age-related differences in memory may be associated with what has been identified as implicit and explicit (or declarative) memory (AARP, 2003). Explicit memory involves areas of the brain that appear to be related to higher cognitive function. It is activated by an intention to remember and is related to specific instructions given to the individual. It involves the conscious recollection of facts acquired through learning. For example, explicit memory is involved in the recollection of names, numbers, or directions. Implicit memory, on the other hand, is associated with the capacity to learn skills and procedures. Because it relies on previously learned skills and behaviors, it occurs without conscious recollection and is not preceded by instructions to remember. Examples of this type of memory include riding a bicycle, playing sports or dancing. Often areas of the brain responsible for motor activity are involved in this memory process.

Recent evidence suggests that age-related differences in explicit memory are more frequent and profound than in implicit memory (Hultsch & Dixon, 1990; Howard, 1992). Could it be that older adults are able to use remote memory when naturally and unconsciously stimulated by their environments, but when instructed to remember, their capacity to recall is less evident? Or is implicit memory more directly tied to crystallized intelligence and explicit memory, therefore more resistant to decay? Another possible explanation is the amount of relationships needed to acquire a complex motor skill, such as playing golf. Once the brain connections are established, it may be easier to retain than single pieces of information for which meaningful associations have not been developed.

Another aspect of memory that has been examined is working memory, which is related to the ability to do two things at once. For example, trying to subtract two large numbers in your head involves retaining the numbers in your memory while also performing the actual subtraction. Focusing on the subtraction may result in forgetting the original numbers. There is evidence that working memory declines in later life (Women and Aging Newsletter, 1996; West, Wincour, Ergis & Saint-Cyr, 1998; U.S. Department of Health and Human Services, 1999; Kemper & Mitzner, 2001).

Backman, Small and Wahlin (2001) provide an expanded view of memory. They contrast non-episodic memory with episodic memory. Episodic memory is more focused and relates to information acquired at a particular time in a particular place. Nonepisodic memory is not bound to a time or place. For example, procedural memory, a type of nonepisodic memory, "underlies the acquisition of skills and other aspects of knowledge that are not directly accessible to the consciousness and the presence of which can only be demonstrated indirectly by action (e.g. walking, skating)" (p. 350). It is related to the gradual acquisition of skills relying on practice for their development. Although the evidence of age related change is mixed, most aspects of procedural memory do not appear to significantly decline with increasing age. A second type of nonepisodic memory is semantic memory which underlies general knowledge of the world, including the meaning of symbols, concepts and words. It also does not dramatically decline in most older people. Episodic memory, including source memory, false memory and prospective memory, appears to change with increasing age and the decline, while relatively slow, commences in early adulthood. Source memory "refers to the specific conditions that were present when a memory was acquired (e.g. the temporal, spatial, and social conditions of the event; the modality through which it was perceived)" (p. 356). Prospective memory is the ability to remember to do something at a future time. Both source and prospective memory reflect age related declines. False memory, for example remembering a word that was not actually in a list of words, appears to increase with age.

Age-associated memory impairment (AAMI) is viewed as a normal part of aging. It involves subjective complaints of memory loss and mild deficiencies in memory performance. There is an absence of dementia or other medical conditions that could produce cognitive disfunctioning (Small, LaRue, Komo, & Kaplan, 1997; Ebersole & Hess, 2001). Estimates indicate that AAMI incidence ranges from 40 percent of all individuals in their 50s to 85 percent of individuals aged 80 and older. Memory decline in some individuals may be attributed to AAMI. However, a number of factors have been identified as interfering with memory in old age. For instance, when a variety of stimuli are presented at the same time, memory losses are intensified. This is not surprising since there is decline in working memory with increasing age. Difficulty is also apparent when background stimuli interfere with the task at hand.

Tasks of a complex nature also seem to pose more problems for recall, particularly when information to be retrieved needs to be modified in some way (Kalish, 1982); an example might be recalling the name of the five last presidents and listing them in alphabetical order. Also, when information is shown in a quick sequence or displayed only briefly, memory ability seems to be affected.

Rate of presentation of information and number of study trials have also been shown to affect memory performance. When task pacing is allowed and more opportunities for studying the materials are given, older adults seem to show improvement in recall (Backman, Mantayla, & Herlitz, 1990).

Differences in memory efficiency are also verified between recognition and recall (MacNeil & Teague, 1992). When the older person is given a list of names and asked to indicate which ones correspond to names of United States presidents, the likelihood of successful responses is greater than when the same person is asked to name as many presidents as possible.

Age-related differences in memory may also be explained by retrieval difficulty. The fact that recognition is possible points to the efficient acquisition of information. Nevertheless, difficulties in recall seem to indicate that older adults' ability to search for stored information is deficient. This deficit may be associated with initial difficulties in encoding information in such a way that allows for ready retrieval.

It has been hypothesized that older adults may experience problems in processing information semantically or in utilizing the mnemonic devices needed to activate processed information (Cook, 1983). Age-related differences are almost nonexistent when support is offered at the stages of encoding and retrieval through semantic associations or category cues. When explicit instructions are offered regarding how to organize materials or how to use imagery or verbal mediators prior to presentation of information, differences are also attenuated (Backman, Mantayla & Herlitz, 1990).

Meaningfulness of material presented may affect not only learning, but also memory. This seems to be confirmed by the fact that experience in a certain area appears to be positively related to high levels of performance in that area (Backman, Mantayla, & Herlitz, 1990; Hultsch & Dixon, 1990). Information that is not considered relevant to the individual may not be adequately encoded. When relationships can be drawn from previous experiences and novel ones, the likelihood of later recall may be higher.

Research has indicated that the nature of materials to be remembered strongly impacts performance. Higher levels of recall are observed when stimuli are presented in a multisensorial way, when they are rich and varied in features, and when they are contextually organized (Backman, Mantayla, & Herlitz, 1990).

There is also evidence that medication impacts memory. According to the Women and Aging Newsletter (1996), a variety of medications are commonly associated with memory problems. These include: Aldomet, Ascendin, Dalmane, Elavil, Equanil, Haldol, Inderal, Mellaril, Miltown, Pamelor, Pepcid, Seraz, Symmetrel, Tagamet, Valium, and Xantac.

Although there are cognitive declines in the later years, most older individuals will not be seriously impacted by these losses. According to a recent report from the Surgeon General (U.S. Department of Health and Human Services, 1999) more than 50 percent of older individuals complain about memory loss, but in most cases there is no actual performance loss. Rowe and Kahn (1998) provide hope for those who fear old age as an intellectual wasteland. They found that few specific cognitive losses are the result of the aging process itself and even in these losses there is great variability among the elderly. In addition, cognitive ability is composed of many functions, and these age at different rates. As a result, declines in some areas of functioning do not interfere with the ability to remain independent and function effectively.

ULYSSEAN INTERVENTIONS

Most of the factors associated with age-related learning and memory differences are amenable to intervention. A number of strategies to facilitate learning and recall will be identified below.

Ebersole and Hess (1998) provided an extensive list of special learning needs of some older adults. They can be effective in developing teaching strategies to use in programs and include:

1. Face the individuals with whom you are communicating so they can see your lips and facial movements.
2. Speak slowly and keep the tone of your voice low.
3. Present one idea at a time.
4. Whenever possible, focus on concrete rather than abstract material.
5. Provide sufficient time for individuals to respond.

6. Keep distractions to a minimum.
7. Use a variety of cues, auditory, visual, and tactile, to enhance learning.
8. Connect new learning to things learned in the past.
9. Use creative teaching strategies.

In addition to the above guidelines, the American Association of Retired Persons (1990) suggests the following:

1. Establish a comfortable environment for learning.
2. Assess the older person's expectations and take advantage of the older adult's interests, attitudes and motivation.
3. Emphasize the older person's abilities and experiences.
4. Establish the connection between new information and old knowledge.
5. Use reassurance, but do not talk down to the older person.
6. Try to retain attention by minimizing distracting background noises or other stimuli.
7. Repeat information when needed and emphasize important pieces of material.
8. Learn to interpret nonverbal signs, such as fatigue; take short breaks to allow for relaxation.

Many of the suggestions presented above apply to both learning and memory. The key words appear to be environmental support. In the area of memory improvement, Harris (1984) has detailed several approaches that may be utilized by programmatic interventions. He divided these approaches into four categories: (a) internal strategies, (b) external aids, (c) repetitive practice, and (d) physical treatments.

Internal strategies include the use of mnemonics. He suggests techniques such as creating a story linking a series of words to assist remembering these words, using the first letter of a series of words to be remembered to create a more easily remembered phrase, or associating a person's name with an unusual feature of that person to help remember that person later on.

External aids are objects used to store information externally or to help trigger a memory. A typical illustration of a triggering mechanism is the string around the finger; another might be leaving a medicine bottle next to the coffee pot to remember to take medication in the early morning. Other examples of the former are agendas, grocery lists, calendars, and written medication schedules. In this age of technology, many devices are available to aid with memory. From computer databases to cell phones and portable PDAs, the average person can store an enormous amount of data, available at the press of a few buttons. For those who need assistance in organizing shopping lists or tasks, portable cassette recorders are also generally available in most electronic stores. Another item that has crossed from the accessibility into the generic market is the phone with storage capacity for phone numbers. Anyone can dial with the touch of one single key; if the phone has space for small photographs, the need to rely on memory is even further reduced. In addition, there are other items such as medication dispensers that can be programmed according to individual schedules; these devices are not only convenient but also a safety measure given the potential danger of overmedication. Similarly, timers can be used in food preparation, thus preventing accidents in the kitchen.

Repetitive practice means repeating or rehearsing important pieces of information. This may be particularly helpful for information such as telephone numbers that need to be maintained in conscious awareness until the individual has a chance to write them down. It may also be helpful in memorizing lists or other types of information for which internal strategies may be difficult to find.

Physical treatments refer to the manipulation of chemical and biological processes on which memory depends. Some drugs, including those listed above, result in memory decline. Conversely, other drugs, such as Piracetam, may aid in memory.

There are several programs designed specifically to improve memory in the elderly. The notion of instituting "memory clinics" in community centers and long-term care facilities is an exciting one.

Such clinics could design strategies and programs to assist older individuals in focusing on their strengths in order to compensate for cognitive losses. Rowe and Kahn (1998) indicate that older individuals can significantly improve cognitive functioning through training and practice. For example, they describe a study that focused on the number of words individuals were able to recall after being shown a long list of words. Older individuals were able, on the average, to recall fewer than five words, while younger participants were able to recall more words. Five training sessions were held during which recall techniques were taught. Participants were taught to group words in clusters rather than attempt to remember specific words. In addition, they were taught to link words to locations or sequences already known. For example, remembering groceries was linked to walking through the kitchen. After the five sessions the older respondents' performance tripled compared to pre-training levels. In fact, the number of words older people remembered after training was higher than the number recalled by untrained young people. According to Rowe and Kahn, "people were amazed to learn that elderly men and women who have experienced some cognitive decline can, with appropriate training, improve enough to offset approximately two decades of memory loss" (p. 137). Clearly, opportunities for Ulyssean living can be enhanced through formal memory training programs.

A program of memory improvement was detailed in the Women and Aging Newsletter (1996) and includes several steps. First, individuals should focus on their strengths. These can be used to compensate for losses in other areas. Some people are good at remembering names, others at faces, others at directions, and others at small details. Organizing skills can be used to replace some aspects of memory. In addition, wisdom accumulated through experience is a useful tool in dealing with memory loss.

The second component of the memory improvement process is to identify reasons for forgetfulness and address those reasons. Research indicates that common reasons identified for forgetting include: distractions, sensory losses such as hearing limiting input, fatigue, anxiety, depression, medications, viewing things as not important, and an overload of things to remember. If an individual is able to isolate the reasons for forgetting, then interventions to address them can be initiated. For example, distractions can be overcome by learning to focus, medications can be altered, and sensory losses can be decreased through prosthetic devices.

The third approach to improving memory is to be attentive. People can learn to concentrate on the matter at hand and not be distracted by other input. Specifically focusing on where you are placing the car keys, rather than haphazardly throwing them down, will help remember where they are at a later time. Consciously thinking about events as they occur, for example, where you park your car, will be helpful in remembering its location.

The fourth approach is to use triggers when necessary to assist memory. Writing things down, putting objects such a keys in the same place all the time, repeating important information over and over again, making associations between items, and reviewing photo albums when seeing people who haven't been seen in a long time will all compensate for some memory loss. An example of using associational triggers recently occurred with one of the authors of this book. He was on an Internet site devoted to puzzles and memory games. One of the games involved looking at nine words arranged in three columns and three rows with one word in each square of the 3 x 3 matrix. The player was allowed to look at the words as long as desired. Pressing the "play" button then resulted in the words disappearing and the 3 x 3 matrix remaining with blank spaces replacing the words. This was followed by a series of trivia questions. The object of the game was to answer each question, using one of the nine words, and then clicking on the space in the matrix where that word had been. For example, one question was "The unproduced stage play 'Everybody Comes to Rick's' was turned into what classic film?" To succeed at this puzzle you not only had to know the answer was Casablanca but also had to remember that Casablanca had been in square four in the matrix. The first time the author played, he knew all the trivia questions' answers but was able to correctly place only four of them. The second game was exactly like the first except there were different words and clues. The second matrix looked like this:

Mia Farrow	Enterprise	Ellen
Scapula	Davey Crockett	Godzilla
Baldric	Friends	Dracula

It was decided to use a different strategy to remember the location of these words. A sentence was constructed for each line. Line one became "Mia Farrow boarded the Enterprise with Ellen." Line two became "The scapular (sic) had pictures of Davey Crockett and Godzilla."

And line three was transformed into "Baldric was friends with Dracula." Not only was the author able to answer the trivia questions correctly, but also was able to place each answer into the correct square on the matrix!

West and Grafman (1998) provide a list of seven memory strategies. Their suggestions, similar to those above, provide a framework that can be used to develop a memory program. Their recommendations:

1. Pay attention—They suggest actively monitoring and examining one's own behavior. For example, when placing car keys in a pocket, a person could say, "I am putting the keys in my jacket pocket."
2. Rehearse and repeat—Rehearsing information, repeating it to one's self, is one way to store it in long-term memory.
3. Chunk—This refers to the process of grouping items together to aid in memory. For example, it may be difficult to remember a 10-digit phone number (864-656-2183) but may be easier to remember three chunks (864, 656, 2183) separately.
4. Use cues—Suggestions for using cues such as imagery and triggers are discussed above. Creating a mental snapshot of what is to be remembered in also an effective cueing mechanism.
5. Get organized—Consistently placing objects, such as keys and medications, in the same places reduces the frustration of struggling to remember where they are located.
6. Mind your P Q R S T—This describes a five-step memory and learning exercise to organize text material, such as the directions for a VCR. PREVIEW the material to identify main points, create QUESTIONS identifying the essential points to learn, REREAD the material to answer the questions, STUDY and understand the answers, and then TEST yourself for understanding.
7. Increase use of external aids—Notes, appointment books, calendars, timers, and clock radios may all serve as external aids.

Social support also impacts cognitive functioning and can be used to contribute to Ulyssean living (Rowe & Kahn, 1998). Social support includes encouragement ("well done," "that's right"), and allowing individuals to do things for themselves rather than doing things for them. In addition, social support can assist in developing self-efficacy (Bandura, 1982), a factor in high cognitive functioning (U.S. Department of Health and Human Services, 1999). Older individuals need accurate, positive feedback in order to be convinced that their cognitive functioning is strong. Rowe and Kahn (1998) found that convincing older individuals that they retain ability in the area of memory results in more time and effort to memory tasks and therefore gains in actual performance as well as in self-esteem.

Individuals who age well in the cognitive domain seem to share a number of characteristics (Schaie, 1994; AARP, 2003). They include:

a) internal locus of control: the ability to maintain self-direction
b) education: continued exposure to formal learning
c) physical activity: particularly aerobic type of exercise
d) favorable environments: such as high income and intact family structure
e) absence of chronic diseases: particularly cardiovascular ones
f) marital status: being married to someone with high cognitive status
g) flexible personality styles
h) satisfaction with life accomplishments

Two factors that seem particularly relevant for activity professionals include mental stimulation and physical activity. A Victoria, British Columbia, study followed 250 elderly individuals for six years. Its findings point to the importance of maintaining intellectual engagement. Activities including story recall, language or card games seemed to protect individuals from later decline (Smith, 1999).

One study that has received a great deal of publicity is the "Nun Study" conducted by David A. Snowdon at the University of Kentucky, Lexington. In 1986, he began to follow a group of 678 members of a religious congregation. The age of the participants in the study range from 75 to 106 years old. Because of the healthy lifestyle experienced by these nuns, most of the intervening variables that complicate other epidemiologic studies are reduced. In addition to undergoing physical and mental examinations, the sisters provided the researcher with samples of their autobiographical writings, composed during their young adulthood. Findings show that linguistic ability in earlier life is negatively correlated to incidence of dementia in later years, that is, those nuns whose autobiographies contained complex grammar and a greater density of ideas had the lowest risk of developing dementia. In addition, the study also indicated that higher education in early life seems to be associated with less cognitive decline in later life (Snowdon, 2001; Sibley, 2002).

Studies on physical fitness also have revealed intriguing connections with mental activity. For example, after 10 weeks of participation in an aerobic exercise program, older exercisers (63 to 82 years old) showed substantially more improvement in alternation speed and time-sharing efficiency than those in the control group. (Hawkins, Kramer & Capaldi, 1992). Researchers at the University of Illinois at Urbana-Champaign studied 55 well-educated men and women, ranging from sedentary to very fit athletes, between the ages of 56 and 79. Results from high-resolution magnetic resonance imaging showed that the brains of those who were more physically fit had lost much less gray and white matter than those who got very little exercise. One of the most relevant findings of this study was that areas that showed the most benefit are the frontal areas of the brain, which are associated with higher-level cognition and linked to mental decline due to aging, such as declines in short-term memory (Dye, 2003). The same researchers conducted a meta-analysis of 18 intervention studies done between 1966 and 2001 involving hundreds of participants ages 55 and older. Fitness training was found to show "robust but selective benefits for cognition, with the largest fitness-induced benefits occurring for executive-control processes." (as reported by Barlow, 2003). The same study produced the following conclusions:

a) Exercise programs involving both aerobic exercise and strength training produced better results on cognitive abilities than either one alone.

b) Older adults benefit more than younger adults do, possibly, Kramer said, because older adults have more to gain as age-related declines become more prevalent.

c) More than 30 minutes of exercise per session produce the greatest benefit, a finding consistent with many existing guidelines for adults (Barlow, 2003, p. 3)

Siengenhaler (1999) has identified several other studies that provide evidence of the link between physical activity and cognitive function. Studies reviewed by the author range from walking programs to moderate intensity exercise classes. One impressive aspect of most of the studies examined is that subjects ranged from the young-old to the old-old and often had no history of continued physical activity; this point indicates that exercise may be a contributing factor for enhancing cognitive skills even when initiated in later life.

CREATIVITY

Creativity can be defined as originality in thought and expression; it can also be described as the ability for problem solving when facing novel situations. This domain of cognition has not received as much attention by researchers as areas such as memory and intelligence, however there seems be a resurgence of interest in the topic. Vaillant (2002) identified creativity as one of the keys to a successful retirement and wrote that it "can turn an old person into a young person" (p. 235). Understanding creativity and its role in later life provides insight into the potential for Ulyssean living as a creative act.

Throughout the 20th century, researchers have focused on three major topics: (a) the existence of an age curve for creative output, (b) the connection between precocity, longevity, and rate of output, and (c) the relationship between quantity and quality of output (Simonton, 1990).

One of the classical studies often cited in literature was conducted by Lehman (1953). The conclusion of this study was that creative output, as measured by high-quality works, reaches a peak around age 30 and declines rapidly thereafter, thus showing a curvilinear relationship to age. Having examined three areas of creativity—scholarship, sciences and art—Lehman also pointed to the difference in patterns among these categories. While mathematics showed the earliest peaks, philosophy showed some of the latest ones.

Lehman's findings were disputed by Dennis (1966), who opposed the measurement of creativity by counting major contributions rather than total output. When creative productivity across the life span was examined, results indicated that although the decade of the 40s seemed to be the most productive, results differed among different fields and, most importantly, decline in output was much less dramatic than Lehman had proposed. The drop off observed was gradual; in disciplines such as history and philosophy it was almost negligible since output had peaked in the sixth decade and remained high for the seventh.

Lehman's proposition of creative output as a curvilinear function of age seems to be confirmed through more recent studies; it seems appropriate to look at this relationship as an inverted backward J-curve, representing the fast rise of productivity to reach a clear peak and its decline at a more gradual rate to the point where it represents about half of the output observed at the peak mark (Simonton, 1988). The location of the peak along the life span varies across disciplines, as does the rate of decline thereafter. Areas associated with the sciences seem to show the earliest peaks (20s and early 30s) and the greatest drop off, whereas scholarship domains tend to show the latest peaks (40s and 50s) and the most insignificant declines thereafter.

The relationship between quality and quantity seems to indicate a positive correlation. High quality appears to be a probabilistic result of large quantity of output. The more produced, the greater the likelihood for exceptional quality work; regardless of age period.

There is a strong connection between precocity, longevity, and output rate. Those who show high levels of production at an early age also seem to be the ones who will remain productive until later years; both precocity and longevity are associated with high output rate throughout the life span.

In spite of the findings of research in the area of creativity and aging, examples of exceptional creativity in old age challenge the belief that creativity universally declines with age. Individuals such as Picasso, Tolstoy, Freud, and Sophocles exemplify great achievement after the seventh decade of life. What may explain these and other renowned cases of creative excellence?

In reviewing the literature, Abra (1989) gathered a number of potential contributors to creativity that may be affected as individuals age. Some of them will be discussed next. Flexibility of thinking is one area; rigidity in thinking and deficits in fluid intelligence may explain a drop in originality, one of the criteria used to judge creativity. When an individual's work relies heavily on originality, it may suffer with aging. This may explain why scientists show greater declines than philosophers. While the former are constantly seeking new directions, the latter often devote their time to perfecting a body of ideas. It seems obvious that the criteria for creativity largely affects conclusions regarding age-related changes.

Related to originality is the notion of enthusiasm. As individuals age, spontaneity and enthusiasm are gradually replaced by experience and sophistication. While enthusiasm leads to great originality, experience calls for more critical eyes and a focus on wisdom. According to Beard (1974), these two forces reach a balance around age 40, which might explain why productivity seems to reach its peak at this stage. It also explains why different disciplines peak at different ages; those relying on energetic pursuits of new forms of expression may peak at early stages, while those emphasizing experience would show high output during the later decades of life.

Another interesting issue is that of persistence. It was previously stated that quality depends on quantity. To generate high-quality work, one needs to be willing to produce in great quantities. Younger persons may be more receptive to the idea of trial and error and constant production, with less critical eyes. Older adults, on the other hand, tend to value accuracy in their work; they may spend more time looking for the perfect output, thus producing lesser quantities. Also, energy levels may interfere with the constant drive to produce.

The need for accuracy may also be associated with self-confidence and expectations. Average people are not expected to be exceptionally creative in old age; society sees individuals such as Grandma Moses as the exception rather than the rule. Older adults do not receive much support to express creativity and may therefore feel they have little to contribute. If the individual is already considered talented and has a history of achievement, old age may be accompanied by the fear of losing it, which may lead to high expectations and a need to outdo previous works.

One intriguing conclusion drawn by Abra (1989) is that "creativity may simply change rather than decline with age, with different stylistic and thematic concerns gaining priority" (p. 105). This would explain why playwrights focus more on spiritual matters as they age. One important factor to consider is that older adults constantly make use of creative abilities to adjust to a continuously changing world. Adapting to physical changes and to social losses may represent the ultimate challenge to creativity, one that wins no prizes because it is done gradually and surreptitiously.

Another issue to consider is the need to study average older adults who show patterns of lifelong creativity. A qualitative study led by Fergunson (1989) examined a variety of topics related to creativity in 20 elderly persons residing in the community or long-term care facilities. One of the findings relates to the fact that for some subjects, retirement opened doors for creative behavior. One subject indicated that "creativity comes after the creative person finds that he can free himself of outside interferences and then he can become more of himself" (p. 136).

Participants also disputed the notion that health hindered creativity. Neither acute nor chronic illness seemed to stop the creative process; on the contrary, some temporary illnesses even allowed them more time to pursue their interests. These two findings seem to point to potential opportunities rather than limitations in old age.

The above study also confirmed one of the reasons why people engage in creative work. According to Fergunson (1989):

> When an individual is able to do something for someone who has helped him/her and is able to give something to that helper, he/she is able to feel as if he/she has reciprocated that help. In turn such actions help him/her remain or feel less dependent; if not allowing him/her to be independent (p. 137).

The need to feel independent and feel that life has purpose cannot be underscored enough when Ulyssean living is the aim.

More recent work (Sternberg & Lubart, 2001) has confirmed that creativity declines in old age. However, the decline is variable across individuals and fields (i.e. the productivity of mathematicians peaks earlier than the productivity of historians), and not universal since many individuals produce creative work throughout life. As in earlier works the authors ascribe the decline in creativity to cognitive, personality, motivational, and environmental changes as individuals age.

Vaillant (2002) provided proper perspective to the question of whether creativity declines in the later years:

> Thus far I have evaded answering the question "Can the elderly be creative?" I shall now stop waffling and reply, "Damned straight!" Monet did not begin his water lily panels until 76; Benjamin Franklin invented bifocal spectacles at 78; Houston heart surgeon Michael DeBakey obtained a patent for a surgical innovation at 90. Titian painted what many regard as his most original, beautiful, and profound works after age 76. Leopold Stokowski signed a six-year recording contract at 94, and Grandma Moses was still painting at 90 (pp. 238-239).

ULYSSEAN APPROACHES

Encouragement may be the major need of older persons in this domain. The need to feel useful guides most individuals' motivations. In a recent qualitative study of the role of leisure in the lives of older black women (Tedrick & Boyd, 1992), one of the participants, an energetic 91-year-old woman, mentioned that she used to make hats, of which she was quite proud. When asked why she no longer engaged in such activity, she responded, "I have no one to make them for." This woman's talent was not being capitalized on by the senior center she frequented.

A suggestion that applies to all settings serving older adults is to assess individuals' past skills and to foster a sense of autonomy and pride by making use of such gifts to keep the individuals connected with their families and communities. Gifts do not need to be confined to the artistic vein. One nursing home made use of the sales skills of one of the residents who had suffered from a stroke. Knowing that the woman had a history of exceptional performance as a salesperson, the staff provided her with a telephone so she could call community members and sell paintings produced by other residents. A good sales speech is definitely a sign of a creative mind; this woman had not only the opportunity to remain mentally active, but also to feel that her work was a contribution to her facility and to the community in general.

McLeish (1976) recommends gathering individuals in small groups and challenging them to awaken their creativity through a series of exercises. Some of the creativity-stimulating activities he suggested were:

1. Make a parody of a nursery rhyme.
2. Name five practical inventions that have not yet been invented.
3. List 10 new ways to use Scotch tape.
4. Take two objects as different as possible—a sock and a lawn mower for example—and identify how they might be paired in creative ways.
5. Suggest three or four historic people and describe how their meeting would create a bizarre, ludicrous, or comical conversation.
6. Describe three new uses for a computer.

The result of participating in exercises of this type will be revitalized creativity and a Ulyssean perspective.

CONCLUSION

Much of what is viewed as a natural part of the aging process is, in fact, pathological. For instance, significant memory loss is partially associated with Alzheimer's disease or other cognitive disorders rather than related to aging, per se. Losses in learning and memory are not significant enough to seriously deter older adults from their Ulyssean journeys. The role of practitioners is to post enough signs along the way as to guide travelers to follow the path.

This brief examination of cognitive processes in the later years provides an overview of intelligence, learning, memory, and creativity. The message is the same as that in Chapter 3: Declines occur; intervention is effective; Ulyssean living is possible.

A few lines of the poem "Ulysses" apply here:

> How dull is to pause, to make an end,
> To rust unburnished, not to shine in use!
> And this grey spirit yearning in desire
> To follow knowledge like a sinking star.
> Death closes all; but something ere the end,
> Some work of noble note, may yet be done
> . . . but strong in will
> To strive, to seek, to find and not to yield.

The potential for Ulyssean living in the later years is greatly increased in individuals with high levels of cognitive functioning. Learning, memory, and creativity are powerful tools for enhancing the quality of life. Although there are some declines in these areas in the later years, the good news is that in most cases the losses are neither overwhelming nor intractable. Indeed, the mind and things of the mind will "shine in use."

FIVE

PSYCHOLOGICAL AGING

The examination of psychological changes that accompany the aging process deals with a variety of topics, such as personality, tasks associated with older adulthood as a developmental stage, adaptation to old age, and mental health of the elderly. The sections below will approach some of the major issues associated with these topics and include recommendations to foster psychological well being in older adults.

PERSONALITY

The study of personality change in aging is pervasive in the literature. It is an extremely complex topic and the findings are often confusing. Work on personality indicates there is little change in personality in some individuals, but not all. Ryff, Kwan, and Singer (2001) wrote, "More than any query, studies of personality in adulthood and aging have been dominated by the seemingly straightforward question, Does personality change as people grow older, or is it stable?" (p. 480). Their answer is a resounding yes to both, personality in the later years reflects continuity as well as change. They also indicated there is great variation in the changes that occur. Whitbourne (2002) examined the work related to personality over time and concluded that the evidence indicates that personality is mostly stable in later life and that studies show a "remarkable consistency over time of adult personality" (p. 14). Kogan (1990) noted, "Interindividual stability of specific traits across extended time periods is quite substantial" (p. 341). This continuity of personality structures over the life span is a consistent finding of most studies on aging and personality (Cook, 1983; Heckheimer, 1989; Ruth & Coleman, 1996). Older individuals have spent entire lifetimes developing strategies for coping and adapting. The evidence indicates these strategies endure as people age. Older individuals are active participants in their lives and most have developed the personal resources needed to survive. Entering old age does not diminish these resources. Such stability does not exclude, however, the possibility of some general personality alterations.

In one of the few longitudinal studies conducted with older adults reported in the literature, Neugarten (1964, 1977) and (Atchley, 1991) uncovered a global trend that begins in middle age and becomes more evident in old age. Such a trend, referred to as "interiority," is defined as a growing introspection, a change in focus from the external environment to the person's interior world. Neugarten's subjects also seemed to adopt a "passive mastery" of the environment, showing accommodation rather than spending their energies trying to change a world that seemed increasingly dangerous and complex.

Another characteristic generally discussed in the aging literature (Haight, 1991) is the tendency for men and women to move in different directions as they age, eventually showing signs of androgyny. That is, while males show more signs of nurturance and affiliation (traditionally considered female traits), females demonstrate more aggressiveness and independence (traditionally seen as male traits). Sex role differentiation thus seems to decrease in old age (Cook, 1983).

Some of the above findings may lead readers to believe that old age is a time of passivity and surrender. It is important to view such results in light of previous discussions regarding motivation and social context. In an earlier chapter, it was shown that the resistance to learn new information could be attributed to the older person's realization of what was meaningful to him or her. Motivation to learn is then associated with an evaluation of worth. After years of experimentation, the older person may come to adopt the same approach regarding where to invest his or her energies. Instead of reacting aggressively toward the outside environment, the individual may pick battles selectively, reserving more energy to spend in other important inner-world processes, such as life review. Such a view is consistent with the components of the selective optimization with compensation discussed in chapter 2.

In terms of social context, it is important to look at the changes in the older population since 1960. Some of the findings of Neugarten's study may have been due to cohort effects, rather than universal, unchangeable characteristics of aging. Although her study used a longitudinal methodology, it surveyed individuals born in the beginning of the 20th century.

An obvious question may be: "Will the next generation of older adults, particularly those in the baby-boomers cohort, exhibit these same traits?" These individuals, men and women, are known for their active involvement in society. They are expected to be healthier, more physically active, more engaged in self-advocacy, and more demanding of high-quality services.

Women are more engaged in the workforce than ever; they share many of the males' stresses that they were previously spared due to their traditional homemaker roles. Men, on the other hand, seem to be sharing the responsibility involved in caring for the family and the household. It will be interesting to see if this group will resemble the subjects in earlier studies.

Let us return to the question that was asked in the beginning of this section: "Does personality change in the later years?" Although the answer depends on how one defines and measures personality, it seems that most of us remain essentially the same. Traumatic events such as disease, disability or loss may bring about changes, but generally our approach to life endures as we age. George Vaillant's (2002) insightful examination of adult development in a cohort of older individuals provides life histories of many older individuals, and one is struck by the consistency in people's lives. Vaillant's respondents typically experienced cohesion rather than radical change as they aged. He summarized his data:

One of the very best indicators of how Harvard men adapted to old age was whether they had been classified an A or C in college! Of the 85 As–those men seen as best adjusted in college–28 were among the Happy-Well and only nine were among the Sad-Sick. In a majority of cases those As who aged badly had developed the personality-distorting illnesses of alcohol abuse or major depressive disorder. Among the 40 worst-adjusted college men–the Cs–only three men at 80 were among the Happy-Well... The past affects the future... Successful adolescence predicted successful old age (pp. 283-284).

DEVELOPMENTAL TASKS

One paradigm of age-related change in personality is based on developmental stage models. These models view later adulthood as a time of continued development and as qualitatively different from earlier stages.

For example, Kogan (1990) identifies the work of Erikson (1950), Loevinger (1976), and Levinson (1986) as representative of this approach. According to Erikson's (1950) psychosocial stages, individuals move from middle adulthood's tasks of "generativity vs. stagnation" to late adulthood's tasks of "integrity vs. despair." While middle-aged adults are concerned with leaving a legacy to their descendants, viewing their jobs and civic responsibilities as their major channels of productivity, older adults strive to find senses of integrity, feelings of closure related to the acceptance of life as lived.

One interesting approach to development is the notion of "maturity," a state of being that is needed to meet the psychological tasks of adulthood, beginning in young adulthood and reaching its full potential in the 50s and 60s (MacNeil & Teague, 1987). The characteristics of maturity, as proposed by Allport (1961) are:

1. Extended sense of self: having concern for others, actively participating in different dimensions of the surrounding environment
2. Ability to relate warmly to others: developing bonds of intimacy and treating others with sensitivity
3. Acceptance of self and sense of emotional security: accepting self and being able to express self, showing increased tolerance to frustration
4. Accurate perception of reality: being able to perceive reality and act accordingly
5. Capability for self-objectification: being aware of personal skills and limitations, possessing self-insights and ability to derive humor from shortcomings
6. Establishment of a unifying philosophy of life: developing meaningful goals and working toward them

Developmental tasks define the things an individual needs to accomplish, adjustments to be made, and problems to solve (Birchenall & Streight, 1993; p. 11). Although a variety of taxonomies of these developmental tasks exist, the Havighurst and Duvall model identified by Birchenall and Streight (1993) (see Figure 5.1) and the system developed by Ebersole and Hess (1998) (Figure 5.2) provide clear evidence of the foci needed in later life.

Examination of these three models yields intriguing possibilities for fostering continued development in the later years. There are clearly two opposite tasks the elderly must address. The first is adjusting to the physical losses that are concomitants of aging. The body declines, health diminishes, and death approaches. An inner peace and acceptance are important in later life. Erikson's ego integrity is a noble goal. However, true development, Ulyssean aging, requires more than acknowledgment and acceptance of loss. It also demands searching for continued meaning in life. As Ebersole and Hess's model shows, there is a need to share wisdom, develop new activities, maintain relationships and become an active member of the community. Acceptance and growth are the twin developmental tasks in the later years. Adaptation is a crucial factor in achieving these tasks.

ADAPTATION

Adaptation has been viewed as resulting from both personal characteristics and environmental conditions and the interaction between the two (Hooyman & Kiyak, 1993). Ruth and Coleman (1996) define it as a "range of behaviors to meet demands, from developing habits to meeting problems and frustrations through managing intense anxiety" (p. 309).

Carp's (1972) components of adult life adjustment remain relevant to most individuals' adaptation to old age: (a) fairly stable personality and behavior, (b) positive attitude toward others, (c) favorable assessment of others, (d) active involvement in life, (e) satisfaction with past and present, (f) positive appraisal of general health, (g) intellectual competence, and (h) ego strength. Some of the resources for coping identified by Ruth and Coleman (1996) should be added to this list: an easy-going or optimistic disposition, internal locus of control, self-efficacy, and social support. Individuals who positively adapt to old age are those capable of dealing with crises without resorting to self-destructive measures, certainly a task that involves the ability to integrate the confronted situations with an overall positive perspective toward life, striving for resolution through the activation of one's internal and external resources. Older adults, in general, seem to adapt to the challenges and stresses old age brings, preserving their self-concept and self-esteem.

Even in the face of environmental forces that threaten their perceptions of self, older adults seem to draw on the notions established in younger years, adjusting such external forces to fit into their internal reality.

MENTAL HEALTH

According to Ebersole and Hess (2001), mental health may be defined as "a satisfactory adjustment to one's life stage and situation" (p. 523). The concept of adaptation appears to be intertwined with that of mental health. Those who adapt to subsequent stages in life retain positive mental health.

Figure 5.1

HAVIGHURST AND DUVALL'S DEVELOPMENTAL TASKS OF AGING

Adjusting to decreasing health and physical strength
Adjusting to retirement and reduced income
Finding meaning in life
Maintaining satisfactory living arrangements
Finding satisfaction within the family
Adjusting to the reality of death
Accepting oneself as an aging person

ERIKSON'S DEVELOPMENTAL TASKS OF AGING

EGO INTEGRITY	VERSUS DESPAIR
Person accepts that life has been what it had to be	Person develops dread of dying
Feeling that life has been good and meaningful	Disgust with oneself and one's failures
One has acted responsibly and led a successful life	Bitter because it is too late to start over and do it better

(Birchenall and Streight, 1993)

The majority of the elderly population is in good mental health (Cohen, 1990). Due to the gradual nature of the aging process, the older person has time to develop coping mechanisms to adjust to the physical and psychosocial losses characteristic of aging. However, the amount of physical and emotional energy consumed in adapting to the changes that result from such losses and recovering from the stress they cause may lead to behavioral responses such as loss of hope, decreased self-esteem, social isolation, feeling of burden, withdrawal, and inability to find alternatives.

Many factors will impact on the ability to cope with stress, such as availability of social support, adaptability of surrounding environment, previous levels of mental health, and the amount of stressors at a given period of time. An individual already vulnerable to stress may have his or her abilities to adapt severely depleted.

Although general statistics for mental disorders in the elderly indicate about 20% to 22% of all individuals aged 65 or over meet the criteria for some form of it (Gatz, Kasl-Godley & Karel, 1996; U.S. Department of Health and Human Services, 1999; Gatz and Smyer, 2001) the percentage for nursing homes may range from 70% to 90%.

Figure 5.2

DEVELOPMENTAL TASKS OF LATE LIFE IN HIERARCHIC ORDER

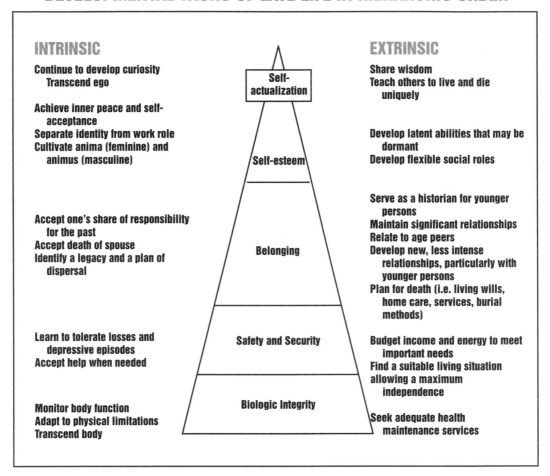

INTRINSIC

Continue to develop curiosity
   Transcend ego

Achieve inner peace and self-
   acceptance
Separate identity from work role
Cultivate anima (feminine) and
   animus (masculine)

Accept one's share of responsibility
   for the past
Accept death of spouse
Identify a legacy and a plan of
   dispersal

Learn to tolerate losses and
   depressive episodes
Accept help when needed

Monitor body function
Adapt to physical limitations
Transcend body

EXTRINSIC

Share wisdom
Teach others to live and die
   uniquely

Develop latent abilities that may be
   dormant
Develop flexible social roles

Serve as a historian for younger
   persons
Maintain significant relationships
Relate to age peers
Develop new, less intense
   relationships, particularly with
   younger persons
Plan for death (i.e. living wills,
   home care, services, burial
   methods)

Budget income and energy to meet
   important needs
Find a suitable living situation
allowing a maximum
   independence

Seek adequate health
   maintenance services

Pyramid levels (top to bottom): Self-actualization, Self-esteem, Belonging, Safety and Security, Biologic Integrity

(Ebersole and Hess, 1998) Reprinted with Permission of Mosby Yearbook Company.

The Surgeon General's report on mental health in older adults (U.S. Department of Health and Human Services, 1999) indicated that older adults experience the same mental health disorders as other adults. However, prevalence and the course of disorders may be different in older people. Assessment and diagnosis is complicated by several factors. First, older adults may have symptoms differing from those of younger people. In addition, mental disorders in older individuals often occur in the presence of other illnesses and this co-morbidity may make detection more difficult. Older individuals are more likely to report somatic symptoms rather than psychological ones, again complicating diagnosis. Finally, mental health disorders may be dismissed as "just aging" rather than as serious problems. For example, depression may be viewed as a natural part of bereavement after the death of a spouse rather than recognized as a problem requiring treatment.

DEPRESSION

Some of the functional disorders most frequently found among the elderly are anxiety disorders, simple phobias, mood disorders and depression (U.S. Department of Health and Human Services, 1999) with depression as the most frequent mental health problem in the aged (Ebersole & Hess, 2001). The National Mental Health Association (2003) reported that more than two million older Americans suffer from some form of depression. Chronic conditions typically associated with aging, such as heart disease, Alzheimer's disease, and cancer can trigger depression. In addition, loss of a loved one can also serve as a trigger. In fact, one-third of widows and widowers suffer from depression in the first month after the death of their spouse and half of them are still clinically depressed after one year. In spite of its prevalence, depression is still misunderstood by many older adults. The National Mental Health Association (2003) found that although depression is very treatable, less than three percent of individuals aged 65 or over receive help from mental health professionals and 68 percent of older adults know almost nothing about depression. The majority would not seek help for depression and instead would deal with it themselves. Remarkably, more than 55 percent of seniors believe depression is a normal part of aging.

Although no one thing causes depression there are identifiable symptoms. The most common include: (a) a persistent sad feeling, (b) sleep difficulties, (c) weight changes, (d) feeling slowed down, (e) excessive worries about health problems and finances, (f) frequent tearfulness, (g) feeling worthless or helpless, (h) pacing and fidgeting, (i) difficulty concentrating, (j) physical symptoms such as gastrointestinal problems or pain (National Mental Health Association, 1996; National Institute on Aging, 2002). Of course any one of these symptoms may not be an indicator of depression. However, the existence of several, lasting more than two weeks, may be cause for concern.

Older individuals may not experience depression until later in life. Late-onset depression does not occur until after age 60 and is marked by greater apathy, and more pronounced cognitive deficits than early-onset depression. Factors related to late-onset depression include widowhood, physical illness, maximum education level at less than high school, impaired functional status, and heavy consumption of alcohol. Late life depression tends to be more chronic, with longer term recurrences, than early life depression. (U.S. Department of Health and Human Services, 1999).

There is evidence that several approaches to prevention of depression are effective, including grief counseling for widows and widowers (U.S. Department of Health and Human Services, 1999). Other preventive measures include trying to prepare for major life changes, having someone to talk to, developing friendships, finding a hobby, staying connected with family, being physically fit, and having a balanced diet (National Institute on Aging, 2002l). If prevention is not enough there are a variety of highly effective treatments for depression. Support groups, therapy, and medications have been proven effective. In some cases electroconvulsive therapy may be the most effective course of treatment (National Institute on Aging, 2002l).

SUICIDE

A major consequence of depression is suicide. Data indicate that older Americans are much more likely to die by suicide than younger people. Although older individuals compose less than 13 percent of the population they accounted for 18 percent of suicides in the year 2000. The highest rate of suicide was among white males aged 85 years of age or older, who committed suicide at a rate of 59 deaths per 1000,000 persons. This is a much higher rate than the 10.6 deaths per 100,000 persons in the total population (National Institute of Mental Health, 2003). Therefore, it is important to understand the factors that might precipitate such action. Men seem to be more at risk than women, perhaps because of the loss of control that may accompany retirement, or severe illness may be harder to accept for men than women, given socialization patterns both groups have been exposed to. Feelings of helplessness may lead to depression, and severe depression may culminate in a suicide attempt.

Potential signs of thoughts of suicide such as continued depression, sudden changes in sleeping and eating patterns, unusual behaviors such as giving possessions away, apparent disregard for previously cherished objects, persons, or activities, and comments such as, "I would be better off dead," or "Life has no meaning anymore" should be taken seriously. There is also a need to be aware of risk factors such as mental or physical illness, depression, death of a spouse, substance abuse, and pathologic relationships (U.S. Department of Health and Human Services, 1999; Ebersole & Hess, 2001). Harbert & Ginsberg (1990) recommend that services such as telephone reassurance and being available to talk be instituted as needed.

SUBSTANCE ABUSE

Another mental health problem experienced by older individuals is substance abuse, although it is often overlooked by family and health care providers. People may become more sensitive to alcohol as they age and as a result, alcohol consumption levels that were appropriate in middle age may be excessive in the later years. In addition, alcohol may exacerbate conditions such as ulcers, high blood pressure and ulcers. Some individuals are heavy drinkers throughout life and continue patterns of alcohol abuse into later life. However, other older individuals develop drinking problems later in life, late-onset drinking, as a result of stressful events such as failing health, loss of loved ones or shifts in employment. Alcohol may become the mechanism for dealing with anxiety, boredom or grief (National Institute on Aging, 2002). In addition to problems with alcohol, older individuals may experience drug-related problems, particularly from over-the-counter drugs.

COGNITIVE DISORDERS

The above paragraphs dealt with "functional" disorders, that is, disorders in which psychosocial factors such as personality and life stresses may lead to impaired functioning. Such disorders do not seem to have consistent biological causes. They differ from the "organic" disorders, which may be traced to physical etiology. The following section will explore the range of organic disorders among the elderly. The remainder of this chapter will utilize the terms "delirium" and "dementia" to describe the two major syndrome complexes experienced by the elderly.

DELIRIUM

According to Whitbourne (2002), delirium is a "cognitive disorder that is characterized by temporary but acute confusion that can be caused by diseases of the heart and lung, infection or malnutrition" (pp. 219-220). Also known as acute confusional state or transient cognitive disorder, this syndrome is characterized by:

1. Disturbance of consciousness (such as reduced clarity of awareness of the environment) with reduced ability to focus, shift, or sustain attention
2. A change in cognition (such as memory deficit) or development of perceptual disturbances not better accounted for by a pre-existing, established, or evolving dementia
3. Development over a short period of time, usually hours
4. Symptoms that fluctuate during the day
5. Evidence that the disturbance is caused by direct physiological consequences of a general medical constitution (American Psychiatric Association, 1994)

Manifestations include memory impairment, language disturbances, learning difficulties, involuntary movements, abnormal mood shifts, and poor-reasoning ability and judgment. Among the precipitating causes for delirium are (a) medication, (b) trauma, (c) infection, (d) malnutrition, (e) metabolic imbalance, (f) cerebrovascular disorders, (g) alcohol intoxication, (h) social stressors, (i) depression, (j) prolonged immobilization, and (k) sensory deprivation.

A report from the Mayo Clinic (1999) provided an in-depth discussion of delirium. It is present in 11 percent to 24 percent of older individuals admitted to the hospital, and an additional five percent to 35 percent of patients will develop it. The fairly rapid onset typical of delirium means that individuals working with the elderly may see completely altered behaviors in a brief time span, for example, drowsiness, normal wakefulness, agitation and excessive vigilance may all occur in rapid succession. The report identified three types of delirium. Hyperactive delirium is characterized by increased motor activity. Hypoactive delirium is marked by decreased motor activity and is a more common form in older individuals. In the mixed type both hyperactive and hypoactive behaviors are seen. In 40 percent of the incidences of delirium hallucinations will occur. A characteristic of delirium often observed in the elderly is sundowning, increased disturbances occurring in the evening. (Sundowning, marked by increased agitation and restlessness during the night, also occurs in Alzheimer's disease.)

Treatment outcomes for delirium are often good. Typically, when the medical problem causing delirium is found, treatment is possible and the individual is able to return to previous levels of functioning. However, there is evidence (Mayo Clinic, 1999) that in some cases symptoms may persist.

DEMENTIA

Dementia is an umbrella term for a brain disorder that seriously affects a person's ability to perform daily activities (Alzheimer's Disease Education & Referral Center, 2003). "Dementia is the loss of memory, reason, judgment and language to such an extent that it interferes with a person's daily life and activities. It is not a disease, but a group of symptoms that often accompanies a disease or condition" (U.S. Department of Health and Human Services, 2002a, p. 6). The Diagnostic and Statistical Manual of Mental Disorders (American Psychiatric Association, 1994) defines dementia as including the following:

1. Development of multiple cognitive deficits including memory impairment and at least one of the following: aphasia (loss or decrease in ability to speak, understand, read or write [burlingame & Skalko, 1997]), apraxia (inability to conduct purposeful, voluntary movements without the presence of impaired sensations, muscle weakness or paralysis [burlingame & Skalko, 1997]), agnosia (decreased ability to know familiar persons or objects [burlingame & Skalko, 1997]), or a disturbance in executive functioning (i.e. problem solving or abstract reasoning).
2. The decline must be serious enough to cause impairment in occupational or social functioning.
3. The decline must represent a decline from previously high levels of functioning.

Individuals with dementia exhibit wide ranges of symptoms. Some of these include the inability to learn new information; loss of memory for information previously learned; difficulties with reasoning and abstract thinking; difficulties in ability to speak, carry out motor activities, and identify objects; personality changes; inability to carry out work or social activities; anxiety, depression, or suspiciousness; spatial disorientation; poor judgment and poor insight; and disinhibited behavior such as crude jokes or neglecting personal hygiene (American Psychiatric Association, 1994; New York Hospital Cornell Medical Center, 1996).

Dementia is not an inevitable consequence of the normal aging process. On average, dementia affects approximately 10% to 15% of the older American population. However, as age increases, so does the probability of developing dementia.

DISTRIBUTION

It is estimated that Alzheimer's disease accounts for 70% of all cases of dementia (Ebersole & Hess, 2001). Other causes of irreversible dementia include: vascular dementia resulting from damage to arteries supplying the brain, caused by a stroke or transient ischemic attacks; fronterotemporal dementia, caused by damage to the temporal and frontal areas of the brain; Parkinson's disease, a nervous system disorder; Lewy body dementia, estimated to be the second most common form of dementia and similar to Alzheimer's disease; Huntington's disease, a degenerative neurological disorder causing loss of control over movement; Creutzfeldt-Jakob Disease, also known as "mad cow" disease; Pick's disease, a rare form of dementia; and HIV-related dementias (Whitbourne, 2002). In addition, there are reversible dementias caused by a variety of medical conditions that impact the brain (Whitbourne, 2002).

Some of these conditions may develop earlier in life, others are extremely rare, and not all will inevitably result in dementia. Two of the major causes of dementia among the elderly, vascular dementia and Alzheimer's disease, will be examined next.

Vascular dementia. These types of dementia, formerly known as multi-infarct dementia, usually occur after age 65. They result from a series of infarcts in the brain, leading to tissue death. The infarcts are a consequence of interrupted blood supply to the brain due to vascular changes produced by arteriosclerotic disease.

The main characteristic of this type of dementia is its "stepwise" progression. In other words, symptoms usually begin suddenly and fluctuate with time. After the first evidence of decline, the individual may seem to improve or remain stable, until another infarct occurs, bringing about increased damage to the brain. Some of the telltale signs of vascular dementia include speech or vision problems and/or weakness on one side of the body. Vascular dementias (VaD) are differentiated from Alzheimer's disease (discussed in detail below) in several ways, including: (a) impaired motor skills are an early symptom of VaD, (b) brain scan shows evidence of stroke or stroke-related changes in VaD, (c) an underlying vascular disorder such as hypertension or heart disease is always present in VaD, (d) abrupt onset, often progressing in steps, with decline slowed by controlling the vascular disorder is characteristic of VaD, (e) some intellectual functions are affected to a greater degree than others in VaD (Alzheimer's Association, 1995).

ALZHEIMER'S DISEASE

Alois Alzheimer in Germany identified the first case of Alzheimer's disease in 1906. Alzheimer noticed distinctive clumps (amyloid plaques) and tangles of fibers (neurofibrillay tangles) in the brain tissue of a woman who died of what was considered an unusual mental illness (Alzheimer's Disease Education & Referral Center, 2003). Since Alzheimer's time a great deal of research has gone into understanding Alzheimer's disease.

In the past, it was not uncommon to hear the word "senile" used as a label for what was actually demented behavior. Such misuse of the term led to general stereotypes, equating "old" with "cognitive decline." Today, it is well known that Alzheimer's may occur either before or after age 65.

Alzheimer's disease is characterized by a progressive neurological decline, accompanied by the following pathological changes in the brain: (a) presence of the amyloid plaques first identified by Alzheimer; (b) presence of neurofibrillary tangles; (c) brain atrophy (shrinking of the brain); (d) loss of nerve cells in the areas of the brain used for memory and mental abilities; (e) decreased levels in the brain of chemicals used to communicate between nerve cells (U.S. Department of Health and Human Services, 2002a; Alzheimer's Disease Education & Referral Center, 2003).

The Diagnostic and Statistical Manual of Mental Disorders (American Psychiatric Association, 1994) identifies Alzheimer's disease as:

A. Development of multiple cognitive impairments manifested by:
   —memory impairment marked by inability to learn new information or recall old;
   —at least one of the following:
        aphasia,
        apraxia,
        agnosia,
        disturbance in executive functioning.
B. The losses cause impairment in occupational or social functioning and are a significant decline from previous functioning.
C. There is gradual onset and continuing
D. The cognitive deficits are not due to other central nervous system conditions that cause progressive deficits in cognition and memory, systemic conditions causing dementia, episodes of delirium, or by any mental illness such as depression or schizophrenia.

This disease affects approximately four million Americans. Approximately 10% of the 65 and over population have Alzheimer's disease (Alzheimer's Association, 1998). Its prevalence shows a dramatic increase with age; approximately 3% of individuals between the ages of 65 and 74 are affected, 19% of those between 75 and 84, and nearly—of all individuals aged 85 and over (Alzheimer's Disease Education & Referral Center, 2003). Since the over-85 age group is the fastest-growing segment of the older American population, a concomitant increase in the number of Alzheimer's cases is expected in the future. In fact, it is estimated that 14 million Americans will have Alzheimer's disease by the middle of the next century.

The financial costs of Alzheimer's disease are staggering. The cost per patient lifetime is approximately $174,000, and the total cost to the nation is $100 billion per year. Alzheimer's is the third most expensive disease, after heart disease and cancer. Typical family care costs are $12,500 per year, while care in nursing home is $42,000 (Alzheimer's Association, 1998a).

The personal costs are also tremendous. As Rowe and Kahn (1998) state: "It robs people of their personalities, their ability to interact with others, and to function effectively" (p. 93).

The search for the cause of Alzheimer's disease continues, and several causes are under examination (U.S. Department of Health and Human Services, 2002a). There is a link between genetic factors and early-onset Alzheimer's disease, which affects individuals aged 30 to 60. There may also be a genetic link causing late-onset Alzheimer's, with scientists focusing on the gene that produces a protein called apolipoprotein E (ApoE) as a potential link. Researchers are also examining the relationship of beta-amyloid, a protein fragment from a protein called amyloid precursor protein (APP), to Alzheimer's disease. It is known that forming beta-amyloid from APP is related to Alzheimer's disease. Another protein, called tau, is also being studied. There also may be a link between risk factors for cardiovascular disease and Alzheimer's. Recent evidence indicates a class of drugs, called statins, used to lower cholesterol may also lower the risk of Alzheimer's disease. Other causes being studied include the role of molecules called free radicals in Alzheimer's, as well as inflammation in the brain and damage to blood vessels in the brain.

Since there is no reliable test for Alzheimer's disease at this time, the only definite diagnostic tool is an autopsy to look for the tangles and plaques distinctive to Alzheimer's disease. However, a number of assessment tools are used to identify the probable presence of Alzheimer's disease, including: (a) a complete patient history; (b) information from family members and close friends; (c) complete physical and neurological examinations; (d) a computerized tomography (CT) scan or MRI of the brain; (e) neuropsychological testing of memory, language, arithmetic and other brain functions (U. S. Department of Health and Human Services, 2002a).

The life expectancy of an individual with AD is quite variable, ranging from two to as long as 20 years, with an average course of four to eight years (Whitbourne, 2002). The progression is gradual and is often classified into three stages according to the type of cognitive and behavioral deficits experienced by the individual as the disease advances (U.S. Department of Health and Human Services, 2002a; Whitbourne, 2002):

Mild Alzheimer's disease (early stage)

- Memory loss
- Confusion about location of familiar places (getting lost begins to occur)
- Taking longer to accomplish normal daily tasks such as remembering shopping lists
- Trouble handling money and paying bills
- Poor judgment leading to bad decisions
- Loss of spontaneity and sense of initiative
- Mood and personality changes, withdrawing from others, increased anxiety
- Recent memory problems such as forgetting to turn off the stove

Moderate Alzheimer's disease (middle stage)

- Increasing memory loss and confusion
- Shortened attention span
- Problems recognizing friends and family members
- Difficulty with language; problems with reading, writing, working with numbers
- Difficulty organizing thoughts and thinking logically
- Inability to learn new things or cope with new or unexpected situations
- Restlessness, agitation, anxiety, tearfulness, wandering–especially in the late afternoon or night (sundowning)
- Repetitive statements or movements, occasional muscle twitches
- Hallucinations, delusions, suspiciousness or paranoia, irritability
- Loss of impulse control (shown through sloppy table manners, undressing at inappropriate times or places, vulgar language)
- Perceptual motor problems (such as trouble getting out of chairs or setting the table)
- Problems in following the content conversations

Severe Alzheimer's disease

- Weight loss
- Seizures, skin infections, difficulty swallowing
- Groaning, moaning, or grunting
- Increased sleeping
- Lack of bowel and bladder control
- Lost ability to speak

The above stages are not the rule for every individual affected by the disease. There is much variance regarding speed and level of decline seen among persons with Alzheimer's.

Some older individuals experience memory loss exceeding that normally expected as part of aging but not as severe as seen in Alzheimer's disease. In addition, they do not have the other factors listed above. These individuals are identified as having Mild Cognitive Impairment (MCI). Some individuals, about 40 percent, progress from MCI to Alzheimer's disease. However, in a majority of cases, 60 percent, MCI is not a precursor to Alzheimer's disease (U.S. Department of Health and Human Services, 2002a).

Although there is no known cure for Alzheimer's disease, there are four prescription drugs—Reminyl, Exelon, Aricept and Cognex,—currently used to lessen symptoms in the mild to moderate category. They delay progression of symptoms for a limited time and may be effective in controlling behavioral symptoms in the short term. However they do not stop the progress of Alzheimer's disease (U.S. Department of Health and Human Services, 2002b).

Another important factor to remember is that individuals maintain certain assets in spite of the losses. Based on a review of literature, Bowlby (1993) identified the following areas of persisting assets:

1. Emotional awareness—capacity to experience a full range of emotions in spite of difficulty in expressing them; need to give and receive affection, memory of feelings associated with past events.
2. Sensory appreciation—capacity to derive pleasure and stimulation from sensorial experiences.
3. Primary motor functioning—strength, dexterity, and motor control stable until later stages.
4. Sociability and social skills—persistence of overlearned, ingrained social skills, such as shaking hands, exchanging social greetings.
5. Procedural memory and habitual skills—ability to remember how to perform certain activities by cuing into triggering aspects of the environment; e.g., being given a bowl with cereal and a spoon and using spoon to eat from the bowl.
6. Remote memory—ability to recall significant events from the distant past, or circumstances surrounding them.
7. Sense of humor—use of humor to cover embarrassing moments and to relate socially.

Remembering that the individual retains such abilities into advanced stages of the disease helps practitioners and caregivers focus on areas of intervention, to delay further deterioration, and to assure a better quality of life for the individual. Some suggestions for working with persons with Alzheimer's will be offered in the following section.

ULYSSEAN APPROACHES

Psychological vitality is important to Ulyssean living. The mind and body must function at the highest level possible to achieve a sense of accomplishment and happiness. The following material provides some examples of interventions used to create conditions conducive to Ulyssean living.

As a general principle, considering the potential causes of functional mental disorders such as depression, practitioners should examine the amount of social and psychological support provided by the environment. Individuals experience a great number of losses, some related to loved ones. Appropriate counseling should be made available to help cope with grieving. Support groups may be created for the elderly to share experiences and find solace among others undergoing similar pain.

Since loss of occupational status is so disturbing to some older adults, leisure education programs should begin prior to retirement and prepare individuals to find productive uses for their leisure time. Also, offering meaningful volunteering opportunities, such as involvement in civic associations or intergenerational programs, may help alleviate feelings of worthlessness and help maintain self-esteem.

Loss of health is often gradual and can be dealt with through approaches discussed previously in the chapter concerning biological aging. If sudden illness or disability set in, the individual will need psychological support through individual or group counseling. As noted above, involvement in recreational activities also has the potential to reduce negative feelings associated with declining health.

Numerous interventions may assist with mental well being. Pet therapy, horticulture, music, and graphic arts are all examples of successful interventions in creating opportunities for socialization and enjoyment.

INTERVENTION TECHNIQUES

As Hellen (1993) indicates, a thorough assessment is crucial for success when working with individuals with Alzheimer's disease. Activities must flow from the results of the assessment. In general, a stable, familiar environment and an established routine are crucial when working with individuals with Alzheimer's disease. Activities should focus on remaining abilities and strengths and be as normal as possible (Alzheimer's Diseases Education and Referral Center, undated). In addition, activities should be meaningful to participants.

The following are suggestions on how to work with persons with Alzheimer's disease compiled from a variety of authors (Bartol, 1979; Greenblatt, 1988; Weaverdyck, 1991; Bowlby, 1993; Hellen, 1993). They also are generally useful in working with older adults with a variety of cognitive impairments.

99 TIPS FOR WORKING WITH PEOPLE WITH ALZHEIMER'S DISEASE

COMMUNICATION:

1. Speak to the person as an adult, do not talk down.
2. Address person by proper title (Mr./Mrs.); use first name only after requesting permission.
3. Reassure by confirming the emotional message, even if verbal message makes no sense (e.g., "You seem to be upset about this, Mrs. Smith").
4. Never argue or disagree if incorrect; instead find positive ways to validate feelings and orient to reality (e.g., if the person says she has not eaten all day, start by discussing types of food liked, then show the menu for the day, and refer to incidents during meal time rather than saying, "You are wrong, you had steak for lunch just an hour ago").
5. Emphasize recognition, not recall.

6. For conversation topics, focus on "opinions" rather than facts (e.g., ask "How do you like to spend Christmas?" rather than "Where did you spend Christmas last year?")

7. Be aware of every aspect of presentation—tone, posture, facial expression—since the person may read non-verbal communication better than the verbal content of messages.

8. Alert the person by touching or saying his or her name before asking questions or giving directions. Make eye contact as you speak.

9. In social situations, always introduce other persons by providing name and orienting information so that the individual will not feel embarrassed for not recognizing others.

10. Eliminate background noise or confusion.

11. Speak slowly and clearly. Use short, simple sentences. Keep voice calm, low, moderated.

12. Do not use abstract language, confusing figures of speech, sarcasm.

13. When referring to names of places or objects, use full titles and descriptors (for example, "We are going to the physical therapy room, the place you go for exercise every morning").

14. Use terms that are most familiar to the person in referring to objects (icebox vs. refrigerator). Use familiar phrases and mannerisms that were common in the person's life.

15. Allow ample time for response.

16. Be ready to repeat information; when doing so, use the same words.

17. Supply the words a person is trying to recall.

18. Avoid using "don't," commands, or ordering the person. Instead, use clear directions such as, "Mr. Jones, I would like for you to throw the ball to me now."

19. Express warmth and caring. Listen even if the speaker is not making sense.

20. If the individual begins to ramble, refocus and rephrase what has been said so far.

21. Never speak about the individual to others in his/her presence as if not there.

SELECTING AND CONDUCTING ACTIVITIES:

1. Use overlearned, familiar activities.

2. Choose simple and repetitive, not overly challenging, but age-appropriate activities (folding napkins).

3. Emphasize sensory experiences.

4. Emphasize overlearned, persistent social skills.

5. Use activities to foster social interaction such as small parties.

6. Maintain exercise program. Encourage ambulation.

7. Stimulate cognitively. Do not assume potential participants are not able to perform activities. Use cuing and simplifying if necessary.

8. Allow for expression of emotions.

9. Take advantage of intact remote memory. Encourage reminiscing.

10. Explain the purpose of activities. Choose activities that are meaningful and have obvious, practical purposes.

11. Use activities that relate to seasonal life themes and experiences from the work environment. Look for activities that reflect acceptable work themes for that generation.

12. Cue or prompt procedural memory by concrete, non-verbal instruction.

13. Break down complex tasks and give instructions in steps. Begin with a step participants can successfully accomplish.

14. If choices are required, offer only two manageable choices at a time.

15. Give immediate but not excessive feedback for responses or attempts.

16. Use consistent routines in the environment and presentation of activities.

17. When working in groups, do not expect to have everyone work on the same step independently. Use a "parallel" format, in which each individual completes each step of the activity in turn.

18. Plan the week or month around a familiar theme and schedule all activities related to major themes to increase consistency for the individual.

19. Use ample, familiar, concrete physical cues and memorabilia. Use multisensorial cues.

20. If participants get restless, reassure, call by name, and distract by asking for help with activity.

21. Use demonstration. Include high-functioning members to model. Keep supplies at hand for those capable of proceeding on their own.

22. When working with groups, sit around a table, maintain seat assignments for following group meetings.

23. Provide a bridge from the general milieu. When beginning groups, introduce participants, orient to time, place, and explain reason for being there. Provide large name tags for participants.

24. Repeat successful activities often and maintain consistency in the schedule.

25. Schedule activities that demand verbalization and cognitive functioning in the morning and those requiring energy spending for afternoon.

26. Use small groups of three to five persons. Plan to meet no longer than 30 minutes.

27. Determine the best time of the day for a resident to do activities.

28. Read short stories and poems to simulate cognitive functioning.

29. Activities such as marching, clapping, walking, and dancing may be effective substitutes for agitated and wandering behavior.

ENVIRONMENT:

1. Keep it safe by removing obstacles.
2. Remove sources of potential illusions, such as glare, unfamiliar noises or objects.
3. Allow space for walking.
4. Avoid wandering into dangerous areas; place warning signs.
5. Use environmental cues to help individuals find their way (e.g., photo on room's door).
6. Maintain environment structured consistently. Keep it unambiguous and understandable.
7. Avoid distractions. Keep things simple.
8. Make the environment as homelike as possible.
9. Compensate for physical deficits.

A report from the Alzheimer's Disease Education & Referral Center (2003) provides a variety of suggestions for working with family members who have Alzheimer's disease. Several of the principles underlying their suggestions are useful for enhancing the possibility of Ulyssean living by individuals with Alzheimer's disease. Suggestions in addition to those listed above include:

1. Follow established routines as much as possible.
2. Simplify tasks and focus on one step at a time.
3. Allow the individual to exercise as much independence as possible.
4. Be as gentle and calm as possible.
5. Don't rush to get tasks done.
6. Adjust your expectations so they match the person's abilities.
7. Be as creative and flexible as possible.
8. Make the environment safe and inviting.
9. React to problems, such as incontinence or emotional outbursts, in a calm manner.
10. Daily exercise is important in reducing excess energy.
11. Provide ample time to respond to requests and questions.
12. Speak in a calm tone of voice.
13. Use simple instructions.
14. Do not overload the person with questions.
15. Be alert for signs of frustration.
16. Do not assume an individual cannot understand what you are saying or asking.
17. Try using eye contact and touch when you respond to questions.
18. If an individual is using repetitive speech, is aggressive or reacting poorly in a situation, try distracting him or her with pleasurable activities such as having a snack, music, or looking through old pictures.

19. If necessary, remove an individual from a stressful situation causing a catastrophic reaction.

20. Keep the environment simple by removing clutter, extra people, noise and overactivity.

21. Do not try to use logic and reasoning (since these are impaired in individuals with Alzheimer's) when dealing with catastrophic situations.

22. Schedule activities that are more involved early in the day.

23. A well-lit environment may reduce sundowning.

24. Do not overreact to inappropriate behavior.

25. Avoid loud and confusing noises.

26. Rather than trying to teach new activities, build on preserved abilities, such as singing or maybe even playing an instrument.

27. Limit activities to no more than 30 minutes.

28. Focus on simple, repetitive activities not requiring a great deal of decision making. Suggested activities include sweeping, walking a dog, shelling peas, and raking.

29. Break activities into smaller pieces. Rather than, "Set the table," you might ask that the plates be set out.

30. Demonstrate desired behaviors.

31. Keep activities, and instructions, at as adult a level as possible.

32. Agitation or frustration should lead to a break or new activity.

The U.S. Department of Health and Human Services (2002c) published Caregiver Guide: Tips for caregivers of people with Alzheimer's Disease to help those responsible for care of a family member. The publication provides excellent advice related to various activities of daily life, such as bathing, dressing, eating and activities. In addition, it provides information on typical problems of Alzheimer's disease, such as hallucinations and wandering. Many of the recommendations are similar to those listed above. A few additional tips:

1. Prepare in advance, making sure you have everything you need before any activity begins.

2. Incorporate enjoyable activities into a person's daily routine and try to do them at the same time every day.

3. Turn off the television when violent or disturbing programs are on.

4. Be sure to secure anything that can cause harm or injury.

5. Keep activity areas free from clutter. Remove scatter rugs or anything else that may cause falls.

6. Keep family traditions that are important and adapt as needed.

7. Encourage visits by family and friends.

8. Avoid crowds, strange surrounding and changes in routines since they may cause agitation or confusion.

The many interventions listed above are intended to provide caregivers with some tools that may be effective when working with individuals with dementia. Much of what has been listed supports the need for individualized programming offered in a stable environment free from unnecessary distractions. Keep activities and directions as slow and simple as necessary, while remembering that you are working with adults. Patience, flexibility, respect and understanding should guide all your interactions with people with Alzheimer's disease.

CONCLUSION

Psychological changes in the later years are varied within and across individuals. Most individuals adapt well to changes and are able to continue with patterns of behavior developed throughout life. The balance between continuity and change is typically maintained without major negative consequences. Unfortunately, another reality for some individuals is that pathological changes in personality and cognition will occur. The specter of Alzheimer's disease looms large in many families. However, even in these cases, Ulyssean living remains a possibility through careful, well-planned interventions such as those discussed in this chapter.

Belief in the value of Ulyssean living requires it be a focus for all individuals receiving our services. People with cognitive impairments such as those described in this chapter may require greater effort to achieve the goals of Ulyssean living. However, they will also be among those who will benefit the most from this approach to life.

SIX

THE IMPORTANCE OF LEISURE

What appears below is a letter received from a couple who attended an Elderhostel program given by one of the authors. It is reproduced exactly as written.

Dear Fran: A short report on leisure at Laurel Vineyards. The "work" part of our life is growing grapes, a vegetable garden and fruits as well as winemaking and selling grapes to home winemakers. Also the regular chores of keeping a home and personal finances in order. Actually leisure seems to be part of the above; a blend of leisure and work. A great deal of effort is made to keep 300 vines growing and producing, then made into wine—and gardening is not all fun, but many parts of our projects are leisure. There are frequent pleasant breaks from routine. A few of our leisure doings:

- Reading to learn or entertain
- A 20-minute walk before breakfast and a look at our beautiful world
- A leisurely second cup of coffee after breakfast with reading or conversation
- After lunch, reading and a nap
- Evening reading or TV (if any), knitting or weaving with good friends one day a week—Mary Jane, P.C. users meeting for Alan
- Lunch out or shopping
- Choosing books at the library
- Planting new plants and varieties of vegetables; Watching the woods as seasons change
- Wine tastings with friends
- Tasting our wines two years after grapes were harvested
- Alan likes the challenge of developing techniques for solving problems using the P.C. Also learning to use new software.

THE ROLE OF LEISURE IN LATER LIFE

Is leisure a central focus in later life as Kelly (1987a) indicated, or is it a con foisted upon older individuals providing small compensation for losses in other roles? The answer is an elusive and often confusing one. This chapter will examine the role of leisure in later life.

Since the question is a multi-faceted one with several levels of answers, this chapter will be equally multi-faceted. There are several ways to examine the role of leisure in Ulyssean living; this chapter will examine its linkage to physical, psychological, affective, and social well being.

WHAT IS LEISURE?

Dychtwald and Flower (1989) created a media furor with their publication of *Age Wave: The Challenges and Opportunities of an Aging America.* It was seen as a major contribution in viewing life in the later years as something positive and to be valued. Leisure and recreation merited its own chapter in this highly entertaining book. Dychtwald and Flower view leisure as the "dominant national pastime for men and women over 60" (p. 119) and see it as "becoming progressively more active and adventurous, and physical as well as intellectual— in short, more intensely gratifying" (p. 115).

Clearly, we are concerned with something very important and even crucial in the lives of many individuals. However, understanding this phenomenon is difficult. Defining leisure is an impossible task. According to Barrett (1989), "Of all concepts, that of leisure is one of the most intractable. Like the concept of time, in the words of St. Augustine, we know what it is when no one asks us, but when they ask what it is, we are hard put to find an answer" (p. 9).

There have been a variety of definitions presented for leisure. Generally, the definitions fall into three broad categories: time, activity, and state of mind (Kelly, 1996). It is tempting to adopt a time definition when examining leisure in the later years. The link between aging and leisure would be relatively easy to make, since in many cases old age is accompanied by retirement and its concomitant unobligated time. In fact, when asked to define leisure, responses from a group of older individuals included: that which occupies time not used to gain necessities; time when you can do what you want without thoughts of duties or obligation, time available when there is no required activity, time to relax and play, time to do things I want to do as contrasted to things I have to do, time to do things you wish to do without any pressure, unconstrained time, time to do things other than those essential, time left over, free time after I take care of responsibilities, time to do what you want, time when I have to answer to no one, unscheduled time.

If free time were synonymous with leisure, then the experience of that time would be superfluous to the leisure experience. That is clearly not the case. For example, 15 minutes immersed in a Clive Cussler novel or watching your favorite football team is not the same experience as 15 minutes spent in a dentist's waiting room. The first may be leisure, the dentist's office probably is not. Yet both are composed of unobligated time.

To limit the leisure perspective to time is to deny its potential centrality in life. It is not solely an event used to fill time. It can be more than that. While it is true leisure resides partly in the world of time, it also resides in a world of activity. In fact, typical definitions of leisure include: doing something you like to do in your spare time; an enjoyable activity that serves a purpose; relaxed reading; relaxation, doing what you desire, meditation; doing what you want at the time, reading; anything I choose to do for a change from work I have to do; things I like to do that aren't work; doing something special; completely different from everyday and/or ordinary activities; sex; an enjoyable activity. This activity perspective is appealing and congruent with a common sense view. However, activity alone is not sufficient as a leisure definition. If it were, the same activity would always be considered leisure. For example, the experience of jogging would be the same whether it was to train for a race, an effort to lose weight, or a chance to interact with your friends. Again, this seems overly simplistic.

A third dimension that appears when older individuals define leisure is the perception of choosing to do something and enjoying it. Some examples provided by older individuals included: being last on the line at the grocery store and not caring; freedom of choice; doing what I want, when I want; a period of life that allows me to pursue a course of pleasure without many of the normal pressures of accomplishment; when you do what you want to do instead of what you must or what you think you must. These descriptions incorporate all three elements of time, activity, and perception.

There is general agreement that two central constructs of leisure are perceived freedom and intrinsic motivation. Perceived freedom is closely aligned with freedom of choice. The participant must feel the activity is chosen, not required. The other element, intrinsic motivation, indicates the activity is chosen primarily for rewards coming from the activity itself. Extrinsic motivation lies in rewards, such as trophies or other forms of recognition, which are external to the activity (Mannell & Kleiber, 1997). The importance of intrinsic motivation in Ulyssean living is discussed in greater detail in Chapter 7. We agree with Iso-Ahola (1989) who believes, "While freedom of choice or self-determination is a necessary condition for the occurrence of leisure, it is not sufficient . . . to have leisure one must experience enjoyment" (p. 256). Therefore, we view leisure as a freely chosen activity done primarily for its own sake, with an element of enjoyment, pursued during unobligated time.

As the letter that opened this chapter indicated, leisure is usually relatively simple. In fact, its allure is often in its uncomplicated nature. The Johnsons take obvious pleasure from the simple things in life. Their leisure revolves around everyday things, often integrated into their "work." But do not be fooled by the simplicity of leisure. It is also one of the most important arenas for personal growth and development for Ulyssean living.

Caudron (1997) addresses the changing nature of retirement and retirees. The baby boomers are entering the threshold of retirement and the impacts will be dramatic. Many boomers will return to work, in some form. Others will "reinvent" themselves through volunteer work, education, or other leisure involvements. The image of the retiree spending the years after work passing time in a variety of "leisurely" pursuits will be even less accurate than it is today. A retiree may decide to return to school, seek part-time employment, or join the Peace Corps. While these activities may not fit the traditional perspective of leisure, they clearly fall under our definition of leisure. In fact, the Ulyssean perspective demands a broader view of leisure than merely the passing of time in some frivolous activity. This huge group of individuals will enter their retirement years expecting a great deal out of retirement, including the opportunity to pursue a Ulyssean lifestyle. An understanding of the role of leisure in later life is crucial.

THE ROLE OF LEISURE

There is evidence that leisure provides a multitude of benefits to older participants (Mobily, Lemke & Gisin, 1991; Haberkost, Dellman-Jenkins & Bennett, 1996; Patterson, 1996; Everard, Lach, Fisher & Baum, 2000; Grant, 2001; Lennartsson & Silverstein, 2001; Silverstein & Parker, 2002). The underlying perspective of much of the research on leisure and aging has been the link between activity involvement and successful aging. Issues such as life satisfaction, interpersonal processes, social interaction, and health (Spacapan & Oskamp, 1989) have been included in the search for optimum aging. This chapter will examine the place of leisure in these processes.

Several years ago, Janet McLean presented an equation summarizing the factors that go into successful aging. With some modification, her formula was: Successful Aging = Health X Meaningful Activity X Being Needed X Financial Security. One way to examine the importance of leisure in later life is to examine its role in each of the components of successful aging.

HEALTH

Many view later life as a time of poor health. In fact this is not the case. (See Chapter 3 for more on this issue.) Health is defined as not only the absence of disease, but also physical, mental, and social well being, and therefore health is best viewed as an indicator of function and disability (Burdman, 1986). Although aging is accompanied by physiological decline, decreasing well being is not a necessary concomitant of this process. Rather, the ability and willingness to take control of one's own health is crucial. According to Burdman, "To age is not to look forward to decrement and infirmity, but rather to continue to use and nourish all remaining capacities to the fullest" (1986, p. 106).

Actions, built around leisure, can be taken to increase health in later life. (See Chapter 8 for an in-depth discussion of the role of physical activity in later life.) There is evidence that many elderly people make efforts to achieve and maintain good health. The 1985 Health Survey indicates individuals over 65 years of age are less likely to smoke, report that stress has adversely affected their health, or be overweight than their younger counterparts. The bad news is that older individuals are also less likely to exercise regularly (U.S. Senate Special

Committee on Aging at al., 1991). In fact, heart disease is the leading cause of death and major health problems in later life. A recent report from the National Institute on Health (2001) reported that the combination of poor diet and lack of exercise is the second largest underlying cause of death, behind only smoking, in the United States. Leisure can play a role in reversing the lack of regular exercise by older individuals and as a result increase physical health. Lifestyle is a major component of health. Exercise, as part of that lifestyle, is crucial.

Fortunately, many individuals realize the role of movement in their lives. Exercise programs are staples of the offerings at many senior centers. Many states have formalized the role of activity by holding annual Olympic games for older residents of their state. The culmination of this institutionalization of exercise is the development of the U.S. Senior Sports Classic. A recent report of the fourth annual version of this national contest, which had a total of 250,000 contestants over the age of 55, in *USA Today* (Dorsey, 1993) allows us a glimpse of the role of exercise in the later years. According to one of the competitors, 67-year-old sprinter Jim Law, "These games showcase a different slant of the aging process . . . It allows everyone to see that it is possible to age and be in control, contributing, creative, and competitive all at the same time."

Lois Scofield, a tennis player in the same event, echoed Law's message, saying, "We are proving that we are not a burden to society in the health sense. This whole industry is the best prescription for Clinton's (health care) administration. My advice to seniors would be to get off the bridge table and get onto the tennis court" (Dorsey, 1993, p. 12C).

Teague (1987), and more recently the National Institute on Aging (2001), supported the need to get out and exercise. He cited evidence that "carefully planned physical activity programs can help prevent or diminish the severity of many chronic conditions affecting the elderly" (p. 60). An optimum physical activity program will incorporate the five components of a balanced fitness program (National Institute on Aging, 2001). They can serve as a guide in developing an effective activity program.

1. Endurance activities increase breathing and heart rate and therefore improve the health of the lungs, heart, and circulatory system. The result is health as well as improved stamina to do activities of daily life such as shopping and climbing stairs. In addition, endurance exercise may be linked to delay or prevention of cancer, heart disease, stroke and diabetes. Endurance activities include walking, jogging, swimming, bike riding, raking leaves and mowing the lawn. Any activity that increases heart rate and breathing can be an endurance activity.

2. Strength activities not only build muscles, but also increase metabolism and may prevent osteoporosis. Working with weights, machines or resistance bands are useful in developing strength.

3. Flexibility activities keep the body limber. They help prevent falling and injuries. Stretching exercises are recommended in building flexibility.

4. Balance activities are effective in preventing falls, a major problem among older people.
5. Teague adds one component to the above list, exercise for weight control.

Unfortunately, concerns about factors such as heart attack and injury may prevent some individuals from initiating programs in this area. There are of course cautions that must be followed prior to beginning an exercise program. The National Institute on Aging (2001) identified the following precautions and recommend seeking physician approval if they occur:

- Chest pain
- Irregular or rapid heart beat
- Severe shortness of breath
- Undiagnosed weight loss
- Infections, such as pneumonia, if accompanied by a fever
- Fever
- Acute deep vein thrombosis
- A hernia with symptoms
- Ankle or foot sores that will not heal
- Joint swelling
- Persistent pain or walking problems after falling
- Eye conditions, such as bleeding in the retina or detached retina following lens or cataract implants or other eye surgery

In addition to being aware of these cautions, it is recommended that recreation professionals instituting exercise programs seek the help of trained exercise experts, including local physical education teachers, university faculty, or exercise professionals from local fitness centers, as the program develops.

Although Paffenberg, Hyde, and Dow (1991) were not specifically examining the benefits of physical activity to older individuals, many of their conclusions are relevant to all age groups. They stated: "Epidemiological evidence supports the concept that sedentary living habits are directly and causally related to the incidence of hypertensive-atherosclerotic diseases, especially coronary heart disease, sudden cardiac arrest, and stroke" (p. 50). The literature (Goldberg & Hagberg, 1990; Fried, Freedman, Endres, & Wasik, 1997; Agency for Healthcare Research and Quality, 2002; National Institute on Aging, 2002; Nied & Franklin, 2002) continues to offer strong documentation for the many benefits of physical activity. Even a partial list of the potential benefits identified in these resources provides overwhelming evidence of the importance of an active lifestyle:

- reduced resting heart rate
- lower blood pressure levels

- reduced blood glucose levels and possible decrease or delay in the development of noninsulin-dependent diabetes mellitus
- decreased fat body mass and increased lean body mass, lowering risk of obesity
- helps prevent osteoporosis and is rehabilitative for individuals determined to be osteoporotic
- increased muscular strength and improved structure and function of connective tissues thereby preventing chronic back pain
- potential prevention of various types of arthritis and benefit for individuals with osteoarthritis
- reduced depression and anxiety neuroses through improved social skills and self-image
- increased life expectancy
- reduced risk of some cancers
- improved quality of sleep
- improved cognitive functioning
- decreased risk of bone fractures
- lower risk of falls and injuries

Clearly, exercise is a wonderful tool for Ulyssean living. It will result in increased health and well being that is vital for a developmental approach to later life.

The Centers for Disease Control (1999) also strongly recommend exercise as a part of aging, even for individuals who have been sedentary most of their lives. At first, such individuals should exercise for a short time, five to 10 minutes, but the ultimate goal should be at least 30 minutes of exercise at least five days a week.

The CDC also provides guidelines for what communities can do to increase the likelihood that older individuals will exercise. These include, offering programs with aerobic, strength and flexibility components, working with malls and other indoor places to find protected exercise locations, encouraging gyms and exercise facilities to accommodate older participants, providing transportation as needed, involving health care providers as advocates for exercise by their clients, and planning community-sponsored activities and opportunities for exercise. To these, the Agency for Healthcare Quality and Research (2002) adds conducting community-wide campaigns to raise awareness, creating walking trails, and improving access to locations, such as trails and gyms, designed for exercise. These suggestions provide a roadmap to increasing exercise by older people, as well as guidelines to help provide them with physical ability needed for Ulyssean living.

The National Institute on Aging publishes a variety of "facts sheets" providing information about a plethora of aging issues. Their "Exercise: Feeling Fit For Life" (National Institute on Aging, 2002k) not only supports the deleterious effect of no exercise and the benefits of increasing physical activity, it also provides information on initiating a program. They recommend that activity be incorporated into daily life. Rather than adding on calisthenics or a formal exercise program, they recommend selecting activities such as walking, bike riding and gardening as vehicles for exercise. The first step, once activities are chosen, is to eventually participate in at least 30 minutes of activity that results in breathing hard. The 30 minutes can be broken into shorter segment of 10 minutes, as long as the daily total of 30 minutes is reached. The 30 minutes meets the need for endurance type activities. However, a well-balanced exercise regimen should also include strength activities, since loss of strength can affect quality of life. The recommended amount of strength related exercise is at least two days per week. The third component of a comprehensive activity program is activities designed to improve balance. Finally, they recommend stretching in order to stay limber. There it is, an activity approach building endurance, strength, balance and flexibility. Although most older individuals can, and should, exercise, the fact sheet recommends that males over 40 and females over 50 planning to participate in vigorous activity (defined as activity that make one breathe and sweat hard) check with their physician. In addition, a visit to the doctor should occur if the individual has health-related problems, such as those noted earlier in this chapter. The key is to start slowly and get help in starting an exercise program. In most cases the dangers of not exercising far outweigh the potential dangers of exercising.

The data related to benefits of exercise in later life continues to grow. If any one activity could be described as "the fountain of youth" it would be exercise! Indeed, if it were possible to offer only one activity, we would make a strong case for that activity being exercise. The Agency for Healthcare Research and Quality (2002) states, "For many adults, growing older seems to involve an inevitable loss of strength, energy and fitness. But it need not be so. The frail health and loss of function we associate with aging, such as difficulty walking long distance, climbing stairs, or carrying groceries, is in large part due to physical inactivity. When it comes to our muscles and physical fitness, the old adage applies: 'use it or lose it'" (p. 1). This statement gives us insight into why exercise is important to older individuals. It is not to build strength, flexibility and endurance because they are nice to have. Rather it is a matter of quality of life and functional ability.

In addition to the individual costs of inactivity, there are also social costs. The Agency for Healthcare Research and Quality (2002) estimates that 18 percent of adults over the age of 65 are obese and an additional 40 percent are overweight, with associated risks for high blood pressure, diabetes and heart disease. The medical costs are in the billions of dollars. Data from Harvard researchers indicate that almost 10 percent of all healthcare costs are accounted for by obesity and inactivity! Injuries from falls among older people cost more than $20 billion every year. Exercise, or lack of exercise, is more than a personal problem.

Health refers not only to physical health, but mental heath as well. Just as there is strong evidence supporting the link between physical fitness and successful aging, there is also evidence linking mental well being to success in later life. Engagement in leisure activities provides the cognitive stimulation and challenge needed for mental health. In fact, the Center for the Advancement of Health (Facts of Life, 1998) indicates that lifestyle choices are crucial to successful aging. Exercising, making friends, and engaging in activities are "three of the most powerful determinants of health and functioning in seniors."

Everard, Lach, Fisher and Baum (2000) provided strong evidence of the health benefits of engagement in a variety of leisure activities. Their review of the literature documents a variety of benefits including increased physical functioning, slower decline in physical functioning, improved health, and survival. Their research supported a link between retention of engagement in instrumental activities (shopping, cooking, paying bills and doing housework), social activities (traveling, entertaining, attending parties, and attending church), high-demand activities (swimming, woodworking, walking and gardening) and higher physical health. In addition, retention of engagement in low-demand activities (sewing, reading, watching television and listening to music) was related to lower levels of physical health. However, maintenance of low-demand activities was related to higher levels of mental health. Everard et al. provide an interesting perspective on their findings. They suggest that a decline in activity may be a precursor of declining health and trigger intervention. They wrote, "If older adults themselves or others notice a decrease in their usual activities, or a replacement of high-demand leisure with low-demand leisure activities, something can be done before the decrease in activity results in functional limitations" (p. S211). The suggestion that engagement in certain types of activities can forestall physical decline is further evidence of the value of leisure in later life.

It is necessary for regular activity to become part of an individual's lifestyle and one role of leisure service providers is to help this occur. Unfortunately most older individuals are not physically active. Remarkably, "Up to 75 percent of older individuals are not physically active at the levels needed to accrue the benefits of exercise" (Nied & Franklin, 2002). The section of Chapter 7 on constraints will discuss reasons why this is so.

MEANINGFUL ACTIVITY

Meaningful activity can take many forms. Meaningful may include instrumental use of leisure to reach goals and the expressive use of leisure to find meaning. It may be a way to find a new identity or a way to reestablish an old one. It may be an instrument for continuity or for change. In a sense, it is having something important to do.

According to Kelly and Godbey (1992), "Perhaps the most common stereotype is that retired older persons have nothing worthwhile to do" (p. 368). Ulyssean adults have much that is worthwhile to do. According to Miller (1965), retirement can be viewed as a crisis. It is a time when individuals are forced to leave a role that has been central to them, and they may be left without a replacement. This is probably congruent with the image many of us have of the later years. If an individual's image is based on what she or he does for a career, what happens when that career is no longer available? If there is any doubt that a job is crucial to many individuals' self-image, you only need to ask people what they do. In many cases, the response will be vocation oriented: "I am a doctor," "I am a carpenter", "I am a truck driver."

It is much less likely people will answer by describing a vocational activity: "I am a square dancer," "I am a rock climber," "I am a jogger." What then happens when individuals lose their vocational identity? Can leisure step up and fill this void? Is it fair to expect leisure to be that central to individuals?

Mannell and Kleiber (1997) examined the psychological benefits of leisure and classified them into "theories" based on shared assumptions. Three of them are particularly germane to our examination of meaningful activity, personal growth, identity formation and affirmation, and buffer and coping.

The personal growth perspective posits that leisure provides "an opportunity for people to develop a clear idea of their strengths and weaknesses, continually develop their skills and abilities, become the kind of people they would like to be and feel good about who they are" (p. 289). Concepts such as self-esteem and self-actualization emerge from personal growth. These benefits, however, will not result from merely participating in leisure. Challenge, commitment, persistence and success are crucial. Growth results from effort and psychological reward from success. The implication of this perspective for Ulyssean living is that older individuals need activities that challenge them. The discussion in the next chapter about flow provides one schema for challenging activities. Another is Stebbins's (2001) concept of serious leisure. Serious leisure is the pursuit of an activity that is complex, involves challenges and is based on knowledge, experience or skill. Furthermore, serious leisure requires perseverance and the pursuit of serious leisure may become similar to pursuing a career, without the salary. Stebbins divided serious leisure participants into amateurs, hobbyists and serious volunteers. Amateurs are involved in arts, sport, science and entertainment. Hobbyists are divided into: collectors, makers and tinkers, activity participants such as hunters and barbershop singers, games such as bridge and poker, competitors in unprofessional sports such as darts and martial arts, and liberal arts enthusiasts who read extensively in an area such as cuisine or history (Stebbins, 2001). The third category of serious leisure pursuers is serious volunteers, defined as individuals who contribute deeply to their communities through sharing knowledge, expertise and skills. The benefits of engagement in serious leisure are many, including a stronger self-identity, sharing and recognition of one's abilities, satisfaction of overcoming obstacles to success, and new friendships. However, serious leisure is also hard work. It is contrasted to casual leisure, which is, according to Stebbins, "immediately, intrinsically rewarding, and relatively short-lived pleasurable activity requiring little or no special training to enjoy it" (p. 53). Stebbins's framework fits nicely with our concept of Ulyssean living. It indicates that meaning in later life can come from in-depth and challenging leisure experiences. Intensity, commitment and competence mark serious leisure just as they mark Ulyssean living. Superficial engagement may bring pleasure, but it is unlikely to bring meaning to life.

Stebbins (2000) discussed methods for educating individuals about serious leisure. He believes in a direct approach, telling individuals about serious leisure and its benefits, as well as how to start their engagement. He suggests developing lists of serious leisure activities, along with a description of each activity, and sharing those with potential participants. An individual might select one or two activities from such as list, and, after exploring the activities, elect one for further engagement. The role of recreation professionals would revolve therefore around helping people identify potential serious leisure activities, and then providing the resources needed to initiate the participation process.

The personal growth perspective fits well with Ulyssean living. It supports the need for older individuals to develop a focus, much like the selective optimization with compensation theory described in Chapter 2, and use that focus as a developmental tool. The use of leisure as a vehicle for personal growth and development holds promise for older individuals as well strengthening the importance of leisure in later life.

Mannell and Kleiber's (1997) identity formation and affirmation theory provides an additional perspective on the potential role of leisure in fostering personal growth and development. Haggard and Williams (1991) believed people use leisure as a tool for identity creation and affirmation. They stated, "Leisure activities symbolize identity images. These images may be seen as an outcome or product of participation in a leisure activity" (p. 116). Identity formation and affirmation reflects this belief.

An individual's identity is based on his or her behaviors and reactions of others to those behaviors. Manell and Kleiber provided an example based on leisure behavior: "Based on the success and failures of an individual's efforts, and the feedback she or he receives from those around her or him, that person may come to see herself or himself as good at fixing things, a lousy golfer, concerned about the environment or fun-loving. To the extent that these images form a somewhat consistent and stable picture, an identity is formed" (p. 293). As older individuals experience loss of roles, for example retirement brings the end to the worker role, there may be a need to form a new identity in order to continue to grow. Whereas an individual's self-identity may have revolved around her or his job, retirement may require a reevaluation and an alteration in identity. Leisure can be one arena for a revised self-identity.

However, the identity of older individuals is influenced by more than behavior and others' reaction to that behavior. Whitbourne (2002) presented a model of identity based on the interaction of biopsychosocial processes, that "incorporates physical changes associated with aging, psychological interpretations of these changes and other experiences, and sociocultural influences caused by the impact of socialization and the environment" (p. 3). She placed biological functioning at the core of identity, particularly when biological and cognitive declines become noticeable. Whitbourne's model is built on the interaction between assimilation and accommodation in identity formation. Assimilation occurs when an individual experiences something that is incongruent with identity, and he or she minimizes or ignores the experience rather than revise his or her self-identity. If however the individual revises self-identity accommodation occurs. Whitbourne uses leisure as an example: "For example, a 65-year-old man has always regarded himself as a good dancer but he has not actually danced in several years. On one occasion, he takes his partner out on the dance floor to do some swing dancing and finds that he is not as limber as he would like to be, or as he recalls himself to be. He even has some trouble maneuvering his partner. Using identity assimilation, he minimizes this experience, attributing it to his being a bit 'rusty.' He still regards himself as a good (i.e. agile and strong) dancer who probably needs some practice" (p. 3). She goes on to describe what would happen if the dancer experienced accommodation: "The out-of-practice dancer draws an ominous conclusion from his failure to perform the desired steps. He is convinced that his failure is a sign that he has gotten 'too old' to dance. Now his identity has changed from that of someone who is a good dancer to someone who has lost the ability to perform an activity that he has cherished for his entire adult life" (p. 4). Whitbourne views "identity balance" as the optimum approach to identify formation. In the balance model change may be necessary (accommodation) in some cases, but should be balanced with finding alternative means of participating in the activity or putting the event into perspective (assimilation). With the balanced approach accommodations are made when necessary. However, many losses previously viewed as necessary components of aging are in fact results of other factors such as poor nutrition or lack of exercise, and do not have to be accepted as inevitable or irreversible.

Can leisure be a vehicle for identity formation? Probably not if leisure is viewed as frivolous, secondary and unimportant in life. However, this formation may come through leisure if an individual views it as meaningful and significant. For example, the discussion of serious leisure presented above indicates that for some people leisure may become a central life interest providing meaning and substance in life. In addition, success in leisure provides evidence that aging is not synonymous with inability and that success in possible at any age. As a result leisure involvement can serve as an arena where individuals can test the reality of their own aging against the myths of aging. The result will be the ability to find the balance between accommodation and assimilation that Whitbourne identified as crucial for successful aging. Leisure can serve, therefore, as both an activity providing engagement that helps define self-identity (i.e., a volunteer, an historian, a competent individual), as well as an activity allowing individuals to test their mettle and determine the extent to which physical and cognitive losses require changes in self-perception.

Mannell and Kleiber also view leisure as having a role in identity affirmation, the process of selecting activities "partially on the identity images associated with them" (p. 294). The affirmation is based on selecting an activity whose "identity image" is congruent with an individual's self-image. Mannell and Kleiber provide the example of rock climbing, with the associated activity image of competence, strength and adventure, as the activity of choice of individuals wishing to be competent, strong and adventurous. The implication of identity affirmation for Ulyssean living is that older individuals need the resources to continue engagement in activities supporting their self-identity or assistance in finding alternate activities reaffirming self-identity if preferred activities are no longer available.

The third perspective we borrow from Mannell and Kleiber (1997) is the buffer and coping theory. Buffer and coping posits that leisure benefits health and well-being by helping an individual cope with life's stresses and negative events. The coping occurs through two mechanisms. The first is social support and the second is a sense of control over what happens in our lives.

The social nature of leisure and the resulting friendships provide ample opportunity to develop social supports and the buffering mechanism they provide. One of the most consistent findings in gerontological research is that friends are crucial to successful aging. Physical and mental health are related to having a circle of individuals who can function as a support network. The number of friendships does not seem as important as the depth of the friendships one has. It is important, therefore, that older individuals have opportunities to strengthen friendships. One arena for doing so is leisure. If you close your eyes and think of your friends, it is most likely that the image you see involves a leisure activity. You may be playing a sport, socializing at dinner, on a road trip or walking in the woods together. The reason is that friendships usually entail doing activities together, and those activities are usually enjoyable and freely chosen. The provision for socialization in leisure should be a goal in fostering successful aging since friends often provide the mechanisms for buffering life's difficult times.

Antonucci (2001) indicated that the role of social support in coping might be particularly germane in the later years. She wrote, "there is increasing evidence that social relations help individuals cope with, and recover from many of the exigencies of life that are associated with aging" (p. 427). Antonucci proposed the idea of a "convoy" to describe and explain how social support helps individuals cope with life's problems. The convoy is composed of people who provide "a protective, secure base or cushion that allows individuals to learn about and experience the world" (p. 430). The convoy assists in meeting the challenges of life while helping the individual grow and develop, resulting in mental and physical health. Membership in the convoy changes as the individual changes, but its role in helping the individual cope and adapt endures. The importance of leisure therefore is in helping strengthen bonds among members of the convoy by facilitating friendships and meaningful social relationships. The link to the socioemotional selectivity theory discussed in chapter 2 is clear. Although social circles, or convoys, may shrink in size with increasing age they do not shrink in importance.

The freedom and control inherent in leisure help accomplish the second component of the buffer and coping theory. There is perhaps no area of life where the individual is more able to exercise control than in leisure. This control extends from activity selection to the outcome of participation in an activity. Leisure is primarily self-determined (Deci and Ryan's theory of self-determination is fully described in Chapter 7) and therefore one of the freest of all areas of behavior. This then provides the capacity to cope with life's changes and emerge with physical and mental heath.

Burdman (1986) related the story of a woman named Helen Ansley. She identified her own formula for mental health: the "As" and the "FFIGs." They provide an excellent framework for understanding the role of leisure in later years. The As were: Acceptance—there is a need to belong and experience the acceptance of others. Appreciation—everyone needs to be needed by others and make a contribution as an individual. Appreciation acknowledges the importance of diversity in contributing to the welfare of a group. Affection—there is a need to be affiliated with others and share in their success and achievements. Achievement—the setting and accomplishment of goals is an affirming experience; It does not lose its importance with increasing age. Amusement—according to Ansley, "Laughter, fun, and games are an important part of the emotional diet."

Ansley's FFIGs are emotions that are potentially damaging to individuals. These include: fear, frustration, inferiority, and guilt. Ansley views the As as being a counterbalance to the FFIGs. When an overabundance of FFIGs occurs, there is a need to act on them. Three techniques for combating an overload of FFIGs were identified by Ansley. Her prescription provides an excellent rationale for providing activities to older individuals.

The first is to seek out people and situations that provide the opportunity to experience the As. Certainly leisure can provide an arena for that contact. Ansley's second suggestion is to take action, particularly exercise, to defeat the FFIGs. Finally, she recommends talking about the negative emotions with someone else. Burdman (1986) summarized Ansley's approach to healthful aging as "keeping interested in the world around us, keeping abreast of the times, caring and reaching out, developing a sense of independence, developing new interests and hobbies, and treating ourselves with dignity" (p. 102). These are sound examples of the potential leisure has on an instrumental activity.

Csikszentmihalyi and Kleiber (1991) discuss the potential role of leisure as a tool individuals use "to explore the limits of their potentialities and to expand the range of their mental, physical, and social skills, what today we might call self-actualization" (p. 92). The importance of such a role in older adulthood for Ulyssean living is apparent. The Ulyssean adult is seeking to explore the limits, seeking to expand life, and seeking to self-actualize.

Csikszentmihalyi and Kleiber identify the activity requirements for self-actualization to occur: "Involvement must be deep, sustained, and disciplined to contribute to an emerging sense of self." They go on to describe the flow experience (see Csikszentmihalyi, 1975 and 1990, for a detailed description), which they identify as the context for self-actualization. The characteristics of this experience would appear amenable to programmatic intervention to assist in their occurrence.

The elements of flow include:

- The merging of action and awareness as the participant becomes part of the activity. The individual becomes lost in the activity and is not separated from it.
- The sense of complete involvement in the activity requires a balance between the demands of the activity and the skill of the participant. If an activity's challenges are too great for the skills of the participant, a state of anxiety will result. When, however, the skills of the participant exceed the demands of the activity, boredom is the inevitable outcome. Locating the fulcrum between activity demands and participant's skills is crucial.
- The activity should provide a clear goal for the participant. The goal, whether it is to complete the marathon or finish painting the deck, provides an opportunity for

feedback and sustains interest in the activity.

- Attention must be focused on the activity to the elimination of all else including worry and unwanted thoughts. If you have ever been so intensely involved in an activity that time seems to stand still, and you find it hard to believe you have been doing it as long as the clock indicates, then you have experienced this level of intense involvement.

The combination of the above characteristics results in an activity becoming rewarding in itself, what Csikszentimihalyi and Kleiber call autotelic. The flow experience emerges when there is an opportunity to explore alternatives and identify what is challenging and using that challenge as an opportunity for growth. Anxiety and boredom can be combated by the development of new skills and concomitant opportunities for new challenges. Although program guidelines for facilitating self-actualization are not firmly established, the work of Csikszentmihalyi and Kleiber, as well as interpretation of their work, does provide some suggestions. These include:

1. Provide participants with opportunities for making choices and exerting control over their own leisure.
2. Provide a range of activities. Offering activities only at novice levels will result in boredom. Activities viewed as overly challenging will result in anxiety. Opportunities for activity progression must be made available so increasing skill levels can be accommodated.
3. Do not underestimate the abilities of older individuals. Myths and stereotypes should not guide program decisions.
4. Provide opportunities to discuss leisure and its importance. Help individuals identify how leisure can be used to challenge, not merely to pacify.
5. Csikszentmihalyi and Kleiber suggest that schools, and the authors would add programs for older adults, can assist in self-actualization by offering "opportunities for reflection, intellectual play, and exploration" (p. 98).

Further evidence of the importance of meaningful activity in later life is provided in the MacArthur Foundation Study of Aging in America (Rowe & Kahn, 1998). The study identified the three components of successful aging: (1) avoiding disease, (2) maintaining high cognitive and physical functioning, and (3) engagement with life. The first two of these were discussed in earlier chapters. Engagement with life is at the heart of meaningful activity. As Rowe and Kahn wrote: "The task of successful aging is to discover and rediscover relationships and activities that provide closeness and meaningfulness" (p. 46). One of the roles of individuals working with the elderly is to assist in finding meaningful activities. Rowe and Kahn identify continued involvement in productive activities as a primary category of meaningful activity.

In many cases these productive activities occur as a result of the third component of the successful aging equation: being needed.

BEING NEEDED

We are social individuals. Not many of us would be satisfied living alone in a cave, and few would be willing to enter the solitary life of a monk. We need other people and hope they need us. The process of being needed is reciprocal. It is an exchange between at least two individuals. Our focus in this section will be on two dimensions of being needed: volunteerism and friendship.

Volunteering by older individuals is a major use of free time and one that has been increasing. In 1989, 41 percent of all Americans aged 65 and over had volunteered in the previous year. This included 47 percent of those aged 65 to 74 and 32 percent of those 75 or older (Chambre, 1993; Rowe & Kahn, 1998). The most common volunteer site for individuals 65 years of age or over was a church or other religious organization, followed by health care locations, including hospitals, social/welfare organizations, civil/political organizations, and sport/recreation organizations. The average older volunteer donated approximately 4.7 hours per week during a 35-week period (U.S. Senate Special Committee on Aging et al., 1991).

The roles of volunteering in later life are varied. At the most obvious level, it is a mechanism to fill time and provide a regular schedule. It is also an opportunity to serve, achieve recognition, be active, use skills, and exhibit mastery and competence. Volunteering also provides an opportunity to achieve a sense of "giving back" to the community, an opportunity viewed as crucial to successful aging (Fried et al., 1997).

Being needed is also part of friendship. One of the consistent findings in the aging literature is the importance of friendship in later life (Crohan & Antonucci, 1989; Mullins & Mushel, 1992; Sabin, 1993; Antonucci, 2001)). Social contact is an important aspect of well being. Friendships provide support for coping with adverse events in life (Schultz & Ewen, 1993). Feelings of attachment based on reciprocity and equality can validate feelings of self-worth and social integration, and provide a role and meaning in life. However, factors such as changes in living arrangements, retirement, and other changes may make friendships vulnerable and threatened. Therefore, there is a need to introduce opportunities for friendship that may counteract the trend toward the diminishing quantity and quality of friendship. Leisure may provide such an arena.

Through planned social activities and programs to identify partners for activities ranging from tennis to travel, support groups and enduring friendships can be built. According to Antonucci (1990), friendships built on reciprocity and a fair exchange are more satisfying and positive than those built on asymmetrical exchanges. The leisure arena is one where reciprocity can be experienced. Participants are on equal footing and may negotiate the giving and receiving of support. There are no expectations that one individual will be the giver of support and the other will be the receiver. An activity, such as a card game, frees all participants to "give as good as they get" over the course of the game.

One of the authors can remember playing Scrabble with his 90-year-old grandmother. There was no need to be hesitant to try to win, no need to coddle or cater to "old age." There was only a need to try hard to win, usually with dismal results. This competitive arena was free of age bias, free of stereotypes, free of caregiving. It was an even exchange of effort, support, and benefits. As a result, it was a special time where age was irrelevant and friendship could develop.

Providers of recreation services can build opportunities for reciprocity into their programs by matching people of equal ability in activities. In addition, providing individuals with responsibility for their own programs can help provide an equitable exchange environment where everyone can bring his or her contribution to the rest of the group. It appears such an approach will assist in friendship formation.

FINANCIAL SECURITY

Some older individuals may use the free time available through retirement to develop a hobby that provides a source of income. This component of financial security may include making and selling crafts, starting a second career, consulting with business or individuals, or using skills such as woodworking to earn an income. Typically, the money earned will supplement Social Security income or a pension. Leisure service providers may be involved in this process through providing classes to teach skills, helping identify opportunities to use abilities, and matching individuals with needs with those able to provide the required services.

SOCIAL-PSYCHOLOGICAL BENEFITS OF LEISURE

George (1990) identified five major themes useful in examining the social psychology of later life. Each has implications for leisure services. The first, frequently identified in leisure and aging literature, is the definition and achievement of "successful" aging. Issues such as morale, life satisfaction, and well being are viewed as aspects of successful aging. George identifies the origin of the interest in successful aging as the debate over activity theory versus disengagement theory.

Although the focus has moved beyond these theoretical frameworks, the issue of social structure and quality of life endures. George (1990) defined subjective well being as the individual's perception of the quality of overall life. Concepts such as happiness, morale, and life satisfaction fall under the umbrella of subjective well being. George identified three social factors as exhibiting strong and consistent relationships with subjective well-being: socioeconomic position, attachments to social structure, and age density of the residential environment.

The second of these is particularly germane to the benefits of leisure in later life. George differentiated between formal attachments and informal participation in primary groups. Formal attachments include labor force participation and membership in formal organizations. Informal group involvement includes interacting with family and friends. The influence of loss of formal attachments appears to have a relatively unimportant linkage to life satisfaction. However, informal attachment involvement is a "strong and robust predictor of subjective well being" (p. 192).

The informal attachments that appear crucial to subjective well being can be developed through organized recreation programs. They are also part of the core of leisure identified by Kelly and Godbey (1992). Core activities are those inexpensive and informal things people typically do. They include socializing with friends, walking, reading, and going shopping.

Some of the greatest contributions to understanding the psychological benefits of leisure result from the work of Tinsley and his colleagues at Southern Illinois University. Although some of this work has been directly related to older adults (Tinsley, Teaff, Colbs, & Kaufman, 1985), much of it is more generic. However, that does not decrease its value to us.

According to Driver, Tinsley, and Manfredo (1991), "Individuals should be able to structure their leisure so as to maximize life satisfaction, raise self-esteem, and facilitate increased self-actualization. To do so however, requires knowledge of the need-gratifying characteristics of the various activities" (p. 264). This knowledge will also help professionals involved in the delivery of leisure services in structuring their program offerings.

The work of Tinsley and his colleagues resulted in the development of an instrument called Paragraphs About Leisure (PAL) designed to measure the extent to which involvement in an activity meets a range of psychological needs. The potential benefits of leisure described by Tinsley and measured by PAL include:

1. Self-expression—resulting from the use of individual talents and recognition of those talents
2. Companionship—resulting from supportive interaction with others
3. Power—resulting from being in control and at the center of social situations
4. Compensation—resulting from experiencing something new and unusual
5. Security—resulting from the ability to experience a long-term involvement free from change and resulting in some form of recognition
6. Service—resulting from providing help to others
7. Intellectual aestheticism—resulting from intellectual and aesthetic experiences
8. Solitude—resulting from the opportunity to be by one's self

The work of Tinsley and Teaff (1983) shows the potential in using the PAL in program planning. Designing a program to ensure balance in activities will maximize the likelihood that needs will be met. For example, offering only activities high on companionship (bingo, bowling, ceramics, dancing, volunteer opportunities, and social group meetings) limits the likelihood of meeting a variety of needs.

Although activity provision will never be as simple as consulting a guide such as that detailed by Tinsley and Teaff, it provides an excellent starting point when designing programs. Actually using PAL with participants would further the process of finding balance in programs.

George's (1990) second theme in the social psychology of later life is social roles. A common perspective of later life is as a time of lost roles. Work roles, family roles, and community roles may be less prevalent with increasing age. Much of recreation for older individuals is viewed as an opportunity to replace these lost roles with a new role, a leisure role. The research findings related to the validity of this position is mixed.

George's third theme is the relationship of life events, such as retirement and widowhood, and well being. The extent to which such events are likely to result in negative outcomes depends on how stressful the individual perceives such events to be. George states that, "Social resources, including socioeconomic resources, attachments to the social structure, and especially involvement in supportive social networks can lessen the impact of stressful life events" (p. 189). For example, Patterson (1996) and Patterson and Carpenter (1994) found some association between leisure involvement and stress reduction for recently widowed individuals.

Leisure can provide an arena for the development of social networks that may mediate the impact of life events. A great amount of leisure is social. Group travel, Elderhostel, potluck suppers, and volunteer work provide outlets for developing and utilizing social networks. They give individuals opportunities to meet others who have experienced similar life events and identify skills and techniques to deal with them. As a result, the events lose some of their potency and become less deleterious.

Age-stratification theory is George's fourth theme. This theory was discussed in Chapter 2. Individuals are viewed as part of an age strata. These strata are viewed in a hierarchical manner. George cites evidence of avoidance by chronologically older adults to view themselves as part of that strata. It may be that leisure can provide a vehicle for decreasing the stigma of older age strata. For instance, the example that opens this chapter provides evidence of individuals whose age is unrelated to leisure achievement. This achievement can function to decrease the perceived stigma of being part of this age group. Achievement can take precedence over stratification.

George's final theme is aging and modernization. Although modernization theory is explored in Chapter 2, a brief restatement may clarify its relationship to leisure. Modernization "as indexed by urbanization and industrialization, leads to decreased social status for older adults" (p. 190).

It may be that this decreased social status results in decreases in the quality of life of some individuals. The extent to which an individual perceives decreased status may be related to decreases in happiness or satisfaction. If that is the case, vehicles for increasing social status must be identified. Within some groups of individuals, leisure may provide an opportunity for increased status.

The work of Leitner and Leitner (1985) supports the role of leisure in psycho-social well being. Their review of the literature indicated leisure activity can provide a variety of benefits, including: "improved health, increased opportunity for social interaction, improved morale and life satisfaction, higher self-concept and improved body image, greater feelings of usefulness and self-worth, improved skills and better ability to function independently, and most of all, fun and enjoyment" (p. 21).

SOCIAL BENEFITS OF LEISURE

Although most of the focus on leisure in later years is on psychological benefits such as life satisfaction, morale, and self-esteem, leisure also has a social payoff. The relationship between leisure and the social system is often viewed from a perspective that leisure is dependent and the system is independent. That is, leisure is shaped by culture. However, in this section, leisure is viewed as the independent variable playing a role in shaping the system. An earlier section of this chapter discussed friendship, clearly a social benefit. However, here social benefits as they relate to the community, rather than the individual, will be the focus.

Unfortunately, this is an area where relatively little is known. According to Burch and Hamilton-Smith (1991), "The available systematic knowledge of the potential and actual social benefits of leisure is very thin and empirical evidence is especially lacking" (p. 369).

Burch and Hamilton-Smith (1991) identify three possible social outcomes of what they term "nonwork opportunities." These include bonding, solidarity, and integration. Bonding, or the establishment of "ties between intimates," results in loyalty to a group or association, as well as encouraging the performance of roles necessary for the continuation of the group. Social solidarity, described as "emotional commitment to a larger social role," results in enhancing individuals' role performance. Finally, social integration, or the linking of elements of society together, results in the efficient operation of the group. Leisure can play a role in all three aspects of the continuity.

Kelly (1991) views leisure as critical to "developing and maintaining bonds of commitment and sharing" (p. 422). A study by McCormick (1993) in two southern communities clearly supports this conclusion. He examined the role of leisure in a residential, lakeside community populated mostly by retired northerners who selected the south as an area for retirement and a nearby rural community composed mostly of individuals who aged in place. A series of interviews with residents of these two communities indicated the crucial role of leisure in the formation of an identifiable entity in the lake community. Leisure played a major role in the bonding process.

Similar results were found by Hochschild (1973) in her study of Merrill Court. She identified the development of an "unexpected community" in this garden apartment development inhabited by older residents. She describes the beginning of the community in this small apartment building for retirees: The story of how a collection of near-strangers became a community has several versions. As Freda, the first "indigenous" leader tells it, "There wasn't nothin' before we got the coffee machine. I mean we didn't share nothin' before Mrs. Bitford's daughter brought over the machine and we sort of had our first occasion, you might say."

There were about six people at the first gathering around the coffee machine in the recreation room. As people came downstairs from their apartments to fetch the mail in the midmorning, they looked into the recreation room, found a cluster of people sitting down drinking coffee, and some joined in. A few weeks later, the recreation director "joined in" for the morning coffee, and as she tells it, the community had its start at this point. The evolution of a group of people from being a collection of individuals to being a cohesive community, marked by bonding, integration, and solidarity, began during a social event easily identifiable as leisure. The need many older individuals have for the establishment of social ties and to feel part of a community points toward the value of using recreation and leisure as a vehicle for social integration.

WORK, LEISURE, AND RETIREMENT

The examination of the importance of leisure in later life cannot be complete without an understanding of the role of retirement in peoples' lives. Some view retirement as one of the most significant changes experienced by older adults. Some fear it, others embrace it. The assumption that the work role is a major contributor to our self-worth may lead some to believe that retirement is likely to cause severe psychological distress or impact physical health. Miller (1965) claimed that retirement had the potential to trigger an identity crisis among the elderly. His position was based on the belief that occupational identity mediated most other roles of the individual, providing meaning to life and status to the person; leisure was not thought to replace work as a source of self-respect, productivity, and social acceptance. The stigmatization resulting from the loss of the ability to "perform" in society's eyes was seen as a cause for embarrassment, identity breakdown, and eventual withdrawal.

However, there is little evidence that retirement is a crisis. As Vaillant (2002) wrote, "Retirement is highly overrated as a major life problem" (p. 220). Rather, it is a process with much individual variation (Quinn & Burkhauser, 1990; Hooyman & Kiyak, 1993) marked by periods of satisfaction and dissatisfaction. Factors such as health, financial security, work experience, and the opportunity for meaningful activity involvement are related to satisfaction with retirement. Vaillant (2002) cited three community surveys, each of which identified retirement as a low-stress event and not a problem for most people. However, he identified four circumstances under which retirement may be a problem. First is if it is unplanned and involuntary. Second, lack of financial resources increases the stressful nature of retirement. Third, if work has been an escape from an unhappy home life, retirement may be difficult. And finally, retirement may be stressful if it has been preceded by poor health.

Ebersole and Hess (1990) identified six retirement issues of relevance to older individuals. They provide an indication of areas where assistance in adapting to retirement may be needed.

1. What provisions have been made for income in retirement? Assistance in financial management may be necessary.
2. What activities are important and available to the retiree? The required skills, abilities, interests, and resources need to be in place in order to participate in the activities.

3. What living arrangements are most appropriate? Factors such as size, physical access, cost, and geographic preference must be considered.

4. What accommodations for role changes are anticipated? Spouses may be spending more time together. Widowhood, grandparenting, and caregiving may become a reality.

5. What health changes can be expected? Health issues must be clarified and examined. Factors such as insurance, change in diet and exercise, and sexuality may be fertile areas of discussion.

6. Have legal matters, such as wills and inheritance taxes, been addressed? Programs to assist in the legal area may be needed.

A study by Bickson and Goodchilds (1989) gathered information from 79 older men regarding retirement. The group of men, half retired and half still employed, formed a task force to study issues related to retirement. The retired members of the workforce in Bickson and Goodchilds's study (1989) were asked to identify the best things and worst things about retirement. Some of the responses regarding benefits were: (a) being creative, (b) no daily routine, (c) being your own boss, (d) no pressure, (e) relief of responsibility, (f) no obligations, and (g) Palm Springs! The most common advantage noted by the subjects was not having to live according to a set schedule. Although almost half the subjects said there was nothing bad about retirement, some of the disadvantages reported were (a) miss the work, (b) miss friends at work, (c) wife is worried about money, (d) wife's criticism of my activities, (e) getting wife to do things, and (f) making up mind about what to do. These responses point to both financial, social and personal concerns in retirement.

Interviews with the retirees and employees revealed that the former were significantly more satisfied with their overall use of time, particularly time spent with a spouse. This higher satisfaction of retirees with time usage seemed to be explained by their ability to vary how their time was spent. No differences were found between the two groups regarding time spent with friends. One interesting finding was that retirees were significantly more heterogeneous in their distribution of time for activities than employees.

In terms of family and social adjustment, regardless of employment status, those men who reported greater amounts of time spent with their spouses tended to perceive themselves as happier with their marital arrangements. Of course, this correlation does not indicate the direction of causation. Is satisfaction a result or cause of spending more time together? The wives interviewed, however, instead of making reference to time, seemed to view adjustment to retirement as related to their need to preserve some personal space. In the social domain, the study showed that retirees made more friends during the project year than the employees. When asked how they would describe themselves, the retirees listed different roles retirees assume including: (a) collector, (b) churchgoer, (c) grandparent, (d) investor, (e) recycled teenager. Rather than representing a loss of meaningful roles, retirement to these men appeared to add new roles to their lives.

George Vaillant (2002) provided another perspective on the importance of leisure in retirement in a fascinating book entitled *Aging Well: Surprising Guideposts to a Happier Life from the Landmark Study of Adult Development*. He used data from a study that followed 824 individuals from adolescence to old age, a period of more than 50 years, and had a deceptively simple goal: identify models of how to "live from retirement to past 80—with joy" (p. 4). Among his many findings was the link between a rewarding retirement and four basic activities: replacing lost work mates with a social network, rediscovering how to play, seeking opportunities for creativity, and continuing lifelong learning. Closer examination of each of these makes it clear that leisure is intimately related to all four, another strong indication of the primary role of leisure in later life.

We have already discussed the importance of friendships and social support in later life as well as the role of leisure in fostering friendship. Vaillant sums it up, "As in the rest of life, the first retirement activity should be to create new relationships as fast as the old ones are lost" (p. 226).

The inclusion of play on the list is significant for leisure professionals. Vaillant views play as a "proper role for both child and retiree" and contrasts play with work: "A career must be of value to society as well as to oneself. Play need be of value only to oneself and maybe to a close few friends" (p.229). He does not hesitate to strongly advocate for the value of play, even if it is frivolous: "Mindless bowling on the green, atrocious golf, and amateurish watercolors can provide great pleasure and, equally important, freedom and meaning. In retirement what is important is to live life fully, and that in many ways is achieved through play and through minimally paid creativity. In retirement you can finally quit your day job and follow your bliss" (p. 229). Vaillant sees the value in an activity others might view as unimportant. Play is marked by freedom from convention, is done for the joy of the activity and is free from the need for approval of others. It is therefore the opportunity to truly be one's self while absorbed in the activity. Play can take any form, the key is that it is done for the pleasure of doing it rather than a long-term goal. Play needs to be joyful and Vaillant's data indicated joy is important to successful aging.

Vaillant's third component of successful retirement is creativity. He contrasts creativity with play by viewing creativity as more goal oriented, serious and passionate than play. We discussed creativity in Chapter 4 and will not repeat the information here. Vaillant expands on our discussion and provides vivid examples of creative individuals and the importance of creativity in their lives. His examples share several traits, not the least of which is talent. The role of leisure service professionals is to help identify and nurture the talent older individuals have. Art classes, creative writing groups, and music lessons may be critical in bringing out the creative nature of individuals. In addition, it is important to provide opportunities for an audience to share the creative products. Art shows, theatrical productions, newsletters, and literary collections are examples of outlets for creativity.

Vaillant's final component of successful retirement, and ultimately successful aging, is lifelong learning. The informants in Vaillant's study continued to learn. Many were taking classes and were regularly engaged in formal learning. Some were involved in Elderhostel, a program offering courses to older learners at facilities throughout the world, others at local colleges, and some at senior centers. They all shared a gusto for learning and were able to find outlets to meet their zest for lifelong learning.

The message from Vaillant and the participants in his study is clear: healthy retirement, and we would add Ulyssean living, is facilitated by engagement in play and creative activities, supportive social networks and participation in lifelong learning. Leisure professionals can make significant and meaningful contributions to successful aging by helping individuals achieve in each of these areas.

LEISURE COMPETENCY

The previous sections detail the role and benefits of leisure in later life. However, these benefits will not accrue unless individuals are able to participate in leisure. In addition, it is possible the role of leisure can be expanded if individuals learn how to become better "leisurites."

A paradox of leisure is that it may take work to achieve leisure. We are not necessarily born with the abilities needed to experience leisure. While a great deal of education is geared to vocational preparation, few efforts are designed to facilitate leisure involvement. The authors of this book are frequently presenters at pre-retirement seminars. One of the points they make is that leisure will not just happen. Free time will occur as a concomitant of retirement and other role losses, but some skill is needed to use this time for leisure. The scuba diver's motto is "plan your dive, and dive your plan." Similarly, a motto for leisure in the later years may be "plan your leisure, and leisurely go about your plan." The following are ways that may be done. It is not the intent of this book to be a treatise on leisure education. However, leisure professionals working with older individuals will benefit from knowledge in this area. There are several useful books and materials that should be consulted for further information.

If leisure is used to develop feelings of competence, meaning, and mastery, then individuals need to learn how to do that. The presence of leisure opportunities is not sufficient to ensure leisure participation. Individuals also need to develop competence in the area of leisure. Competence assumes that the knowledge, attitudes, and skills required to participate in available activities have been acquired.

For example, Atchley stated that many older people are reluctant to engage in activities such as art, music, and writing, at least due in part to the individual's feelings of incompetence in activities.

The work of Bandura (1982) indicates a need for feelings of self-efficacy prior to entry into freely chosen activities. Self-efficacy is a belief that you have the ability to successfully participate in an activity. If an individual does not expect success in an activity, then participation is less likely to occur. Therefore, it is necessary to impart a sense of efficacy to individuals if participation is to occur. According to Bandura, efficacy can be increased through direct or vicarious experience with the activity.

There are four stages in Tedrick's (1982) leisure competency model. The first involves clarification of attitudes toward leisure and exploration of the role of leisure in life. Many instruments exist to assist in this exploratory phase. They include books and instruments such as the Leisure Diagnostics Battery. Such materials can be useful in exploring attitudes, values, and activity preferences. This exploratory phase will be concluded by decisions related to leisure, its role in life, and leisure goals.

The second stage of the leisure competency program involves the learning of new leisure skills and activities. Instructional classes and seminars may be effective techniques for this leisure education component. These can either be conducted in segregated settings, such as multi-purpose centers, or in age-integrated programs. It is possible that individuals may be more comfortable in an age-segregated setting; however, this is a decision best left to the participant.

The third phase of the program involves gathering information about leisure opportunities in the community. Some communities have directories of leisure opportunities. For example, Greenville, South Carolina, has a central clearinghouse where individuals can call to learn about outlets and opportunities. Such an information and referral service can be useful in identifying available activities. A search of the multitude of activity sources to be found in most communities can be used to develop a resource list. Sources of activity information are listed in Table 6.1.

Table 6.1
Some Sources of Activity Information

Friends	AARP
Radio Station	Television
Newspapers	Board of Education
Libraries	Community Rec. Department
Churches	National Park Service State Travel
Community Colleges	or Visitors Bureau
Country Extension service	Adult Education Programs
YMCAs and YWCAs	Volunteer Action Center
Travel Clubs	Craft Groups
Elderhostel	Yellow Pages
Museums	Chambers of Commerce
Health Clubs	Travel Agencies
Bookstore	State Depts. of Parks and Recreation

The goal of the leisure competence program is to assist individuals in being able to take advantage of the leisure opportunities that exist. If successful, the opportunities to make choices and exert control over a major area of life will be increased. The program is a dynamic one marked by evaluation and feedback, and therefore, as individuals change and their circumstances change, the program will assist them in making alterations in their leisure lifestyle. It can be an effective approach to Ulyssean living.

The leisure education content model (Peterson & Gunn, 1984) provides an excellent overview of the components needed to "facilitate the development and expression of a satisfying leisure lifestyle" (Stumbo & Thompson, 1988, p. 18). The model includes four components: leisure awareness, social interaction skills, leisure resources, and leisure activity skills. The incorporation of these components into a leisure competence program will assist in preparing individuals for Ulyssean living.

McDowell (1978) developed an approach to achieving leisure well being. Although his work was done several years ago, the message is still a useful one. McDowell defines leisure well-being as "a measure of how well prepared you are to assume and maintain responsibility for an enjoyable, healthful, satisfying, and dynamic leisurestyle" (p. 4). As a result of lack of leisure experience or failure to develop leisure skills over the life course, some older individuals may have a difficult time developing leisure well being. McDowell's model can help facilitate its development.

Leisure well being has four components. Each is crucial in developing effective leisure habits.

Coping is the ability to manage boredom and guilt. In addition, it is the ability to move beyond what McDowell identifies as "I can't" compulsiveness. Some indicators of ineffective coping include: oversleeping, compulsive busyness, alcohol or drug abuse, watching television because it is easy, and not trying new activities.

McDowell's second component is leisure awareness and understanding. This includes an examination and understanding of the influence of work and duty on leisure. Viewing leisure as a reward for work or an event to re-create one to return to work is not an accurate perspective on this realm of behavior. It is particularly inappropriate for older individuals, many of whom are retired and therefore not able to "justify" leisure based on work. Individuals should be assisted in viewing leisure as valuable for its own sake. To do so requires realization of the value of leisure. Some areas to assist in examining leisure awareness include: reflecting on the role of leisure in life, examining the value of leisure in life, and looking at the excuses used for not doing activities.

Knowledge about leisure, including interests, resourcefulness, and fitness, is also part of leisure well being. Issues such as the breadth and balance of leisure, knowledge of talents and interests, and the role of physical fitness are part of knowledge. Sample questions useful in identifying extent of knowledge include: What is one's leisure breadth and balance? What common interests are shared with others? Is there time to be alone in leisure? Are the activities selected reflective of a variety of interests?

The route to leisure well being is a personal one. Unfortunately, other people may make it a more difficult journey than it needs to be. McDowell's final component in his model is assertion. Assertion is built around McDowell's "bill of rights" including:

1. The right to do nothing
2. The right to procrastinate
3. The right to be uncertain
4. The right to be alone
5. The right to be playful
6. The right for self-expression
7. The right to be childlike

These seven items provide a strong statement of a "bill of leisure rights" for the later years.

A more recent program designed to enhance control and competence was described by Searle, Mahon, Iso-Ahola, Sdrolia, and van Dyck (1995). They designed an intervention that successfully enhanced feelings of leisure control and competence. The program included 12 units:

1. an examination of what participants did for their recreation;
2. an examination of participant's motives for activity involvement;
3. an analysis of the components, physical, mental, and social, required for each activity;
4. a self-assessment of abilities and their impact on activity involvement;
5. an explanation of how to adapt activities and equipment;
6. an examination of barriers to participation and how to avoid them;
7. a goal-setting session to make long- and short-term leisure plans;
8. an examination of alternate activities and the skills needed to participate in them;
9. an identification of support people and how to use them;
10. an assessment of personal resources such as finances and transportation;
11. an examination of community resources and how to take advantage of them;
12. a reassessment of leisure goals.

If individuals are to realize the meanings available in leisure, they must develop the competence needed to use leisure. The materials presented above can be used to develop programs to assist in doing that.

CONCLUSION

There are a variety of definitions of leisure, ranging from time to activity to state of mind. It is interesting that there is more agreement on the benefits of leisure than on its definition. Clearly, leisure can play a major role in the lives of older people. It has the potential for providing physical, social, psychological, and health-related benefits. It can help establish social networks, provide meaningful activities, assist in the formation of identity, enhance physical functioning and provide focus in later life. Activities can provide vehicles to reach a variety of personal goals and are potentially a primary means of Ulyssean living. Leisure service providers can therefore assist in the search for Ulyssean lifestyles by facilitating the development of leisure competency.

Some individuals will choose leisure as a central life interest and use it to meet their social and psychological needs. Other individuals may not share the same degree of commitment to leisure, but it will still have a major impact on their lives and on their communities. Successful aging incorporates meaningful activity, and it is a misperception to view older adults as sitting around with nothing to do. Most older adults are active and find personal affirmation through their involvement. Ulyssean living requires nothing more and nothing less if it is to be a reality.

SEVEN

ENHANCING THE LEISURE EXPERIENCE:
MOTIVATIONS AND CONSTRAINTS

If leisure is useful as a vehicle for Ulyssean living, there is a need to understand what motivates or inhibits this experience. This chapter will examine both these factors. What will become clear as you read is the power of leisure to have a meaningful role in later life. The needs and motives discussed in this chapter can be met through leisure engagement. The ability of trained leisure professionals to structure leisure in order to help address these motives and needs is a crucial component in helping older individuals achieve Ulyssean living. We will continue our search to understand leisure in the later years and how this leisure can be used to achieve a Ulyssean lifestyle. We will continue to explore the primary role of leisure in people's lives. The next chapter will directly relate leisure to the Ulyssean lifestyle, but here we are interested in focusing on further elucidating the richness of leisure and understanding its roots. The model of motivation described by Mannell and Kleiber (1997) provides the definitional starting point for this chapter. The model postulates that behavior is preceded by a need or a motive. Engagement in the behavior may result in fulfillment of the need that originally motivated involvement in the activity. Feedback on the success, or failure, of the activity in meeting needs results in the continuation or cessation of the activity. Motives are a crucial part of the leisure experience. In fact, Losier, Bourque, and Vallerand (1993) identify motives as the most important factor affecting the leisure experience. This chapter will examine the motives that drive leisure choices. Let us start by looking at the leisure of Victor Logan.

> The light entered the workshop from one dusty window and fell on Victor Logan, playing in and about the grooves and wrinkles of his face as he bent patiently over a piece of wood on the workbench. The only sound was the scraping of Logan's chisel on the curley maple. The smell was of wood and dusty oldness. High on the dark shelves there were mysterious and wonderful boxes tied meticulously with string and labeled for nails, bolts, and screws. Well-used and worn tools of the trade lay in disarray.

On a clothesline in one corner two violins hung, awaiting the final touch of the master craftsman. Logan was a master craftsman, a violin maker for more than 40 years.

"I've never sold one," he said, tightening the strings of one of his violins. "Not that I haven't had offers. I do it for fun, and besides, I like having them just hanging around here."

His handsome red-headed wife stood outside the shop and gazed affectionately at her husband. "He's got the gift," she said. "He just loves to work with his hands."

He has never had any formal music training, but he taught himself and now "plays anything he can get his hands on." He is even the church organist at Bostic Presbyterian.

"I built my first violin in 1932. I had nothing to copy, cause we farm boys had no money like that. So I borrowed one and built mine just by guess, and when it was done, well, it came out pretty close to the real thing," he said, dusting off the front piece of the violin he was working on.

Logan used only old wood and hand tools just as Stradivari did. Time in plentiful amounts and patience were the other shared ingredients. "I'd say it takes me about a year to build a violin," he explained, picking up his favorite.

He was slow to admit he could even play the violin, but finally picked up his favorite, tuned it carefully, and tucked it under his chin. His bow sawed across the strings, and the strains of "Christ the Lord is Risen Today" filled the workshop. He finished that piece and then went right into "In the Sweet By and By."

And so Victor Logan, violinist and violin maker, became Victor Logan, old-time fiddler. He let his right foot tap the tempo to the sprightly "Soldier's Joy," a haunting melody reminiscent of a highland bagpipe fling. His fingers flew like the feet of dancers he might have been imagining while he played the fiddle he had patiently built with his own hands years before—not for money, not for fame or glory, but, as he said, "just because I love the music" *(Greenville News Piedmont)*.

Victor Logan is an individual who has been able to continue leisure patterns developed throughout life into his later years. This pattern of continuity is typical of many older individuals. Logan's involvement in creating musical instruments is a lifelong one. It is not a new leisure activity developed after retirement to help fill time. Rather, it is an activity he has found satisfying and fulfilling; it provides meaning in his life and is part of him. This chapter will examine the motivations and meanings of leisure and focus on understanding why people, such as Mr. Logan, do what they do.

LEISURE MOTIVATION

When we ask people why they engage in leisure activities, the typical answer is because they are enjoyable. That is seen as sufficient motivation—we do what we enjoy. However, there is a great deal of evidence that leisure is more than a pleasure provider. It is a rich area of behavior from which we should expect a great deal more than enjoyment. The Ulyssean approach requires a great deal more!

Examination of the meaning of leisure is a difficult task. Leisure revolves around personal, individualized activity and therefore is difficult to classify or categorize. Each individual brings his or her own history, physical and mental state, emotional needs, and intellectual perspective to an activity, and these influence the meaning of the activity. For example, participation in tennis may have five different meanings to five different participants. One person may do it for the status, another for the exercise, another to be with her spouse, one to emulate a role model, and one to socialize with friends.

The difficulty of attaching meaning to activities is further complicated by the differential nature of activities to the same person. An individual may jog because it is a fitness activity on one day and for socialization the next day. As Kelly summarized after examining the "career" of one activity, dancing, "In the end it is the meaning to the participant that is crucial. It is that meaning, that definition of the activity for a time and place, which determines whether doing the activity is primarily expressive leisure, social leisure, or activity that is required by social or professional roles" (1996, p. 25).

In spite of the difficulty in specifying leisure meanings, examination of this area will provide insight into leisure in the later years. Understanding why people do what they do has practical importance. Iso-Ahola (1989) indicated that knowledge of motivations can provide a powerful tool in program planning, since motives are linked to desired outcomes of participation. In fact, he views motives as internal factors driving behavior. As he stated, "If social interaction, for instance, is the main motivator among nursing home residents, then it would be foolhardy to plan recreation programs around activities that do not facilitate social contacts" (p. 247).

Ryan and Deci (2000) offered a clear definition of motivation, "to be motivated means *to be moved* to do something" (p. 54). They continued their discussion by specifying that someone who is motivated is "energized or activated toward an end." They also link motivation to professional practice, "Practitioners of all types face the perennial task of fostering more versus less motivation in those around them" (p. 54). Our questions are what motivates people toward engagement in leisure, and what can leisure service providers do to cultivate these motivations.

REASONS FOR PARTICIPATION

Some of the earliest work into the meanings of leisure was done by Havighurst (1961) as part of the Kansas City Study of Adult Life. He asked individuals to identify their favorite leisure activity and then classified these activities into 11 categories:

1. participation in formal groups including social clubs, fraternal organizations, and church groups
2. participation in informal groups
3. travel
4. sports participation
5. watching sports
6. television and radio
7. fishing and hunting
8. gardening
9. manual-manipulative activities such as sewing and woodworking
10. reading and imaginative activities
11. visiting friends and relatives

Havighurst then used these activity classifications to determine why people participated in activities. Eight leisure meanings were identified:

1. just for the pleasure of it
2. welcome change from work
3. new experiences
4. chance to be creative
5. chance to achieve something
6. contact with friends
7. make time pass
8. service to others

The meanings found were more determined by the personality of the individual than by age, gender, or social class.

EXPRESSIVE LEISURE

A classic examination of the meaning of activities in later life was conducted by Gordon and Gaitz (1976). They defined leisure as "discretionary personal activity in which the expressive meanings have primacy over instrumental themes, in the sense that gratification of present needs, wants, desires or objectives is given precedence over practical preparation for later gratification" (p. 311). This definition clearly identifies leisure as being defined by meaning attached to an activity rather than the activity itself. The need therefore to understand why an activity is done becomes a necessity to understanding leisure.

Based on an extensive review of the literature, Gordon and Gaitz identified five major "objectives of leisure," including: relaxation, diversion, self-development, creativity, and sensual transcendence. They conceptualized these objectives as being ordered along a continuum of intensity of expressivity, with relaxation being very low and sensual transcendence being very high, and then categorized activities along the five dimensions.

Relaxation was defined as activities providing variety and recreation for the body. Activities such as sleeping, resting, and daydreaming were classified as relaxation. Activities providing a change of pace and relief from tension and boredom were classified as diversion. Light reading, hobbies, and socialization were identified as diversion. Developmental activities, such as learning to sing or dance, participation in clubs and organizations, and involvement in cultural activities, are often intrinsically enjoyable. In addition they result in increases in knowledge, physical capacity, and more abstract ways of interpreting daily experience. Activities such as playing an instrument or serious discussion about a topic were identified as creative activities and involve actively performing in a manner to create new cultural productions. The final classification, sensual transcendence, involves the pursuit of pleasure, including both sexual pleasure and activation of the senses.

Gordon and Gaitz do not imply any one type of activity has a higher value than any other since only the participant can decide value. However, before individuals are able to attach a value or meaning to an activity, they must be given the opportunity to participate. This indicates a need to provide individuals with a variety of activity opportunities, encompassing all five realms of meaning.

Limiting opportunities to some areas while eliminating others will limit the potential of leisure to contribute to life and Ulyssean living. For example, not providing opportunities for sensual transcendence, whether as a result of accepting a myth that old age is marked by a loss of sexuality or from a puritan ethic, deprives individuals of a needed leisure experience. The choice should lie with the participant, not the leisure provider.

Gordon and Gaitz examined the association between age and level of expressive involvement. They found that relaxation and solitude showed an upward trend, while developmental activity and creativity showed moderate declines across the life span, whereas diversion and sensual transcendence were marked by strong declines with increasing age.

According to Gordon and Gaitz, "These most 'pleasure oriented' and 'hedonistic' leisure categories in our sample are found to be almost the exclusive province of the relatively young"

(p. 330). They interpreted this finding as indicating that older individuals had decided to trade the opportunity for high levels of happiness and joy obtainable from such activities for a more sedate existence. However, it may also be that older individuals do not have equal opportunity with their younger colleagues for such activities, and these age differences are related to opportunity rather than desire. A further explanation may be that older individuals have never done such activities and therefore have not "traded" one activity for another, but have experienced continuity in their leisure.

In any event, it is worth noting that not all individuals in the Gordon and Gaitz study avoided sensual transcendence or diversion. Therefore, outlets to meet the search for those meanings in leisure should be provided.

Kelly and Godbey (1992) identified an alternative perspective on the search for leisure meaning by suggesting simplifying the definition of leisure to incorporate the global concept of "leisure activity," which transcends the environment and form of the activity. For example, they identify six components of meaning based on "leisure activity." These include:

1. psychological—a sense of freedom, enjoyment, involvement and challenge
2. educational—intellectual challenge and knowledge
3. social—relationships with other people
4. relaxation—relief from stress and strain
5. physiological—fitness, health, weight control, and well being
6. aesthetic—response to pleasing design and environment
    (Kelly & Godbey, 1992, p. 234).

Lawton (1993) provided an updated explication of the meaning of leisure to older adults. His list of meanings supports the value of leisure in later life and included the following benefits:

1. solitude
2. intrinsic satisfaction
3. diversion
4. relaxation
5. intellectual challenge
6. health
7. personal competence
8. expression and personal development
9. creativity
10. social interaction
11. opportunity for service
12. social status (p. 29)

Other attempts to understand leisure motivations have focused on a smaller number of primary motivations rather than the more general approach illustrated above (Iso-Ahola, 1989). A series of motives, including competence, socialization, flow, arousal, and seeking and escaping have been examined.

SELF-DETERMINATION

A characteristic of leisure is that it is primarily intrinsically motivated. Intrinsic motivation is

> The doing of an activity for its inherent satisfactions rather than for some separable consequences. When intrinsically motivated, a person is moved to act for the fun or challenge entailed rather than because of external prods, pressures, or rewards (Ryan & Deci, 2000, p. 56).

Simply put, intrinsically motivated behaviors are the "activities that people do naturally and spontaneously when they feel free to follow their inner interests" (Deci & Ryan 2000, p. 234).

Deci and Ryan (2000) expanded on the importance of intrinsic motivation in their development of self-determination theory (SDT). Underlying the theory is the position that people pursue their goals to satisfy basic psychological needs. SDT focuses on three needs: competence, relatedness and autonomy as individuals pursue goals. Meeting these needs is critical for well being, integrity and continued growth (Ryan & LaGuardia, 2000). Our position is that these needs can be meet through the leisure experience and indeed are inherent in that experience. Deci and Ryan (2000) point out that people "experiencing reasonable need satisfaction" engage in activities they find interesting and important not necessarily to meet specific needs. They provide an example from the leisure arena:

> A man who, in the evening, sits at the keyboard and begins to play a piece of music may become lost in its beauty and experience great pleasure. He would not experience the pleasure if coerced to play, or if he felt unable to master the music. Thus, the need satisfaction, which in this case means experiences of autonomy and competence, is necessary for the enjoyment of the activity, but his explicit purpose in playing the music is not likely to be need satisfaction. He would be doing what interests him, and he would experience spontaneous pleasure as long as the activity was self-organizing and the task appropriately challenging (pp. 230 -231).

This passage illustrates the power of leisure. It serves as the activity context for enjoyment as well as the vehicle for meeting basic needs. It is the ultimate behavior—it is not only pleasurable, but also good for you!

Within the self-determination perspective, Ulyssean living will be enhanced if individuals can meet their need for competence, autonomy and relatedness. We will examine each of these further.

Competence. Deci and Ryan (2000) indicated why competence is important to the individual, it is a catalyst to self-development and growth. Seeking competence leads the individual to explore, experiment, persist and succeed.

Others have viewed competence as a primary leisure motivation. This primacy of a drive toward self-perceived competence is supported by Kamptner (1989). She wrote, "Theories of motivation emphasize that individuals have a need to feel effective and interact competently with their environment" (p. 170). However, declines in "autonomy and personal control, which may come about by changes or losses in one's work or family status, income, social network, and physical capacities, or through social devaluation," may make it more difficult to achieve this sense of competence. Leisure can play a major role in the search for competence, particularly if individuals pursue the Ulyssean course.

Since leisure is freely chosen and largely self-determined, it provides an opportunity to select and succeed at activities that will result in perceptions of competence. Climbing a rock, creating a quilt, mentoring an at-risk youth, or completing the Sunday *New York Times* crossword puzzle allow participants to succeed or fail based on their ability and effort. Leisure maximizes the chance to succeed since the activity is selected by the participant and is not imposed by external agents. The result will be an affirmation of self-efficacy (Bandura, 1982) and mastery of the environment.

While people seek relaxation and escape in leisure, it is also an arena for action. Therefore, programs must offer opportunities for challenge and progression from introductory to advanced levels. In many cases, this progression will be most easily provided through age-integrated programs that provide all participants the opportunity to seek their own optimum level of action. However, it may also be necessary to start individuals at a very basic level and in an age-segregated setting until they have enough belief in their own ability that they will enter into age-integrated programs.

For example, a woman would only participate in a water aerobics program that was held in the swimming pool in her retirement community. The pool was for residents only and met her desire to be only with other older individuals. When asked why she did not participate in the program at the local YMCA, her response was that she was not comfortable being seen in her bathing suit in a public pool. It is possible she may have eventually progressed to the point of participating in the more advanced Y program, but the choice had to be hers.

Similarly, programs such as Elderhostel are designed to serve older individuals. Factors such as pacing, competition, and intensity are less than they might be in an age-integrated program. Certainly, many individuals in Elderhostel could do very well in regular academic classes, and many probably do, but the level of "action" provided in Elderhostel is that sought by many. If meaning comes from finding action contexts given the opportunity to demonstrate competence and mastery, then the job of the leisure service professional is to identify, and if necessary provide, as wide an array of opportunities as possible.

Autonomy. Autonomy within self-determination theory refers to the need for self-organization and self-regulation of behavior and is contrasted with heteronomy, being "regulated by forces felt to be alien to the self" (Ryan & LaGuardia, 2000, p. 149). An autonomous individual has a sense of control over activities and outcomes and is able to regulate his or her actions in response to changing needs and environments. It is important to note that autonomy is not the same as independence. Ryan and LaGuardia (2000) allow for the possibility that an autonomous individual can also be dependent upon others, particularly if functionality or well being has declined. The implication of this is that older individuals with health problems can still meet their need for autonomy. The key factor in autonomy is the need for intrinsic motivation, self determination and self regulation. The findings of a great deal of research related to autonomy are clear: "a more autonomy-supportive climate fosters greater initiative and well being in old age" (p. 161).

Mannell and Kleiber (1997) discussed ways of creating autonomy-supportive environments. Providing opportunities for choice and control appears particularly important in helping individuals develop a sense of self determination. Providing older adults with the opportunity to make decisions about their leisure, including types of activities and schedules, assists in developing autonomy. In fact, leisure itself, since high levels of perceived freedom and intrinsic motivation mark it, is an autonomy-supportive behavior.

The need for autonomy requires leisure service providers to alter traditional views of their role. Rather than functioning as a leader, the role of facilitator is more appropriate. Any choices that can be made by participants should be made by them. Rather than offering activities and forcing potential participants to bend their preferences to participate, a controlling approach, service providers need to determine what participants want to do and then find ways to help them do it, an autonomy-supportive approach. Several years ago Bengston (1973) provided a model illustrating ways to introduce autonomy into long-term care facilities. The model he proposed was called "social reconstruction" and he contrasted it with "social breakdown." In social breakdown, older individuals are subjected to a downward cycle of decreasing autonomy and self-determination as a result of social devaluation. Social reconstruction results in empowering individuals to be autonomous and self-directed. It requires three "inputs" into the lives of older people. First, there must be a mechanism to free individuals from inappropriate perspectives of status. For example, if status is defined by employment or economic definitions of productivity, someone who has retired may need assistance in finding alternate means of self-judgment. The gerotranscendence theory described in Chapter 2 identifies some possible alternatives. Volunteer work, community contributions, leisure time use or intergenerational connectivity may provide realistic determinants of self-evaluation and status. The second input is removing conditions reducing independence and control. Many of the issues related to social conditions and biological aging discussed earlier in this book would be included. For example, poor health, lack of transportation or low income may reduce independence and interventions to reduce their impact would be necessary to increase autonomy and control. The third input into social reconstruction is development of an internal locus of control. This is facilitated through providing older individuals opportunities for control and choice in their leisure. The result of social reconstruction will be increased autonomy and ultimately Ulyssean living.

Relatedness. Although relatedness, defined as "feeling connected, cared for, and a sense of belonging with significant others" (Ryan & LaGuardia, 2000, p. 150), is an important factor in intrinsic motivation and self-determination, it is not a crucial as competence and autonomy. Some activities, such as hiking or crossword puzzles, may be intrinsically motivated but done alone. However, according to Deci and Ryan (2000), "Intrinsic motivation will be more likely to flourish in contexts characterized by a sense of secure relatedness" (p. 235). As they indicated, relatedness provides "a secure relational base." or a sense of being supported, loved and cared for. This need for relatedness is related to the socioemotional selectivity theory (Ryan & LaGuardia, 2000) discussed in Chapter 2. Relatedness may become more central with increasing age as individuals reduce social ties while seeking more depth in those they retain. Therefore, programs providing opportunities for intimacy and meaningful social ties are important in meeting the need for relatedness.

Mannell and Kleiber (1997) also identified the need for relatedness as a key motivator of leisure. They view relatedness as revolving around being needed by others and having a sense of being part of something larger than one's self. The previous chapter addressed the role of leisure in community building. Since social integration is a primary motivation for leisure, strong programs will be those focusing on developing relationships. In fact, it has been said that one measure of program success when working with older adults is whether marriages occur between participants.

The author at one time worked in a camp limited to individuals at least 60 years of age. During the summer, a man and woman met during camp and became partners during the morning hikes. Hiking together blossomed into romance, and the couple eventually wed. Clearly, this was a program success.

In another case, during the course of interviewing candidates for the position of center director, one of the authors was confronted with typical answers to the question: "If you were hired, what programs would you initiate?" Answers included travel clubs, potluck dinners, exercise class, and bingo. One candidate said she would start a dating service. She was hired. Kelly (undated) suggests programs providing opportunity for continuity (see Chapter 2 on theories of aging for more on the concept of continuity) in the personal and social realm are those that permit the "expression of ability and community." Clearly, relatedness is an important goal to include in programs.

FLOW

One of the most cited efforts to explain leisure behavior has been Csikszentmihalyi's (1975) notion of "flow." Flow is viewed as the state when individuals' skills are harmonious with the demands of the activity in which they are engaged. When an activity is overly demanding for an individual's abilities, anxiety will result. Contrarily, when skills exceed demand, boredom results. Individuals seek to optimize flow experiences and avoid boredom and anxiety-producing experiences.

This motivation can be effectively used in program design. For example, individuals with low levels of skill should be motivated to seek beginner-level programs. However, if the program does not become more demanding as they develop higher skill levels, boredom will result and dropping out of the program may occur. More odious than dropping out is the possibility the individual may continue to participate in the boring activity, thereby reducing the likelihood it will be a leisure experience.

If activities are viewed as too demanding, it is probable individuals will avoid them since the result of participation will not be personal or social development, but rather anxiety. Therefore, it is necessary that a progression is provided.

There is probably greater danger of underestimating the abilities of older individuals than overestimating their abilities as a result of myths, stereotypes, and ageism. The skills of many individuals are mistakenly viewed as diminishing and deficient. Programs based on those misconceptions will result in boredom. In fact, the low level of involvement in community-based "senior citizen" programs may be at least partly the result of programs viewed as boring by older individuals. If the focus was on meeting the motivation for flow, perhaps public programs would attract more participants. (see Chapter 6 for more on flow).

SEEKING AND ESCAPE

Iso-Ahola's (1989) work supports a more focused perspective on motivation. In fact, he stated, "There are only two fundamental dimensions to leisure motivations: seeking personal and interpersonal intrinsic rewards, and escaping personal and interpersonal environments through leisure experiences. Leisure motivation is not a matter of either seeking or escaping, but of both" (p. 269).

These are two components of the intrinsic motivation that are necessary for leisure. In order to achieve the benefits of leisure discussed in the earlier chapter, individuals must be free to exercise choice and self-determination in their leisure, and this choice revolves around seeking and escaping.

The interpersonal realm refers to the social contacts, while the personal realm focuses on personal rewards, including competence, resulting from participation. Seeking and escaping are presented as motivational forces and not single motives. According to Iso-Ahola, both are present at all times in leisure behavior, but the strength of each varies. Figure 7.1 presents Iso-Ahola's model of seeking and escaping.

Figure 7.1
Model of Seeking and Escaping Behaviors

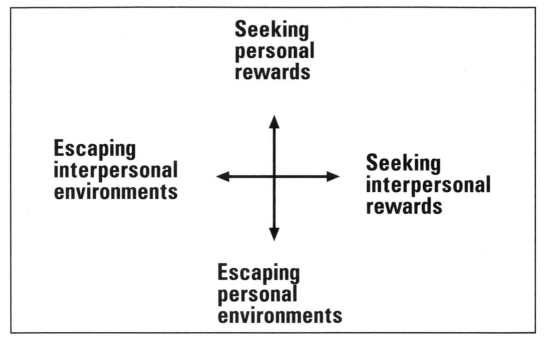

(Iso-Ahola, 1989)

An example may help clarify this model. An individual may look forward to retirement and welcome the free time it will bring. However, she also views this time with trepidation, since boredom is not a desirable outcome. An opportunity to become a volunteer in an intergenerational program with at-risk youth is available in the local community. The individual would like to join since it would provide an opportunity to meet new friends (interpersonal seeking), while breaking away from work mates (interpersonal escaping), and an opportunity to use her skills in new ways, while learning new things (seeking personal rewards), while disengaging from the work role (escaping a personal environment). However, she does not want the same demands on her time as work required, since the escape component is important. If the volunteer role became too rigid and structured, too work-like, she might cease volunteering if the opportunity for escape is no longer present. The wise project director will be aware of the seeking and escaping dimensions and work to keep them in balance.

OPTIMUM AROUSAL

Ellis (1973) identified optimum arousal as a primary leisure motivator. Individuals seek to be in a state of uncertainty and stimulation. This is often achieved through novelty in activities. The freely chosen nature of leisure makes this a behavioral arena where optimum arousal is likely to occur since participants have the freedom to alter their activities to introduce novelty, and the accompanying incongruity, into their activities. For example, an aquatics exercise program can be made stimulating by the introduction of new exercises, equipment, or members into the class. Similarly, challenging activities, such as rock climbing, backpacking, and kayaking, can be incorporated into an individual's leisure repertoire to allow opportunities for optimum arousal. Mannell and Kleiber (1997) indicated that arousal beneath, or above, an individual's optimum level is "unpleasant," and movement toward optimum arousal is pleasant. Therefore, people seek optimum arousal through novelty, incongruity, challenge, and uncertainty when they are sub-optimally aroused. When overaroused (supraoptimal arousal) individuals will seek things that are familiar and predictable.

Many programs for the elderly do not provide enough opportunities for optimum arousal. They are often made up of introductory level activities that underestimate, and underchallenge, the skill of the participants. The result is participants who are sub-optimally aroused. In these cases there is a need for stimulating, novel and challenging activities. However, the losses that accompany aging may result in a supraoptimal level of arousal in some individuals. If that is the case, familiar, predictable activities are most appropriate.

FINDING PERSONAL MEANING IN LEISURE

Reker and Wong (1988) provide an excellent examination of the search for personal meaning in the later years. They view the seeking of meaning in human existence as fundamental to life and are strong proponents of an interpretive science perspective on aging. This perspective has two major premises (p. 216):

1. Humans are viewed as "conscious, active, purposive, self-reflecting organisms capable of symbolization and symbol manipulation." The individual constructs reality rather than merely responding to reality. As a result, "aging may be viewed as a process of change in personal construction over time." Aging is therefore an individual process, "giving the person the power to accommodate and transcend both personal and societal limitations."
2. The physical attributes of the natural world are secondary to the meanings people attach to objects and events in searching for reality.

What is the role of leisure in finding personal meaning in later life? This meaning can only be identified by the actor. In fact, people are motivated by the search for personal meaning in life. Programs designed to assist in this search will help individuals find purpose in living. Although Reker and Wong are more theoretical than practical in their presentation, there arc some clear paths to using the interpretive perspective for programmatic direction. Sources for personal meaning, resulting from values and beliefs, include:

1. personal growth
2. success or achievement

3. altruism
4. hedonism
5. creativity
6. religion
7. legacy

The development of meaning in life accrues from several values, and as a result greater variety contributes to greater meaning. The result is what Reker and Wong call the breadth postulate:

"An individual's degree of personal meaning will increase in direct proportion to his or her diversification of sources of meaning" (p. 225).

Further postulates provide additional programmatic fodder. The depth postulate states:

"An individual's degree of personal meaning will increase in direct proportion to his or her commitment to higher levels of meaning" (p. 226).

The highest level of meaning rests in values that relate to the ultimate purpose of life and cosmic meanings. That is heady stuff that may be difficult to incorporate in a recreation program.

Victor Logan may have reached this level of meaning, but it is probably not accessible to all. However, the lower levels of meaning may not be as problematic. The lowest level of meaning is seeking pleasure and comfort. Many recreation programs are designed at this level. However, the depth postulate suggests a need to move beyond pleasure.

The second level of meaning is the devotion of time and energy to the realization of our potential. This would include areas such as creativity and personal growth. The Ulyssean perspective espoused in this book comes close to this level of meaning.

The third level of meaning revolves around altruism, and service to others with dedication to a larger social or political cause is part of this level. Opportunities such as mentoring, political action and community will contribute to this level of meaning. The depth postulate indicates the need to provide opportunities to find meaning at all these levels.

Individuals reflecting both breadth and depth in their personal meaning systems are viewed as healthy. They are able to cope and adapt in a shifting world while accepting personal limitations. In fact, the meaning system postulate addresses the value of a comprehensive meaning system.

The personal meaning system of an individual who has available a variety of sources of meaning and who strives for higher levels of personal meaning will be highly differentiated and integrated. (p. 226)

Although Wong and Reker develop other postulates, these are the most germane to the leisure topic. The finding of meaning in later life is personal. However, that does not mean individuals working with the elderly have no role in the search for meaning. In fact, the following postulates derived from Reker and Wong may explain our potential role:

Breadth Hypothesis: The opportunity to find personal meaning will increase in direct proportion to the number of potential leisure opportunities available.

Depth Hypothesis: The opportunity to find personal meaning will increase as activities providing opportunity to find higher meaning are provided.

Based on these hypotheses, it is recommended older individuals be offered a variety of experiences that will facilitate the finding of meaning in later life. Opportunities must exhibit depth and breadth if they are to be effective.

LEISURE CONSTRAINTS

The outcomes of leisure involvement described in this chapter will only accrue if individuals are able to engage in desired activities. There has been a great deal of research examining factors limiting or prohibiting participation in leisure and therefore much is known about why older individuals do not participate in desired activities. (See McGuire and Norman forthcoming, for a full description of the leisure constraint and aging literature.) Any factor interfering with the pursuit of leisure, such as poor health or lack of opportunities for active engagement, may be viewed as a constraint. The impact of these constraints will be aging that falls short of the possibilities open to older people. In that sense constraints not only restrict or limit leisure involvement, they also prohibit Ulyssean living.

Some of the concomitants of aging may themselves function as constraints. For example, decline in visual acuity may result in the loss of the ability to drive and therefore lack of transportation may become problematic. Similarly, reduced income resulting from retirement and reliance on social security as a major source of finances may magnify the effects of not having enough money. Constrains may also arise from perceived loss or decline, such as fear of falling (Bruce, Devine & Prince, 2002; Murphy, Williams, & Gill, 2002), and limit engagement in activities.

There has been a great deal of research related to constraints to participation in specific activities. Perhaps the largest area of such study has been exercise. Exercise is recognized as a crucial factor in health in the later years. As a result, exercise programs, many designed for older people, such as mall walking or water aerobics, have become common. Concomitantly, questions are asked about why more people do not participate in physical activity. Grant (2001) identified factors such as childhood socialization, limited early life opportunities, physical and social vulnerability (particularly among women), fear of injury, and cultural values such as perceptions of what is age appropriate, as constraints to involvement in physical activities by older people. Nied and Franklin (2002) listed several additional constraints to participation in physical activity, including low self-efficacy (one's belief that one is able to successfully engage in an activity), discomfort and disability, poor balance, and lack of an environment for pursuing activities.

Another activity studied is travel. For example, Fleisher and Pizam (2002) explored tourism constraints among older Israelis, recognizing that "The senior market is of significant size and importance to many countries." They surveyed Israelis 55 years of age and over and found that the decision to take a vacation was dependent on two variables, self-assessed health and income. Age did not matter. However, income, health, past vacation experience and age (where the relationship is not linear but rather increases and then decreases over time) affect the length of a vacation. This study supports the findings of most of the literature on leisure constraints in later years, income and health are critical factors in facilitating or limiting engagement in leisure.

Rogers, Meyer, Walker, and Fisk (1998) used focus group interviews to assess constraints in the daily lives of 59 healthy older individuals, ranging in age from 65 to 88. They addressed four issues: in what ways do older adults encounter constraints in everyday life; what is the source of the constraints; how do older adults respond to constraints; and can intervention help to minimize constraints. The focus groups began with participants asked to discuss the last time they "really got frustrated trying to use something," and concluded with participants asked to review a list of everyday activities (transportation, new technologies, using the library, remaining healthy, consumer-related issues, hobbies and entertainment, communication, cooking and eating, money management, home maintenance, and housekeeping) and discuss problems related to each area. The results indicated constraints could be sorted into motor-related problems such as problems with bending, balance and walking, as well as fine-motor difficulties, visual and auditory problems, cognitive limitations including memory and procedural knowledge, external limitations such as fear of crime and dependence, and general health limitations. The study also examined responses to limitations. The most common response was activity cessation with nearly half of all responses being curtailment of task performance. It is particularly noteworthy that physical limitations were the cause for cessation in a variety of leisure activities including walking, swimming, reading, dining out, traveling, library use, visiting family and friends, and dancing. Perseverance, often marked by reduced speed or accuracy in performance, was another response to constraints. The study participants also used compensation as a strategy to overcome limitations. This approach included using a tool to assist in task completion, changing the environment or changing the steps in the task. A final approach to negotiating limitations was self-improvement. For example, rehabilitation after a stroke, concentrating more to accommodate memory loss, or learning a new skill such as how to use a computer were identified as self-improvement mechanisms. The final purpose of the study was to identify interventions professionals could use in helping reduce constraints. The authors found that approximately half of the identified problems were not correctable through training or redesign. Of the one-half that were open to remediation, a number could be addressed through training (information on how to exercise safely) or redesign (providing lightweight tools for gardening).

Deci and Ryan (2000) provided a more theoretical discussion of leisure constraints within the framework of self-determination theory. Any environment that is excessively controlling, over challenging or rejecting can hinder self-determination. The implication is that an environment allowing individuals to control activities and outcomes, balancing participant skills with activity demands, and providing supportive social interactions will facilitate social determination and the benefits accruing from autonomy, competence and relatedness.

The research on constraints in later life indicates factors such as money, time, facilities, companions and health impact opportunities for Ulyssean living. In addition, lack of opportunities for autonomy, competence and relatedness will also reduce the likelihood that leisure will be a vehicle for successful aging. One task of leisure professionals is to help individuals identify and remove barriers whenever possible. Mannell and Kleiber (1997) discuss the concept of leisure affordance, "conditions that will promote and support satisfying leisure styles" (p. 345). They identify a variety of strategies for facilitating involvement, typically revolving around the identification and removal of constraints. Providing transportation, assistive devices, managing activities to make them accessible an enjoyable, providing leisure companions, keeping activity costs down, scheduling during the day since older individuals may have difficulties driving at night, creating leisure competence as described in Chapter 6, and increasing a sense of self-efficacy are some suggestions for creating leisure affordance.

CONCLUSION

This chapter has examined the motivations underlying leisure involvement. Long lists of potential reasons for participating in leisure have been developed by a variety of authors. As this chapter has shown, these lists accurately reflect the multitude of reasons for being involved in leisure without telling us a great deal about why any particular person is involved at any point in time. The answer to why people do what they do is a deeply personal one. This is probably more true in leisure, one of the most personal of all behaviors, than in many realms of behavior. Therefore, the information provided in this chapter should be viewed as a point of departure rather than an arrival. Obviously, it gives us a perspective on the richness of the leisure experience. However, this richness demands activities be based on the needs and desires of participants rather than the judgments of leisure providers. Although people are pushed into activities by motivators such as competence, relatedness, arousal, and seeking and escaping, the nature of the activity selected to respond to the call for action will vary across individuals. It is crucial that leisure service professionals provide environments and opportunities where motivations can be translated into meaningful activities.

The presence of constraints will make Ulyssean living more difficult to achieve. Leisure service providers should work with participants to identify and overcome barriers to successful aging.

EIGHT

TIME AND ACTIVITIES IN RETIREMENT

Both leisure and the aging of society and individuals exist within a broad socio-cultural context that shapes what transpires—trends in average workweek affect leisure time, opportunities for young female athletes may translate to awareness on the part of recreation agencies that adult females may desire competitive events, and the economic significance of leisure within the economy resulting in many services available as examples. This context also helps to determine meaning of activity. If health and fitness are priorities in society, participants may see such activity as necessary and valued. Society and individuals must deal with questions about the importance of leisure in later life, the degree of status attached to freetime activity, and whether relevant leisure is a viable substitute for paid employment. Retirement and the options therein do not exist in a vacuum; the issues and trends in the broader society act to influence choices in late life pursuits.

Among these current trends are the *speed*-up of life with instantaneous communication in a 24-7 world, perceptions of time famine–there is so much going on and so little precious time to partake of it that uneasiness and stress follow, and the societal ethos that busier is always better and multi-tasking is the only way to operate. Such forces may run counter to the expected and desired pace of retirement. Some may eagerly embrace a slowed pace upon retirement, others may need a period of decompression to adjust to a world without pagers and lines of unread emails, and some, undoubtedly, approach retirement with attitudes carried over from work, "I'd better knock off eight items on my leisure to-do list today, and the quicker the better, or the day won't be a success." Ekerdt (1986) echoed this sentiment in a paper entitled "The Busy Ethic" in which he argued that retirement is legitimized through productivity. Whatever pattern or approach is adopted, there will be a connection between societal-level happenings and how these affect individuals.

Economic trends or shifts in the period immediately preceding and following the year 2000 greatly impacted spending for leisure, career planning for younger and older workers, and individual choices about retirement. The healthy economy and stock market prior to the year 2000 brought much discretionary spending frequently on leisure-related items such as vacation homes and expensive trips. Retirement portfolios grew and financial plans for retirement were carefully analyzed as wealth increased for many. Yet even in this robust climate, many firms were downsizing and eliminating staff in order to improve the bottom line and keep stocks attractive. The downturn immediately following this boom period left many without jobs, and many looking for comparable positions to the ones they had held found the prospects quite dim. Most older workers reconsidered a host of retirement issues as future pensions were being depleted by the negative stock market. Such trends existing at a macro level became part of the decision process for those about to exit the workplace and those already retired.

A final societal trend to be noted that is directly linked to older adults and the realm of leisure is the general aging of the population. The next 30-to 40-year span will bring an older society in a manner that has not been experienced before. Not only will a massive baby boom cohort move into their senior years, but in addition, the old-old will grow dramatically. How society grapples with these changes will have a direct impact upon notions about aging, the aged, and what roles older citizens may be expected to occupy. Many issues are already being debated—changes in Social Security and Medicare—while others are playing out—older family members/grandparents/parents as care recipients or as care providers in watching grandchildren or others in need. This central issue of roles (What is to be encouraged? What is deemed necessary? And the balance between obligatory and discretionary activity for masses of older adults) is one tied to leisure meanings and choices. Optimists may view this future as one with unlimited potential, perhaps many will achieve self-actualization through leisure, and a true Ulyssean journey will unfold as most take full advantage of the retirement years. Whatever transpires, notions of aging and of leisure are likely to undergo scrutiny and analysis in the decades to follow.

Have you ever thought seriously about how we use time and how typical retirees spend their hours and minutes? Before beginning this next section dealing with time use, make an estimate as to how different groups spend their time. Create a number of categories in which people spend their time—one might be personal maintenance (sleeping and bathing, etc.), another might be time spent eating, another might be chores (housework, cleaning, preparing food, washing clothes, etc.). The realm of leisure time might include social activity (time with friends, visiting, phone conversation, etc.) and time spent on hobbies. You decide what the major categories should be and then make an estimate of time use as a percent of daily time or in terms of hours/minutes per day.

Once the categories have been established, make your estimates for three different groups:

A) All adults (include work time for this group)
B) All retirees
C) Yourself during your retirement

Compare the three groups of estimates. Keep these in mind as you review the next sections on time use and activities.

CONCEPTUAL PERSPECTIVES IN THE EXPLORATION OF TIME AND ACTIVITY

Before presenting an analysis of time use and activity preferences in later life, perhaps the reader should briefly pause and consider the perspective or viewpoint taken in reviewing such material. When time is considered, an obvious approach similar to the exercise above could be used—develop common categories and observe these in percents of all time available or in units (hours/minutes per day or week). Perhaps some key demographics such as gender or age group (the young-old and the old-old) could also be utilized to explore differences. This type of analysis would lend itself to generalizations and perhaps a normative approach to aging (Neugarten, 1977). Most older adults retire within a certain age span and then spend their time on various activities, and a time expenditure in those activities can be assigned as a percent of total time.

Another view could consider two major periods—pre- and active retirement. Bolles (1978) noted three major periods or "boxes of life" as education/learning (our youth), work (our adult years), and leisure (our older adult years). Comparisons in this vein might emphasize changes in time categories and activities in the adult working years with changes seen when retirement occurs.

Chapter 2 offers theoretical perspectives on personal aging, described as disengagement, activity, and continuity theories. Features of time and activity would be of greater or lesser importance according to these perspectives. Disengagement would expect a decline particularly in social involvements; time and activity would be charted looking for drops except in areas of an individual nature. Activity theory would pay attention to total amounts of participation with focus on the maintenance or decline over the adult years. Continuity perspectives would hypothesize continuance of a number of activities with some adaptive shifts or adjustments possible and note differing styles of aging and leisure. Here some could be very focused on types of leisure (athletics or crafts), and a central focus of volunteering might be displayed in a variety or roles and organizations. Those with life-long tendencies for exercise would be analyzed for continuing participation and for any shifts necessitated by health or advancing old age. Likewise, Kelly's (1983) core and balance model would project "a group of constant, accessible activities that would account for a percent of available time; these core activities would be contrasted with others (balance) that round out the leisure repertoire and are seen as high investment pursuits—special in the sense of time required or energy and resources needed for participation."

A longitudinal or human development viewpoint focuses on change over time. This view follows subjects through extended periods of time, and comparisons of activities and time allocations would note similarities and shifts as aging progressed with attention to key variables associated with change (declining health, death of a spouse, etc.).

Finally, McLeish's Ulyssean model sees the time and activity canvas as one truly blank. Choice is foremost. Each has the ability to select, to challenge, to shift, and to repeat the enjoyable. Here, those who vary from the norm in terms of time use and activities are worthy of examination because of their uniqueness. Qualitative methods exploring those who stand apart would provide insight. Those who read or exercise quite a bit more than most, those who rise at 5:30 each day because they wish to begin with the peace this time affords, and those who vary substantially from the norm in terms of time and activity would all be subjects of interest within the Ulyssean framework. These orientations are worth considering as the review of time and activity preferences proceed in the next sections. The reader may wish to revisit Chapter 2 and keep in mind the dominant theories of personal aging as time and activity are described.

WORK AND LEISURE IN SOCIETY

Since the exiting of the work role with the movement into retirement is a major transition for the majority of older adults, the balance of the work-leisure relationship is one worth considering for all adults. As mentioned earlier, a number of trends in society at large were affecting the nature of work and leisure as a new century/millennium began in 2000. Most adults were striving for a better work-leisure balance. Combining stress levels in the workforce and a general quickening of the pace of daily life, many struggled to gain adequate amounts of leisure and to enjoy that time in a manner devoid of speed and productivity. In terms of recent historical time, the past 20 or 25 years, analysts debated whether more work and less leisure was the norm for the employed. Perception entered the debate, as well, with some (Robinson & Godbey, 1996) claiming that working hours had remained relatively constant while the public's feelings about overwork and stress had changed for the worse. Schor's (1991) frequently quoted examination of hours for the typical worker from the late 1960s to the late 1980s concluded that Americans were working an extra month (approximately 160 hours) a year and this was in part due to employers favoring overtime for existing workers rather than hiring additional employees with fringe benefit costs, the rise of low-paying service jobs in the economy requiring many to work a job and a half or more to break even (see also Ehrenreich's 2001, account of the plight of the hourly worker), and the standardization of a long week (50, 60 hours) for white-collar management and professional types whose extra hours benefited the company's bottom line.

Other observations offered a differing view of average weekly hours. Data from the Bureau of Labor (see Jones, 1963: U.S. Department of Commerce, Statistical Abstract of the United States, 1955-2001) showed a relatively stable work week in manufacturing jobs (this analysis is not reflective of many managers and professionals) since the end of World War II with an average of slightly less than 40 hours a week. For sub-groups of workers in the economy—poorly paid service workers, most in retail sales, and the majority of managerial and professional workers—the 40-hour standard was not a reality.

Contrasted with work, leisure in recent years had declined significantly, remained about the same, or undergone a tremendous growth spurt depending on definition. As related to dollars spent, leisure in the sense of personal consumption had grown from $10.8 billion in 1950 to $65.5 billion in the mid-1970s to $292 billion in 1990 and more than $534 billion by 1999, with older consumers contributing to those amounts (Statistical Abstract of the United States, 1951-2001). As related to participation, many areas of leisure and sport showed growth over a sustained period, and as reported in following sections, seniors were responsible in part for such growth in many categories. As a measure of time, free or discretionary, authorities differed as to the extent of leisure and whether it had been growing or declining depending on the frame of reference. As we will see, many analyses as probably expected, showed the older population with most retired to be advantaged in terms of free time. Schor (1991), referring to the late 1980s, claimed work was increasing with leisure in decline. The Harris Polls (Taylor, 1998) portrayed consistently long work weeks as estimated by respondents, about 50 hours a week during the 1990s and 47 to 49 in the 1980s, but these may have been inflated due to the question including commuting and housekeeping with hours spent in paid employment. Robinson and Godbey (1999) have noted the tendency of those working long hours to overestimate and discrepancies often occur when time diary data are compared with estimates of work time.

In contrast the Harris Polls were consistently among the lowest for reported leisure with a nadir of 16.6 hours in 1987 and rising through the 1990s to 19.4 hours in 1998. Part of the reason for such low estimates may be traced to the wording of the questions asked; specific leisure activities were presented in the question, and respondents may not have included periods of time when no activity was occurring, yet such time should be considered as free and discretionary. Analyses of leisure by Robinson and Godbey (1989, 1999) portrayed a much different picture. Their figures placed weekly leisure at 40 hours per week for adult males and 39 for females in 1985. By the mid-1990s all men had gained about three $1/2$ hours (43.6) while women had stayed nearly the same (a slight drop to 38.5). Females saw most of their gains in leisure during the 1965-1975 decade primarily due to less time spent on housework. Older groups consistently enjoyed the most leisure. Thus, depending on the source and the frame of comparison (recent periods versus a longer historical view), one could find differing accounts of the amount of leisure and whether it had been declining, expanding, or remaining constant. Some of these differences had their roots in methodological and definitional inconsistency regarding what "leisure" meant and how it was to be determined.

RETIREMENT AGE AND STRESS

In addition to the amount of leisure in hours per day or week, a consideration of prime importance when exploring time use in older adulthood is the age at onset of retirement and the average number of years until death. Closely associated with retirement and noted earlier as a general trend in society is the problem of stress. Logic would suggest that a prime benefit of retirement is the shedding of work-related stressors and research has supported the supposition that older adults are less susceptible to stress (in the sense of work and general time pressures, other types of stress connected to personal factors and health status do show links to older adults) than other age groups.

Gerontologists and demographers have used as a measure of life expectancy not only the predicted span of years from birth to death, but also the projected time from the age of 65 until death. This period of time has been growing for adults in the United States during the last century. In 1900 a 65-year-old could look forward to about 12 more years of life; this span had increased to 18 years by 1996 (see Chapter 1). Recent trends in retirement age had recorded a movement away from (lowering) the traditional age of 65 and had shown decreasing percentages of men in the workforce in their fifties (Gendell & Sigel, 1992, 1996). For males the median age of retirement dropped from 66.9 in 1950-1955 to just over 62 in 1995-2000 with a projected median of slightly less than 62 for the period 2000-2005. In addition to the lowering of the median age for retirement, the percent of males aged 55-59 working had dropped 10 percent from 1950 (90 percent) to 79.4 percent in 1995. The percent of older women working actually increased as more women entered the workforce after 1960; most ended their employment at about the same age as men. Taken together, these two trends of a longer period of life after the age of 65 and a median retirement age lowered to the early sixties meant an extended period of leisure in later life would be the norm for most.

Another positive factor associated with older age and retirement is reduced stress as reported in national health surveys. One in Canada (Zuzanek & Smale, 1997) and another in the United States (Robinson & Godbey, 1998) demonstrated that older age groups perceive the least amount of stress of all adults. In fact, retirees are likely to score about $1/2$ of what working adults will report. Adults in their thirties and forties are most susceptible to high levels. That is not to say that certain older groups—those recently widowed, those suffering from health problems, and those struggling economically—will not endure significant stress, but older persons as a group enjoy a benefit of lowered stress. Stress, along with a number of other psychological constructs including morale, well being, and additional quality of life measures have been connected with leisure participation and these relationships will be highlighted in succeeding sections.

THE USE OF TIME IN LATER LIFE

From previous commentary, a number of positive forces are present as time use in later life is considered. Even with legislation barring forced retirement, the general trend is toward a lowered age of about 62 with more workers opting to leave in their mid- to late fifties. Future economic trends, no doubt, will be a factor in the continuance or modification of the move toward earlier retirement. An extended retirement with more years from ceasing employment until death is the expectation. Further, foregoing fulltime employment is associated with lower stress; the hassles of the workplace behind them, retirees can approach time and activities without the worries and stress connected to employment. Thus, time use presents positive features to those retired that differs from the perspectives held by many in society. Not all, however, share in these advantages. Victims of pension fraud or corporate shifts resulting in severely reduced payments to pensioners may be forced to extend the working years. The popular press has brought attention to segments of the elder population who have outlived their retirement resources and by necessity returned to work at an advanced age. Others, when unexpected health crises occur to themselves or their spouse, face a much different reality in terms of how time will be allocated than what was originally planned. These strata of aging adults must be considered with the generally favored position of all older persons.

A recently reported analysis by Gauthier and Smeeding (2000) used large-scale, national time budget data collected from daily diaries and focused on adults in the age category of 55 to 64. United States data were from the 1985 Americans' Use of Time Project. They were interested in comparing males and females in this age span who were still employed with those who had retired. Six nations were used for a cross-national perspective; Canada and Finland were found to be similar to the United States.

Seven categories of time were used: personal maintenance, paid work, housework, unpaid work (childcare and volunteering), active leisure (hobbies, physically active sport/exercise), social leisure (eating out, parties), and passive (media use, television, reading). The major conclusion reached was that as people retire, their leisure pattern resembles how they spent time on non-work days while they were still employed. Continuity of activity pattern was suggested. There were some differences in males and females in the United States sample when those working were contrasted with those retired. Working males averaged 6.7 hours of leisure (categories of active, social, and passive) compared to 9.6 for retirees. Retired men also spent more time on house chores. For women, those retired had an extra three hours of leisure daily (8.5 versus 5.7) compared to their working counterparts. Retired women also spent more time (1.8 hours daily) on housework. The results indicated that retirees do not substitute unpaid work (civic volunteering or childcare) to any significant extent for paid employment upon retiring. Again, findings supported a continuation or continuity of time allocation. As one retires, the pattern resembles the way hours were spent on weekends and other non-work days while still in the workforce.

Zuzanek and Smale (1997) used general social surveys in Canada (1981 and 1992) to examine time expenditure and notions of stress or time pressure (cited in previous section) and when older women and men (65+) were contrasted with younger subjects, advantages in free time and low stress were noted. Since most were retired, the 65 and over group reported much less time in paid and unpaid work. Older persons had by far the most free time; 8.8 hours a day for men and 7.7 for women. Older men (3.7 hours) and women (3.0) spent the most time in daily television viewing of all groups. Feelings of being rushed or pressured for time were rare in the senior group.

A national study conducted in the early 1980s (United Media Enterprises, 1983) in the United States reported attitudes and behaviors relative to leisure time and activities. The sample was divided into relevant groups in terms of a lifespan perspective: teenagers, single adults, those married with no children, traditional parents, dual-career parents, single parents, parents with grown children, and seniors (65+). Results pointed toward differing issues and problems in time and activities from younger to older age. Free time was most abundant for those at opposite ends of the age spectrum—the 65-and-over group with 43 hours a week and the youngest (teens) with 41 hours a week. Those disadvantaged for free time included dual-career, traditional, and single parents. Opinions about wasting time varied by age, as well. Seniors were the least likely to feel they wasted time while teenagers were by far the most likely to indicate that time was wasted. The oldest group also said that time rarely weighed heavily on their hands. One could conclude that most seniors are more than capable of dealing with the time available to them.

In a series of reports utilizing data from the Americans' Use of Time Project, Robinson/Godbey and colleagues (see Robinson, 1989; Robinson & Godbey, 1996, 1998, 1999; and Robinson, Werner & Godbey, 1997) have explored leisure within the context of a changing society. The picture emerging from the starting point of the mid-1960s through the mid-1990s is one of constants (television viewing assumes the bulk of our leisure, sleep has remained relatively constant for adults), changes (women doing less housework through the years) and surprises (men and women, overall, are becoming more alike in their allocation of time). As expected, older age, has been a variable linked with discretionary time and certain patterns of activity.

The latest analysis (Robinson & Godbey, 1999; Robinson, Werner & Godbey, 1997) using time diaries collected from 1993 to 1995 revealed some changes in the way older adults use time compared to earlier studies in 1975 and 1985. Persons aged 65 and over now have about 60 hours of leisure a week and this amount has increased 10 hours since 1975 and seven since 1985. Compared to the earlier reports, seniors are less likely to work for pay and less time is spent in sleeping, eating, and grooming, however, the average for sleep is still a healthy 8.5 hours daily. Gains in free time have gone to TV viewing (about $^1/_2$ of the gain), personal communication, and travel to visit or attend social events.

For older males, free time breaks down in the following order (amounts are in hours per week): TV (26.7), communicating (7.8), reading (7.2), visiting (6.5), hobbies and sports (3.7 each). Small amounts are spent weekly in organizational activity, religion, and educational events. The pattern for older women is nearly the same: TV (26.6), communicating (8.0), reading (6.8), visiting (6.5), and hobbies (4.4). Women spend less time on sports than men do. Women also spend more time on house chores than men (six hours a week) and both groups see an increase in time spent in housework after retirement (Robinson, Werner & Godbey, 1997).

The older-old, those 75 and over, differ in some ways from the younger-old (65 to 74). Persons past 75 have an extra hour of leisure daily and tend to spend less time on housework and eating out. The oldest group compared to younger seniors have increased amounts of media activity—television viewing, radio, and reading the paper. The differences in time allocation between the 75 and over and the 65 to 74 groups are not as large as the gaps between pre-retirees and post-retirees (Robinson, Werner & Godbey, 1997).

A few conclusions appear warranted when time use is considered for adults in later life. The period for leisure in the sense of a block of years and days is growing as earlier retirement and longer life result in a span of 20 or more years for many. Retirement is a major life event that creates blocks of discretionary time and amounts differ for mature adults still in the workforce and those who have stopped working (Gauthier & Smeeding, 2000; Robinson, Werner & Godbey, 1997), yet the pattern of activity may be set in the pre-retirement years (Gauthier & Smeeding, 2000). Not only is time allocation impacted but suggested through the findings on stress (Robinson & Godbey, 1998; Zuzanek & Smale, 1997) is that the approach to activity in retirement is less rushed and without time pressures felt while still in the workforce. While not directly explored in the reviewed studies, there is an implied notion that the pace and rhythm of time use are more leisurely in retirement and one study (Zuzanek, Robinson & Iwaski, 1998) has suggested that the pace of activity can be important in keeping stress at bay. As to what occupies time, one can't escape the persistent presence of television as a gobbler of free time for the old as for all others. From the perspective of analyzing time use, it is the foundation from which the remainder is segmented into other activity.

LEISURE ACTIVITIES IN LATER LIFE

The preceding comments on time use provide an excellent background for exploring activities in retirement. Time analysts use categories to divide time and one of these is usually labeled "uncommitted, discretionary, or leisure" activity. Amounts of time devoted to various activities give a sense of priority or rank order. We continue in this vein here focusing on the most popular to least popular activities of seniors. Comparisons will be offered of all adults with the 65-and-over population. Researchers are frequently interested in using independent variables such as gender, age, health or economic status in exploring differences in activity use; examples will be shown here. Frequently, leisure participation is also connected with various dependent variables. Researchers wonder about the links of activity participation with well being, morale, or life satisfaction. These links will be discussed, as well. Chapters 6 and 7 provide insight into the role and importance of leisure in later life and the motivations or "why" of participation. Readers may wish to quickly review these chapters as the importance, benefit, and reasons for activity involvement will be apparent. Not emphasized here are the areas of exercise/fitness, sports and competitions, and travel; these are detailed in succeeding sections. Numbers given are percentages, except where noted.

For a snapshot of what the general adult public does with its free time the Harris Poll provides a national sample that is representative and has tracked preferences over the years (Taylor, 1998). When adults were asked to give their top two or three favorite activities (note this is favorite, not what occupies the most time), reading ranked first (30 percent), followed by television (21 percent), and spending time with family (13 percent). Gardening grew significantly throughout the years and ranked next. Other favorite activities at the top of the list were fishing, team sports, going to the movies, sewing, walking and swimming. As seen previously, from a time and preference perspective, research indicates TV viewing as the top activity.

The United Media Enterprises study (1983) asked about daily participation in various activities. For the oldest group, 65 and over, the rank order with daily participation was: reading the newspaper (87 percent), watching TV (81 percent), talking on the phone (47 percent), hobbies (39 percent), reading books (35 percent), and exercise (34 percent). Gardening and visiting friends were next. Compared to empty-nesters, most of whom were working and had grown children, the 65-and-over group recorded higher percentages of daily participation, and rankings were the same for the top three categories. Gardening was ranked higher for empty-nesters while reading books was lower. The benefit of having greater amounts of daily leisure for the 65-and-over group can be seen in the higher daily percentages when compared to the empty-nesters who were frequently still employed.

Milletti (1984) surveyed retired college professors and administrators, a group higher in average education and income than the norm for all older adults. Favored activities were: reading (92 percent), time with friends (75 percent), gardening (71 percent), travel (66 percent), hobbies (61 percent), followed by creative arts, church and volunteer pursuits.

Rankings of leisure in the sense of time spent by older adults from the 1993 to 1995 period by research from Robinson, Werner, and Godbey (1997) placed TV viewing in first place accounting for about half of all free time and three times as much as the second-place activity, communicating with friends. Reading, visiting, and hobbies were also near the top but received far less time daily compared to television. For men, sports occupied sixth place and for women religious activity assumed this spot.

Older women living in Florida were surveyed (Gibson, Ashton-Schaeffer & Sanders, 2000) and noted primary leisure involvements as socializing with friends and family (70 percent) and reading (69 percent). Religious activity (51 percent), television (50 percent), talking on the phone (50 percent), and gardening (33 percent) were also popular. A significant relationship was found between attitudes toward leisure and life satisfaction for the women.

As a sub-set of leisure pursuits, use of local parks by aging adults was examined in two recent research studies. An urban sample was selected by Payne, Mowen, and Orsega-Smith (2002) who looked at attitudes and behaviors. Age was the strongest predictor (older persons classified as 50 and over) in feeling that no more land was required for the park system. Older persons were less likely to visit parks than younger ones and preference for active recreation versus passive functions was indicated by those over 50. Contrasts by race included blacks favoring the expansion of park land, the preference for recreation over conservation uses, and the desire for organized rather than nature activities, and less visitation of parks when compared to whites.

Gender, ethnicity, and age were used to examine park use and perceived benefits in Chicago in a recent study (Tinsley, Tinsley, & Croskeys, 2002). Older subjects ranged in age from 55 to 93 and neither age nor gender was found responsible for differences. Ethnicity, as divided into four groups—Asians, Hispanics, African-Americans, and Caucasians—did account for predictive power with Asians and Hispanics more likely to visit with family or an organized group and Caucasians more likely to use foot or bike paths and more likely to come to the park alone. Highest rated psycho-social benefits by all older adults were: the immediate sense of pleasure provided by the park, enjoying nonchallenging activity, affiliation, exercise, and escaping a sense of duty.

LEISURE DURING THE OLDER YEARS: A LONGITUDINAL PERSPECTIVE

One of the intriguing issues about aging concerns change—how much and what types of change will be seen as an adult passes through later life? Will time be spent differently (discontinuity) or will patterns of activity remain relatively stable (continuity)? How might changes in other areas of life (health, income, marriage) affect leisure? These questions are answered with some level of agreement in a group of studies focusing on leisure participation over time (a longitudinal view) as related to pertinent variables such as gender, health, and well being.

Summarizing the issue of change in personal circumstances and in activity, Verbrugge, Gruber-Baldini, and Fozard (1996) comment:

> "As people age, their activities change due to shifts in preferences, constraints, attitudes, and health. The changes occur in many ways—the specific activities a person does, procedures to accomplish them, frequency, and duration. Stated briefly, these features are what, how, how often, and how long. Together, frequency and duration determine the amount of time spent on an activity in a day or a year" (p. S30).

Using one of the most important data bases available to gerontologists, the Baltimore Longitudinal Study of Aging, change in activity associated with advancing age was investigated from three differing perspectives: cross-sectional age difference (comparison of 50- 60- 70- year-olds at a given time point), longitudinal changes (how the same persons differ over time), and secular changes (what events occur in society that might be responsible for differences when activity patterns are contrasted by decade). Both the power of the data base and the level of analysis regarding change were notable in this research. Begun in 1958, the Baltimore Longitudinal Study of Aging allows for an analysis of change over time by collecting data from the same subjects for extended periods. A battery of exams and questionnaires are administered every two years and more than 1,800 persons were used in the analysis here (Verbrugge, Gruber-Baldini, & Fozard, 1996) between 1958 and 1992. Fourteen categories of activity were available for examination with five classified as discretionary leisure (socializing, entertainment, public service, hobbies/leisure, and sports).

Analyses found general stability over time (differences within persons over time were much smaller than differences between persons at different ages), and if change was seen, it occurred gradually over time. Support was found for the contention of Robinson, Werner, and Godbey (1997) that leisure activities are similar by gender; however, men did spend more time devoted to sports and women to hobbies. Cross-sectional results discovered that many committed and discretionary activities showed a curvilinear pattern when age groups were contrasted—lower in the younger and older ages and higher for those in the middle. Overall, the picture portrayed in their work was one of a narrowing of the leisure repertoire for groups of older adults. Decreases were noted by decade in the leisure categories of socializing, entertainment, sports, and walking for men, but most activity categories held their relative rank when age groups were compared. Time spent in hobbies increased with age group. As to secular or societal changes, earlier retirement, more workers leaving employment in their fifties or early sixties, more women working, and decreases in time spent on housework (all noted in previous sections) were factors associated with activities in later life. Comparisons by decade from the 1960s to the 1990s revealed men socializing more and spending more time in sports and hobbies and women increasing in these areas as well, but in smaller increments than males. Thus, stability and change were seen; individuals displayed a general pattern of stability over time, yet differences by age cohort and by decades based upon societal-level trends were noted.

Smale and Dupuis (1993) were concerned with activity change or consistency during the lifespan and how well being might be related to leisure. A national sample of more than 4,000 people in Canada included younger, middle-aged, and two older-aged groups (50 to 64, 65 to 80). A particular focus was social and passive leisure as distinguished from physical forms of activity. For all females, more time was spent in social organizations and walking compared to men who swam more often and spent more time in crafts. As age groups were compared, older groups spent more time in crafts/hobbies and walking for exercise. In terms of well being, the oldest group scored highest, and a number of activities were linked to higher well being. Craft activity and visiting friends were related to well being for older age groups. Television use was negatively correlated with well being particularly in late life. A conclusion for all age groups was that passive activities showed stronger relationships with well being than did physically active ones.

Activity connected with morale and physical health was researched longitudinally by Freysinger, Allessio, and Mehdizadeh (1993) with a group of older, white, rural men and women over a period of six years. Most were in their 50s and 60s at first assessment and 60 or 70 at final data collection. It was found that morale was high overall and a significant, but slight, increase was seen over the six-year period. Decreases were noted in perceived and functional health and in levels of leisure activity. A key difference was related to gender; as women aged, leisure participation correlated strongly with morale. For men the relationship was not significant except in the earlier years. Men displayed a linkage of perceived health and level of morale. Thus, health and leisure activity were found to operate differently for older men and women as related to the outcome of morale.

In another longitudinal exploration, Stanley & Freysinger (1995) tracked 164 older adults for a 16-year span. Age, health, and gender were predictor variables as levels of activity were followed over the time period. Six activity categories were used: informal social, home activity, volunteer and organizational, spectator/travel, crafts/hobbies, and sport participation. Women showed less change in activity participation with advancing age. Only for sport participation and volunteer activity did a decrease occur with age, and increases were noted with home and social activities. Males, on the other hand, showed lower participation with advancing age in all six categories. Men also appeared to be particularly affected by health problems over time. At the last assessment five of the six activities showed significant positive correlations between health status and activity level. For women this occurred for only three categories of activity. Thus, change in terms of health status and activity level appeared to be more prominent for older men than women. A strong recommendation was given for the consideration of physical activity as an element of total programming for any type of senior center or other setting where older adults gather.

Using a longitudinal view and focusing specifically on males, Singleton, Forbes, and Agwani (1993) analyzed changes in activity over a 20-year span from middle adulthood (age 45 at the beginning of the study) to older adulthood at the age of 65. A number of demographic variables such as marital status, health, income, and others were explored in connection with leisure. Overall, findings supported stability of activity from mid-to older adulthood for the men. The top-ranked activities were non-organized recreation (21.3 percent), social engagements (20.5 percent), and individual, mechanical activity (18.5 percent). Income was found to be connected with the likelihood of taking on new activities. Overall, the pattern discovered gave support to continuity theory.

Extending the perspective of continuity theory, Iso-Ahola, Jackson, and Dunn (1994) investigated how many activities were started, stopped, or replaced at different life stages. Levinson's (1978) human development model, which portrayed differing developmental tasks at each life stage (four stages from childhood to late adulthood), was the conceptual basis for the research. A national sample of approximately 4,000 households in Canada was utilized and activity was categorized into seven groups: exercise, outdoor, team sports, hobbies, home-based, mechanical outdoor, and other. Starting a new activity was greatest in the two earlier life stages and lowest in middle and late life. Ceasing activity showed a slight decline from early to late adulthood periods; seniors were least likely to stop an activity. Replacing an activity was highest when young and uncommon thereafter with middle-aged adults (44 to 63) being the least likely to replace activities. Older men, however, were slightly more likely to replace a stopped activity than were older women, and usually replacement came from hobbies or other home-based activity. The highest percent of aging persons could be described as "continuers" with a pattern of maintaining the same activities over adulthood. Similar to the findings of other research in this section viewing participation over time, Iso-Ahola, Jackson, and Dunn described a pattern of leisure which is established by later life. Time is devoted to favorite activities and if health or other factors intervene and certain activities must be abandoned, consideration will be given to replacement. Hobbies and home-type activities are possibilities in these instances.

EXERCISE AND PHYSICAL ACTIVITY

As a sub-category of total leisure activity, exercise and other fitness activities appear to be keenly relevant to the aging process. The frequently heard adage of "use it or lose it" brings an urgency to physical involvement in the retirement years as biological and physiological change is a significant part of the aging process. Fitness is also susceptible to trends. As reported by Robinson and Godbey (1993), the level of physical activity in the population had dropped about 10 percent from the mid-1980s to the early 1990s, and an active minority of exercisers accounted for a large part of total activity hours or days related to fitness activities. Without the physical stamina or condition to participate in a desired activity (the state of having "lost" it) modification or ceasing participation is the likely outcome. As to motives, many older adults may view exercise as a way to delay or minimize the biological declines associated with aging; others may be more interested in feeling good on a daily basis and some, no doubt, see physical activity as a way to extend life. Exercise is seen as a major part of a healthy lifestyle which hopefully will result in a lengthened retirement period.

The societal context of fitness activity at the turn of a new century was one offering contrasts. Knowledge about healthy lifestyles and media attention given to the topic were such that few were unaware of the importance of staying physically active. A barrage of media advertisements and reports broadcast the image of healthy and active humans enjoying life to the fullest. In marked contrast, however, were the warnings and research studies portraying a society overweight and inactive. Of particular concern was the daily pattern of too many youth who were far too sedentary. For example, only 13 percent of children in grades one through nine exercised 20 minutes a day at least three times weekly (U.S. Department of Health and Human Services, 2000). Fitness for older adults constituted part of the larger picture, but knowledge and attitudes about what to do seemed to be interacting with behavior in a less than desirable manner.

For a snapshot of current health and fitness levels of the United States, *Healthy People 2010* (U.S. Department of Health and Human Services, 2000) provides background statistics and recommendations to improve overall health. Data from reports are sub-divided into many relevant groups, among them the older population in categories of 65 to 74 and 75 and over. Generalizations on low rates of physical activity included: women less active than men at all age levels; African-Americans and Hispanics getting less exercise than whites; a general need for physical forms of activity for those with disabilities and about two thirds of the oldest-old (75 and over) engaging in no regular physical activity. As to concerns about excessive body weight, only about one third of the 60 and over population was deemed to be at a healthy weight.

The recommendations given from experts were aimed at reducing a host of problems associated with low levels of physical activity. These included reducing the numbers of adults who obtained no leisure time physical activity, increasing the percentage of those who exercised 30 minutes a day for at least three times weekly, and focusing on fitness activities that provided cardiovascular, strength, and flexibility benefits. In many categories of fitness the 65 to 74 age group of seniors was not much different from middle-aged adults and decreases in participation were evident for seniors above 75. Data from the report (U.S. Department of Health and Human Services, 2000, section 22) showed about one half of 65- to 74-year-olds and as mentioned above, two thirds of those beyond 75 getting no leisure-related physical activity. One third of adults 65 to 74 and one quarter of those 75 and over engaged in 20 minutes of physical activity for three or more days weekly. Further, strength-related activity was uncommon (10 percent of the 65 to 74 group and seven percent of those over 75), as was stretching and flexibility exercise with about 25 percent of both groups involved here. The conclusion reached was that older adults would benefit greatly in terms of health status as a marker of quality of life through increased amounts of activity demanding strength and some degree of endurance.

The next paragraphs will examine physical activity through published research focusing on selected variables (male-female differences, older versus younger seniors, etc.) and outcomes of physical involvement (feeling better, lowered stress, improved mood, etc.). Most studies examining overall activity or time use contain categories of physical activity. As a percentage of all available time or ranked as a daily or favorite activity, the expectation might be that physical activities would not be among the top activities as units of 30 minutes or rates of three or four times a week may be all that is needed for desired benefits.

For the "why" of exercise involvement in later life, one needs to look no further than the position statement of the American College of Sports Medicine (Mazzeo, Cavanagh, Evans, Fiatarone, Hagberg, McAuley, & Starzell, 1999). After an exhaustive review of nearly 250 current studies, they concluded: "Participation in a regular exercise program is an effective intervention/modality to reduce/prevent a number of functional declines associated with aging. Further, the trainability of older individuals (including octo- and non-agerians) is evidenced by the ability to adapt and respond to both endurance and strength training. Together, the benefits associated with regular exercise and physical activity contribute to a more healthy, independent lifestyle, greatly improving the functional capacity and quality of life for the fastest growing segment of our population" (p. 142).

The review of literature on exercise serving as the basis for the statement was divided into five areas: cardiovascular improvements, effects on muscle mass and bone density, posture and flexibility, connections with psychological function, and exercise for the very old and frail. To be expected in such a review are problems of generalizing or summary based upon a variety of methodological issues, but the bottom line conclusions gave a strong endorsement for the efficacy of exercise in later life. Clearly in the first two categories of cardiovascular functioning and maintenance of muscle mass and bone density, the preponderance of empirical evidence showed the value of strength and resistance exercise combined with some type of aerobic activity. Better posture and reduced likelihood of falls, a particular problem for the old-old, were shown to result from physical activity. Further, many studies have used very old subjects, those over 80, and seen positive effects. From a meta-analytic standpoint, the review and position statement strongly asserted the value of physical activity in later life.

EXERCISE AS A CATEGORY OF LEISURE FOR AGING PERSONS

As we begin the review of physical activity as a part of total leisure in later adulthood, there may be a few expectations. Noted before was the possibility that exercise may not be ranked or rated highest when time or daily activity are analyzed. Another expectation might be that as one ages through middle and older adulthood, the most physically demanding pursuits (running) will decline in favor of those that are less demanding (walking). We might also speculate that women and men will differ in certain ways when fitness activities are compared. These hypotheses will be tested as the following research is presented.

For adults of all ages as discovered by the Harris Poll (Taylor, 1998) physical activities do represent only a small portion of favorite leisure involvements. After TV and reading, percents drop off dramatically with gardening (14 percent), walking (seven percent), swimming (six percent), and golf (six percent) all requiring exertion and near the top of favorite things to do. As consumers, the 65 and over population does purchase fitness equipment although at a rate (six percent of total) only about one half of their proportion in the total population (13 percent) according to the National Sporting Goods Association (2003). Spending on golf equipment is also notable for older golfers at 11 percent of total spending in 2001 (National Sporting Goods Association, 2003). Thus, choices are made with expenditures as well as activity selection.

When queried about daily activity (United Media Enterprises, 1983), exercise (34 percent) and gardening (30 percent) were ranked in the middle for older adults after reading the newspaper, TV, phone use, and hobbies. Again, the question specified daily participation. In 1991, Sports Illustrated (see Leiberman, 1991) conducted a national survey and explored participation in a variety of sports and fitness activities. As a sub-group seniors (over 65) showed lower rates than other adults, and women were involved less than men in most activities. Aerobics and horseback riding were female-dominated. The highest categories of participation (done at least once in the past 12 months) for seniors were: working out on exercise machines (20 percent), swimming (16 percent), biking (12 percent), bowling (12 percent), and golf (11 percent). A pattern of decline could be observed when younger groups were compared with older persons in this survey.

A survey of outdoor activity in Pennsylvania (Becker & Yost, 1991) brought attention to two important aspects: activity by age cohort (those 45 to 54, 55 to 64, 65 to 74 and 75 and over were segmented) and intensity (the number of days involved per year). In many activities, participation days increased for the younger seniors (65 to 74) compared to the pre-retirement group (55 to 64, many undoubtedly still working). After sightseeing, the most popular outdoor activities requiring a degree of exertion were jogging and walking (no distinction made) at 62 percent, hiking (32 percent), swimming (27 percent), and biking (19 percent) for 65-to 74-year-olds. Similar rankings were seen for the oldest group, 75 and over, although marked decreases in percents were noted.

While not representative in terms of the entire United States, a Cigna survey (Aldana & Stone, 1991) in Arizona showed relatively high levels of activity for senior adults. About two thirds of those 65 and over said they engaged in regular exercise with top categories being slow walking (41 percent), fast walking (25 percent), swimming (18 percent), calisthenics (15 percent), and biking (14 percent). With few exceptions older women's levels were lower than those of men's. Only three percent indicated they lifted weights.

Older adults in the Robinson, Werner, and Godbey (1997) research showed minor weekly involvements (3.7 hours for men, 1.2 for women) in sport-related activity demanding physical stamina, while the TIAA-CREF survey of college retirees also found sport and fitness activity (33 percent involved) as a lower category compared to others (Milletti, 1984). Returning to the expectations cited in the opening paragraph, the empirical work does suggest that when ranked or analyzed as a component of all leisure time, pursuits involving physical activity are not top priorities. The methodological nuances must be kept in mind. Some ask about participation (at least once) in the past year, some inquire about "favorite" activities, and few track activity days per year (the Pennsylvania survey is the exception here). Findings agree with a contention that physical activity tends to drop with age particularly for demanding forms and particularly after the age of 75. Older women typically display lower levels of fitness-related activity than older men and tend to participate more frequently in aerobic-type classes. Reference was made earlier to the data used for the *Healthy People 2010* report which portrays a more urgent call for involvement than a number of the studies cited in this section.

EXERCISE IN LATER LIFE: RESEARCH FINDINGS WITH ATTENTION TO PREDICTOR AND OUTCOME VARIABLES

The relationship of stress, health status and physically active leisure was explored by Zuzanek, Robinson, and Iwasaki (1998) for adults in various phases of the life cycle. Data were from national health surveys conducted in the United States in 1985 and 1990. Measures of stress and health status were subjective self assessments while physical activity involved a subjective perception and a score based on participation in 22 possible physical activities such as walking, running, aerobics, golf, etc. As noted previously in the chapter, older adults in this investigation also scored lowest of all age groups in terms of stress levels. However, while older men were about one-third the level of all men, older women were only slightly below all other women in 1990. Perhaps the most interesting and unexpected finding was that perceived level of activity involvement, rather than actual participation rates, was the better predictor of low stress levels and this was especially so for older persons. The investigators were not sure as to why actual participation failed to link with reduced stress. Participation in physical activity did correlate positively with assessed health in all age groups.

Focusing primarily on gender, Robinson and Godbey (1993) explored participation in 21 different fitness and sport activities using national samples in 1985 and 1990. Respondents reported which of the activities they had engaged in as well as the number of occasions during the past two weeks. Overall participation dropped 12 percent during the span, and the most significant declines were seen in younger adults aged 18 to 34. Only slight declines were noted for older men and women (65 to 74); however, men participated about five times during the period as opposed to about three and $^{1}/_{2}$ for women. The most significant reduction seen was in women aged 18 to 34, clearly a finding in opposition to the thrust of Title IX intent. Supporting continuity theory, the authors concluded that relative consistency exists in physical activity between the ages of 35 and 74.

A complete review of the research literature on exercise in older adults is beyond the scope and space constraints of this section and chapter. Briefly, however, a few selected studies that explored a number of outcome variables (strength improvements, reduced falls, balance, and psychological benefits) are noted. As will be seen, exercise has demonstrated benefits in a variety of different ways. The effects of strength and endurance training upon balance, falls, gait and the use of health services were tested in a recent study of older (68 to 85 years) persons living in the community (Buchner, Cress, deLateur, Esselman, Margherita, Price & Wagner, 1997). The training involved both resistance exercises and endurance (stationary bikes) for an hour, three times a week for about half a year. Increases in strength were found and older exercisers had fewer falls and fewer visits to health clinics than control subjects not involved in the training. Desired improvements in gait (speed and length of stride) and balance were not seen. A similar study (Schlicht, Camaione & Owen, 2001) using older adults (61 to 87 years) ran for eight weeks with exercise sessions three days a week. Again, strength increases were found, and in this experiment walking speed did increase, however, balance and the time it took to move from sitting to standing did not.

Psychological outcomes through exercise have also been of interest to researchers. Mood and anxiety were explored as outcomes in an exercise program of older women (mean age of 68). As with other studies, strength improved and body fat also declined for exercising women, while mood improved and anxiety decreased, demonstrating a connection between exercise and positive psychological status (Tsutsumi, Don, Zaichowsky, Takenaka, Oka & Ohno, 1998). Sigenthaler (1999) conducted a literature review of exercise and aging and divided outcomes into three areas: biological, cognitive, and psychological. Six studies were included in the psychological section with positive outcomes noted in lowered depression, reduced stress, enhanced mood, and higher overall psychological well being. A conclusion from the above is that benefits of exercise for aging adults appear to extend beyond strength and include positive psychological enhancement.

MOTIVES AND INCENTIVES FOR PHYSICAL ACTIVITY

In addition to psychological outcomes of exercise-related activities, the nature of motives or incentives to participate in exerting activity in the retirement years has been a topic of interest to researchers. Heitman (1986) with a group of middle-aged and older female exercisers (three groups used, 40 to 59, 60 to 69, and 70 and over) and older men who engaged in regular physical activity (two groups, 60 to 69 and 70 and over) utilized six different motives as incentives to participation. Comparison of the older women's and men's groups showed no differences with health reasons, social opportunities, and coping to be the primary motives for exercise. Appearance, achievement, and aesthetics were ranked lowest. For middle-aged women (40 to 56) health was followed by appearance and achievement. Allmer (1992) used a very small sample of exercisers and divided them into age categories of 30s, 40s, and 50s. Those in their 50s differed slightly from younger adult groups. All groups ranked maintenance of health as the top incentive. Fifty-year-olds assessed self-experience and improving individual capacity as next most important. Another important incentive for exercise perceived by the oldest group was the structure it provided in daily life. Older exercisers differed from younger groups in regard to personality development as an incentive; they viewed this as less important than did younger adult groups.

Smith and Storandt (1997) divided a group of older (55 and over) men and women into three classifications based on participation in sport and exercise activities: competitors (those who exercised regularly and participated in events such as senior games), non-competitors (regular exercisers who were not in competitions), and non-exercisers.

They sought to explore differences among the groups in four areas: life history (involvement in sports and competitions throughout life stages), beliefs about health, motivations, and personality. Attention here is drawn to the non-competitors who exercised about four times a week and averaged about 40 minutes during each workout. Compared to the competitors, the non-competitive exercisers had a history of withdrawing from competitive sports in their 30s through their 50s. They also valued regular exercise as something important and were more negative in attitudes toward smoking than non-exercisers. Benefits of activity such as maintaining weight, muscle mass, reducing stress, and being with friends were rated lower by non-competitors than by the competitive group. Non-competitive exercisers saw the outcomes of appearance and feeling better as more important than did the non-exercisers. In terms of personality, non-competitors were particularly open to new experiences. The profile of competitors will be detailed in the succeeding section.

From the material cited within the section, we could conclude that exercise and fitness occupies a small percent of total leisure time available for older adults and this is as expected as benefits from exercise can be seen with 20 or 30 minute sessions done three times a week. The national health agenda as detailed in *Healthy People 2010* portrays an older population in need of physical activity. Of concern is the high percent (50 percent) who report no physical activity on a daily basis. The benefits of activity requiring physical exertion for those in later life are clearly delineated in the position statement of the American College of Sport Medicine and they include gains in strength and endurance, improved posture and flexibility, and links to positive psychological states. The bulk of empirical work reviewed points to benefits in health, in daily functioning, and in feeling better if physical activity becomes a priority in the retirement years.

SPORTS, ATHLETICS AND COMPETITIONS IN LATER LIFE

In two editions of photographs and brief biographies of older competitors, Clark (1986, 1995) provides a vivid snapshot of what sports and athletics mean on a personal level in later adulthood. Perhaps more importantly, the power such images have in creating a positive statement about aging is visualized. Aptly titled *Growing Old is Not for Sissies: Portraits of Senior Athletes (Volumes I & II)*, the reader is drawn to the health and vitality portrayed by athletes in their 60s, 70s, 80s and 90s. Examples include (Clark, 1995):

> Helen Zechmeister—a 91-year-old weightlifter who works out with her husband Joe three times a week and deadlifts 200 pounds. Her suppleness is such that she can do a full split.

> Fred Ullner—a long-distance runner at 76 who battled weight problems and drug and alcohol addiction in adulthood and began serious running at the age of 60, culminating in completion of marathon races in his 70s. *'Running is my life, because running gave me life.'* (p. 57).

> Ed Longner—who started bowling at the age of 74 and rolled a 600 series at the age of 90. Active in senior competitions, he regularly wins in the 80 and above bracket. Ed advocates a vegetarian diet and stands on his head for five minutes daily describing it as "reverse aging." (p. 112).

As one element of total leisure time or the variety of activities available during retirement, sporting and athletic competitions represent a significant category of involvement for at least three reasons. Such participation, often of a serious nature and conducted through a number of years, can greatly impact the lives of those involved. As Fred described above, running gave him life. Secondly, while the general pattern of involvement in physically demanding activities including sports such as track and field, softball, or competitive swimming as illustrations is one of decline from younger adulthood to later periods of life or lower levels of participation when older and younger aged cohorts are compared, the numbers of senior athletes playing at some level of competition are such that notice must be taken of those who see no need to forgo competition because of an artificial age marker. Whether on local tennis courts or in formal competitions such as Senior Games or Masters events, many older athletes possess the desire to compete and see this as one segment of their leisure choices. Lastly, as briefly cited in the opening paragraph, the images connected with senior athletics are powerful statements about the possibilities and potentials of aging. Through photographs, through profiles, and by word of mouth, the notion that growing numbers of seniors are drawn to the fields or courts of play is a statement that counters negative stereotypes linked to the process of aging.

As a review of sport in older adulthood is begun, some foundational questions may emerge. Are there frameworks from the fields of gerontology or leisure and sport that offer perspectives in analyzing competition in the senior years? For example, do human development models from a lifespan view offer connections to these competitive endeavors? Basic questions about the types of sports that are most common for older adults and the motives, meanings, and benefits associated with them arise. Performance could be a consideration. Research has examined peak performance by age category, but the larger issue might be that of how older athletes conceive of performance and what comparisons are made. One might also wonder about degrees of involvement. Causal observation might yield categories of senior athletes ranging from what appears to be rather social and fun approaches as typified by a weekly bocce group or tennis players who gather at a regular time and place. At a slightly higher level of commitment and intensity are those who play in a league or two and regularly schedule practice time. Investments are made in equipment and winning or losing matters for this group. At the highest level are the super-competitors or elite athletes who train and compete regularly and choose sanctioned events such as Senior Games to test their prowess against themselves and others. The motives and benefits of participation at these progressive levels of seriousness might differ, we would hypothesize. This section unfolds with a look at some of the frameworks that are applicable to sport in adulthood and proceeds with a highlight of participation rates in answering the question about most popular sports. The issue of performance related to aging is addressed, and the final area discussed is that of Senior Games and similar formal competitions.

THEORETICAL PERSPECTIVES ON SPORT AND AGING

Stebbins' (1992, 2001) work on amateurs, professionals, and serious leisure appears useful as a framework for studying the ways in which older athletes commit to sport. Based on analysis of participants in eight differing fields ranging from sports (baseball and football players) to performers (magicians, comedians, and musicians) to those in more academic interests (astronomers and archaeologists), Stebbins was able to document varying levels of involvement and distinctions between professionals and amateurs. From the leisure perspective, one could be classified as a dabbler (occasional participation aimed at fun), a novice (a step-up in commitment but not really concerned with proficiency), a participant (willing to devote more time and energy than a novice), or a devotee (serious and committed to the pursuit). Stebbins (1992) defined serious leisure as:

"the systematic pursuit of an amateur, hobbyist, or volunteer activity that is sufficiently substantial and interesting for the participant to find a career there in the acquisition and expression of its special skills and knowledge" (p.3).

Further analysis of the eight groups showed that those who were amateurs and who represented "serious leisure" involvement displayed six qualities: 1) they persevered—the journey with the activity held ups and downs but they stayed with it over time; 2) there was evidence of career progression beginning with novice skills and moving to levels of accomplishment and ability; 3) they had expended personal effort in the endeavor that was based on acquired knowledge, training, and skill; 4) they could describe benefits (eight categories) such as self-actualization or enrichment to renewal to social interaction; 5) they felt a part of a sub-culture as in being in the world of musicians and knowing how that world operated; and 6) having a strong personal identity with the activity of their choice. What is applicable here is the usefulness of the schema to the realm of older athletes. The profiles of Helen, Fred, and Ed commencing the section describe a group of committed, continuously involved athletes who had persevered, progressed, and benefited in many ways. They exemplified "serious leisure." The earlier statement about categories of older athletes from the casual bocce player to the elite competitor fit the categorization of dabblers/novices to devotees. The senior competitors in the Smith and Storandt (1997) study illustrated the serious side of leisure or sport. The group designated as competitors not only trained about four days a week but competed regularly in senior Olympic events. Motives included exercising to help prepare for events, being with friends, meeting goals and reducing stress. Their profile indicated a serious approach to sport. Thus, participation in sport and competitions for older adults provides a continuum of involvement, seriousness, and benefit ranging from rather casual intent to deep and long-standing levels of commitment.

Rudman (1986) analyzed sport from a developmental perspective assigning primary goals and outcomes in differing life stages. When younger (children/adolescence), the intent and benefit frequently involve socialization and status in the peer group, while during adulthood a primary focus of sport is family and community connectedness, either doing things as a family or maintaining social links as parents coach, attend games, and develop friendships with children and parents of teammates. Rudman described the nature of developmental tasks and applied them to senior adults engaged in sport. For example, tasks have both internal pressures (what is seen as appropriate by the individual) and those that are external (what peers or others in society see as the norm), and at times older athletes might encounter negative attitudes by being too competitive or serious. Also, the nature of the tasks are likely to change over the life course (differing motives and benefits may emerge over time) and completion of certain developmental tasks leads to transitions such as the decision to forgo active competition as a player and become involved in coaching or some administrative role in the sport. The model was applied to national survey data with attention here on the oldest

(55 and over) group of athletes. Fourteen sports were used, and decreasing involvement was seen from middle to older adulthood in most sports (golf and aerobics held fairly constant). Socio-economic factors were seen to be particularly significant in later life in sports and activities such as golf and gym memberships. The social aspects of sport are often rated highly in later life and frequently competition becomes less important for the average sportsperson. The model and subsequent analysis portrays involvement in sport over adulthood as one in which negotiations and challenges occur (continuing involvement at a certain level or decreasing practice or competitive level) as internal meanings are blended with biological and age-related changes as well as societal expectations about sport in the golden years (too much practice and super-competitiveness may be frowned upon).

Similar notions about older adult sport have been expressed by O'Brien-Cousins and Burgess (1992) who echoed the internal (wanting to strive for excellence and playing to win) versus external (many viewing sport only as non-serious and non-competitive) debate over participation. A friendly approach to matches or games accompanied by practice time or conditioning that is moderate may be seen as acceptable for aging athletes. For the serious competitor, however, a keen desire to excel and a willingness to train such that physical limits may be tested are conditions that many outside the circle of senior sports may frown upon. While calling for a common sense approach to training backed by sound physiological principles, O'Brien-Cousins, and Burgess raise the possibility that minimal expectations and fears based on stereotypes or outdated concepts of aging will not be suited to older athletes who have trained regularly for a number of years and want to improve performance. They call for more coaches and trainers of aging athletes who have the ability to listen and use judgment that is sound in the sense of gerontological physiology, yet not crippling for those who wish to test their athletic abilities. They note that many older competitors will choose a relative performance standard that combines the realities of growing older, the amount of training they have invested, how long they have played the sport, the level of their opponent's abilities, and how they feel on a given day. Mixing these factors they give their best, are willing to enjoy the challenge of competition, and in the end make some assessment of their performance. The perspective is positive, encompasses varying levels of proficiency, and captures the serious athlete such as Helen, Fred, and Ed described in the opening paragraph.

Using continuity theory as a framework and employing a case study based on narrative inquiry, Langley and Knight (1999) detailed the sporting life of Art Kahn (pseudonym) from childhood to his active status as a tennis player, a serious one, in his late 60s. Athletics had proven to be a central focus of his life and were connected to significant events such as friendships as a child and adult, job opportunities through those he had played or coached with, and even meeting his spouse in a bowling league. Art's history of participation evidenced continuity according to the authors as it displayed both internal (development of a strong self-concept through sport over a lifetime) and external consistency (his friendships and social networks were primarily from acquaintances through sport). As he competed in tennis matches in his late 60s, Art described losing skills and making adaptations in his game. The desire to compete and to win remained strong. Primary benefits at this stage of his athletic career were remaining physically fit and enjoying the friendships developed through tennis. His lifetime of sporting participation fit the categorization of serious leisure or devotee from Stebbins' model (1992).

Another conceptual perspective, feminist theory, was used in analyzing participation in marathon races by women in a paper by Vertinsky (2000) titled, "Externally Wounded Women? Feminist Perspectives on Physical Activity and Aging or A Woman's P(l)ace in the Marathon of Life." Noting that both ageism and sexism have existed until recent times—women were not allowed to compete in the Boston Marathon until 1972 and in Olympic marathons until 1984—Vertinsky offers an historical account that contrasts and differentiates the roles of males and females relative to vigorous physical exercise and competitions such as marathon running. The norm for athletic participation has always been one based on strength and muscle; female athletes and their competitions were viewed as deviations from men and how men approached and played sports. Women were seen to age differently and more quickly than males, a concept connected to the cessation of childbearing function and its significance as a gender marker. Many historical eras dismissed female participation in vigorous sports or fitness activity even when concurrent trends promoted the same for men. All of these examples cited by Vertinsky pointed to the prominence of gender in vigorous physical activities such as marathoning. Despite the barriers faced by women, and older women in particular, female competitors in their 50s and 60s are now racing in marathon events. One such runner noted, Nina Kusczik, is in her 60s and has completed 80 marathons. These images of older women marathoners will actively counter the ageist and sexist notions mentioned above.

To briefly summarize, sports and competitive events in the senior years have been examined through conceptual approaches such as human development throughout the lifespan, continuity and feminist theories. Profiles or narrative stories of the athletic accomplishments of senior athletes have illustrated concepts such as continuity or a progression of skills or challenges in the sport occurring over a long period of time. Athletes are likely to face consistency (enjoying the sport for what it offers and the benefits seen) and challenges (modifying the level of involvement or performance due to injury or facing society's expectations that competition should not be taken too seriously in later adulthood). The nature of sport for seniors ranges from rather casual, non-serious participation (dabblers or novices according to Stebbins, 1992) to medium-level involvement where some practice is undertaken and winning or losing is a consideration to the highest level of competitiveness where personal performance is a major concern and training is a regularly scheduled activity (O'Brien-Cousins & Burgess, 1992; Smith & Storandt, 1997: Stebbins, 1992). Feminist theory (Vertinsky, 2000) notes that female athletes, especially those beyond middle adulthood, have faced outright prohibitions, restrictions, or lowered expectations such that a female over the age of 40 or 50 who wishes to remain actively competitive is seen as an oddity. Current examples of female marathoners in their 50s or older may bring about changes in the way we conceive of female athleticism in later life.

LEVELS OF SPORTING PARTICIPATION
BY OLDER ATHLETES

The purpose of this section is to give a sense of the most popular sporting activities for the 65- and -over population. As we begin, a few caveats or reminders are offered. Most surveys do not delve into definitional distinctions related to the degree of competitiveness or seriousness attached to a sport, hence an activity such as swimming that many would pursue for fitness or relaxation might fit loosely into a categorization of sport or would perhaps be better considered as a leisure activity. Motives attached to competitiveness or seriousness are often not explored, and for the purposes of this review a rather inclusive definition is used for sporting activity.

As noted in the section on physical activities and exercise, the general pattern of lower levels of participation for older persons when compared with younger groups holds for sporting activity as well. The more demanding the activity, marathon running as an example, the more likely the expectation that fewer older athletes will participate as opposed to all adults below 65. An exception to this general pattern is that when 65-and-older groups are contrasted with 55- to 64-year-olds, the percents or numbers of participants can be larger for the older group due to full-time working commitments of many in the 55-to-64 category. Data from the 2002 Statistical Abstract (U.S. Census Bureau, Statistical Abstract of the United States, 2002) showed greater numbers of 65- and-older adults active in swimming and golf and bowling than their counterparts aged 55 to 64. Another area, intensity or degree of participation, has shown that 65- to 74- year-olds may participate more frequently than younger (55 to 64) adult groups in the sport or activity of choice as measured by time or activity days (Becker & Yost, 1991). Also to be kept in mind is the fact that a small minority may be responsible for a great deal of the total participation in a sporting endeavor—an active minority is engaged frequently in what they enjoy (Howard, 1992; Robinson & Godbey, 1993).

As statistics, figures, and percents are presented, it should be reminded that even relatively small percentages of the total 65-and-over population can represent a significant number of participants. With more than 35 million seniors (2001 figures, Statistical Abstract, 2002), 10 or 12 percent represents 3.5 to 4.2 million active in a given sport.

For many seniors, swimming represents a relaxing or fitness activity rather than a sporting or competitive one, yet its popularity is demonstrated in surveys that rank leisure or physical activity in later life. After walking, it usually is one of the most popular fitness pursuits. The 2002 Statistical Abstract (U.S. Census Bureau, Statistical Abstract of the U.S., 2002) counted 3.8 million older (65 and over) swimmers and other surveys have placed the percent of all older adults who swim within a range of 15 percent to 25 percent (Aldana & Stone, 1991; Becker &Yost, 1991; Leiberman, 1991).

Golf, as a recognized lifetime sport, is also popular with 3.1 million seniors (Statistical Abstract, 2002). As noted earlier, older players represent about 11 percent of all golf expenditures, which nearly matches their percentage of the total population (National Sporting

Goods Association, 2003). A recent qualitative analysis of golf's contribution to successful aging (Siegenthaler & Thomas, 2001) found four types of senior golfers: those who viewed golf as a core or central focus of their lives, the group (*joie de vivre*) who enjoyed the game but weren't too serious about their performance, social golfers who saw it as a means to meet people, and those who identified with the therapeutic aspects of golf allowing them to cope with physical and emotional challenges. Benefits were noted as preventing disability, keeping mentally challenged, and providing social contacts.

Bowling trails golf slightly (2.1 million participants according to the Statistical Abstract, 2002) in popularity with senior competitors and remains one of the top-ranked activities when senior games or competitions are held. As Ed Lonergen exemplified in the opening section, it is an activity that can be done successfully into the eighth and ninth decades of life.

Tennis has seen a decline in participation throughout the last 10 years (dropping from 14.2 million players in 1993 to less than 11 million in 2001) according to the National Sporting Goods Association (2003), but still is a relatively popular activity for the over 65 set (486,000 involved in 2000, Statistical Abstract, 2002). What is also of interest when one scans statistics of older adult participation in sporting activity are the numbers of athletes in sports associated primarily with younger age groups. For example: 244,000 older basketball players, 136,000 enjoy softball, 37,000 play volleyball, and 74,000 adults 65 and over find martial arts appealing, and an estimated 44,000 senior adult hockey players exist (2000 figures from the 2002 Statistical Abstract). While the level of seriousness and degree of competitive spirit may vary for older athletes, their range of interest in the realm of sports is substantial.

SPORTS PERFORMANCE—OLDER ATHLETES

Researchers have shown interest in exploring aging as it relates to performance and adaptations that are made over a long career with a particular sport. As physiologic change is a reality accompanying growing older and certain changes (decreased reaction time, decreased maximum heart rate, and the likelihood of weight gain during adulthood with a change in the ratio of muscle to fat) are likely to affect performance in specific sporting events or skills (a short sprint versus a medium-length or long-distance run or the maximum weight lifted or the distance a golf ball can be driven), analysis has focused on which specific skills and events may be affected and the degree to which serious training may counter age-related declines. Since records have been accurately kept for masters competitions in track and field, this area has been used for comparative purposes. The following studies are examples of this stream of research.

Elite distance runners were tracked for 22 years in a longitudinal design exploring physiological change and its effects on performance (Trappe, Costill, Vukovich, Jones, & Melham, 1996). Males (53) who were serious runners and in their late 20s through their 40s were tested initially and then re-examined 22 years later. Four categories of participation were found at the second testing. The highest training group had trained and competed the most; they were serious and still very competitive. The next group had remained active in running, but did so primarily for fitness reasons. The next group had stopped competitive events and had not trained in five years and the last group was the oldest with a mean age of 68 years who had remained active for 20 to 25 years with fitness as a dominant motive. Findings expressed the reality of biologic aging tempered with the positives that serious exercise over long periods can bring. A number of physiological measures were taken (weight, maximum oxygen intake, ventilation efficiency and heart rate on a treadmill test). As might be expected, the performance measures all showed declines at the second testing with the highest training group affected the least and the group who had stopped running impacted the most. Even though the oldest group had trained for a number of years, they still displayed significant declines in most areas and had only about two thirds of the aerobic power of the younger highest trained group. The authors concluded that when aerobic efficiency is monitored over a period of time, there are likely to be effects traced to both aging and training factors.

In an effort to discover the impact of chronological age on track performance, Fung and Ha (1994) compared records in running, jumping and throwing events from an international veterans event. Not only was change by age group of concern but the researchers were also interested in exploring the specific type of event most affected as related to physiological principles of aging, i.e., would a sprint, a middle-distance run or a long-distance run be most affected when age groups were compared? Age groups were created in five-year spans beginning at 40 for men and 35 for women. Most events showed only negligible declines by group until about the age of 60 or 65 after which declines (or increases in running times) were greater. The events most impacted by age were the 400-meter run, the long jump, the javelin for men and the discus for women. In analyzing the demands for performance in the 400-meter race, the authors noted the combination of anaerobic and aerobic efficiency and requirements of different types of muscle fibers that are affected by aging. The long jump would require explosive muscle power, an area also affected by the aging process. Thus, under examination maximum performance may remain relatively stable through the fifth or sixth decade, however, certain skills or athletic requirements are more likely than others to be impacted negatively by the process of aging.

Another study (Starkes, Weir, Singh, Hodges & Kerr, 1999) found support for the above finding that decline is likely to be greatest after the age of 60. Records from different masters competitions were analyzed in four races ranging from 200 meters to 5,000 meters and the distance found most affected by age was the 800 meters. Diaries from serious masters runners revealed that many had been running for more than 30 years and averaged about seven hours of running a week, a figure certainly notable but far less than they had maintained in their prime as a competitor. It was noted that analysis of records by age group must consider the amount of training (as one grows older, demands are different than at earlier life periods and injury is a reality for many as they age) which is likely to be less than the peak years and restrictions imposed by biologic aging processes. That being said, there are exceptional older athletes who have the ability to suspend the aging clock and are able to produce times nearly identical to what they clocked in their late teens. One such example is Bill Collins who, at the age of 52, holds world records (masters) in the 60-meter indoor, and 100- and 200-meter outdoor (Bloom, 2003). His 100 meter time of 10.95 seconds is only a few ticks slower than what he ran as a high school state champion. Collins wears long stretch leg coverings to keep muscles warm and shuns the starting blocks using a standing start. His 40-plus-year career has been nearly injury free and the training regimen used includes heavy weights, 2,000 situps a week, and three weekly running sessions. Collins feels that his 200-meter time of 22.78 can be improved.

Not only should older athleticism be considered within a context of slower times or reduced distances, but the positives of aging—experience and the ability to adapt—must be recognized as well. Over and Thomas (1995) discovered the quality of adapting when older and younger golfers were studied. Their method involved analyzing how the game was played and approached through a series of psychological measures in addition to concrete markers such as length of drives, number of putts, and greens hit in regulation. A group of younger golfers (mean of 33 years) was matched against an older group (mean of 62) and both were of comparable ability (similar handicaps). Findings revealed a slightly different game being played by the two groups. Older players did not drive the ball as long as their younger counterparts and both were similar in greens hit and putts per round. They differed in the mental side of the game. Older golfers were less susceptible to negative emotions on the course and they used a more conservative approach to shotmaking. The authors noted the strength of youth may be "compensated for by the greater reliance on skills that either improve or remain stable with age" (p. 1).

This focus on performance raises the issue of comparison. What is the standard to be used in assessing older athletic ability? For elite athletes, the standard remains existing records in their age category and how their time/score/distance compares with others in a comparable age grouping. It is interesting to note that age-graded tables have been developed for masters athletes allowing them to calculate their times (multipliers are used based on age) and determine if world class or national level status has been reached (Starkes, Weir, Singh, Hodges & Kerr, 1999). In addition to peers, self-comparison offers many possibilities—how today's game or outcome measures against last Tuesday's, whether performance has improved since the beginning of the season, and whether new skills or strategies are being learned and utilized. In this vein sport is a growing experience at any age. Hopefully most older recreational athletes can resist the temptation to contrast current performance with peak skills in their 20s or 30s.

FORMAL COMPETITIONS—SENIOR GAMES AND MASTERS EVENTS

Opportunities for elder athletes to compete and test their prowess against others, individually or in team sports, have grown remarkably over the past 20 or 25 years such that a number of formal organizations are sanctioned and active in the promotion of senior athletic events. While a major goal of their mission is the conduct of the competitions, nearly all are also heavily involved in education and the enhancement of healthy lifestyles. A quick glance at the websites of these senior sport governing bodies (see www.nsga.com for the National Senior Games Association, for example) reveals that offering a competitive outlet is of primary concern, but encouraging athletes to train properly and eat well in addition to recruiting new senior athletes at the local level are important objectives as well. In essence, competitive gatherings of thousands of older athletes is the focal point through which education and the recruitment of new senior athletes can occur. Below senior games and masters/veterans events are highlighted as examples of governing bodies involved in senior sport so that the reader may be introduced to the scope of competitive opportunities available to athletes beyond middle age.

NATIONAL SENIOR GAMES ASSOCIATION

This organization, with ties to the United States Olympic Committee, coordinates activities through a number of state and local providers of senior games or olympics. National events are held in odd-numbered years for the summer events, the Summer National Senior Games, and in even-numbered years for the Winter National Senior Games. June of 2003 saw 10,717 athletes (Phil Godfrey, Vice President, NSGA, personal communication) athletes gather in Hampton Roads, Virginia for more than 800 events at the ninth national competitions for summer sports. Future summer games have been awarded to Pittsburgh (2005) and Louisville (2007).

The scope of competition and participation is noteworthy and underscores the growth of older athleticism in recent decades. While national summer meets now draw in the 10,000 to 12,000 range, roughly 25,000-30,000 athletes qualify by way of state and local meets, and the National Senior Games Association estimates that 250,000 older athletes are active at some level of training and competition (National Senior Games Association, 2003). As opportunities for competition become more widely available and as more seniors become aware of what their peers are accomplishing, the participation curve will trend upward in coming decades. A snapshot of participation notes the following: average age of athletes is 65 with track and field the most popular individual event and softball the most popular team sport for women and men. Swimming, tennis, and volleyball draw large numbers. Growth has been substantial since the inaugural summer games in St. Louis (1987) attracting 2,500 participants (National Senior Games Association, 2003).

MASTERS/VETERANS ASSOCIATIONS AND COMPETITIONS

Masters athletics or competitions are generic terms associated with senior athletics (although here "senior" begins with competition for men at 40 and women at 35) and often are thought of in connection with track or swimming, however the range of events extends to many individual and team sports. "World Masters Athletics" (formerly the World Association of Veteran Athletes or WAVA) is the administrative body of masters athletics worldwide (World Association of Veteran Athletics, 2003) and their functions include hosting major sport competitions at international and national levels for athletes 35 and beyond for women and 40 or older for men, keeping accurate records in five-year age groups, fostering international friendship among participants and promoting education and training information to all concerned. A visit to their website finds schedules of upcoming international meets, articles on how to stay fit and healthy, and information on products and techniques. One can access rules for competition, and accurate records are available by event and age bracket. As to the scale of competitions, in 1994 Brisbane, Australia, hosted 24,000 athletes from 71 nations. This was the largest international multi-sport event ever held World Association of Veteran Athletics, 2003). Edmonton, Alberta, has been designated the site for the games in 2005.

Similar in intent and function but operating on a national level, United States Masters Swimming (USMS) organizes major swimming events for masters athletes, keeps and publishes records for each event by age category, offers many tips and training guidelines, and promotes a social atmosphere for middle aged and older aquatic participants. Records speak to the competitiveness of these mature swimmers. As an example, in the men's 70- to 74-age bracket, top times in the following events are on record for 2003: 50-meter freestyle: 12:31, and 400-meter individual medley: 5:34 (www.usms.org/comp/tt/toptenlist, 2003). Again, the focus of the USMS website is to inform all people of meets to come and provide a forum for discussion on relevant topics. The article of the month for May 2003 (Parks, 2003) discusses the management of stress and how swimming in adulthood can serve as a positive factor. If one considers the demography of aging projected in previous chapters, the growth of these associations devoted to senior competitions will likely continue. It is evident that many older athletes view competition as an integral part of their lives and that training is one component of a healthy lifestyle. Others may be less serious about competition, seeing it connected to social friendships resulting from meets and gatherings. Both groups will contribute to the demand for the organization and governance of senior sporting competitions.

TRAVEL AND MATURE ADULTS

What activity could be more representative of the Ulyssean ideal than travel? Literally, travel represents a journey, and the growth of this retirement activity has not gone unnoticed by those marketing and providing tourism, resort, lodging, and transportation services to adults in middle age or beyond. These journeys represent the best of what aging and retirement can offer—the chance to be creative in the selection of sites and sights, the opportunity to encounter new experiences at whatever pace and degree of adventure one desires, and the occasion to benefit in multiple ways from socialization, to learning, to challenging one's self. With discretionary dollars to spend and with a degree of control over time that working adults do not possess, retirees have become a force within the tourism and hospitality industries.

A cursory review of the professional literature in topical areas such as activities and aging or tourism and hospitality points to the growth of travel by senior adults. Most articles cite the demographic reality that nations are aging and most older adults are arriving at retirement in relatively good health and with years to live. Finances for many are such that travel is well within their means. Demand is high as well; travel is typically at the top of the list of things to pursue in retirement. Articles aimed at providers of travel and lodging services offer hints on how to promote or advertise, the likes and dislikes of 55- and-over travelers, and the varied segments that exist within the senior travel market. A visit on the world wide web using descriptors such as "senior travel" produces numerous sites emphasizing the growth and diversity of this segment of tourism. It becomes quickly apparent that senior travel is expanding rapidly and that those offering such services are becoming more sophisticated in marketing and in delivering what is desired.

The following review will include the scope and significance of senior travel as noted in the professional literature and on the internet. The needs and desires of mature travelers as revealed by surveys will be given. Next, research reporting the segmented nature of senior travel will follow and examples of these varied segments, such as Elderhostel serving those with a strong education or learning motive will conclude the section.

A GROWING SENIOR TRAVEL MARKET

With titles such as "Have Pension Will Travel" (Blanding, 1993) and "Aging and the Future Travel Market" (Penalta & Uysal, 1992) the professional literature has noted that those 55 and over are on the move and this market will trend decidedly upward in the next three decades as baby boomers retire and seek destinations of interest. Available time allowing for longer vacations and off-season travel combined with adequate financial resources are two factors cited when mature travelers are discussed (Chon & Singh, 1995; Penalta & Uysal, 1992; Teaff & Turpin, 1996; Wills, 2003). The 55 and over group represents nearly 80% of vacation dollars spent in the United States according to Teaff and Turpin (1996). Like most travelers, mature persons want value but they are also willing to pay for the kinds of services and amenities such as bathrooms designed for comfort that are highly rated in importance. This literature notes that the senior travel market is not a single, homogeneous group but rather many sub-segments identified by such characteristics as differing demographics (older—younger, degrees of wealth, varying education and health, and experience with travel), and motivations that result in variety as to the types of excursions taken. Travel is usually at the top of the list in terms of retirees' desires (Teaff & Turpin, 1996), and authorities agree that providers will need to stay flexible and active in meeting the demands of this sizable segment of global tourism.

The internet offers many services and sites to the older vacationer and demonstrates as well the varied pieces of this market. As to choices and selections, it is clear that it would be a mistake to assume that retirees only use a trusted travel agent in the neighborhood. "Senior travel" linked to a search engine generates many, many organizations and destinations eager to assist and attract middle-aged and older adults. As brief examples, "Senior Women's Travel (for the 50-plus woman with a passion for travel)", (2003) pays particular attention to the needs of women travelers (security, shopping, need for a single room, etc.); many trips are packaged and can be accessed on the site. The state department has compiled a list of travel tips for older Americans that are worth considering if international travel is to be undertaken. (U.S. State Department, 2003) Consular information sheets are available in foreign lands that update factors such as health conditions, any security concerns, and even give tips on how to pack and what types of insurance to consider. A final example, "Transitions Abroad" (2003) is aimed at international travelers and offers sites for those who might wish an extended stay, perhaps to practice or learn a foreign language. It is evident by scanning such sites that senior travel is quite comprehensive and diversified and companies are reaching the mature information seeker via the internet.

CONSIDERATIONS OF OLDER TRAVELERS: AMENITIES, SERVICES, COMFORT

As the tourist industry has become more familiar with older guests and courted them specifically through advertising and direct marketing, some elements, notably lodging and tour operators, have begun to accommodate their interests by providing design features and amenities aimed at satisfying the desires of these customers. Specific firms have approached the task through proactive measures—hiring architects and designers aware of physiological change brought on by aging and skilled in principles of universal design. This concept, universal design, operates from a foundation that the best design is that which meets the needs of all concerned, and if a person with some disability or an older adult in need of particular consideration can be satisfied with the environmental elements present, then it is highly likely that all will benefit through such provisions. Revisiting some of the biological changes discussed in Chapter 3, it is easy to understand that older guests could benefit through attention to lighting and glare in rooms (changes in the lens and visual threshold), safety and ease of access in bathrooms (musculoskeletal changes, balance), as well as size and print quality in signage and menus, etc. (presbyopia). Universal or barrier-free design has been noted as a guiding principle for rooms and general areas within hotels and motels (Marvel, 1999; Miller, 1996). Bathrooms with easily used, sturdy fixtures and adequate grab bars in tubs, large print on clocks, phones, television remotes, and menus; high levels of lighting with reduced glare in rooms, and doors requiring modest levels of pull to open are among design features that the lodging industry has incorporated to satisfy seniors. Marvel notes that 90 percent of Holiday Express units are barrier-free and 25 percent of Choice Hotels' Rodeway chain are specifically outfitted for senior travelers.

Beyond design and physical features, mature tourists seek other types of amenities. Obviously price and quality matter. Surveying hotel chains in America and abroad, Marvel

(1999) found much greater use of standard discounts for room rates and meals stateside and off season or non-peak reductions in rates in Europe for the 55-and-over tourist. A survey of 200-plus older (59-plus) and younger (under 59) travelers in the United States found the two groups to differ in terms of prioritizing services and amenities (Ananth, DeMicco, Moreo, & Howey, 1992). Security concerns were important to both groups but particularly so to the older respondents with well-lit hallways and garage areas being deemed essential. A nightlight in the bathroom was a noted safety feature, and having extra blankets for comfort is a good idea for senior guests. The survey confirmed the tendency of mature adults to travel with 87 percent having done so in the previous year and 55 percent having taken one to four trips during that period. A final consideration discussed by the authors was employee attitudes and behavior. Older guests do not want to be singled out as needy or different, yet staff should make every attempt to spend time necessary to satisfy requests. This might mean repeating directions if necessary and checking to see that communication has been effective on both ends. It is apparent that guests and clients who are over 55 can articulate the kinds of services and features they find pleasing when staying overnight and many in the lodging industry are listening. This trend will likely continue as projected growth unfolds.

SEGMENTATION OF THE SENIOR TRAVEL MARKET—MANY GROUPS, NOT ONE

This section will turn to the research literature as the basis to explore the travel interests of middle-aged and older persons, and as will be seen, the earlier point that the older market for travel consists of many, not one, varied segments will be emphasized. The type of trip and mode of transport, the desired outcome, and the location chosen are as varied as the faces and lifestyles of the older population. Along the way the research reviewed will answer some of the basic questions focusing on travel and tourism. How often and where do seniors travel? What categories or kinds of trips (motorcoach, guided, ecotourism) do they choose? What are the benefits or outcomes received? Results will connect independent variables (such as background characteristics of participants) with dependent or outcome variables (what has been gained, or perceived benefits as illustrations). A trend in the research methodology of senior travel has been the use of factor analytic or discriminant techniques to explain and to guide practice, for example, the type of group that might be targeted for a certain kind of marketing campaign.

Plog (2004), based on findings from the American Traveler Survey, divided mature travelers into two groups, middle-aged (45 to 64 called "new freedom") and older (65-plus termed "mature explorers") and noted they were similar to all adults in the number of trips per year (between two and three), yet tended to take longer trips and spend more money. This was particularly true for the 65-plus group who averaged 9.1 nights per trip, almost double the average of all adults and spent about 25 percent more on the trip or vacation. Mature explorers also visited more destinations (about eight) over a three-year period and favored cruises (33 percent to 21 percent) when compared to all adults.

Javalgi, Thomas, and Rao (1992) surveyed a large group of adults (4,500) in the United States and divided them into three groups: the non-seniors (55 and under), the 55- to 64- aged group and those over 65. The two older groups were found to prefer touring vacations, cruises, and trips to visit friends and relatives compared to those 55 and under who were more likely to take outdoor and resort vacations or visit theme parks. This younger age group was more highly educated, had higher income and was much more likely to be working than the two older groups. As to mode of travel, the older groups used air and bus travel more than the younger groups, although personal auto was the preferred mode for all groups. Other findings related to senior travelers showed their high use of motel or hotel and friends and family for lodging, their favoring of group package tours, and a greater use of travel agents for booking (although 74 percent of seniors did not use a travel agent). Price and quality, as found in many surveys, were of significance to older travelers.

Using a Canadian sample of seniors (65-plus) and focusing on distance of travel, Zimmer, Brayley, and Searle (1995) employed factor-analytic techniques to explore relationships among background characteristics and preference for short or lengthy trips. Age (those older being less likely to travel), education (higher levels associated with greater travel), and health and mobility (poorer condition linked to less travel) were found significantly related to travel. Higher income showed a positive relationship with travel as well. In terms of travel distance, older rural residents took shorter trips, while those with higher education, income, and life satisfaction traveled further distances. This research demonstrated the heterogeneous nature of senior travelers.

Another study that demonstrated that the senior travel market can be segmented was that of Shoemaker (1989), who identified three clusters of 55 and over travelers from a sample in Pennsylvania. The top motives for travel for the entire sample were to visit new places, escape routine, and experience new things. "Family travelers" were identified through factor analysis as taking shorter trips often to see family and friends, staying in economy motels, and not desiring a planned agenda. This group was more likely to be still working and had a mean age of 63. The second group, "active resters" enjoyed seeing new destinations and wanted a level of activity on their trips—visiting historical places and doing physical things such as hiking or golfing. They would frequently use motorcoach tours and often planned their trips using guidebooks. The last group, the "older set," averaged 69 years of age, were primarily retired, enjoyed bus tours and liked the concept of one price that included everything. They had a higher percent than the other two groups who toured three times a year or more. Shoemaker gave marketing suggestions for each type of older traveler. The last group would be a prime market, he felt, for package tours.

Similar to Shoemaker's approach, a team of researchers employed cluster or factor analysis that resulted in three types of mature travelers that were labeled "novelty seekers," "active enthusiasts," and "reluctant travelers " (Lieux, Weaver & McCleary, 1994). Background characteristics of each were explored in relation to their preference for type of lodging. The first two groups were similar in demographic makeup and they were more upscale in their preference for lodging, often choosing mid-price or luxury hotels and motels. These groups also enjoyed bed and breakfast accommodations. The "reluctant travelers" were older, lower in income and education and tended to travel less. They typically looked for bargains in lodging and rarely stayed in luxury hotels. Again, the usefulness of this type of methodology was shown as marketing strategies were apparent for each type of traveler.

A group of senior tourists (mean age of 70 with about one-half married and one-third widowed) were assessed using a formal instrument measuring psychological well being both before and after an escorted tour to determine if the trip would be responsible for improved well being (Milman, 1998). While no significant change was found in this indicator, happiness was found to be associated with the number of activities engaged in on the trip. Favored activities included sightseeing, dining, visits to historical places, shopping, and gambling. Overall, this sample of older travelers was quite content with the trip (90 percent satisfied), and Milman speculated that perhaps a longer period of touring, more than a one-week period in this study, is needed to influence well being.

Hawes (1988) used national survey data and focused on older women tourists in creating three different types of travelers based on factor analytic methods. General trends revealed younger women being less likely to have traveled abroad and those under 60 to be less satisfied with their overall leisure. The group termed "travelers" held a strong orientation to vacations and had traveled more often. They were often single, had active lifestyles, and had higher income and more education than the other older women. Group two, "laidback travelers," primarily enjoyed domestic travel and they enjoyed an unhurried, relaxing pace and would not use credit to pay for their trip. The last type were called "dreamers" and they viewed travel mainly as fantasy and often drew upon television for images and stimulation.

Similar to Hawes' approach of identifying profiles, Backman, Backman, and Silverberg (1999) analyzed senior (55 and over) nature-based tourists using factor analysis that resulted in five differing psychographic profiles. These were described as: education and nature, camping and tenting, social, relaxation, and information seeking. The profile predicted the style of nature-based travel and the benefits sought. Younger senior travelers were less interested in the education and nature benefits and older seniors were less inclined to favor camping or tenting.

African-American tourists, most of whom were 45 or older, were surveyed by Ken Backman and colleagues (1998) to explore demographic characteristics, trip features and patterns, and factors influencing the destination of choice. Nearly two-thirds of the respondents were over 45 with about one-third between the ages of 55 and 74. The group was predominately married, of middle income, and 70 percent had at least some college education. The two most popular types of trips were to visit family and friends (26.5 percent of all trips) or nature-based activity (21.4 percent), with the latter being connected with higher socio-economic status. Personal auto was by far the preferred mode of travel and lodging preferences showed most to stay in motels and hotels on trips with four to six nights being the average away from home. Persons in this study took 2.4 trips per year. Top motivators for travel included time with family, having fun, seeing as much as possible in available time, and going to places that offered safety and security. The report noted that efforts such as this will help tourism officials better understand a viable African-American travel market.

As another example of segmentation within senior travel, Chacko and Nebel (1993) surveyed motorcoach tour operators and discovered that about 50 percent of their business was related to mature adults. Trips were about evenly split between those regularly scheduled and advertised and those that were customized for groups and organizations with the latter becoming more popular. The primary type of lodging used was three-star hotels indicating mature travelers' preference for quality and price. In terms of seasonal popularity, summer, fall, and spring were about equally scheduled with a slight drop in the winter. The types of trips planned included those that allowed the group to customize their itinerary, those going to special events, and those where general sightseeing was the main focus. Customers were reached through direct mail (93 percent), group presentations, and by newsletter. Chacko and Nebel suggested that an aging population will mean continued business and, again, the senior market consists of a number of sub-segments rather than one indistinguishable group.

A final illustration to highlight the diversity of older adult tourism is a survey of those living in continuing care retirement communities (Brewer, Poffley & Pederson, 1995). Conducted in Pennsylvania, two-thirds of respondents were between 76 and 85 years of age, and travel was found to be a favored leisure activity second only to reading. A substantial number, 41 percent, had plans to travel in the next year and most took longer trips with 50 percent touring eight to 21 days when they traveled. Most said they preferred going to new places rather than past vacation destinations, and about one-quarter of this older group perceived themselves as adventurous. Results suggested that even the older segment of the total senior population should not be dismissed as a group prepared to travel.

EDUCATIONAL TRAVEL

A number of categories of travel have been mentioned thus far in the review, among them: cruises, outdoor or nature-based, trips to historical sites, motorcoach tours, and resort vacations. Many of these reflect an element of education as a motive for the visit. As future cohorts of senior adults will possess higher levels of formal education, and as formal programs such as Elderhostel will continue to prosper in years to come, the area of educational travel by mature persons is discussed as a probable growth segment.

In a three-part series of *Leisure Today* (February-April, 1998) the topic of leisure and life-long learning was addressed and attention paid to the desires that many adults have to connect travel and learning experiences when they consider vacations. Authors offered conceptual perspectives on learning in later adulthood (MacNeil, 1998), presented research findings about older learners (Gibson, 1998), and described the characteristics of successful, current programs (Bodger, 1998). MacNeil stressed that while many do not think of old age as a time for learning and that much of our education is focused on vocational outcomes, perhaps learning in the mature years is of significance because most are seeking it for intrinsic reasons—to learn for the sake of gaining knowledge, which models the ancient Greek ideals of purity and purpose of such activity. Current retirees have the time and many are experiencing the joy of learning in their local communities or through visiting various sites nationally or internationally. Among the personal benefits highlighted by MacNeil related to educational endeavors were developing new interests and skills, forming new social contacts to counter disengagement, allowing for creative talents to flourish, and improving fitness levels by way of any program that includes physical activity. He concluded that growth will be seen in educational initiatives aimed at seniors and the links to travel were easily seen.

Gibson, based upon doctoral research, focused on gender differences in educational purposes and involvements of those in middle age and beyond. Her results found interest in educational travel to be at a peak for women in their 50s and early 60s, while men of this age were less inclined to pursue such ventures, perhaps because many were in the adjustment period of retirement. Those men who favored educational travel were affluent and well-educated and women displaying interest tended to be college-educated as well. Personal growth and self-discovery were primary motives for those seeking educational travel.

A successful program at the University of Nottingham includes both weekend stays on campus and longer trips to places such as Australia or China. Bodger (1998, p. 2) defines educational travel as "a program in which participants travel to a location as a group with the primary purpose of engaging in a learning experience directly related to the location." Based on his tenure as director of the program at Nottingham, he noted that many aspects must be considered when older learners are involved. For example, instructors must have many qualities beyond just a command of the subject or topic; seniors will want time to discuss informally and intineraries must be carefully thought out to allow the right balance of active learning and time to reflect or to pursue individual interests. Attendees at Nottingham have been primarily female with most being older than 56. For such programs to be successful marketers must be conscious of image—always stressing the fun and exciting side of the ventures. He predicts growth of educational travel for adults in the next two decades.

Elderhostel, claiming more than 200,000 annual participants 55 and older in more than 10,000 programs located in 90 countries, has clearly seen and met the need for education and for travel related to this notable niche within the educational travel market ("Elderhostel: Adventures in Lifelong Learning," 2003). Begun in 1975 with fledgling programs in five colleges and universities in New Hampshire, the concept nurtured by its founders Marty Knowlton and David Bianco, was one in touch with the needs of many senior adults (Elderhostel, 2003). Explosive growth during the next 25 years reached the point where international travel became a staple of the offerings and educational categories include: traditional programs (visits, lectures, tours on almost any topic of interest), exploring North America (itinerary-based programs in such areas as national parks, cultural arts, food and wine), active outdoor (hiking, biking, kayaking trips), service programs (hands-on projects often linked to research or to assist special groups), adventures afloat (floating classrooms incorporating learning connected to rivers and waterways), and intergenerational (young and old come together to learn and share). All programs stress the fun and adventure of learning, and travel is a major component of many of the activities. Formal research by Thomas and Butts (1998) explored motivations for a group of international Elderhostel travelers and compared them with a group of commercial sightseeing tourists. Intellectual stimulation was a prime motive for Elderhostelers, and many would explore sites on their own or visit museums in town rather than resting for the next day's trip. They enjoyed learning by doing and most had a high level of formal education. The commercial group placed more emphasis on the social aspects of travel as a motivator than did Elderhostelers, although the latter group saw this as a pleasant part of travel related to overall satisfaction. The authors urged further research to better understand older travelers interested in the Elderhostel experience and indicated such knowledge should assist those who plan travel schedules and sites to be visited.

Given key demographic projections of the aging population to come, particularly the baby-boom generation with high levels of formal education and many retiring with adequate financial resources and a history of vacationing and traveling throughout their early and middle-adult years, it appears that education and travel will continue to merge and result in a variety of tourism experiences where learning is at the foundation of the venture. Private operators and college and universities have already recognized this interest in education on the part of mature adults and combined this with travel and visitations to satisfy this market segment. It will indeed be interesting to follow the new offerings and programs in years to come, but there is no doubt that demand will increase.

SUMMARY

A number of sub-topics have been addressed in this chapter focusing on time use and activities in retirement and the overall theme of Ulyssean aging, or life seen as a journey, has been the guiding foundation. The following serve as broad summary points from the chapter sections:

Retirement occurs within a context of societal factors and trends; a speeding-up or quickening of the pace of daily life, economic conditions, and the general aging of society are among those affecting time and activity decisions in retirement.

Debates and analyses of the amount of work and leisure time in society have resulted in differing conclusions based upon definitions and methodologies used and the length of comparative periods. Most surveys or polls show older adults advantaged in terms of leisure time.

Conceptualizing or generalizing a retirement age (often thought of as 65) is a difficult task with many opting for earlier retirement in their late fifties or early sixties. Taking an historical view, more adult women had entered the workforce over the last 40 years and most decided to retire in their mid-sixties or earlier.

Compared to other adults, retirees typically experience more freetime and report lower levels of general stress. Time analyses show they engage in a variety of activities with television use and other at-home pursuits being quite popular. Activity patterns may be similar to those established in the middle adult years.

Formal research has explored leisure activity and aging using a variety of independent and dependent variables. Researchers have wondered whether activity patterns remain the same or vary in later life and what might be responsible for change. Characteristics such as gender, health status, and age (the younger and the older-old) have been analyzed in relation to activity participation.

Exercise and physical activity are important to aging adults especially considering the overall status of physical condition and inactivity within the entire population (*Healthy People 2010*). Excessive body weight combined with little physical exercise are major concerns.

Most surveys of physical activity and older adults do not reveal large amounts of total time spent in such involvement, yet notable percents do engage in activities such as walking, swimming, biking, and using exercise equipment. A core of users probably accounts for much of the participation in terms of time spent. Results from most of the research involving benefits of exercise well into the older adult years has been positive with gains demonstrated in areas such as strength, mood, reduced likelihood of falls, and better balance.

More older adults are interested in the challenges offered through athletic competitions. They have been athletes throughout their adult years and see no need to relinquish their status as a player/competitor. They offer positive images to all in society about the aging process. Stebbins' (1992) work was cited indicating the serious manner in which many undertake their sport. Vertinsky (2000) places older female participation in marathoning within the framework of feminist theory'– many barriers have been overcome to reach a point where serious competition can offer adult women the challenge they deserve.

The growth of organizations aimed at providing serious athletic competitions, the National Senior Games Association and World Masters Athletics as two examples cited, provides evidence that the challenge involving self and/or others is a goal for many aging athletes. Beyond competition, socialization, networking, and sharing training information are benefits that participants enjoy.

Travel was noted as a true Ulyssean venture with opportunities for creativity, learning, friendships, and challenge as prime motivators. The senior travel market is growing and many in the travel, resort, and hospitality industries are considering the needs of older tourists in areas such as physical design, pricing, and staff training. The senior travel market has been shown to be one that is segmented – many groups exist based on a number of demographic/ psychographic features.

Educational travel as exemplified by the types of programs available through Elderhostel is a popular type of travel for seniors and is projected to grow in the future given the demographics of the baby boom cohort. Universities and other providers can be expected to develop creative programs whether short-term on the campus or of a longer variety to national or international sites to meet the needs of those who view travel linked to learning.

NINE

ETHNICITY AND GENDER:
IMPACT ON LEISURE FOR OLDER ADULTS

If the Ulyssean journey through older adulthood stands as a central theme of this book and its application to leisure and retirement is a corollary concern, then the effects of ethnicity and gender upon that journey, particularly with regard to activities and their meaning, deserve consideration.

With a broad, sweeping stroke we may describe "typical" retirement, but as will be shown, differences due to one's ethnicity have been reported in the types of leisure pursuits enjoyed and their functions or meanings on a personal level.

Similarly, gender in virtually every investigation completed has been used as an independent variable when activity participation is being analyzed. Hence, the purpose of this chapter is to (a) review current literature in the areas of ethnicity and gender as applied to activities in adulthood (particularly older adulthood), (b) address major theories that have evolved surrounding one's race or ethnic background and how leisure is impacted, i.e., ethnicity, marginality, acculturation, or assimilation, and the more recent differential access model (Taylor, 1992), (c) offer a critique of the strengths and weaknesses of the current research and theory at this point in time, and d) explore leisure through the context of aging, ethnicity, and gender as noted in recent work (Allen & Chin-Sang, 1990; Allison & Geiger, 1993; Boyd & Tedrick, 1994; Brown & Tedrick, 1993; Tedrick & Boyd, 1999).

STRENGTHS AND WEAKNESSES OF EXISTING RESEARCH KNOWLEDGE

Discussion of cutting-edge theory related to leisure, aging, ethnicity, and gender is hampered by two major flaws related to samples drawn for research studies: (a) few studies are specifically concerned with older adults and therefore "adult" is often operationally defined as anyone over 18 or 21, and (b) if "older adulthood" is a focus of the study and ethnic background is introduced as a variable, sample sizes typically end up being smaller than desired, even when oversampling of certain ethnic groups occurs.

There are exceptions to the above, yet studies with smaller numbers of minority members such as Brown and Tedrick (1993) are more common. Here a nationwide outdoor recreation survey was used for secondary analysis; while 1,600 older adults (60 and over) were among those sampled, older blacks totaled only 136. Existing qualitative studies (Allen & Chin-Sang, 1990; Allison & Geiger, 1993; Boyd & Tedrick, 1994) obviously contain small samples while stressing the interpretive paradigm.

The first factor, lumping all adults together or excluding older adults, must be weighed carefully as life-cycle theory and cohort effect are considered. Findings from research exploring activities, meaning, and ethnicity where adults age 21 to over 70 are aggregated can provide only hints or speculation when leisure and aging in later life is of concern.

Assimilation or acculturation for a 25-year-old recently immigrated to the United States might be very different from that of a 70-year-old who arrived in this country 50 years ago. In short, we must be very cautious of applying the work on leisure, ethnicity, and gender to older adults when the samples comprising these studies have excluded this subpopulation.

The second issue, small sample sizes of older ethnic groups, frequently compromises generalizability. Floyd (1998) noted small samples in ethnic studies may lead to "false homogeneity" by reducing demographic variability and may eliminate the use of sophisticated multivariate statistical procedures that require large sample sizes. If ethnic groups are further sub-divided (educational level, social class, or gender), cells can become very small. Thus, it must be kept in mind that generalizability in studies involving older adult ethnic groups and their leisure may be less than ideal.

Furthermore, activity lists used in many of the larger-scale outdoor recreation surveys are designed for a younger adult population and are used for purposes of resource management, planning, and visitor use strategies. These lists do not capture the essence of daily (outdoor or otherwise) activity for many older adults, and frequently the lists appear inappropriate for aging or ethnic adults (Taylor, 1992).

For example, one study (Brown & Tedrick, 1993) using a nationwide survey included: horseback riding, outdoor team sports, kayaking, primitive camping, motorized vehicle use off improved roads, ski touring, and snowmobiling as possible activities for senior adults. While these pursuits certainly reflect outdoor management considerations, they are less than desirable in capturing typical retirement interests.

Another failing present in the empirical work on leisure and ethnicity is that conceptual clarity is often lacking when key terms such as race, ethnicity, or ethnic background are used. Race and ethnicity may be interchanged incorrectly (as variables or in narrative discussion); often a checkmark in the demographic section of a questionnaire serves as the basis for identification (Floyd, 1998; Taylor, 1992).

Kelly and Godbey (1992, pp. 163, 164) note that race differs from ethnicity and includes social identification that cannot be altered; racial identification is permanent. Ethnicity or ethnic background, on the other hand, is a complex term and includes feelings or perceptions on the part of the subgroup member. The depth of feeling one has regarding ethnicity may vary for each person. Terms such as ethnic identity, acculturation, ethnic consciousness, generational status, structural assimilation, etc. have been used in measuring and discussing the concept of ethnicity (Carr & Williams, 1993; Floyd & Gramann, 1993; Taylor, 1992).

Recent studies involving leisure have carefully looked at individual perceptions of ethnicity (Allison & Geiger, 1993; Carr & Williams, 1993; Floyd & Gramann, 1993; Shaull & Gramann, 1998; Stodolska & Jackson, 1998; Taylor, 1992), yet in many others the above-mentioned confusion or oversimplification can be found.

Other weaknesses within the existing body of knowledge include the use of theoretical models that are simplistic; too often race and class are used when a number of activities is the dependent variable and other intervening factors are never considered (Taylor, 1992). Another failing is the monolithic aggregating of all sub-groups into one, e.g., the group "Hispanics" is not further divided to include the considerable variation based upon country of origin (Floyd, 1998; Floyd & Gramann, 1993; Taylor, 1992); Taylor (1992) notes that black leisure participation has been perceived as deviant, perhaps stemming from studies of outdoor-wildland participation that have shown "underutilization" by blacks. This ethnocentrism or "norming" of activities based upon a white, middle-class orientation has been mentioned by others (Allison & Geiger, 1993).

Considered together, these weaknesses should not overshadow what has been reported about ethnic variation in leisure pursuits. Specialists in outdoor recreation (Baas, Ewert, & Chavez, 1993; Carr & Williams, 1993; Dwyer & Gobster, 1992; Ewert, Chavez, & Magill, 1993; Floyd, 1998; Floyd & Grammann, 1993; Johnson, Bowker, English, & Worthen, 1998; Stodolska & Jackson, 1998) have contributed much toward an understanding of how ethnicity impacts upon selection, use, and meaning of outdoor-related activities.

The largest gap remaining, from our perspective, is the speculation and hypothesizing that must occur because of the dearth of studies including older adults, their leisure, and ethnic considerations. For example, how did assimilation play out 30 or 40 years ago when ethnic group members of today's elder cohort were making leisure choices in a different period of their lives? How did location, access, and historical time shape their leisure then and perhaps for years to come? Likewise, how were female roles different years ago, and did the feminist movement affect leisure positively for those 60 or 75 today?

An interesting approach to the above question is a recent study by Bialeschki and Walbert (1998) that combines historical and leisure studies perspectives in contrasting the leisure of white female textile workers with that of African-American females employed in tobacco factories during the period of 1910 to 1940. Historical factors such as the attitudes of factory owners concerning the provision of company-sponsored leisure and the role of the church and early union efforts give meaning to leisure opportunities and choices for these women in the industrial new South.

There aren't many retrospective studies that can fill in the leisure timeline from early adulthood through the retirement years. We do have studies that report the current status of leisure for ethnic groups and for males and females. We must, however, be cautious in applying findings about leisure and ethnicity to the older adult population when they have been largely excluded from samples.

THEORIES EXPLAINING LEISURE PARTICIPATION

This section reviews the dominant theories proposed and empirically tested concerning leisure (most often outdoor-related) and subgroup variation. Marginality, ethnicity, assimilation and acculturation, and the differential access model are presented with commentary and synopses of supporting studies. The reader is again cautioned that generalizations to older adult populations involve risk as few studies have sampled aging persons.

MARGINALITY

Marginality theory is closely linked to socioeconomic status and the negative consequences stemming from limited access (Taylor, 1992; Washburne, 1978). Recreation resources available at the local level are likely to vary greatly; poverty and various forms of discrimination brought on by meager financial means have direct impact on the kinds of leisure opportunities available or not present. Styles and meaning of participation are therefore affected. Marginality theory embraces constraints and barriers as powerful shapers of personal leisure. Related to the wildland outdoor experience, it proposes that many urban poor adults grew up with very limited chances to enjoy overnight camping, visit state or regional parks, or learn to appreciate outdoor recreation. Cost, transportation, availability of adult supervision, and nonexisting instructional programs could all have been barriers. In summary fashion, Floyd, Shinew, McGuire, and Noe (1994, p. 156) describe marginality in the following manner, "Stated differently, by occupying a subordinate class position, minorities have had limited access to society's major institutions, which negatively affects life-chances and lifestyles, which is reflected in reduced participation in certain forms of leisure."

Washburne (1978) tested the marginality thesis using a California survey of urban residents that oversampled blacks. Without controlling for residence or other socioeconomic factors, blacks were shown to be more involved in team sports and spectator sports, while the participation for whites was significantly higher for wildland-outdoor recreation, travel outside of their community, overnight camping and day camping, and walking, hiking, and climbing. When residence and socioeconomic status were controlled (matching whites and blacks on these indicators), differences in participation still held for most activities based upon race. Wasburne (1978) concluded that support could not be found for the marginality theory, and the latter analysis appeared to favor differences based upon race.

Two other research thrusts are linked to marginality. Leisure sociologists as early as the 1950s used social class as a predictor variable when comparing lower-, middle-, and upper-class groupings. Among them, Burdge, (1969); Cheek, Field, and Burdge (1976); Clarke (1956); and White (1975); all found differences in participation based on social class.

Gottlieb (1957), as an example, explored the use of taverns by the lower class. Gerontologists concerned with ethnic factors have also contributed to the dialogue on marginality. Rather than comparing ethnic groups while controlling for social class, their approach has more often been to look at constraints and barriers and demography in explaining service underutilization and other quality of life factors.

Double or triple "jeopardy" has been used (Jackson, 1972; Jackson, Kolody, & Wood, 1982) to describe the forces of ageism, racism, and poverty as daily life is considered for many minority-aged persons. The notion pertaining to leisure would imply restricted access, limited opportunity, and difficulty in working within existing systems. Yet, as will be shown later in this chapter, older minority adults do develop meaningful leisure patterns and are able to overcome many obstacles.

Brooks-Lambing (1972), who implicitly considered marginality, found differences in the leisure of three groups of retired blacks; those with the fewest economic resources displayed the narrowest range of activities.

Floyd's (1998) recent review of marginality theory as represented by the work of leisure researchers noted the following weaknesses: often the concept has not been clearly defined, and it has not been shown how socioeconomic differences (middle- versus lower-class, for example) affect the theory. Further, discrimination has not been analyzed as a factor in most marginality studies, and while participation rates have been used as the dependent variable, rarely have meanings and values been tied explicitly to marginality theory.

ETHNICITY

Ethnicity theory related to leisure patterns attempts to explain differences (between minority groups and the majority population or among varying ethnic subgroups) in participation based upon the values, orientations, norms, and socialization processes inherent within the subcultures being examined (Allison & Geiger, 1993; Floyd et al., 1994; Kelly & Godbey, 1992; Taylor, 1992).

Also referred to as the "subcultural" theory or hypothesis, it is a multi-faceted framework that has frequently been treated in a simplistic fashion without exploring the meaning of what ethnicity means to those participating in the study (Allison, 1988; Allison & Geiger, 1993; Kelly & Godbey, 1992; Taylor, 1992). Attitudes, behaviors, and lifestyles stemming from the cultural origins of subpopulations are of interest, as is the context in which leisure activity occurs. Floyd (1998) also noted that ethnicity is often treated in a static manner and that researchers have not been able to capture the changing, dynamic nature of ethnicity.

Critics have faulted some research for failing to analyze intragroup variation, e.g., results are presented under the label of "Hispanics" or "blacks" when ancestry (Mexican, American,

Cuban, African-American, or Jamaican) may be a crucial concern (Kelly & Godbey, 1992: Taylor, 1992). Taylor (1992, p. 97), for example, reported differences in participation in ethnic festivals between Jamaicans and African-Americans. The notion of a black subculture pertaining to leisure has also been challenged (Taylor, 1992) in that variation can be found when the black population is sub-divided.

Many studies have lent general support to the ethnicity theory (a word of caution is introduced again—some studies have not probed ethnicity sufficiently and have failed to uncover the degree of ethnic identification, ancestry, generational status, etc., instead relying only on a "race" designation as part of a questionnaire).

Frequently cited is the Stamps and Stamps (1985) investigation of 750 urban adults, two-thirds black due to oversampling, which found relatively high correlations in activities for lower-class whites and blacks (R = .79) and middle-class blacks and whites (R = .55). A higher correlation, however, was found between lower-class and middle-class blacks (R = .89).

Blacks ranked socializing and partying, television and radio, sports participation, reading, and listening to music as their top five activities, while whites ranked listening to music, television and radio, outdoor recreation, sports, and sewing and needlework as their favorite activities. Comparison by race and class showed middle-class blacks favoring socialization and partying and resting and relaxation, while middle-class whites ranked outdoor recreation significantly higher. These were the only significant differences out of 22 activities. Lower-class blacks and whites differed in only two areas, whites favoring reading to a greater degree, and blacks ranking resting and relaxation higher.

Washburne (1978), noted earlier, while exploring marginality, found differences between blacks and whites when social class was controlled, which aligned with theory based upon ethnic differences. Other notable investigators include Dwyer and Hutchinson (1990), who used regression analyses for a sample of Chicago residents. Race, gender, and age were included in the regression equations, and while only small amounts of variance were explained by the combination of variables, race was significant in three-fourths of the analyses.

The Pennsylvania Outdoor Recreation Survey (Becker & Yost, 1991) showed participation rates higher for whites in many of the outdoor activities (birdwatching, boating, fishing, golfing, hunting, sightseeing, and swimming), while blacks participated significantly higher in basketball and football. Comparable levels of participation existed for baseball and softball, bicycling, horseback riding, jogging or walking, and picnicking.

Using a stratified, nationwide sample of 1,600, Floyd et al. (1994) explored both race and social class. Class was determined subjectively by study participants. A moderate level of association was found regarding the activities of whites and blacks (R = .53), with blacks ranking social activities and exercise activities higher, and whites favoring outdoor and individual pursuits. Associations between middle- and lower-class blacks (R = .73) and middle- and lower-class whites (R = .86) were higher. Low associations were found for lower-class whites and blacks (R = .42) and black and white females of lower class (R = .23), leading the authors to conclude that ethnicity theory may operate differently at the lower socioeconomic levels, and that gender should be analyzed, particularly when meager economic resources are present.

Recent, late 1990s studies have continued to use ethnicity as a framework in exploring leisure. Stodolski and Jackson (1998) focused on discrimination of ethnic whites (Polish) by using qualitative and quantitative techniques. In contrast to earlier studies, little discrimination was experienced in leisure settings; more often the workplace or governmental bureaucracies were the locations of jokes or references to language difficulties. The concept of "ethnic enclosure," participating in leisure or other social contacts only with those of similar ethnic ties, was discussed as a possible outcome of discrimination.

Marginality and ethnicity were examined in a study focusing on wildland recreation visits in the rural South (Johnson, Bowker, English, & Worthen, 1998). A series of logistic regression models incorporating a variety of sociodemographic variables were used to estimate visitation to outdoor sites. In contrast to the findings of previous research, poorer rather than higher-income African-Americans were found to visit wildland sites more often, although, overall, whites visited more frequently. It was suggested that rural urban differences should be accounted for in marginality and ethnicity studies and that the two orientations probably work in combination to explain racial differences.

ACCULTURATION/ASSIMILATION

Closely linked to work on ethnic variation is the acculturation or assimilation perspective, which describes the degree to which ethnic groups "blend" with the dominant or majority population. Labeled the "melting pot" thesis by Allison and Geiger (1993), acculturation has received scrutiny from many different social scientists. Pfister (1993) notes that generational status, education and income, age, years of residence in the adopted country, ethnic density of the neighborhood of residence, occupation, religion and kinship networks may all be crucial factors influencing acculturation. A type of ethnocentrism may also exist on the part of the dominant ethnic group (Allison & Geiger, 1993) in thinking that assimilation is or should be a goal of all ethnic subgroups; some members may embrace the idea, while others will resist attempts except where absolutely necessary. Generational differences may exist, with first and third clinging to the native culture in contrast to second generation children and adults making a conscious effort to adopt the lifestyles, dress, and behaviors of the majority group (Kelly & Godbey, 1992).

Of particular interest here is the role played by recreation and leisure regarding assimilation. Leisure may enhance assimilation, or it may take forms associated with native customs and thus help to perpetuate a strong sense of ethnic identity (festivals, celebrations, dishes, reading material). For a group of elderly Chinese Americans, leisure was found to both support assimilation (reading English and watching popular television shows) and to assist with ties to ethnic culture through activities such as Tai Chi, mahjongg, or reading newspapers printed in Chinese (Allison & Geiger, 1993).

Assimilation and acculturation are complex concepts and may be viewed on a continuum ranging from resistance (retaining the native or "old" ways) to complete acceptance with overt attempts to adopt the diet, language, customs, habits, and religion of the majority. Floyd and Gramann (1993) note that structural assimilation refers to the process of ethnic group members entering into the mainstream through participation in the workforce, education, and civic affairs. This involvement occurs through warm, personal ties with members of the majority group (primary structural assimilation) and through less intensive contacts made in institutional or community settings (secondary structural assimilation) such as attending school functions or non-intensive relationships in the work setting. Recreation, due to its often social forms, obviously offers opportunities for primary and secondary structural assimilation.

Using the above conceptual framework as a base, recent studies (Carr & Williams, 1993; Floyd & Gramann, 1993; Gramann, Floyd, & Saenz, 1993) have probed outdoor utilization and meaning as related to the degree of assimilation present on the part of the various ethnic groups. This research thrust improves upon the earlier noted weakness of many studies that failed to explore ethnicity in any detail. In measuring assimilation for Mexican Americans in the metropolitan Phoenix area, two techniques were used (Floyd & Gramann, 1993; Gramann, Floyd, & Saenz, 1993): the degree to which English was used and understood as the primary language and the degree to which friends of the same or other ethnic groups were selected for recreational visits (primary structural assimilation).

Results suggested the notion that assimilation is a factor should be considered in analyzing recreation patterns. Mexican Americans who scored highest on the acculturation scale were similar to Anglos in four out of five activity categories, while the least acculturated groups participated significantly less than Anglos in all but one category (Floyd & Gramann, 1993).

When benefits were explored (Gramann, Floyd, & Saenz, 1993), differences were noted between Mexican Americans (divided into three groups based upon acculturation scores: least, intermediate, and highest) and Anglos. Mexican Americans highest in acculturation valued family togetherness significantly more than did Anglos or the other two groups of less-acculturated Mexican Americans. Some benefits were perceived in the same fashion by all groups, but distinctions were evident in most categories based upon acculturation. The authors concluded that selective acculturation may occur where certain views mirror the majority population, yet others remain distinct from the dominant group.

Degree of acculturation was also part of a three-pronged approach in describing ethnicity (ancestral group membership and generational status were the other elements) in a study of Hispanics of Mexican and Central American origin and Anglos in the national forests in Southern California (Carr & Williams, 1993). Mexican Americans were found to be more acculturated than Central Americans and variations were found both in activity usage and reasons for participation. Visits with extended family described Mexican Americans, while

Anglos were more likely to be visiting with friends. Variation within Hispanic groups was a theme both in leisure style and perceived benefits. Meanings and activities (baptisms, for example) linked to religion were found in the forest.

In an attempt to explore the earlier noted weakness of leisure ethnicity research, its lack of focus on values and meanings (Floyd, 1998), Shaull and Gramann (1998) compared Hispanics and whites regarding values placed on family-related leisure experiences and meanings attached to nature-based activities. Assimilation-acculturation was assessed through a self-reporting of English or Spanish use and comprehension. Hispanic participants were divided into three groups ranging from least (Spanish most often used) to most (English used predominantly) acculturated. Hispanics classified as bicultural (between the two extremes) held higher family values regarding leisure than did whites, although the least and most acculturated Hispanics did not differ from whites in this orientation. Also, the least acculturated Hispanic group were most favorable toward nature-related values when compared to whites and more acculturated Hispanics. It was cautioned that a monolithic perspective, viewing any ethnic group in a homogeneous fashion, may fail to capture intragroup differences.

Since the work described above with the exception of the Allison and Geiger study (1993) does not focus on adults of retirement age, interesting considerations emerge when aging is added to the descriptions of acculturation and its relationship to leisure. Length of time in the adopted land and one's age at the period of immigration would be two factors worthy of study.

Perhaps retrospective studies where older adults could describe leisure at different ages would be helpful in clarifying assimilation connected to aging. Immigration at 15, 25, or 40 might be expected to reflect different patterns of leisure and the desire to assimilate. The age at which African Americans, for example, experienced the civil rights movement or overt discrimination in attempting to use recreation resources could be expected to shape attitudes and activities that might well carry on for years. Woodard's (1988) analysis showed factors such as age, discrimination, prejudice, and urban or rural upbringing were responsible in shaping the leisure patterns of black Americans.

Did structural assimilation hold a unique interpretation when separate but equal was the order of the day? These and other questions are ripe for exploration when the effects of aging are added to what has been written about acculturation and assimilation and leisure.

DIFFERENTIAL ACCESS MODEL

Another recent interpretation having a tie to earlier work on ethnicity is Taylor's (1992) differential access model, which sees life's chances being affected by the different or unequal manner in which individuals are or are not able to tap a variety of resources in the community. Taylor (1992) describes these discrepancies as follows:

> Unequal life chances arise because of differential access to societal resources.
> Inequalities emanate from systematic, institutionalized historical and

contemporary discriminatory practices based on factors such as racial characteristics, ethnic origins, social class background, and gender. These factors in addition to family and friendship networks, place of residence, life cycle stage, and community ties are important factors in leisure participation (pp. 15-16).

As far as leisure is concerned, the unequal circumstances may affect leisure in five ways: (1) knowledge of and (2) participation in recreation activities, (3) the breadth or repertoire of activities, and (4) the distribution and (5) quality of recreation resources available. Using a sample of 144 residents in New Haven, Connecticut, including two groups of blacks, African Americans and Jamaican Americans, and two groups of whites, Italian Americans and other whites, Taylor (1992) analyzed ethnic leisure participation (hangouts, cooking, media use, and festivals) and local park use according to the variables of race, class, neighborhood and time at the residence, life cycle, marital status, age, gender, family, friends, and most importantly, ethnic identity.

The latter was assessed by ancestry and whether respondents perceived themselves more as members of ethnic groups or as simply more generic "Americans." Ethnic identity accounted for 16 percent of the significant effects relative to leisure participation. Gender was a successful predictor in the areas of knowledge of ethnic hangouts (males), ability to list hangouts (males), and participation in festivals (females). Race and gender were important when park use was analyzed; twice as many females (43 percent) as males said they did not use neighborhood parks, and black women (52 percent) had the highest reported non-use of parks of any group. In terms of age, 46- to 99-year-olds had the lowest visitation rate of local parks. Both race and self-assessed ethnic identity were noted as important in predicting leisure as measured by ethnic pursuits and park usage.

Using Taylor's differential access model as a theoretical foundation, Juniu (1997) explored the work and leisure lives of 18 adults who had immigrated to the U.S. from South America. Obtaining adequate leisure was a problem for most as work assumed a primary importance in their lives. Access to leisure and types of activities were related to a variety of factors, with social class and the ability to use English being primary discriminators. Middle-class and professional immigrants were much more likely to associate with the mainstream culture in personal and work-related engagements, while working class individuals participated most often with extended family and others of South American descent during free time. Gender, age, and family situation also accounted for differences in leisure. Similar to Taylor (1992), Juniu's analysis supported a framework consisting of many variables to understand the behaviors and meanings attached to leisure for this group of South American immigrants.

GENDER AND LEISURE

Leisure participation as differentiated by gender has been an object of concern for social scientists and recreation planners alike for decades.

Feminist perspectives (Henderson, Bialeschki, Shaw, & Freysinger, 1989, as one example) have created an awareness of the special leisure concerns of women (access, cost, availability based on schedules, crime and attendant fear, lack of opportunities, etc.) and have challenged the status quo. When looking at older women, the effects of cohort (Was working "outside" the family encouraged? How was the feminist movement interpreted personally and at what age?) mixes with gender as changes in such areas as increased athletic opportunities at the interscholastic and intercollegiate levels have been enjoyed by today's younger women but were absent for many females years ago.

Before exploring gender differences connected with leisure, this brief capsule of typical retirement is introduced. Ordinary retirement, as described in two reports by Kelly (Kelly, 1987; Kelly & Westcott, 1991), was characterized by continuity of roles and interests, with a core of activities being enjoyed by both males and females. The samples were primarily whites in blue-collar occupations who lived in the Midwest. Adults were relatively satisfied with retirement living, poor health and disruptive family circumstances (death of a spouse, divorce) having expected negative impacts. Daily patterns had stabilized after a honeymoon period, and family contact was at the center of social involvements.

As for activities, a core of accessible, low-cost pursuits dominated leisure for most (Kelly, 1987; Kelly & Westcott, 1991). Television, contacts with others, informal entertaining, home and yard projects, and selected crafts (primarily women) were the most popular free-time engagements. Fitness or high-exertion activities, such as swimming or hunting, were not favored, and little involvement was seen in formal organizational offerings (senior centers, etc.) or volunteer work.

For this sample of seniors, male-female differences emerged in the following: men were more likely to have a fix-it type project in progress around the house and to drive more often. While family involvements were important, the role played by men differed from that of their spouses. Women occupied the nurturing or organizational roles in dealing with family, and they spent more time in conversations with friends and family. Kelly (1987) notes this role division of men as "providers" and women as "caretakers" being a significant factor over the life cycle in regard to leisure and family interactions.

Finally, high-investment activities requiring special equipment or locales, friends, or high levels of skill for participation provide the "balance" to the "core" of home-based activities that dominate leisure in retirement. Camping, hobby clubs, and sports such as golf require such an investment.

FEMINIST PERSPECTIVES ON LEISURE

A group of authors and researchers has focused recently on the special concerns of women in regard to leisure (Allen & Chin Sang, 1990; Bialeschki & Henderson, 1991; Henderson, 1990a, 1990b, 1992; Henderson & Rannells, 1988; Henderson, Bialeschki, Shaw, & Freysinger, 1989; Horna, 1991; Melamed, 1991; O'Neill, 1991; Teaff, 1991). The major themes have been the inequality of women regarding leisure, a basic difference in the way that men and women conceptualize and experience leisure, and changes, both societal and within the delivery systems of leisure, that should be made to better meet the circumstances of women.

Females beyond their teen years often face the task of keeping the family operating in addition to holding down a full-time job; the disparity in unobligated time for males and females has been frequently reported (Henderson, 1990a; Hochschild, 1989; Horna, 1991; O'Neill, 1991; Robinson, 1989a, 1989b).

Because of upbringing and the traditional role of nurturer, many women feel they have no right to enjoy leisure; the concerns of others must come first (Henderson, 1991). The very meaning and interpretation of leisure may differ for men and women. Deem (1986) suggested that women emphasize friendship and togetherness, less competition and decreased aggression as compared to men, and enjoyment of simple experiences during free time.

Leisure constraints or barriers differ by gender, as well; time pressures due to family obligations, personal safety, and health issues are viewed as primary concerns for women (Henderson, 1991). Taken together, these issues, concerns, and female-male differences are significant when leisure participation is examined.

To what extent did the issues raised in this section affect the older women of today, particularly in regard to leisure? Certainly, prescribed roles in the family, rather rigid in years past, influenced leisure greatly for women. The time budget studies have shown a trend over the years of greater male participation, although females do a disproportionate amount of work around the home (Robinson, 1989b).

The notion that "a woman's work is never done" rang true for most of the current group of older women, even to the point of blurring the distinction between work and leisure when free time did exist. Canning, baking, quilting, or crafts with a utilitarian purpose were often done when regular chores were completed. During interviews, many older women have relayed to this author that husbands were in complete control of finances and were not expected to lift a finger around the house. Shared decision making, whether present or not, would affect leisure as it would other homemaking tasks.

Attitudinal barriers kept many women from pursuing desired interests, particularly in regard to sports or competitive activities. It was simply not expected that a young woman might desire to excel in the competitive arena. Even if attitudes could be overcome, lack of opportunity, poor equipment or coaching faced many women who desired to be athletes. Lack of exposure might then carry over into adulthood.

Did the feminist movement have positive effects for cohorts of now-retired women? Was there liberation that resulted in broader or changed notions of leisure? As with most movements, the degree of influence here most likely varied due to personal and philosophical circumstances, yet the connection to leisure is intriguing and is worthy of exploration, perhaps through retrospective interviews.

Patterns of labor force participation for females 60 and beyond today as contrasted with the current higher percentages of working women with career orientation is another factor to consider. Staggered working cycles arranged around child rearing or calls to work in wartime are descriptive of some 70- and 80-year-old women. How leisure blended with cyclical working schedules is a topic worthy of speculation.

Finally, race or ethnicity and socioeconomic variables must be factored into consideration of feminist perspectives on leisure. The contrast of working-class women, black and white, in the South as explored by Bialeschki and Walbert (1998) is an example of how meanings for church activities or simple monotony-breaking techniques at work, like singing, can differ based upon race. As has been noted previously and will be emphasized in the following section, race, cultural norms, and educational and economic status exert significant influence upon leisure for females and males. Availability of recreation resources, discrimination confronted, and influences of the church differ for selected subgroups of women. Studies such as Taylor's (1992) employing multivariate techniques have been helpful in untangling the web of forces that determine leisure behavior.

THE INTERSECTION OF AGING, ETHNICITY, GENDER, AND LEISURE

One of the earlier studies to focus on the leisure of retired blacks used three categories: professionals, former semi-skilled workers, and a group on public assistance (Brooks-Lambing, 1972), who were all living in Florida. Findings revealed strong social class differences, with the former professionals expressing the broadest repertoire (12.8 activities average) with greater involvement in civic and community roles and intellectual activities than the other two groups.

Travel was important to the former professionals (mainly teachers), and they also differed from the others in expressing a greater desire for new activities in retirement. The former semi-skilled workers displayed a much narrower range of activities (6.3 average, half of what the professionals noted) consisting primarily of television, radio, reading the Bible, and house projects. They were active in the church but not typically in leadership or organizational roles, and many had ceased participating in activities since retiring.

Those on public assistance had a very narrow range of activities (mean of 4.1) with radio, television, reading, and Bible study being dominant activities. Among the desired new pursuits were learning to sew and improving reading and writing skills. Gender differences were noted; women tended to fish more often, with the authors noting that the social aspects were important as fishing tended to occur in groups.

Women also favored handicrafts such as quilting and sewing, while men typically worked on home-related projects and in the garden. Also of note was the restriction on card playing from a religious perspective. Both education and income were positively correlated with activity participation, yet health status showed no effects.

The 1982-84 Nationwide Recreation Survey was used for secondary analysis comparing older black and white groups on outdoor activities and constraints (Brown & Tedrick, 1993; McGuire, O'Leary, Alexander, & Dottavio, 1987). In terms of leisure constraints, older blacks were significantly more likely than whites to experience the following barriers: money, transportation difficulties, safety concerns, lack of information, and lack of an activity companion. Older blacks, compared to whites, favored picnicking, fishing and crabbing, spectator sports, traveling, volleyball, visiting zoos, jogging, and training animals. Overall, however, it was concluded (McGuire, O'Leary, Alexander, & Dottavio, 1987) that similarities, not differences, characterized the two groups.

Using a composite of number of activities and frequency of participation, Brown and Tedrick (1993) compared older whites and blacks on 22 activities (some from this nationwide survey were probably inappropriate for this population; possible activities included primitive camping and use of off-road vehicles). Comparable to other studies reporting lower levels of outdoor and wildland activity for blacks, this analysis showed significantly greater participation, for whites, with fewer than 25 percent of the older blacks reporting any participation at all.

When income, age, education, and gender groups were compared, racial differences still were found. Older black females had the lowest participation score of any age group analyzed. The authors (Brown & Tedrick, 1993) concluded that the special concerns of older blacks should be considered relative to outdoor leisure planning and participation, and that problems exist when pre-established activity lists are used to assess certain subpopulations.

OLDER AFRICAN-AMERICAN WOMEN

Leisure in the lives of older African-American women has been explored in two recent studies using qualitative techniques (Allen & Chin Sang, 1990; Boyd & Tedrick, 1994). The interrelationship between a lifetime of work and leisure was the foundation for Allen and Chin-Sang (1990) when interviews with 30 older (average age 75) women involved in urban nutrition and activity programs in Florida were analyzed.

Perhaps it was not unexpected that only 13 of the group said they had experienced any leisure prior to retirement, and half of those described their leisure connected to work or service. Work had typically started in childhood on farms, and throughout life, farm labor, domestic jobs, and food and health care service were the most common types of employment. When retirement came for these women, leisure was appreciated and perceived as something earned. In late life, leisure was defined by two-thirds of the group as free time or time for personal enjoyment. Other definitions included relaxation or taking it easy, having no work, or time for the church or Bible study.

When looking at descriptions of current activities, leisure overlapped with work activities (things such as house duties and service-oriented pursuits). Favorite leisure engagements (in rank order) were attending senior centers, television, church or prayer meetings, crafts, and exercise. Church was viewed as a context for leisure and service, and in the senior center, work and leisure roles were combined. Many spoke of center activities they enjoyed and important roles such as helping others or doing tasks around the building.

According to Allen and Chin-Sang (1990), these women were survivors, having displayed decades of self-reliance. Leisure, in purpose and in function, was linked to a lifetime of work and represented in later life a continuing way to serve others.

Similar to the above study, Boyd and Tedrick (1994) conducted in-depth interviews with 11 older African-American women attending an urban senior center. A life course framework was used to discuss leisure, work, and family histories. In addition, leisure meanings, attitudes, satisfactions, and barriers were discussed.

Life satisfaction was tapped using a formal instrument, the open-ended Life Satisfaction Index B (Neugarten, Havighurst, & Tobin, 1961). The older women (aged 65 to 94) were predominantly widowed, living on their own with meager financial resources, and had contact with children and grandchildren. With one notable exception, the women rated high in life satisfaction. Statements such as, "I feel fortunate to have lived this long" captured the essence of aging at this point in their lives. Friends, family, grandparenthood (or great-grandparenthood), and God or the church were themes interwoven with questions about life satisfaction.

Using Kelly's (1987) conceptualization, seven of the 11 represented a straight-arrow life course (life events occurring at about the same time as others of their age); the other four had experienced a major life trauma such as personal injury or family problems that had forced them to make major readjustments. As with many of their birth cohorts living in the North, eight had moved from the South prior to their 20s. Descriptions of life growing up centered around school, the family, church, and rural or farm lifestyles.

Childhood activities were noted as playing ball, short trips to parks or zoos, church-related social and religious gatherings, and games, both indoor and outdoor. The decade of their 20s was marked by marriage and childbearing; few mentioned paid employment. The late teens and early 20s were the most active leisure periods with social (friends and courting) activities; parties, gatherings, picnics, movies, dancing, and church functions.

Middle life, as described by the older women, tended to blend as did remembered leisure pursuits. Descriptions of children growing, housework, and paid employment were given, and activities with their children mirrored their own early years going to parks, zoos, picnics, outside activities, and church events.

The fifth or sixth decade brought change such as health problems (cancer) personally or for a spouse, stoppage of work for the husband, and leisure, as described, was not much different from earlier periods.

Widowhood intruded in the 60s and 70s, which forced new social patterns—the senior center became a focus of interaction for most and continuing involvement in the church or Bible study, although actual church attendance began to drop and previous roles (singing) were given up, most often because of health issues.

Beyond church or center involvement, leisure in later life centered around a "core" (Kelly, 1987) of home-based, somewhat passive activities headed by television and radio (often religious-oriented programming), praying, and less frequently, visiting others and sewing. One older female carried on a type of street-corner ministry, attempting to reach teens. The youngest of the group was decidedly more active with a much broader repertoire including travel, cooking, and riding a bike. Regular exercise as an activity was rarely mentioned.

Major themes or findings from the interviews included the following (Boyd & Tedrick, 1994); (1) Family and religion had served and continued to serve as major focal points throughout their lives; both were directly linked to leisure, and this was in agreement with other researchers (Allen & Chin-Sang, 1990; Taylor & Chatters, 1986). (2) A core of leisure activities existed that centered on home-based experiences as well as the senior center and church. (3) Leisure, as a concept, was not easily described (free time or time without obligation was the primary notion), yet it was seen as enjoyable, important, and connected with relaxation; leisure appeared to permeate or intermingle with other aspects of daily life. (4) Few desired to attempt or pursue new activities, and barriers were noted as health problems, lack of money, and neighborhood crime. (5) One older African-American woman stood in marked contrast to the others; her life satisfaction was extremely low because she had been separated from family early in life, was unable to access appropriate services as an adult, and was not accepted at the center. The value of qualitative methods was emphasized as her descriptions of life provided much meaning relative to leisure in a way that would have been much different had quantitative methods been employed.

OLDER AFRICAN-AMERICAN MEN

As a follow-up to the previously cited study on females, older African-American men were interviewed to explore their leisure and how it might differ from women (Tedrick & Boyd, 1999). An urban senior center was again selected as the site and 15 men comprised the sample. Beyond male-female comparisons, the study focused on current and past time use patterns, leisure activities, and meanings. Preliminary findings resulted in the identification of three themes. The first of these was labeled "opportunity" and described differences in life circumstances that had made it easier or harder for the males to access leisure at different times throughout their lives. As an example, migration to the North resulted in different leisure patterns and opportunities during the life course. Those who had grown up in the South often described life on the farm and having little free time. Dropping out of school to work was common. Those who had moved North at a younger age typically remained in school longer, which meant opportunities in school sports. Military experience was common in the latter group, which meant exposure to travel that carried on to a degree during post-military adulthood. While having an effect on the breadth of leisure opportunity, those who grew up on farms spoke positively of this life that was linked to a certain type of leisure style. Family and church were important and served as a focal point for leisure time. There was no indication that leisure opportunities were missed because of life on the farm.

A second theme revolved around the connection of active church involvement and what Kelly (1972) termed "relational" leisure. Men who were active in volunteer roles or assisting at their churches mentioned the notion of being with or helping others—the relational motive. "If you just go to the service and then leave, you're not contributing." For many there had been a high level of involvement in organized religion throughout their lives, and even as health declined or the aging process made it more difficult to attend services, the desire to help in any way remained strong. As told by one older male, "The Lord has been good to me and my family, and I said if I were able to retire and lie long, I'm going to put something back into the system. People are my life." By comparison, while many African-American women in later life were also active in supporting roles in their churches, they spoke more frequently of the personal impact of church and religion through worship at services, prayer, Bible reading, etc. Men most often recounted an active role or visiting someone when the topic of religion arose.

A third theme derived from the interviews was the role of the senior center in their lives, and how participation was influenced by health status and the presence of physical ailments. Center attendance provided a structure to daily time use; most came four or five days a week, and the routine of getting up, awaiting transportation, eating a meal at the center, and returning in mid- or later-afternoon was a pattern they described frequently. Daily time use was centered around this important activity. Participation style at the center was greatly affected by health status. "When it comes to activities, I can't do so much because of my heart." The relational motive (Kelly, 1972) was again present in connection with the senior center, "I come here to help those who can't help themselves."

Further analysis will focus on male-female differences, but it was clear that connections exist between religion and church and leisure for both older African-American men and women, although purposes or reasons for involvement may differ slightly. Males also spoke of the social club, a topic less frequently voiced by women. As expected, certain personal factors—health status as a prime example—shape leisure participation and meaning. The social or relational aspects of senior centers, religious organizations, and other forms of leisure are valued by both African-American men and women in retirement.

CHINESE-AMERICAN ELDERLY

Allison and Geiger's (1993) examination of elderly Chinese Americans is noteworthy for two reasons: the lack of empirical work with this population regarding free-time pursuits and the analysis of leisure as a means to maintain cultural identity and a way to seek assimilation through sharing the popular activities of the majority population.

The authors cite a previous study by Cheng (1978) showing gardening, relaxing at home, reading, television, and crafts to occupy the bulk of leisure time activities for older Chinese Americans.

The pattern uncovered by Allison and Geiger (1993) was similar, yet broader. As a group (10 males, 15 females ranging in age from 64 to 85 at a senior center) television, walking, reading, and exercise were top rated. Men were more likely to read, walk, and watch television, and women were a bit broader in their free time, including interests such as sewing, helping others, Tai Chi, mahjongg, and church activities. Reading materials were used to maintain ties to China (71 percent read Chinese papers, etc.) and to "learn the American way" (40 percent read items printed in English). Television was also used to become a part of the mainstream culture. It was noted that further studies examining assimilation should explore the ways in which leisure is used as a link to the old and the new.

THE ULYSSEAN JOURNEY FOR OLDER ETHNIC ADULTS: CONCLUDING THOUGHTS

For many older minority adults, daily life exemplifies the Ulyssean journey: indeed, "triple jeopardy," being exposed to the negative influences (constraints including access to services) due to age, ethnicity, or gender, may be challenges faced by many of this group.

In the context of MacLeish's (1976) notion of life defined by adventure and creativity, leisure offers the opportunity for self-actualization. That is not to say that the bulk of the leisure repertoire of older minority adults is filled with jaunts across the globe, rock-climbing expeditions, and creating various artworks in the garage studio. The core of daily leisure is a more mundane, home-based series of activities emphasizing accessible media, tasks (many blending work and leisure motives or functions) that are generally enjoyed and done without pressure, and maintaining social contacts through family and friends. The more adventurous or challenging engagements, taking on new hobbies or extended trips, punctuate the patterns of daily life, providing balance (Kelly, 1987).

The finding by Allison and Geiger (1993) that older Chinese Americans use leisure to maintain Chinese identity (reading material about China and printed in Chinese, mahjongg, Tai Chi) and to learn about America (television, local newspapers printed in English) deserves further consideration and exploration. Investigators should undertake similar interviews using life course perspectives with other ethnic group members of older age. Many intriguing questions arise: How does age impact upon the desire to assimilate (or not), and what forms of leisure are used at different ages to maintain ethnic ties or to embrace the culture of the majority population? Do answers to the above questions differ when various ethnic groups are compared? How do minority adults who have immigrated to America use leisure as a link to the past and as a bridge to the new culture if assimilation is desired? Hopefully, further investigation will determine if what is generally accepted about ethnicity and leisure holds true for aging persons.

Taken as a group, the theoretical perspectives of marginality, ethnicity, acculturation and assimilation, and the differential access model all offer speculation into late life leisure for ethnic subgroups, although few studies have sampled the elderly specifically. Viewed together, rather than singularly or as competing explanations, they offer much insight.

Marginality, focusing upon constraints, barriers, and limited opportunities, is particularly relevant when low socioeconomic status is present.

As examples, older blacks on public assistance (Brooks-Lambing, 1972) spent most of their free time on radio, television, reading, and the Bible; for urban, older, African-American women (Boyd & Tedrick, 1993), activities beyond the home, church, and senior center were not frequently mentioned.

Ethnicity theory is particularly helpful in noting intergroup differences; Stamps and Stamps (1985) reported higher correlations in activities for lower- and middle-class blacks than for whites and blacks of the same social class. Intragroup differences have been explained by the level of acculturation or assimilation on the part of ethnic subgroups. The ways in which Hispanics of differing ancestries use the outdoors has been a theme (Floyd & Gramann, 1993; Gramann, Floyd, & Saenz, 1993).

Taylor's (1992) recent analysis leading to the differential access model was significant in a number of ways. Ethnic leisure was a focus (festivals, reading matter, cooking, etc.), and care was taken in assessing ethnicity from the perspective of the respondent.

A future goal tied to both research and policy formulation is to better understand leisure throughout later life as related to gender and ethnicity. Ulyssean leisure implies a journey interpreted most appropriately in individual terms. Thus, consideration must be given to qualitative methods emphasizing symbolic interactions (Samdahl, 1987) and the subjective. Measuring the Ulyssean journey through life stories blending age, ethnicity, and gender is a task worthy of our attention.

TEN

LIVING ENVIRONMENTS

Providers of services to the elderly operate in a variety of settings, and the structure of the environments in which an individual functions is becoming an increasing concern to gerontologists. Rather than viewing the environment as a static setting into which people come to perform activities, it is being seen as a dynamic milieu that can be either penalizing or prosthetic. Therefore, it is important that people working in the environments of the elderly understand its impact and learn how to use it in such a way that it will be a positive factor in Ulyssean living.

Schaie and Willis (1999) examined "everyday competence" and aging. One of the frameworks they discuss is the congruence, or "fit," between environmental demands and an individual's cognitive competence. They indicate that, "Competent behaviors occur when the capabilities of the individual match the environmental demands and resources" (p. 181). Therefore, understanding how the environment enhances or inhibits competence is crucial in helping individuals achieve Ulyssean living. Within the person-environmental fit perspective, individuals are viewed as having lower-level needs, such as food and shelter, and higher-level needs, such as affiliation, privacy and social interaction. The three needs identified as part of self-determination theory earlier in this book, autonomy, competence, and relatedness, might be viewed as higher order needs. The role of leisure service providers within this framework would include providing environments matching an individual's abilities with the appropriate environmental structure in order to meet needs. For example, providing many opportunities for social interaction in a long-term care facility for a person with a need for relatedness would help match the environment to abilities.

This chapter will focus on the role of the environment in that process. It will provide an introduction to the role of the environment in general as well as its specific role with older individuals. This chapter will be followed by two brief chapters focusing on three environments, the age-integrated community, the age-segregated environment, and the long-term care facility.

Before examining the role of the environment in the lives of older individuals, it is necessary to determine the link between leisure and the environment. In many cases, the environment as it relates to leisure is often limited to the outdoor environment. However, that perspective does not provide the level of understanding we seek.

According to Wall (1989), "A full understanding of recreation is unlikely to be achieved in the absence of an appreciation of the attributes of the places in which people recreate, and of the ways in which environmental factors contribute to and detract from the qualities of recreational experiences" (p. 451). He identifies three components of the recreation experience: the individual and his or her attributes, other people, and the environment where the activity occurs. Although all three elements are interconnected, the focus in this chapter is on the third element.

In its most elemental form, the environment encompasses the settings where activities occur. Water is needed for swimming, outdoor areas for hiking, lighted areas for reading, and fields for baseball. However, environment is more than that. It includes "all aspects of the world around us" (Wall, 1989, p. 454). Unfortunately, the examination of environment and leisure has not developed beyond an understanding of the natural environment.

ENVIRONMENTAL CONCERNS

Human behavior is a complex phenomenon influenced by a variety of factors. This complexity contributes to the difficulty in studying behavior. However, there are approaches to interpreting behavior that are helpful. The field of environmental psychology provides an established approach. According to McAndrew (1993), environmental psychology "is the discipline that is concerned with the interactions and relationships between people and their environments" (p. 2). The focus is on the content of the environment as well as the reactions of the individual. For example, we will examine how the built environment of a long-term care facility shapes the behavior of individuals in that environment. However, we will also examine how the individual influences the environment.

McAndrew identifies several types of environments. Each can influence behavior and should be considered when examining the experiences of older individuals. The ambient environment includes factors such as sound, temperature, illumination, and odor, which provide constant sensory input that influences and affects physical well being. Think of the conditions you experience every day: the temperature of your dorm room, the smell in the cafeteria, the color of the walls in your classrooms, or the lighting in the library. You may not be aware of these things until there is a problem. At that point, you may feel uncomfortable, unable to reach your goals, or you may actually get sick. These factors may affect older individuals in the same way. Color is an excellent example of how the ambient environment can influence individuals. McAndrew's review of the literature on color reveals several interesting findings (pp. 65–66):

1.   Colors are associated with moods in the following ways:
     blue—secure, comfort, serene, calm
     red—defiant, exciting, protective
     orange—upset, distressed

purple—dignified

yellow—cheerful

black—despondent, powerful

2. Lighter-colored rooms are perceived as more spacious and bigger than dark-colored rooms.

3. Colors differ in their ability to arouse. Red is a highly arousing color. For example, research has found people walk faster in hallways of warm color (red or orange) than in cool-colored hallways, and pink rooms reduce anxiety more than red rooms.

Factors such as noise and crowding can have equally significant impacts on behavior. Excessive levels of either can result in psychological, and possibly physical, distress. Individuals working with older people need to be aware of the environment and its effect on behavior.

Parmelee and Lawton (1990) indicate that little empirical work has been done in the area of environments and aging in the previous decade. Much of what we know developed in the 1960s and 1970s. However, the older work has contemporary value and provides an exciting overview of this field.

According to Parmelee and Lawton, the primary dialectic in the field is between autonomy and security. Autonomy is defined as "the state in which the person is, or feels, capable of pursuing life goals by the use of his or her own resources; there is thus minimal need to call upon other people's resources" (p. 465).

The heart of autonomy is perceived freedom and independent action. However, the counterbalance to autonomy is security. This is defined as "a state in which pursuit of life goals is linked to, and aided dependable physical, social, and interpersonal resources. The term thus emphasizes not only physical safety or psychological peace of mind, but also the communality rather than the separateness of the person" (p. 465). The authors view the autonomy-security dichotomy as being at the heart of person-environment relations, since the independence and freedom of early and middle life should continue into later life. We all need to exercise choice and control over daily activities. Autonomy is crucial to happiness in the later years.

Parmelee and Lawton indicate that personal safety and security are major concerns among the elderly. In fact, fear of crime is a major factor in limiting involvement by older individuals. The earlier chapter on physical aspects of aging in this book indicated that factors such as poor vision, balance problems, hearing difficulties, and slower reaction time may put older individuals at greater risk of accidents than their younger counterparts.

Clearly a balance between autonomy and security is needed. Steinfeld and Shea (undated) stated, "An environment that provides a high level of safety and security is likely to have a lower level of privacy, independence and choice" (p. 1). Absolute security might be guaranteed by a closed environment with a great deal of control by facility managers, but this would minimize autonomy. Contrarily, completely independent living in an age-integrated community may assure autonomy but ignore security needs.

The approach to balancing these two needs is often presented within a person-environment fit model, which seeks the point at which the demands and characteristics of the environment are congruent with the needs, preferences, and abilities of the individual. The ultimate goal related to the environment is to achieve congruence between the demands of the environment and the abilities of older individuals (Lawton, 1989).

The environmental press model (see Figure 10.1) depicts this ideal situation. The "zone of maximum comfort" is the condition where the environmental demands are lower than the competence of the individual. Lawton describes this as the zone "characterized by the maintenance of appropriate behavior, together with a favorable level of psychological well being consisting of restfulness, relaxation, or pleasant lassitude" (p. 139). The area where the demands of the environment are greater than the individual's competence is labeled the "zone of maximum performance potential." Lawton indicates: "Provided the mismatch between demand and competence is relatively small, this situation is one where new learning and novel experience occurs" (p. 139). Either of these zones will be desirable based on the needs of individuals.

When the congruence between the demands of the environment and the competence of the individual is out of balance, an individual enters a state of stress (beyond the zone of maximum performance) or boredom and atrophy of skills (beyond the zone of maximum comfort). Seeking renewed congruence is necessary.

Figure 10.1
Ecological Model of Adaption and Aging

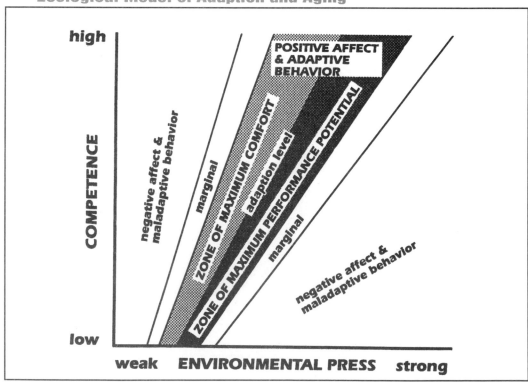

(Lawton, 1989)

Wahl (2001) updated the work of Parmelee and Lawton (1990) and reviewed recent work in the area of aging and the environment, structuring his work around the three basic functions of the environment: maintenance, stimulation, and support. Wahl looks at each of these in relation to the home and institutional environment. Maintaining one's environment is a desirable goal for older people. The evidence cited by Wahl supports the importance of retaining one's home or apartment since there is a sense of attachment to that place. The sense of being "at home" is significant in quality of life for older people. Structuring the environment and experiences to help individuals feel at home, extending even to the long-term care facility, is an appropriate role for leisure service providers. Think about the things that make you feel like the place you reside is home. You probably altered your dormitory room or apartment to make it more homelike. You exerted your own control rather than moving into a place and not shaping it in desired ways. You may have built a loft, put personal belongings in place, bought food you like, or possibly even brought your pet from home. Your desire to maintain your own home required a sense of control and ownership. Older individuals require a similar sense of ownership.

FACTORS INFLUENCING THE ENVIRONMENT

An understanding of behavior relies on an examination of the forces that operate in the environment. Crandall (1980) differentiates between the "people effect" and the "thing effect" in the environment. The people effect includes five components:

1. The type of people in the environment: Are they alert or feeble? Are they old or young? Are they open- or closed-minded?
2. The number of people in the environment: Are there enough to interact with? Are there so many it is stressful?
3. The type of interaction that occurs: It is verbal or nonverbal, equal or one-sided, personal or impersonal?
4. The amount of interaction: Is there too much or too little. Is it constant or sporadic?
5. What are the norms of behavior in the environment?

According to Crandall, the "thing" effect of the environment consists of two parts: the physical aspects of the environment, such as the arrangement of furniture, temperature, and wall color (these are similar to aspect of the ambient environment discussed above) and the non-physical aspects of the environment, such as privacy and territoriality. All these aspects of the environment influence the behavior and well being of the individual. Crandall cites research indicating the environment plays a role in an individual's physical and mental health.

Territoriality is a crucial aspect of privacy and safety. There is a need to have space we can identify as our own. As you will see in the chapter on long-term care environments, this need is often met by allowing individuals to retain some of their furniture and use it in their rooms.

Environments can also be differentiated as either "micro" or "macro" environments. The micro environment can be viewed as the identifiable places in which a person lives or interacts with others. Examples include an individual's house, a multi-purpose center, or a long-term care facility. The macro environment encompasses a broader living milieu such as the neighborhood, community, or city (Schwartz, 1975). Examination of the environment at both these levels is necessary to an understanding of behavior.

An increasing number of older people are "aging in place." In fact, approximately 70 percent of older Americans spend the rest of their lives in the place they celebrated their 65th birthday (Barbara Krueger & Associates, 1996). Successful aging in place requires environments that are safe, accessible, usable, predictable, and accommodating. Pynoos and Golant (1996) identified four strategies useful in helping people age in place: increased financial assistance, more helpful household arrangements, home modification, and responsive home and community services. Household arrangements will be discussed in Chapter 12. The sections of this chapter that follow focus on modifications of the micro and macro environments.

THE MICRO ENVIRONMENT

Several authors (Charness & Bosman, 1998; Ebersole & Hess, 2001) expounded on the value of environmental modification as a pragmatic intervention strategy. It is clear that purposive intervention into the microenvironment can play a significant role in the development of Ulyssean lifestyles.

Understanding the role of living places in individuals' lives is also important in understanding the role of the environment in later years. According to Cox (1993), the elderly are more restricted to their home environments than any group other than small children and individuals in institutions, and as a result, the "house, neighborhood, and community environment, is, therefore, more crucial to older persons than it is to other age groups" (p. 214).

The place where older individuals live provides opportunity for mastery, competence, interaction, privacy, and stimulation. Clearly the living environment is more than a static setting providing an envelope for living. It is a dynamic creation that is a factor in the quality of life experienced by individuals. Therefore, it is important to understand how the environment can be improved. Although much of the work in this area has specifically applied to the living environment, it is likely many of the suggested manipulations can apply in other environments.

Schwartz (1975) provided very specific interventions useful in using environments to improve the quality of life. Although offered several years ago, his suggestions are still appropriate today. According to Schwartz, such interventions are important in development of positive self-regard. He wrote:

> The essential concept in the design of micro-environments for the aged
> must be aimed not only at ameliorating stress, minimizing the effects of

losses, and compensating for deficits, but must do so in ways which enhance the individual's effectiveness, support their competence, and thus maintain self-esteem (p. 289).

According to Schwartz, three dimensions are relevant when considering environmental intervention: environmental cues, environmental stimulation, and environmental support. Environmental cues are necessary:

1. to identify spaces and distinguish personal or private spaces from public and shared spaces;
2. assist people in finding the way to individual areas;
3. anticipate unforeseen hazards such as stairwells, changes in slope, and slippery spaces;
4. locate needed persons;
5. locate service areas, utilities, and materials and supplies.

Suggested techniques to provide necessary cues include:

1. signs with recognizable symbols, easily read from walking or wheelchair eye level;
2. reinforcing signs at frequent intervals when crossing large spaces;
3. use of brightly colored doors and symbols to identify entry ways, utility areas, service areas, etc.;
4. use of lighting to enhance quiet areas;
5. use of textures to identify hazard areas;
6. auditory cues such as chimes to signal events such as meals, activity time, and other events;
7. automatic devices, such as sliding doors and elevators, as needed;
8. large print newsletters, and calendars;
9. other program cues.

A second area of concern is environmental stimulation. According to Schwartz, it is important to:

1. promote the use of all the senses;
2. enhance new learning behavior;
3. introduce variety into the environment;
4. challenge individuals through activities;
5. provide success experiences;
6. maximize associative inputs.

Environmental stimulation can be increased by:

1. use of bright colors;
2. use of contrasting colors;
3. introduction of changeable materials such as plants and art work into the environment;
4. enhancement of bare walls through paintings, murals, wall hangings, and the like;
5. use of multimedia programs for entertainment, discussion, and information;
6. use of materials such as oversized books to compensate for sensory losses;
7. initiation of formal sensory stimulation programs;
8. introduction of exciting foods, beverages, and spices into meals;
9. introduction of pets for stroking, observing, and loving;
10. opportunity for intergenerational contact.

The final area of concern is environmental support. Such supports are necessary to assist individuals in establishing control and competence in their environments. It can be built into the environment through techniques such as:

1. providing programs that allow real choices and control;
2. individualizing programs, activities, and leadership approaches;
3. providing prosthetic devices to compensate for losses;
4. "non-infantizing" of individuals;
5. providing opportunities for self-management even if some risk is involved;
6. designing furniture to be assistive rather than penalizing, including seats with arms or lift devices;
7. using oversized knobs and handles on doors and windows;
8. using in-house phone systems to reach staff and activity areas;
9. personalizing living and activity spaces;
10. meeting personal preferences in eating, activities, seating, etc.;
11. providing access to reading lights that are low glare, magnifying glasses, and earphones for radio and television;
12. providing personal identification for staff and others with whom the elderly will have contact.

The above listings are not comprehensive. Rather, they should be viewed as illustrative. Any intervention that will assist individuals in the mastery of their environment is legitimate.

Weiner, Brok, and Snadowsky (1987) and Ebersole and Hess (1998) echoed Schwartz's earlier concern about providing prosthetic environments to older individuals. However, Weiner et al. recommended an approach focused on more general features of helpful environments. These included:

1. prostheses for life-maintenance activities focusing on safety concerns such as non-slip floors;
2. prostheses for perceptual behavior emphasizing use of visual stimulation in the environment;
3. prostheses such as color-coded doors and hallways to aid in cognitive behavior;
4. prostheses to aid in self-maintenance skills in areas such as cooking and toileting;
5. prostheses to enhance morale;
6. prostheses to aid in retaining a sense of time (clocks and calendars), sense of self (mirrors and retention of personal objects), and autonomy (space for privacy);
7. prostheses to encourage social interaction with staff and others, including the engineering of space.

The gradual decline of the senses, discussed in Chapter 3, requires a higher threshold of sensory input be provided for stimulation. Sounds, sights, smells, and tactile sensations may need to be heightened. Older individuals may experience sensory deprivation in dull, monotonous, and nonstimulating environments. This can result in impaired thought processes, childish emotional responses, and organic deterioration. As a result, there is a need to create stimulating environments.

The living environment must be designed to incorporate sensory stimulation through the use of lighting, shapes, changeable materials, lively conversations, and any other techniques needed to activate the senses.

Facilities may need to be designed to compensate for limited mobility of the resident. The use of one level in facilities, if at all possible, is recommended. If that is not possible, an elevator may be needed for residents to use programs and facilities on the second floor. Thresholds into rooms should be eliminated to facilitate movement by wheelchairs. Good lighting in corridors and over any existing steps are important in reducing accidental falls. Handrails in traveled areas and in bathtubs are useful prosthetic devices. Slippery surfaces and loose rugs should be avoided. Logic should prevail in the design of facilities, and any potential hazard or barrier should be eliminated. In addition, it is important to include individuals with mobility impairments in planning and designing facilities.

All individuals need privacy. Crandall (1980) suggests two ways of providing privacy: physical barriers and the establishment of social rules. Setting areas apart through walls and dividers would be examples of physical barriers. Rules identifying areas as quiet areas or certain times as quiet times are examples of social rules.

The final area discussed by Crandall is comfort. The individual needs to feel at ease and comfortable in the environment. Aspects such as safety, temperature, and color are all aspects of the environment that contribute to its comfort.

Concern with environmental intervention has become evident even in the popular culture. It is no longer the domain of gerontologists and architects. Dychtwald and Flower's best-selling book (1989) included a chapter entitled "Redesigning America," detailing environmental modifications that help make life more livable. Their suggestions are extensive and too numerous to identify here. However, a partial listing will help establish their focus:

1. covering floors with carpeting or textured surfaces to reduce glare;
2. automobile dashboards with fewer reflective surfaces;
3. steering wheels with controls for lights, heating, etc. in the center;
4. elimination of high-glare fluorescent lights;
5. talking appliances, providing orally what currently is only available visually;
6. custom-programmed television and radio to compensate for hearing difficulties;
7. specially designed kitchen utensils;
8. non-skid surfaces in bathtubs and kitchens;
9. bathtubs made of resilient materials providing safety and comfort while keeping water hot;
10. street lights that change more slowly, giving pedestrians ample time to cross;
11. verbal command systems in the house and the automobile.

Charness and Bosman (1990) identify the credo for design of environments: "Know the user." Earlier chapters of this book detail changes experienced by individuals as they age. Physical, social, cognitive, and effective factors should be considered when examining environments. Charness and Bosman provide extensive resources for environmental modification, and although space does not permit complete reporting of their information, several of their suggestions are particularly useful and will be detailed here. Their guidelines for the visual environment include (p. 452):

1. avoid sudden and large shifts in illumination;
2. control glare by shielding light fixtures and using non-reflective materials on walls, ceilings, and floors; place furniture away from sources of glare; use overhangs on windows; do not locate windows at locations where falls are more likely to occur;
3. difficult color discriminations should be avoided including discriminations in the blue-green range and colors of the same hue;
4. the size of visual objects should be enlarged; use increased contrasts to identify hazards.

A series of modifications in the auditory environment are also listed:

1. background noises such as air conditioning and piped-in music should be controlled;
2. high-frequency sounds (defined as above 4,000 Hz) should be avoided;
3. the volume of important sounds should be increased;
4. visual cues should be used in addition to auditory cues.

A group of housing researchers, planners, and designers met in 1990 to address the issue of environments that would adapt to the changing needs of individuals as they age. Among the suggestions generated at the conference were 12 principles helpful in designing for older users. These included:

1. privacy;
2. social interaction;
3. choice, control, and autonomy;
4. orientation and wayfinding;
5. safety and security;
6. accessibility;
7. stimulation and challenge;
8. familiarity;
9. aesthetics;
10. personalization;
11. adaptability;
12. sensory aspects.

These design principles can be incorporated into activity areas, day care programs and recreation facilities as well as living areas.

While the goal of providing a non-penalizing environment is an important one, it is just as important not to do too much. If all risk and challenge is removed from an environment, individuals will not be challenged. The result of such an environment will be boredom and stagnation.

Baltes, Wahl, and Reichart (1991) recommend applying the principle of "just manageable difficulty" when deciding how much help and compensation is needed. This principle suggests that the demands placed on older individuals be "just manageable" by them and that their success be determined by the ability to effectively negotiate the environment at that level. Demanding too much or expecting too little are both contrary to this approach.

According to Schwartz (1975), "Any environment which tends to infantize the older person will subvert his sense of self-worth and self-esteem, and will ultimately defeat many of the positive effects which can be envisioned for an environmental design program for older people" (p. 291). The goal in environmental design is to provide a setting that allows an individual to be as independent as possible while also meeting needs for safety and security.

THE MACRO ENVIRONMENT

Ebersole and Hess (1998, 2001) included an extensive discussion of the role of the environment, specifically as it relates to safety and security. They divide space into personal and life space and suggest that the needs of each are different. Personal space is viewed as the individualized component of multiple life spaces and is more private than the largely public life space. Much of the discussion above focused on personal space. However, it is also important to focus on the larger milieu.

At the community level, environments can facilitate activities and satisfaction with life. In addition, environments provide stimulation to users, and this stimulation is important in shaping behavior (Wahl, 2001). A crucial requirement for stimulation and successful aging is the ability to move around in one's environment. According to a report from the Canadian Division of Aging and Seniors (2003), mobility is an essential element in independence and is linked to self-esteem. The report states, "Freedom to move is freedom itself." A variety of factors, personal and environmental, impact mobility. Strength, agility, sensory ability, weather, perceptions of safety, transportation availability, and the layout of streets and sidewalks can be either supportive or deleterious to mobility. A crucial factor in mobility is the ability to either drive one's self or find transportation.

Transportation is a crucial concern when working with older individuals. Many older people may be deprived of transportation, a "critical link in the ability of the elderly to remain independent and functional" (Ebersol & Hess, 2001, p. 473). Lack of a car, failure of public transportation to meet needs, poor driving skills, and economic constraints may result in limits in mobility. It is noteworthy that Ebersole and Hess view transportation for pleasure and recreation as a crucial need that often goes unmet. Some suggested solutions to transportation problems include:

1. use of volunteer drivers;
2. reduced or subsidized fares on public transportation;
3. transit systems designed for older users, including appropriate routes and schedules;
4. charter bus trips;
5. sponsorship of safe-driving programs.

Programs that fail to take transportation needs into account will exclude many participants. Planners need to always keep this crucial service in the forefront when planning programs.

A second crucial life space issue is crime. Many older individuals identify this as a major concern, greater than safety and health concerns. This fear can deprive an older person of opportunities for Ulyssean living and therefore should be addressed by service providers. Crime prevention programs may be excellent additions to the list of recreation opportunities available to older individuals. In addition, care should be taken in scheduling activities since evening programs may be problematic for many.

The life space concept is related to Regnier's (1975) concept of critical distance. Although the work he cited was done more than 25 years ago, it does point toward a focus we should retain. Critical distance is the distance individuals are willing to travel for a service. For example, some services are viewed as "core," and the desire is to have these within walking distance. A bus stop, grocery store, drug or variety store, bank, post office, and church are included in this core. If transportation is not available, the core can be expanded to include a hospital, senior center, park, library, dry cleaners and luncheonette or snack bar. Other services and facilities, including movie theaters and bars, may be located farther than walking distance and still be viewed as accessible.

The distance at which services and facilities become inaccessible will of course vary as a result of factors such as health and fitness of the individual identifying the critical distance, topography, and weather. What is important is that service providers be aware of the impact of the location of things in the macro environment and plan accordingly.

Weiner, Brok, and Snadowsky (1987) introduced the concept of "radius of activities" to address issues similar to those identified within the critical distances framework. Understanding an individual's spatial world allows service providers to identify ways to expand that world since environments may restrict the sphere in which people operate.

Weiner et al. suggest discussing the radius of activity with individuals in hopes of identifying restricting factors and broadening involvement. They recommend focusing on the variety of locations where activities occur and identifying the potential barriers to behavior within each. These locales include:

1. Home
2. On my block
3. Within a five-block area of home
4. Neighborhood
5. Other neighborhood in town or city
6. State
7. Outside state
8. Outside the United States

Reviewing the activities and barriers within each locale will provide an effective tool for expanding the possibilities for Ulyssean living. For example, one of the authors of this book recalls working with a senior center that was moved from the activity room in a high-rise apartment for older residents to a nearby building that had been converted from a school to a multipurpose center. The new location was a much better facility than the earlier one. It had more space, more services, and more activities. However, many people who had attended the programs at the original site did not come to the new location. After much speculation about why this had occurred, it was decided to question those who had stopped attending. It was found that a traffic light on a street that had to be crossed by many individuals who wanted to walk to the center did not stay green long enough for them to safely cross. Changing the timing on the light had a dramatic effect on participation.

Identification of locales may point toward self-imposed limits on movement that may restrict Ulyssean living and should be removed. Weiner et al. (1987) concluded: "Anyone who works with an older population must pay particular attention to the influence of environmental factors on observed behavior. This is especially true if the aim is to help motivate an exploratory attitude" (p. 25—emphasis added). It is this exploratory attitude that facilitates the Ulyssean lifestyle.

Howe (1992) discusses the need for "linkages" in the macro environment. If any part of the environment is inaccessible or penalizing, the entire environment is suspect. As Howe indicated, a state-of-the-art bathroom in a senior center that has a gravel-topped parking lot is of no use to an individual in a wheelchair. Similarly, an excellent program at a facility that does not provide transportation will not be successful. Involving older individuals in the planning and design process is one way to ensure all elements in a facility are linked and usable.

Cox (1993) identified several techniques for deciding what environmental modifications are desirable. The extent to which older individuals are involved in the process varies. These approaches can be revised into the following three perspectives:

1. The older individual plans and initiates changes in the environment. This self-directed approach is desirable for Ulyssean living. If older individuals are made aware of the role of the environment in their lives and educated in ways of manipulating the environment, the likelihood of this approach occurring will be increased.
2. The older individual can work collaboratively with other individuals in redesigning the environment to achieve a desired goal. Architects, planners, recreators, social workers and counselors could play a role in the design process.
3. Experts, such as architects, design the environment for older individuals. The outsiders design a prosthetic environment based on their knowledge of the needs of older individuals.

All three approaches could yield designs conducive to Ulyssean living.

Howe (1992) summed up the need for designing user-friendly macro environments: "Planning for an aging society means planning for people. It means recognizing the diversity within our population and facilitating the development of a built environment that accommodates rather than confronts this diversity. Keeping in mind the needs of older Americans will help create vital communities that are good places in which to live and grow old" (p. 7).

CONCLUSIONS

The environment in which individuals live and play has a significant impact on behavior. Ulyssean living can be enhanced by the creation of prosthetic environments designed to help compensate for the physical and cognitive losses that accompany the aging process. In most cases, the creation of optimal environments will not require a great deal of effort. In fact, minimal changes are often preferable to major renovations that may reduce autonomy. Individual needs should determine the extent of environmental modification. Issues of choice, control, independence, stimulation, security, and safety must all be considered.

Changes may be needed in environments that are essentially personal, such as living spaces, as well as the larger environment, such as a neighborhood. Optimum modification will consider both levels while retaining the individual as the central focus. This will ensure modifications follow the principle of "just manageable difficulty" and are therefore prosthetic without overcompensating for losses.

ELEVEN

LEISURE AND RECREATION IN LONG-TERM CARE

Judith E. Voelkl

Traditionally when one hears the words "long-term care" he or she will picture a nursing home facility. In recent years, partially due to the growing number of older adults and the broad range of their abilities and needs, we find a number of different long-term care services designed to support the independence and quality of life of older adults. Long-term care ranges from home-health care to adult day health care centers, assisted-living facilities, and nursing homes.

Most frequently we find recreation and leisure services provided in residential long-term care settings such as assisted-living facilities and nursing homes. In this chapter we will discuss residential long-term care facilities and present information on the older adults who reside in such facilities, as well as the programming principles that guide recreation services in such settings. Community-based long-term care services, including home-health and adult day care centers, will be discussed in Chapter 12 Community Services.

WHAT IS LONG-TERM CARE?

Long-term care has been defined as "assistance given over a sustained period of time to people who are experiencing long-term inabilities or difficulties in functioning because of a disability" (Kane, Kane, & Ladd, 1998, p. 4). Typically, we find that older adults seeking long-term care services have one or more chronic conditions, such as arthritis, hypertension, or diabetes, that impair their day-to-day functioning. For instance, some older adults have conditions that result in loss of independence in activities of daily living (ADLs), including such as dressing, eating, or bathing. The same chronic conditions may also impair an elder's independence in instrumental activities of daily living (IADLs), including such as shopping, managing their money, or making telephone calls. Long-term care environments, therefore, are in the unique position of providing care for elders' chronic conditions as well as supporting elders' independence in ADLs and IADLs.

Although older adults, their family members, and health care providers may initially focus on the impact that chronic conditions have on activities of daily living, increased attention is being given to how these same chronic conditions may impact an older adult's social relationships and engagement in meaningful leisure activities (Kane, 2003; Kane, Kane, & Ladd, 1998). For example, Mabel, who is an 83-year-old widow living in an assisted-living facility, recently had a stroke that has impaired her mobility. Mabel, her family, and the staff at the facility were concerned initially with how Mabel would continue to live independently in her apartment and arranged for support with house cleaning and bathing. Several months later her daughter began to notice that her mother's contact with friends via weekly bridge games and church socials had ceased. Mabel's friends had difficulty in assisting Mabel in and out of their cars. The lack of transportation resulted in Mabel decreasing her social network and meaningful engagements. Mabel and her daughter began to consider increasing involvement in the recreation programs offered within the assisted-living facility as well as encouraging her weekly bridge group to meet in one of the facility's lounges. Such support would allow Mabel to maintain her preferred level of social engagement and continued involvement in a life-long bridge group.

Long-term care environments vary in the degree of attention given to both independence in functional abilities (i.e., activities of daily living) and independence in social relations and leisure pursuits. Such variability is linked to whether a long-term care facility adopts a health model, a social model, or a 'hybrid' model that combines the medical and social model (Kane, Kane, & Ladd, 1998). As depicted in Table 11.1, the model chosen to guide service delivery in an agency will influence the roles and relationships among care staff and residents. For example, service delivery based on the traditional health model focuses on the maintenance and improvement of the older adult's physical and mental functioning. In such cases a recreation professional may lead a daily current events group in which she reads and discusses newspaper articles with residents in order to support the maintenance of residents' cognitive functioning. In contrast, service delivery based on a social model results in the active involvement of the older adult in designing services that promote his or her subjective well being. For instance, Jack who has a life-long passion for tailgating, plans the football tailgates for all residents who are interested.

The third and final model, the hybrid model, which is increasingly prevalent in long-term care facilities, combines the health and social models and addresses residents' functional abilities and quality of life. In facilities using the hybrid model, the recreation professional provides a broad range of activities, with some activities designed to maintain and enhance residents' physical and cognitive functioning, such as walking, current events and jigsaw puzzles, while other activities provide opportunities to maintain involvement in life-long leisure pursuits and maintain or develop meaningful social relationships.

Table 11.1. Care Models (Adapted from Kane, Kane, and Ladd, 1998, p.191)

	Health	Social	Hybrid
Goals	Physical and mental health; focus on therapeutic goals.	Quality of life; care compensates for impairment; focus on older adult's life goals.	Therapeutic and compensatory goals.
Role of Care Provider	Identify health problems and solutions.	Facilitate consumer identifying needs to promote well being.	Both care provider and consumer identify needs.
Role of Older Adult	Consent or refuse treatment.	Older adults make all decisions; constraints to choice due to legal or functional competence.	Extent of older adult choice is unclear.

PROMOTING FUNCTION AND QUALITY OF LIFE THROUGH RECREATION AND LEISURE

Recent legislative actions, primarily the Omnibus Budget Reconciliation Act of 1987 (OBRA) for nursing homes and recent legislative hearings on quality control in assisted living (U.S. Congress, 1987; U. S. Senate, 2002), have changed the nature of care in long-term care facilities and moved long-term care toward a social or hybrid model of care. More specifically, OBRA mandates that all nursing home facilities provide "activities designed to meet the interests and the physical, mental, and psychosocial well being of each resident" (U. S. Congress, 1987), suggesting the need for a hybrid model in long-term care. As recreation and leisure service providers we are faced with the several important questions:

- What role should a long-term care facility take to improve residents' functional abilities? Quality of life?
- How may such a role differ from one aimed at merely making residents' lives more comfortable?
- Is the notion of Ulyssean living applicable in the lives of older adults residing in long-term care facilities? More specifically, can residents of long-term care facilities grow and develop? Can they experience old age in a positive way?

We know, based on previous research (Langer & Rodin, 1976; Saul, 1993; Voelkl, 1993), that activity opportunities and involvement have been found to increase residents' self-esteem, happiness and self-concept (see Table 11.2 for an example of an activity calendar). Ultimately,

Table 11.2
Example of an Activity Calendar
The Courtyard (provided by Jennifer Carson)

Sunday	Monday	Tuesday	Wednesday	Thursday	Friday	Saturday
1 **Morning:** Dancing **Afternoon:** Hymns & Bible Story; Life Work: Chop Vegetables **Evening:** Classic Stories	**2** **Morning:** Beauty Salon; Outdoor Strolls **Afternoon:** Manicures; Piano Music **Evening:** Living Legacies	**3** **Morning:** Dancing **Afternoon:** Gazebo Social; Scenic Drive; Guitar Music **Evening:** Reminiscing	**4** **Morning:** Life Work **Afternoon:** Rabbit Visits; Patriotic Sing-a-Long **Evening:** Hymn & Bible Story	**5** **Morning:** Set Dining Room Tables **Afternoon:** Souvenirs; Scenic Drive; Backyard Adventure **Evening:** Foot Baths/Pedicures	**6** **Morning:** Outdoor Strolls **Afternoon:** Beauty Basket & Men s Grooming; Tying Flies **Evening:** Living Legacies	**7** **Morning:** Life Work: Folding Laundry **Afternoon:** Classic Stories & Tea; Guitar Music **Evening:** Reminisce Group
8 **Morning:** Gardening **Afternoon:** Hymns & Bible Story; Life Work: Wash Car & Work on Boat **Evening:** Classic Stories	**9** **Morning:** Beauty Salon; Outdoor Strolls **Afternoon:** Manicures; Accordion **Evening:** Living Legacies	**10** **Morning:** Dancing **Afternoon:** Gazebo Social; Scenic Drive; Guitar Music **Evening:** Reminiscing	**11** **Morning:** Life Work **Afternoon:** Fast Food Delivery!; Jazz Guitar; Painting Demonstration **Evening:** Hymns & Bible Story	**12** **Morning:** Set Dining Room Tables **Afternoon:** Tea Cup Collections; Scenic Drive; Backyard Adventure **Evening:** Foot Baths/Pedicures	**13** **Morning:** Outdoor Strolls **Afternoon:** Beauty Basket & Men s Grooming; Creative Painting **Evening:** Living Legacies	**14** **Morning:** Life Work: Sorting Objects **Afternoon:** Classic Stories & Tea; Guitar Music **Evening:** Reminisce Group
15 **Morning:** Gardening **Afternoon:** Hymns & Bible Story; Life Work: Folding Laundry **Evening:** Classic Stories	**16** **Morning:** Beauty Salon; Outdoor Strolls **Afternoon:** Manicures; Guitar Music **Evening:** Living Legacies	**17** **Morning:** Dancing **Afternoon:** Gazebo Social; Scenic Drive; Guitar Music **Evening:** Reminiscing	**18** **Morning:** Life Work **Afternoon:** Simple Craft; Family & Staff Apple Pie Contest **Evening:** Hymns & Bible Story	**19** **Morning:** Set Dining Room Tables **Afternoon:** Art Collection; Scenic Drive; Backyard Adventure **Evening:** Foot Baths/Pedicures	**20** **Morning:** Outdoor Strolls **Afternoon:** Beauty Basket & Men s Grooming; Guitar Music **Evening:** Living Legacies	**21** **Morning:** Life Work: Fill Birdfeeders **Afternoon:** Classic Stories & Tea; Happy Hour **Evening:** Reminisce Group
22 **Morning:** Dancing **Afternoon:** Hymns & Bible Story; Life Work: Polishing Silver **Evening:** Classic Stories	**23** **Morning:** Beauty Salon; Outdoor Strolls **Afternoon:** Manicures; Accordion **Evening:** Living Legacies	**24** **Morning:** Dancing **Afternoon:** Gazebo Social; Scenic Drive; Guitar Music **Evening:** Reminiscing	**25** **Morning:** Life Work **Afternoon:** Music Therapy; Ice-cream Sundaes!; Simple Painting **Evening:** Hymns & Bible Story	**26** **Morning:** Set Dining Room Tables **Afternoon:** Doll Collections; Scenic Drive; Backyard Adventure **Evening:** Foot Baths/Pedicures	**27** **Morning:** Outdoor Strolls **Afternoon:** You-Can-Sing Foundation Perf; Gazebo Social **Evening:** Living Legacies	**28** **Morning:** Life Work: Stacking Wood **Afternoon:** Classic Stories & Tea; Guitar Music **Evening:** Reminisce Group
29 **Morning:** Gardening **Afternoon:** Hymns & Bible Story; Life Work: Grinding and Making Coffee **Evening:** Classic Stories	**30** **Morning:** Beauty Salon; Outdoor Strolls **Afternoon:** Music Therapy; Piano Music **Evening:** Living Legacies	**31** **Morning:** Dancing **Afternoon:** Gazebo Social; Scenic Drive; Guitar Music **Evening:** Reminiscing	**Resident Birthdays!** Elizabeth 07/05 Harold 07/14 Pauline 07/16 Callie 07/26 Minnie 07/31	**Staff Birthdays!** Bill 07/01 Jennifer 07/11 Chuck 07/23 Cynthia 07/29	**Volunteers Wanted** Mondays, 10:00 am-3:00 pm, In-House Beauty Salon Companion Tuesday & Thursdays, 2:00-3:30 pm, Scenic Drive Assistant	Use what talents you possess: the woods would be very silent if no birds sang there except those that sang best. Henry Van Dyke

activities have been found to improve quality of life in what has traditionally been viewed as a stagnant, penalizing environment. One of the benefits provided by activities is a sense of involvement and individuality within institutional settings. The long-term care environment may make it more difficult to achieve continued growth and development but it is possible. Increased efforts on the part of trained, professional staff is needed. Recreation professionals are a necessary part of this effort. Efforts at creating resident councils (Wells & Singer, 1988), encouraging independence and success in activities (Voelkl, 1986), taking activities to residents when needed, maximizing control, and addressing residents' needs are crucial.

In the following sections we will discuss the characteristics and residents of nursing homes and assisted-living facilities, as well as approaches to designing and delivering recreation programs that may enhance residents' Ulyssean living. Program strategies designed to promote choice and control, increased involvement in activities, validate residents' experience, as well as program models such as treatment protocols for dementia care, Eden Alternative, and a family model, all have the potential for promoting Ulyssean living among residents of long-term care facilities.

LONG-TERM CARE FACILITIES

ASSISTED-LIVING FACILITIES

Assisted living, a relatively new option in the long-term care continuum of services, provides a welcome alternative to residency in a nursing home. Seniors seeking assisted living typically need less medical care than nursing home residents. Seniors moving into assisted-living facilities may select either studios or one-bedroom apartments and, in many cases, residents may choose to furnish the living space with cherished belongings from their life-long homes. Residents may have private bathrooms or, in some facilities, shared bathrooms. Just less than half of assisted living-facilities offer kitchens within private living space, with 25 percent of facilities offering kitchenettes and 19 percent offering full kitchens (National Center for Assisted Living, 2003).

Assisted-living facilities are known by numerous names, which may make it difficult to initially identify the assisted-living facilities in your community. They may be touted as residential care, boarding homes, or adult congregate care, to name a few. According to the National Academy for State Health Policy, as of the year 2000 there were 32,886 licensed assisted-living facilities in the United States with 795,391 beds (National Center for Assisted Living, 2003).

There are several characteristics common to all facilities that fall under the umbrella of "assisted living." For instance, assisted-living facilities are:

- "congregate residential settings that provide or coordinates personal services, 24-hour supervision and assistance, activities, and health-related services;

- designed to minimize the need to move;
- designed to accommodate individual residents' changing needs and preferences;
- designed to maximize residents' dignity, autonomy, privacy, independence, choice and safety; and
- designed to encourage family and community involvement" (National Center for Assisted Living, 2003).

The services provided by assisted-living facilities suggest that service delivery is based on a hybrid model that addresses both functional abilities and quality of life. The impetus for assisted living, however, was to focus predominately on a social model when designing services for residents (Carder, 2002).

According to the National Center for Assisted Living (2003), the typical resident of an assisted-living facility is a woman (69 percent females) who is 80 years of age. Eighty-one percent of residents need assistance with one or more ADL (i.e., bathing, dressing, transferring, toileting, eating). The average number of ADLs for which residents need assistance is 2.25. A vast majority of residents (93 percent) receive assistance with housework as well as help with daily medications (86 percent).

Little work has been done to document and understand the activity and social engagement of residents in assisted-living facilities. One recent study conducted by Zimmerman, Scott, Park, Hall, Wetherby, Gruber-Baldini, and Morgan (2003) provides us with some insights into the engagement patterns of 2,078 residents residing in several different types of assisted-living facilities, including small facilities with less than 16 beds, "new" facilities (built after 1987) with more than 16 beds, and "old" facilities (built prior to 1987) with more than 16 beds. Residents fell into three different activity patterns with the first group participating at high levels in private activities such as writing letters, reading, working on hobbies, and talking on the telephone, the second group participated at high levels in group activities such as arts and crafts, cards and games, and religious services, and the third group participated at high levels in outings such as eating, shopping, and walking. In general, residents of "old" facilities tended to participate in private activities at high levels. Whereas residents in "new" facilities participated in group activities and outings at high levels. Although further work is needed to understand both the facility characteristics and personal characteristics that may influence residents' activity patterns, the findings of this study suggest that regardless of type of facility, residents do engage in high levels of activity. Such activity patterns speak to residents' continued growth and active involvement, which supports the notion of Ulyssean living among residents of assisted-living facilities.

NURSING HOME FACILITIES

Nursing homes are residential facilities that are licensed by the state. Based on a health model, or in some instances a hybrid model, the primary concern in most nursing homes is the care for residents' chronic conditions.

Older adults residing in nursing homes typically live in "semi-private" rooms which are small bedrooms that are shared with one roommate. Meals are served in a common dining area. Residents are expected to adjust to the institutional routine of the nursing home, which typically begins with morning wake-ups at 6 a.m., followed by staff assistance with dressing and toileting, and breakfast in the dining room. Morning hours consist of bathing and current events and exercise groups. Following lunch in the dining room, there are typically large group activities at 2 or 3 p.m. in the afternoon. Dinner is served at approximately 5 p.m.. Most residents go to bed between 7 and 9 p.m.. This routine is followed day after day (see Kidder, 1994, for a detailed description of nursing home life).

According to the National Nursing Home Survey of 1999 (Jones, 2002), there are 18,000 nursing homes with a total of 1,879,600 beds in the United States. A majority of these nursing homes are for-profit (67 percent) and less than one-third are non-profit facilities (27 percent). Three levels of care are provided in nursing homes. The level of service will depend on the needs of the individual. Tedrick and Green (1995) identify the levels of care as:

a.   skilled nursing care—intensive, 24-hour-a-day care, supervised by a registered nurse and under the direction of a physician;

b.   intermediate nursing care— involving some nursing assistance and supervision but less than 24-hour nursing care;

c.   custodial care—room and board, with assistance in personal care, but not necessarily health care services.

The majority of older adults residing in nursing homes in the United States tend to be female, age 75 or older, and in need of assistance in more than three activities of daily living (e.g., dressing, bathing, toileting; Jones, 2002). More specifically, as we consider the characteristics of the 1,628,300 older adults residing in nursing homes, we find that 16.4 percent of residents are between the ages of 65 and 74 (i.e., young-old), 35.1 percent are between the ages of 75 and 84 (i.e., old), and 36.8% are 85 years of age and older (i.e., old-old). Female residents outnumber male residents 62 to 38. A majority of residents need assistance with bathing (93.8 percent), dressing (86.5 percent), and toileting (56 percent). Residents' impairments are also evident in their need for eyeglasses (62 percent) and use of wheelchairs (62 percent).

Throughout several decades, investigators have examined residents' time use in order to begin to address the issue of quality of life in nursing homes. In a recent study by Shore, Lerman, Smith, Iwata, and DeLeon (1995) residents' time use was examined. Based on 85 observations conducted on four units, they reported that residents were most frequently engaged in no activity (51.4 percent), followed by engagement in appropriate non-social activities (34 percent; e.g., ambulation, TV, eating), and appropriate social activities (12.1 percent; e.g., conversation, receiving care or instruction). When comparing time-use on weekdays to weekends, residents were found to spend significantly more time in no-activity on weekends and significantly less time in appropriate social and non-social activities on weekends.

Efforts have also been undertaken to describe the characteristics of those residents who participate in group activities. Based on a sample of 3,008 nursing home residents, Voelkl, Fries, and Galecki (1995) reported that residents' mean time in activities was less than four hours per week (mean time of 217 minutes per week). In terms of characteristics that predict time in activities, the results indicated that resource use (time receiving nursing care), cognitive abilities, depression, activity preferences, sense of initiative and involvement, location preferences, gender, and a facility indicator, were each statistically significant. More specifically, those residents receiving high levels of resources (i.e., nursing care) spent little time in activities. Those residents with moderately-severe or severe cognitive impairments had high levels of time in activities and residents with very-severe cognitive impairments had the lowest mean time in activities. Residents who were non-depressed and those with a high sense of involvement in the facility had high levels of activities in comparison to those residents who were depressed and those with a low sense of involvement. Residents with a preference for the day area had high levels of time in activities in comparison to residents with preferences for their own room or no preference. Lastly, women were found to spend greater amounts of time in activities than men.

These studies (Shore, Lerman, Smaith, Iwata, & DeLeon, 1995; Voelkl, Fries, & Galecki, 1995), as well as previously conducted studies (Gottesman & Bourestrom, 1974), speak to the concern that residents of nursing homes may have limited opportunities for Ulyssean living. In particular, there is a need to target recreation opportunities for residents with low levels of activity participation, including those who receive high levels of nursing care, those who are depressed, and those with very-severe cognitive impairments. There is also a need to consider how to design inviting and comfortable activity spaces for residents who typically prefer staying in their own rooms. In the following sections we will address strategies and programs that have been used successfully to promote engagement in meaningful, growth-producing activities among all residents of nursing homes.

RESIDENT BILL OF RIGHTS

All nursing home facilities are required by law to provide each resident with a copy of his or her rights. Frequently, states outline the rights of residents of nursing homes and provide a template of resident rights that may be used by individual facilities. Assisted-living facilities are also beginning to provide residents with a bill of rights. In the state of North Carolina, for example, the Division of Aging has outlined a bill of rights for (a) adult-care homes (see Table 11.3), including assisted-living facilities, and for (b) nursing homes (see Table 11.4). Many of the rights articulated in such bills are directly related to activity programs and services, such as the right to be treated with respect, the right to communicate with persons and groups of one's choice, and to enjoy privacy. We encourage readers to review residents' rights and to discuss the impact they may have on the role of the recreation professional as well as the design of activity programs in long-term care settings.

Table 11.3. North Carolina's Adult Care Home Bill of Rights (North Carolina Division of Aging, 2003).

"Every Resident shall have the following rights:

1   To be treated with respect, consideration, dignity, and full recognition of his or her individuality and right to privacy.

2   To receive care and services which are adequate, appropriate, and in compliance with relevant federal and State laws and rules and regulations.

3   To receive upon admission and during his or her stay a written statement of the services provided by the facility and the charges for these services.

4   To be free of mental and physical abuse, neglect, and exploitation.

5   Except in emergencies, to be free from chemical and physical restraint unless authorized for a specified period of time by a physician according to clear and indicated medical need.

6   To have his/her personal and medical records kept confidential and not disclosed without the written consent of the individual or guardian.

7   To receive a reasonable response to his or her request from the facility administrator and staff.

8   To associate and communicate privately and without restriction with people and groups of his or her own choice on his or her own or their initiative at any reasonable hour.

9   To have access at any reasonable hour to a telephone where he or she may speak privately.

10 To send and receive mail promptly and unopened, unless the resident requests that someone open and read mail, and to have access at his or her expense to writing instruments, stationary, and postage.

11 To be encouraged to exercise his or her rights as a resident and citizen, and to be permitted to make complaints and suggestions without fear of coercion or retaliation.

12 To have and use his or her own possessions where reasonable and have an accessible, lockable space provided for security of personal valuables.

13 To manage his or her personal needs funds unless such authority has been delegated to another.

14 To be notified when the facility is issued a provisional license or notice of revocation of license.

15 To have freedom to participate by choice in accessible community activities and in social, political, medical, and religious resources and to have freedom to refuse such participation.

16   To receive upon admission to the facility a copy of this section.

17   To not be transferred or discharged from a faculty except for medical reasons, the resident's own or other residents' welfare, nonpayment for the stay, or when the transfer is mandated under State or federal law."

Table 11.4. North Carolina's Bill of Rights for Nursing Home Residents (North Carolina Division of Aging, 2003).

"Every Resident shall have the following rights:

1   To be treated with consideration, respect, and full recognition of personal dignity and individuality.

2   To receive care, treatment, and services that are adequate and appropriate, and in compliance with relevant federal and state statues and rules.

3   To receive at the time of admission and during stay, a written statement of services provided by the facility, including those required to be offered on an as-needed basis, and of related charges.

4   To have on file physician's orders with proposed schedule of medical treatment.

5   To receive respect and privacy in his medical care program. All personal and medical records are confidential.

6   To be free of mental and physical abuse. Except in emergencies, to be free of chemical and physical restraint unless authorized for a specified period of time by a physician according to clear and indicated medical need.

7   To receive from the administrator or staff of the facility a reasonable response to all requests.

8   To associate and communicate privately and without restriction with persons and groups of the patient's choice at any reasonable hour.

9   To manage his/her own financial affairs unless other legal arrangements have been implemented.

10   To have privacy in visits by the patient's spouse, and if both are patients in the same facility, they shall be given the opportunity, where feasible, to share a room.

11   To enjoy privacy in his/her room.

12   To present grievances and recommend changes in policies and services personally, through other persons or in combination with others, without fear of reprisal, restraint, interference, coercion, or discrimination.

13   To not be required to perform services for the facility without personal consent and the written approval of the attending physician.

14   To retain, to secure storage for, and to use his personal clothing and possessions, where reasonable.

15   To not be transferred or discharged from a facility except for medical, financial, or their own or other patient's welfare, nonpayment for the stay or when mandated by Medicare or Medicaid.

16   To be notified within ten days after the facility's license is revoked or made provisional."
(North Carolina Division of Aging, 2003).

PROGRAM STRATEGIES AND MODELS

Recreation programs in long-term care facilities are designed to enhance and maintain residents' functional abilities and/or promote residents' quality of life via engagement in meaningful activity pursuits. Predominately, we find that recreation programs in long-term care to be based on a social model, with leisure service providers paying careful attention to how their programs support residents' continued growth, development, and Ulyssean living. As we introduce you to effective program strategies and models used in long-term care, keep in mind that little has been written about strategies and models used in assisted-living facilities. Although the strategies and models discussed reflect state-of-the-art nursing home care, we believe that many of these approaches may be adapted for assisted-living facilities.

PROGRAM STRATEGIES

Increased Control

An important goal of programs in long-term care facilities is to increase residents' perceived control (Bocksnick & Hall, 1994; Martin & Smith, 1993). According to Saul (1993) most residents of long-term care facilities experience a perceived loss of personal control. Indeed, institutionalization by definition requires giving up a degree of control over one's own life. Saul believes individuals should be given "active control" over their own lives. Allowing residents to plan, organize and conduct activities as much as possible will restore some control to participants. A variety of programs have been used to do this. Two will be detailed in this section.

Langer and Rodin (1976) studied the effects of enhanced personal responsibility and choice on residents of a long-term care facility. They believed most long-term care facilities to be decision-free environments and saw a need to return choice and control to the residents. They created a "responsibility-induced group" and a control group in order to assess the effect of choice on residents' lives. The responsibility-induced group was told they were responsible for their own actions and then were asked to select a plant and were given responsibility to care for it. In addition, they were told movies were shown several nights a week and were asked to choose the night they would like to attend. The other group was given a plant and were told the staff would care for it. In addition, individuals in this group were told what night they were to come to the movie. It was found that the group given choice and control in their own lives were happier, more active, spent more time visiting with other residents, spent more time visiting with people from outside the institution, spent more time talking to staff, were rated as being less passive, and had higher movie attendance.

A similar study by Banziger and Roush (1983) used bird feeders to introduce personal responsibility and control into a long-term care facility. One group of residents received a verbal message that they were responsible for making their own decisions and for their own lives. They were also told birds were having a difficult time surviving and each person was requested to care for a bird feeder placed on their window. A second group of residents was told the staff were responsible for their care and were not given the opportunity to maintain bird feeders. A third group received no verbal message and no bird feeder. It was found that the residents given responsibility experienced an increase in life satisfaction, an increase in self-reported control, increased happiness and increased activity levels.

Research by Shary and Iso-Ahola (1989) as well as Vallerand, O'Connor and Blais (1989) has supported the crucial role choice and self-determination has in the quality of life for residents of long-term care facilities. The ability to make choices related to mealtime, personal care, room decoration, and encouragement of self-initiative by staff were related to life satisfaction.

Recreation and leisure professionals may promote residents' perceptions of control through the following strategies:

- Assess residents' preferences. Build on that information by providing opportunities to participate in preferred activities.
- When necessary, adapt preferred activities to ensure a level of participation that is rewarding and provides a sense of control and mastery.
- Provide residents with the opportunity to lead and facilitate preferred activities.
- Provide opportunities for residents to plan large group activities, i.e., cookouts, outings, music groups, etc.
- Build opportunities for residents to express choice and experience autonomy in every activity!

Validation Therapy

Validation therapy was developed by Feil (1993) and provides care providers with an effective means of interacting with older adults with cognitive impairments or some type of dementia. According to Toseland, Diehl, Freeman, Manzanares, Naleppa and McCallion (1997) validation therapy is based on the belief that the behavior of older adults with dementia, regardless of how unusual, occurs for a reason. Individuals adapt to their illness by using whatever abilities remain intact. According to Toseland et al. "when short-term memory is impaired, older adults with dementia use memories and feelings from the distant past to help them continue to communicate with others. Similarly, when language abilities are lost, older adults rely on repetitive vocalizations and motions and on effective responses to communicate" (p. 32). These adaptations are survival techniques and explain what may appear to be unusual behaviors.

Validation therapy accepts the behavior of the individual as a starting point and does not attempt to impose the staff's reality on the older person with dementia. It de-emphasizes the relevance of orientation while exploring the meanings and motivations for the observed behaviors (Scanland & Emershaw, 1993). The approach is marked by respect for the older person's feeling in whatever time or place is real to him or her (Gagnon, 1996). The techniques used in validation therapy are based on empathy and unconditional regard for the individual and are designed to stimulate communication while tuning into and validating the communication of the older person (Toseland et al., 1997).

A validation therapy group typically consists of five to 10 individuals in a structured situation designed to stimulate energy, social interaction, and social roles. It includes music, talk, movement and food (Gagnon, 1996; Validation Training Institute, 1997). Toseland and his associates described a validation therapy group they ran as part of a study of its impact. Their program was divided into four segments of five to 10 minutes each. The session began with warm greetings, hand holding and singing in order to stimulate participants. This was followed by bringing up a topic of interest and encouraging reminiscence about the topic. This was done to encourage interaction and communication. The third stage of the program focused on an activity such as singing or poetry reading. The session closed with refreshments and saying good-bye to each member individually and thanking them for coming. During the session, the leaders used the techniques common in validation therapy:

1. the use of nonthreatening, concrete, simple words;
2. using a low, clear, empathetic tone of voice;
3. rephrasing and paraphrasing unclear verbal communication;
4. responding to the explicit and implicit meaning in verbal and nonverbal communications;
5. mirroring nonverbal and verbal communication (Toseland et al., 1997).

Data examining the efficacy of validation therapy are limited and the findings related to its efficacy are ambiguous. Toseland and his co-authors identified five studies in the literature and these were flawed in their methodology. Nevertheless, validation therapy is becoming more widespread and accepted as an effective technique to use with confused elderly.

Environmental Design

In recent years the long-term care industry has paid increased attention to environmental design and its impact on the lives of residents and care staff (e.g., Calkins, 1988; Lawton, 1986; Lawton, Weisman, Sloane, Norris-Baker, Calkins, & Zimmerman, 2000). Such efforts involve examination of the social environment, the organizational culture, and the physical environment. More specifically, the social environment, which includes the characteristics, numbers, and roles of residents, family members, and care staff, the organizational culture, which includes the norms and policies that influence the roles and behaviors of residents, family members, and care staff, and the physical environment all interact to create the overall long-term care environment.

Frequently, we find that recreation professionals employed in long-term care are being called upon to carefully analyze and design common areas that promote a level of social interaction and activity engagement that matches the model of care espouses by the facility. For example, a recreation professional employed in a facility that espouses a social model and is seeking to create a home-like environment may be asked to participate in the design of "family rooms" that foster social and activity engagement. In such an instance, the recreation professionals may begin by evaluating the social environment by asking who currently uses the family rooms and whether or not changes need to occur in use patterns. The recreation professionals may also consider how roles and norms may influence current behavior patterns. For instance, do staff sit in the family rooms to do their daily charting, thereby communicating that the family room is really a staff room? If this is the case the recreation professional would need to work with the administrative team and care staff to consider how changes can be made so that care staff use the family room for behaviors typical of such a space, such as sitting and talking with a resident, working on a puzzle with a resident and family member, or sharing the colorful pictures from a favorite cookbook with a resident. Finally, the recreation professional would consider the placement of furniture and resources in order to support residents', family members', and care staff's independent engagement in social and recreational pursuits. Pre- and post-design pictures show how two recreation therapists and an architect resigned a sunroom on a special care unit to foster social interaction and engagement in meaningful recreation pursuits (Carson, Battisto, & Voelkl, 2003; see Figures 11.1 and 11.2). Intimate seating areas and the provision of recreation resources were used to foster residents' active engagement.

Figure 11.1 Sunroom Prior to Re-configuration

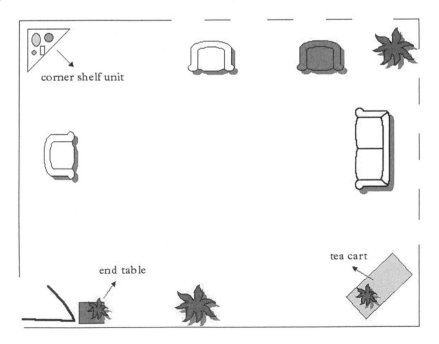

Figure 11.2 Sunroom Designed to Promote Engagement

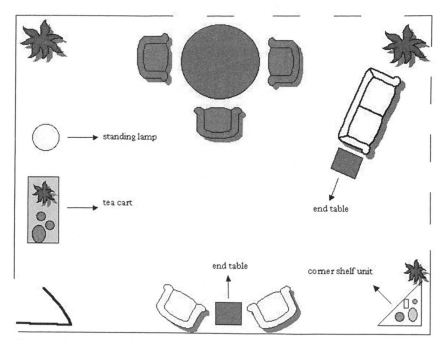

With the environmental innovations currently taking place in long-term care (Calkins, 2002; Marsden, Calkins & Briller, 2003), specifically the movement towards household models, we may find increased numbers of recreation professionals working in settings that contain several households. Household models consist of physical space that enriches the lives and relationships among residents, family members, and care staff. Each household typically has private bedrooms for eight to 12 residents, a living room, kitchen, and access to a courtyard. There are strong visual and physical connections to the outdoor, natural environment. The design of the environment portrays a sense of coziness, is welcoming and reflects the relevant and meaningful furniture, photos, and mementos of the people who live and work in the household. These objects recall the presence of human life, the friendships, personal achievements, family events, community associations and extensions of one's identity. Photographs from the Evergreen Retirement Community in Oshkosh, Wisconsin (see Figure 11.3) provide an example of the household model.

Recreation professionals involved in environment design may benefit from examination of the Therapeutic Environmental Screening Survey for Nursing Homes (TESS-NH) that targets the elements of the environment in need of consideration (Sloane, Mitchell, Weisman, Zimmerman, Foley, Lynn, Calkins, Lawton, Teresi, Grant, Lindeman, & Montgomery, 2002).

The TESS-NH includes the following subscales:

UNIT AUTONOMY

- Is the nursing station used for paper work? Charting in common areas may communicate staff ownership of common areas.

Figure 11.3

- Is the living area/unit used as a walkway between units or is it enclosed? Enclosed space creates a more intimate, home-like atmosphere. Units used as walkways communicate a work rather than a home environment.
- Are meaningful activities provided in the living area/unit, giving it a home-like quality?
- Are courtyards and outdoor areas enclosed to facilitate residents' independent use of such areas?
- Are privacy curtains the only means for residents to mark off their space?

SAFETY/SECURITY

- Are exit doors disguised? Exit doors that are disguised have been found to decrease resident anxiety over not being able to exit the living area.
- Are there alarms and keypads for each exit and elevator?
- Are the floor surfaces safe?
- Are there handrails in hallways?

CLEANLINESS/MAINTENANCE

- Are common areas and resident rooms maintained and cleaned on a regular basis?
- Are there odors in hallways? Resident rooms? Common areas?

STIMULATION (LIGHTING, VISUAL/TACTILE, NOISE)

- Is the lighting glare-free in the hallways? Resident rooms? Common areas?
- Do a majority of resident rooms have a view of the courtyard or common areas? Such views may trigger engaged, independent behaviors in contrast to views of hallways which may trigger agitation and increase confusion.
- Do common areas have views of courtyards that are accessible to residents?
- Is visual stimulation provided in common areas? Are there pictures or paintings on the walls?
- Are televisions blaring in common areas?
- Is there intercom noise? Such noise communicates an institutional environment rather than a home-like environment and may increase resident agitation.

SOCIALIZATION

- Do resident rooms contain chairs?
- Are there natural pathways (hallways) that lead to a place to sit? Socialize?

PERSONALIZATION/HOMELIKENESS

- Are public areas homelike?
- Is there a kitchen available to residents?
- Are there pictures and personal mementos in resident rooms?
- Is the furniture in common areas non-institutionalized?
- Are residents dressed and groomed appropriately for social engagement?

ORIENTING/CUEING

- Are residents' names posted on their doors?
- Are current and old pictures of residents posted on their doors or in their rooms?
- Are there objects of personal significance in residents' rooms?
- Are bathrooms visible from residents' beds?
- Are common areas that foster active engagement visible from residents' rooms?

PROGRAM MODELS

Treatment Protocols: A Focus on Dementia Care

Dementia is characterized by loss of intellectual functioning, memory loss, loss of functional skills, and behavioral symptoms. While dementia is not a disease in itself, it is a syndrome, a group of symptoms. It is an umbrella term that encompasses 70 different diseases or causes. The cause and rate of progression of dementia is variable and depends upon the individual and type of dementia.

One out of every 10 Americans who are 65 years of age or older have some type of dementia (Alzheimer's Association, 2003). Furthermore, half of all nursing home residents have Alzheimer's Disease or a related disorder. These statistics speak to the need for recreation and leisure professionals who work in long-term care to understand the symptoms and functional decline associated with dementia.

Using a health model to guide program delivery, Buettner and Fitzsimmons (2003) state that the role of the recreation professional is to provide therapeutic programs that will effect the "bio-psycho-social well-being of clients" (p. 1). Older adults with dementia have been observed to display a range of disruptive behaviors, ranging from apathy, depression, physical aggression (i.e., kicking, hitting), wandering, repetitive vocalizations, yelling, to name a few. These disruptive behaviors are viewed as representing unmet needs on the part of the older adult with dementia. Such unmet needs may include the need for companionship, communication of one's needs, happiness, or hunger. The health care provider is faced with the task of understanding and identifying the needs expressed through the disruptive behaviors as well as how to assist individuals in meeting such needs.

Buettner and Fitzsimmons (2003) have developed 82 evidence-based protocols designed to address the disruptive behaviors of older adults with dementia (see Table 11.5 for an example of one protocol). The "evidence" suggests that the effectiveness of the protocols have been established through experimental studies, descriptive studies, or case studies. Another common feature of these protocols pertains to the structure of the intervention. According to Buettner and Fitzsimmons, each protocol:

- is conducted in small groups of six or fewer residents,
- contains challenging tasks that match the skills of the residents,
- is conducted in a restraint-free environment,
- contains tasks that are meaningful and promote functional abilities,
- uses sensory stimulation and gross motor integration for relaxation.

The activity content of these protocols ranges from Life Stories to Postcard Collectors, Airmat Therapy, Animal-Assisted Therapy, Wheelchair Biking, Social Dance Club, Music and Motion, Sensory Cooking, Newsletter, Dominoes, Sensory Beach Discovery, Group Drum Circle, Photo Therapy, Gardens Alive, Wave Machine, Sensory Bird Club, Hooked on Golf Club, and Sensory Travel Club.

The treatment protocols for dementia care provide one approach to maintaining or enhancing residents' functional abilities. The inherent challenge in this area of programming is how to ensure that the activity used is meaningful for the resident. This is particularly important if a recreation provider supports a hybrid model and seeks to provide recreation services that enhance both functioning and quality of life among residents.

Table 11.5. Example of a Protocol: Social Dance Club (from Buettner & Fitzsimmons, 2003, p. 118-119).

Purpose: To improve function, mood and behavior through the use of a social movement program.

Entrance Criteria: Demonstrated poor physical function, need to improve or maintain strength and flexibility, depression, passive behavior and deconditioning. If used as an afternoon group, includes restless individuals who become agitated at "change of shift" time. For clients in all stages.

Exit Criteria: Able to exercise 10 to 20 minutes without tiring and free of disturbing behaviors and/or passive/disruptive behaviors.

Group Size: Up to four clients per staff member.

Duration: Three times per week either mid-morning (for passive or deconditioned clients) or mid-afternoon (for restless and agitated clients) for 30 minutes.

Safety: Room with enough space for movement. Client has sturdy, non-skid footwear and assistive devices. Fluids provided at end of program. Clients with COPD avoid overexertion.

Facility & Equipment: Room large enough for up to 10 people. Recorded music and player. Pitcher of water and cups. Gait belt.

Methods: Have music type selected ahead of time from a variety of different styles and tempos. Invite family and other staff members from different departments to come and join. Alternate slow tempo and faster tempo music types. Have theme type dances such as Sock-Hop, Country Square Dance and decorate the room. Also arrange for volunteers, staff or other to come in and demonstrate various types of dances that they know. Have clients do a little stretching before beginning. (further instruction given for low-functioning clients and for high-functioning clients).

Possible Client Objectives:
- Improved or prevent regression of levels of health.
- Maintained or improved strength, muscle endurance, and flexibility.
- To provide active movement program at high need time of day.
- To alert passive clients and to calm restless clients.
- Improved small group socialization as evidenced by verbalizing with at least one other person in the group during each session.
- Improved mood as evidenced by positive comments about experience and/ or by a happy expression.
- Decreased wandering by remaining in program.

Eden Alternative

A national movement, called the Eden Alternative, specifically focused on creating a ew nursing home environment, has begun. Its founder, Dr. William Thomas, defines the ovement as "the creation of a human habitat where people thrive, grow and flourish, rather an wither, decay and die." Simply put, the Eden Alternative creates long-term care facilities that are as "home-like" as possible. Animals, cats, dogs, birds and rabbits, co-exist with residents in Eden Alternative facilities. Plants are prominent in the plan to normalize the living environment and children are frequent visitors. The intent of creating this environment is to reduce the use of medication while increasing the residents' contact with the outside world. An Eden Alternative facility follows 10 basic principles (The Eden Alternative, 1999):

1. Realizes loneliness, helplessness, and boredom account for the bulk of suffering among the frail elderly;
2. Commits itself to surrendering the institutional point of view and adopts the Human Habitat model which makes pets, plants and children the axis around which daily life turns;
3. Provides easy access to companionship by promoting close and continuing contact between the elements of the Human Habitat and the people who live and work within;
4. Creates opportunities to give as well as receive care by promoting elders' participation in the daily round of activities that are necessary to maintain the Human Habitat;
5. Imbues daily life with variety and spontaneity by creating an environment in which unexpected and unpredictable interactions and happenings can take place;
6. De-emphasizes the programmed-activities approach to life and devotes these resources to the maintenance and growth of the Human Habitat;
7. De-emphasizes the role of prescription drugs in elders' daily lives and commits these resources to the maintenance and growth of the Human Habitat;
8. De-emphasizes the top-down bureaucratic authority in the facility and seeks instead to place the maximum possible decision-making authority in the hands of those closest to those for whom we care;
9. Understands the Edenizing is a never-ending process, not a program and that the Human Habitat, once created, should be helped to grow and develop like any other living thing;
10. Is blessed with leadership that places the need to improve resident quality of life over and above the inevitable objections to change. Leadership is the lifeblood of the Edenizing process and for it there is no substitute.

These 10 principles fit nicely with the Ulyssean perspective espoused in this book. The clear focus in Eden Alternative facilities is on the resident. His or her well being is primary and it is achieved through active involvement in a facility as home-like as possible. The facility, and its staff, exists to help residents achieve maximum functioning and the highest quality of life possible (Barba, Tesh, & Courts, 2002).

A Family Model

Given the increased concern with resident quality of life, efforts in recent years have addressed the need to move toward a social model in long-term care. Although the shift to a social model may be positive, concerns still exist as to whether it may be lacking if staff draw on a hospitality approach and treat residents as guests rather than people with needs and abilities to develop intimate, meaningful relationships with other residents and staff (Green, 2003). Voelkl, Battisto, Carson, and Green (2003) have suggested that as we undertake a paradigm shift toward a social model that consideration be given as how we may honor and capitalize on the strengths and abilities of residents, their family members, and care staff. For instance, how may resident-staff interactions build on similar interests, thereby fostering meaningful social bonds? How may family become active members of the unit culture and community? In an effort to promote meaningful social relationships among residents, family members, and care staff, Voelkl, Battisto, Carson, and Green have proposed a family model in long-term care (see Figure 11.4).

Figure 11.4 Family Making (Voelkl, Battisto, Carson, & Green, 2003)

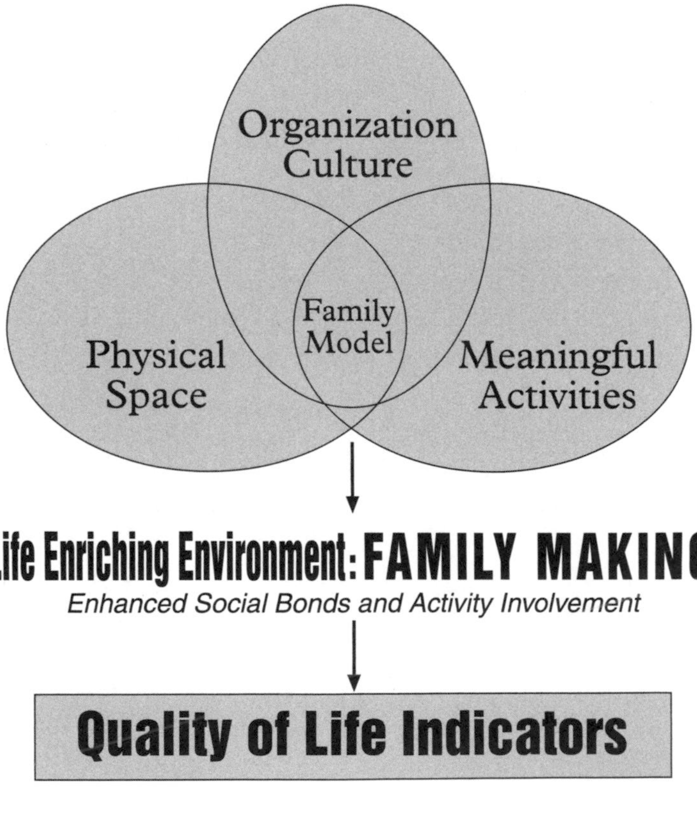

Life Enriching Environment: FAMILY MAKING

Enhanced Social Bonds and Activity Involvement

Quality of Life Indicators

The potential richness of the relationships among residents, family members, and staff of a nursing home speaks to the social bonds and shared experiences that may be cultivated. Family making, coined by Bella, provides a useful way of conceptualizing the potential that is inherent in such environments. Family making is "the process through which we develop relationships that are enduring, caring, and intimate" (in press, p. 10) and is characterized by (a) enduring relationships, (b) caring relationships, and (c) shared domestic space. Family making occurs, for example, when a staff member and two residents sit on the patio, drinking iced tea, and discussing and admiring the flowers they just finished planting. Perhaps they also discuss gardens from long ago, cherished homes or the current home of the staff member.

Eating meals in a dining room, socializing with friends and family in lounge areas, and planting spring flowers on a patio represent the experience of shared domestic space that may foster enduring and caring relationships. Although all nursing homes have shared domestic space, many questions remain as to whether these spaces truly support experiences of sharing and caring. Nursing homes in which residents perceive staff as "owning" shared domestic space, as was expressed by a resident on a traditionally designed nursing home who stated, "We can use it [lounge area] if the girls [care staff] let us" (Voelkl, Winkelhake, Jeffries, & Yoshioka, in press), would not promote family making. In contrast, common areas that promote equal use by all interested parties, allow both residents and staff to take responsibility for the care of such space, and contain furniture and resources that promote social and activity engagement, would promote family making among residents, family, and care staff.

The experience of caring relationships is another aspect of family making that is central to the creation of family-like bonds. Many aspects of caring are inherent in the "running" of the nursing home environment. For example, the act of organizing care activities, as well as the task of staff providing direct care to residents through assistance with bathing and providing medications, speak to a staff's role in caring relationships. Although many staff members have stories as to how residents have expressed care for them through advice on how to handle a difficult life event or shared laughter, these reciprocal moments seem to occur in spite of the institutional environment. For nursing homes seeking to honor and heighten caring relationships, it is important to consider the creation of shared activities that promote meaningful, reciprocal relationships rather than the inequity frequently found in resident:staff relationships. For example, two residents and one care staff with interest in gardening may spend an afternoon repotting and watering plants in the living room, all the while talking over past gardening success stories! Engaging in shared activities based on mutual interests appears to be one important strategy for developing caring relationships among residents, family members, and staff.

As a nursing home creates shared domestic space and promotes reciprocal caring relationships among residents, family, and staff members, the family-like bonds created will be enduring over time and through the course of life events. The enduring nature of these family-like bonds buffer the devastation of a resident losing a spouse or a staff member's distress over an early morning argument with her teenage child. Such bonds have the potential to foster life-enriching environments for direct care staff, thereby promoting job satisfaction and job retention. Such bonds may also enhance the content and quality of residents' daily experiences. Such social bonds extending to family members may result in an increase in the frequency and quality of family visits. Such outcomes further promote and strengthen family making among residents, family, and staff.

Most likely nursing homes vary in the degree of family making that is experienced. As depicted in Figure 11.4, Voelkl, Battisto, Carson, and Green (2003) have suggested that the level of family making is dependent on the interaction between organizational culture, physical space, and opportunities for engagement in meaningful activities. An organizational culture that creates opportunities for care staff, residents, and family members to have a voice in decision-making and takes steps to care for and nurture all members of the community may increase the sense of belonging experienced by residents, family, and staff. Physical space that promotes equal ownership and use of shared domestic space may increase opportunities for interaction among residents, family, and staff, thereby enhancing the development of caring and enduring relationships. The design of a meaningful activity program that builds on the mutual interests of residents, family, and staff, may also be key in the promotion of caring and enduring relationships.

Meaningful activities have been defined as "self-motivated activity that gives joy and purpose and is free of stress" (Jones, 1999, p. 173). Unfortunately, most traditional nursing home activity programs fall short of meaningful measures. Often diversional in nature, traditional nursing home activities such as bingo, arts and crafts, and current events may offer opportunities for only superficial, temporary, and short-lived pleasures. In contrast, the benefits of meaningful activities are genuine and, therefore, greatly contribute to one's quality of life.

In the provision of meaningful activities in a nursing home setting, it is imperative that each person is known and responded to as an individual, complete with life experiences, preferences, strengths, needs, and daily patterns of many sorts. Each individual in the nursing home is constitutionally different from any other individual and a meaningful activity program must reflect these differences. While there is an abundance of individually meaningful activity possibilities, most fall within one or more of the following categories: socialization; family and community involvement; intimacy and touch; work-related and purposeful activities; movement; nature and the outdoors; relaxation and reflection; spirituality; personal growth; and new experiences. Without involvement in these meaningful activities, life is merely existence.

Old age, physical impairments, even dementia does not preclude one's ability to lead a meaningful life because so many of the activities that give life meaning are simple. Activity programming in the family model ensures that *everyone,* residents, families, and staff alike, feels useful, appreciated, and successful whether by watering the garden, delivering the mail, or frosting a cake.

CONCLUSIONS

With the growing number of older adults in the U.S., we will continue to see growth in long-term care services and a need for recreation professionals who are dedicated to the provision of quality services in long-term care settings. Recreation professionals working in long-term care will be called to provide services that support Ulyssean living among residents through programs that maintain residents' functioning and enhance their quality of life. Furthermore, recreation professionals who are successful in long-term care will need a diverse knowledge base in order to creating meaningful programs, use strategies to further engage residents in programs, and design environments that are inviting and comfortable.

TWELVE

THE COMMUNITY ENVIRONMENT

An overwhelming number of older individuals live in age-integrated communities. They live in the places they have always lived: New York City, Dayton, Ohio, Central, South Carolina, Provo, Utah, and everywhere else. In most cases, they live without being noticed or labeled as a special group. At the same time, a continuum of care exists in many communities that allows people to remain in their homes with a little help from their friends, neighbors, and the social system. Many of these services and programs are provided by Area Agencies on Aging, county offices on aging, parks and recreation departments, churches or other non-profit organizations.

A STATISTICAL PROFILE OF COMMUNITY-RESIDING ELDERS

As was indicated in Chapter 1, most older individuals lived in family settings in 2002. Nearly 80 percent of males and 58 percent of females live either with a spouse or other relative. However, many older individuals live alone. Indeed, 40 percent percent of older women and 17 percent of all older men lived alone in 2000. Most older people, whether living alone or with others, prefer to age in place (Pynoos & Galant, 1996). They do not want to give up their homes and live elsewhere. Many individuals' ties to the past are in their homes, and they do not want to surrender those ties. As one of the author's grandmother said, "I can still smell the popcorn from all the Christmases we spent in this house." In fact, 65 percent would secure assistance, such as help for household chores, in order to remain at home (Vierck, 1990).

Vierck (1990) provided insight into community life of the elderly. Sixty percent were either unaware of the services available to them or were not interested in age-segregated activities. Eleven percent used at least one community service, 15 percent attended senior citizen centers, and four percent used transportation services. Fewer than four percent received home-delivered meals, homemaker services, or home-based health services. Ten percent were very active in their communities, 16 percent were fairly active, and 23 percent somewhat active. Fifty-nine percent visited friends at least three times a week, and 57 percent regularly attended social gatherings. Half of them spent time in activities related to religion.

Seventy percent of older individuals viewed themselves as being in good health. Twenty-five percent of older women and 33 percent of men claimed to exercise regularly. The vast majority (72 percent) of people 65 years of age or over were satisfied with life, and 82 percent did not experience frequent difficulties in life.

HOUSING OPTIONS

According to the National Association of Counties (undated a), "The vast majority of older persons age in place in their own homes and communities" (p. 1). Wahl (2001) documented the preference of most older people to remain in their own homes. He views the home as a supportive environment assisting in the negotiation of later life changes and playing a role in the quality of one's life. Therefore, it is necessary that the community living environment includes a variety of housing alternatives to meet the diverse need of this population and allow people to "stay at home" for as long as possible. These options increase the likelihood an older individual will not be placed in a nursing home inappropriately by providing resources needed to help maintain independence. Some of the options include (Heckheimer, 1989; Ebersole & Hess, 2001; AAPR, undated a; Administration on Aging, undated):

1. Conventional home ownership—retaining one's own home and living independently. In some cases home modification focusing on improving a home's design to make it more resident friendly may be sufficient to allow a person to continue in residence.
2. Accessory apartment—a private unit built within a single-family house.
3. Board and care—a housing option typically including room, meals and help with daily activities.
4. Congregate housing—a planned and designed multi-unit facility with private apartments for residents, and including services such as meals, transportation, housekeeping, and recreation.
5. Domiciliary care home—a group living arrangement with supervised meals, housekeeping, personal area, and private or shared sleeping rooms in a setting that is typically licensed and required to meet design and operating standards.
6. ECHO housing, also called a granny flat—a free-standing, removable unit adjacent to a single-family house and occupied by a relative on the same property.
7. Elderly housing project—a rental unit designed specifically to meet the needs of older residents with a variety of services designed to support independent living.
8. Foster care home—a single-family home including an older person living with a foster family, responsible for providing meals, housekeeping, and personal care.
9. Continuing care community—a planned housing development designed to provide a range of accommodations and services to older people, including independent living, congregate living, and medical care. An individual may move from one level to another as needs change.

10. Retirement community—a development designed for older individuals with home ownership and rental units available.

11. Assisted living facility—a facility where personal care assistance, such as help with medications as well as with bathing, grooming and dressing, is provided to residents. (See Chapter 11 for an extensive discussion of assisted living.)

12. Home sharing—Two or more individuals can share a home or apartment along with household duties.

The variety of housing options available to older individuals provides an opportunity to meet the needs for shelter. The nature of an individual's housing will shape the leisure services available to him or her. The next section will examine leisure in community settings.

LEISURE LIFE IN THE COMMUNITY

Altergott's (1988) work profiles daily life in later life. She examined involvement in leisure, obligatory activities, and social interaction among older people. Her findings provide a good starting point for examining the lives of community-dwelling elderly. On the average, the participants in Altergott's study spent approximately one hour per day in social leisure (visiting, conversing, parties, social gatherings). Approximately two-and-a-half hours were spent in television watching each day. Passive leisure (radio, reading, writing letters) consumed approximately one-and-a- half hours. None of the other activities examined—active leisure, religion, volunteerism, creative leisure, entertainment, education, or travel—averaged more than 30 minutes per day. Overall, older men averaged seven hours and 19 minutes leisure per day and older women averaged six hours and 31 minutes.

As can be seen in Table 12.1, there were age differences in leisure involvement. Leisure hours peaked between the ages of 65 and 74 for men and 75 or over for women.

Although the above provides some insight into how older individuals residing in the community spend their days, it focuses on activities. While knowledge of what people do is important to program development, it is also necessary to understand the paths they take in negotiating later life. This perspective provides understanding into the patterns of life.

Kelly (1987) provides a great deal of information on the community life of older residents of Peoria, Illinois. One thing that is clear from Kelly's work is that each individual takes a unique path through life. As Kelly wrote, "The journey of life is singular. No two life journeys are alike" (p. 1). However, some commonalities can be identified. In fact, Kelly identified several approaches to later life.

1. Balanced investors remain invested in life. They are committed and invested in at least two of three life domains: family, work, and leisure. These individuals are likely to participate in community organizations, such as the church. These individuals follow the activity theory approach discussed in Chapter 2 on aging theories.

2. Family-focused individuals found most of their support in the family. Their investments and meanings revolve primarily around their family. The leisure focus is the family.

3. Individuals identified as work-centered were rare. Nevertheless, it appears some older individuals progress through life with a dominant work orientation.

4. In contrast to the work-centered individual is the leisure-invested person. This small group of individuals found meaning and importance in leisure. However, this was not a highly satisfied group.

5. Faithful members focused primarily on the church in later life.

6. Individuals labeled as self-sufficient relied on their own resources for dealing with changes in life. They were not engaged in work, leisure, or community groups.

7. An accepting adaptor reacted to change by accepting it and approaching life in a passive way. They are compliant individuals who react to change by changing. This approach to life is marked by low life satisfaction.

8. Resistant rebels, on the other hand, were angry individuals who tried to change their environments.

Table 12.1
Gender and Age Patterns in Leisure Activities:
Daily Average Hours and Minutes

	Men			Women		
	55-64	65-74	75+	55-64	65-74	75+
Active leisure	:32	:26	:09	:08	:08	:06
Passive leisure	1:13	2:06	1:26	1:02	1:24	1:52
Television	2:34	3:08	3:40	2:10	2:24	2:28
Social leisure	1:13	1:18	:59	1:23	1:20	1:22
Religious Practice	:14	:14	:18	:16	:20	:30
Volunteerism	:08	:10	:09	:12	:14	:04
Creative leisure	:04	:06	:29	:24	:28	:38
Entertainment	:03	:06	:01	:03	:04	:07
Education	:07	:07	:01	:03	:02	:05
Travel for leisure	:26	:26	:26	:17	:25	:13
Total Leisure	**6:34**	**8:05**	**7:35**	**5:49**	**6:49**	**7:23**

If you work in a community-based program, such as a senior center, leisure may play a role in the lives of older individuals. However, it is not a panacea. Not all the types of individuals described above will embrace leisure as a vehicle for dealing with change in later life. It would seem that balanced investors and leisure-invested individuals will be the most likely participants in organized programs. Most older individuals in the community will pursue their leisure interests outside the framework of organized programs such as centers or clubs.

COMMUNITY CONCERNS

Weiner, Brok, and Snadowsky (1987) identify five areas where older residents in the community may experience problems and state that "The goals of any comprehensive rehabilitation or service program could only be truly achieved by helping the elderly deal with all these problem source areas successfully" (p. 160). The problem areas and potential areas of stress included:

1. Economic—Income loss and retirement may result in less income in the later years. Some modifications in lifestyle may be needed.
2. Physical—As we indicated in an earlier chapter, old age is inarguably a time of physical loss and decline.
3. Social—Role losses, such as retirement, loss of friends, or other social roles, may result in need to find replacement roles. The role of leisure independent of work may need to be evaluated.
4. Psychological—Growing old may result in a reevaluation of the self. New developmental tasks emerge. Kelly (1987a), for example, identifies this as a time of culmination marked by attempts to pull life together and find meaning.
5. Philosophical—This issue revolves around "coming to grips with existential and/or religious issues" (p. 160). Questions about the meaning of life and the individual's place in the world become important issues.

Weiner et al. (1987) recommend life enrichment counseling as a technique for assisting in these five areas. The focus of life enrichment is congruent with the development of a Ulyssean approach to later life. Shared factors include:

1. The individual needs to take an active approach to life. The individual actively seeks and finds ways to construct the life she or he desires.
2. The older individual must function as an "open system" seeking new ideas and information rather than being a closed system unwilling to examine new ideas.
3. The importance of going outside the self and making an impact on others remains as a focus. Ulyssean lives are shared lives.
4. The individual should continue involvement in meaningful activities. What is meaningful is subjective and an individual choice.
5. Weiner et al. (1987) view the need to retain spontaneity and a sense of humor as being part of self-enrichment.

Clearly, leisure can be a major factor in achieving each of these components of enriched living. Assisting older individuals in identifying appropriate activities can be a function of community-based programs.

COMMUNITY PROGRAMS AND SERVICES

A variety of community-based services exist (see for example, Atchley, 1991; Gelfand, 1988; Harbert & Ginsberg, 1990; Administration on Aging, undated a) and include: (1) in-home services, (2) protective services and legal services, (3) volunteer and employment services, (4) information and referral services, (5) day care services, (6) transportation services; (7) friendly visiting and telephone reassurance, (8) escort services, (9) center services, (10) nutrition services, and (11) educational services.

In-home services are provided to the person in his or her own home in order to maintain self-sufficiency and independence. They include chore services designed to assist in performing household repair and other light work needed to enable the person to remain at home. A chore service program might provide a person to replace window panes, install handrails, minor plumbing repair, and insect and rodent control.

A second type of in-home service is home-delivered meals. Many communities have a meals-on-wheels program to deliver at least one hot, nutritious meal per day to people in need. Homemaker services provide assistance in tasks of daily living, including housework chores such as laundry and cleaning and needed assistance in personal care. The fourth type of in-home services are home health services, including the provision of health services to the homebound. Part-time nursing care, occupational therapy, and physical therapy are examples of home health care.

Protective services include activities needed by individuals with a physical or mental dysfunction who are unable to carry out activities of daily living and unable to manage their own affairs. They may also be unable to protect themselves from abuse or neglect. A caseworker providing protective services might assist the individual in finding needed financial care, arrange legal services, find housing, and ultimately act as a court-appointed guardian if needed. Families also benefit from protective services through programs offering assistance related to financial services, insurance needs, and health care choices.

Volunteer services include the provision of formal volunteer opportunities with a variety of groups in the community. A 1998 survey of volunteers found that more than 26 million individuals aged 55 or over gave more than five billion hours in volunteer labor (Administration on Aging, 2003). This was done through local programs such as hospitals, delivering meals on wheels, or serving on committees or boards as well as through a variety of national volunteer programs such as: The Senior Medical Patrol, a program using retired professionals to help Medicare and Medicaid recipients; Family Friends, older volunteers working with special needs children; the Experience Corps, placing older volunteers in schools and youth serving organizations; the National Senior Service Corps, including Foster Grandparents, Senior Companions and the Retired and Senior Volunteer Program (RSVP); the Service Corps of Retired Executives, providing assistance to small business owners; and Volunteers in Parks, working with the National Park Service (Administration on Aging, undated b).

Many older individuals would like to work, and efforts designed to assist in their search for employment should be part of a comprehensive community program. Employment services could range from vocational counseling and retraining to the initiation of a job referral or exchange service where older workers are matched with requests for workers from the community.

Information and referral services involve receiving calls in a central location from individuals needing assistance and providing referrals to these services. Usually the service will include a brief assessment followed by the provision of relevant information to the caller. Many agencies also publish a book of community programs and services, including recreation services available to the older individual.

The Federal Government has established a centralized information and referral program called Eldercare Locator, a rich source for locating resources to support older adults. The Eldecare Locator (www.aoa.gov/elderpage/locator/html) is contacted through a toll free phone number (800-677-1116 at the time this book was published) and is frequently the initial step in finding community services and resources, such as home care services, meal delivery programs, housing options, senior centers, day care programs, financial services, legal services and specialized services related to illnesses such as Alzheimer's Disease, cancer and heart disease. A trained specialist answers calls and provides information on the best services and resources to meet a caller's needs.

Some older individuals cannot be left alone during the day, and day care programs for the elderly are becoming increasingly common. They provide a range of services within an organized setting for periods less than 24 hours. Prior to the initiation of day care, the only solution would have been placement in a long-term care facility. The origination of day care provided a sheltered location where the individuals could spend the day and return home at night, providing needed respite to caregivers.

Services at a day care program might include health services such as physical therapy, recreation therapy, and mental health services. The day care program will also include a planned program of recreational activities and a hot meal. The program allows the individual the opportunity to stay at home as a result of the provision of needed services while also providing relief to the caregiver who no longer needs to be available and involved 24 hours a day. As a result, both the individual and his or her family benefits.

Although many older individuals retain their drivers license, many people aged 65 and over are identified as "transportation disadvantaged" (see Chapter 10), meaning they lack adequate public transportation and do not, or cannot, drive an automobile. Data indicate that over 600,000 individuals aged 70 or over stop driving each year (Administration on Aging, undated c). Such individuals require transportation services in order to get to needed services and activities. As a result, the provision of transportation is a major service of many agencies.

Atchley (1991) proposed an "ideal" transportation program. It includes fare reduction on all public transportation, public subsidies to ensure adequate scheduling and routing of public transportation, reduced taxi fares, and funds to senior citizen centers for the purchase of vehicles to be used in transportation programs.

Other transportation programs include the use of volunteer drivers, sharing of vehicles by senior centers with other groups, such as the Easter Seal Society, or corporations using vans for car pooling of employees, use of school buses, and contractual arrangements with transportation providers, such as taxi cab companies.

Regardless of the method used to provide transportation, it is an integral part of any program. No matter how good a program is, it will not be used unless people can get to it.

Telephone reassurance and friendly visitor programs are designed to provide daily contact between the older individual and the community. Telephone reassurance systems are built around a phone call to the individual on a preplanned basis. The call is a way to be sure the individual is doing well and does not need any assistance. If the individual does not answer the call and has not previously informed the caller this would be the case, a call is made to an emergency contact such as a neighbor or friend. This individual will then visit the older individual to determine why the call went unanswered. The impetus for telephone reassurance programs was the knowledge that older individuals can have accidents in the home, such as a fall and resulting broken hip, which would go unnoticed. The telephone call is a method of avoiding such a catastrophe. A friendly visitor program is similar, except a personal visit replaces the telephone call.

Escort services provide accompaniment for older individuals needing assistance in negotiating their environment. This may include trips to the doctor, shopping, or recreation activities.

The senior citizen center has become one of the mainstays of the organized system or services. The Administration on Aging (undated d) estimates there are between 10,000 and 16,000 centers in the United States, funded by governments, non-profits such as the YMCA and churches. The Older Americans Act provided the impetus for the development of many of these centers. They are crucial as a focal point for the delivery of services. Although relatively few older individuals actually participate in center programs, few communities do not have a center that serves as the focal point of aging services.

Centers today typically function as multi-purpose centers offering a variety of programs and services. The attempt to become locations allowing "one-stop shopping" has resulted in the placement of recreational programs, social services such as food stamp and social security information, meals counseling services, and information and referral in the center.

The National Council on Aging (undated) recently identified seven programs exemplifying "best practices" in the area of senior center services. These programs show the richness of center services and the role they play in successful aging. For example: a center in Fullerton, California offers a program designed to reduce the risk of falls by high-risk older individuals by improving their balance and mobility; The Senior Citizens Council in Augusta, Georgia offers a comprehensive exercise program including muscle-building training, aerobic exercise, nutrition information and medication management. Participants have the opportunity to participate in tai chi, line dancing, and resistance training; The White Crane Wellness Center in Chicago offers seniors a "health and wellness outreach initiative," featuring a smorgasbord of services including health education workshops, health screening, healthy eating programs, podiatry education, flu shots, mental health services, tai chi, and yoga.

A variety of educational programs should be made available in the community. These could include programs developed and offered locally, such as classes at centers or community colleges, as well as national programs such as Elderhostel. The opportunity for continuing education is crucial to Ulyssean living.

Nutrition services occur at a variety of levels. Services include direct provision of meals, through senior centers as well as programs such as meals-on-wheels. In addition, many community programs include nutrition education, recognizing the crucial role of proper dietary habits in successful aging.

Two groups may be in particular need of community services: widows and caregivers. Family and friends provide a network for reciprocal relationships which have been identified as a "crucial concomitant of an older person's well being and autonomy" (Hooyman & Kiyak, 1993; p. 266). This "convoy of social relations" (Antonucci, 1990; 2001) affecting health and well-being in later life may be more important since the moving of children out of the house (although it is important to note that about one in five older individuals do not have children) and death of a spouse may increase the need to develop strong bonds with others.

Widowhood can be a time of severe crisis for older men and women. According to Ebersole and Hess (1998), "Losing a partner, when there has been a long, close and satisfying relationship is essentially losing one's self and one's core" (p. 729). A lifelong relationship with a spouse usually provides bonds of intimacy, interdependence, and belonging. The involuntary breaking of such bonds may have serious emotional and social implications for the older person. Feelings of grief, loneliness, and depression may result. The loss of companionship may be difficult to overcome, especially if social support from other sources is not readily available. As a result of widowhood, the role of spouse is lost, leaving some individuals with an identity problem. Opportunities for social interaction may also diminish once a partner is gone, creating a sense of isolation.

A role that may be assumed by spouses as they age is that of caregiver. According to Ebesole and Hess (2001) and the AARP (undated c) in about 25 percent of American households a person over age 18 had served as a caregiver at some time during the previous year. Ebersole and Hess reported that relatives provide 79 percent of all care to noninstitutionalized women and 84 percent of all care to noninstitutionalized men over the age of 85. The majority of care, over 70 percent, is provided by women and there is a strong likelihood that a woman will function as a caregiver at some point during her lifetime.

Although the role of caring for a loved one may be fulfilling to an individual, it is impossible to ignore the potential problems associated with it. Such problems range from issues directly related to the illness or disability to emotional reactions displayed by care-receivers. Many studies report "burnout," a behavioral manifestation of stress. In a manual for caregivers developed by the Pennsylvania Department of Aging (undated), burnout is described as having three components. The first is emotional exhaustion, which results from a sense of energy depletion. The second, depersonalization, is associated with negative feelings toward the care-receiver. Lastly, reduced personal accomplishments stem from the feeling of total immersion in the caregiving role, leaving no time or energy to invest in anything else. Burnout may be hazardous to mental and physical health, and it may eventually have a negative impact on the caregiver/care-receiver relationship.

A conceptual model developed by Pearlin, Mullan, Semple, and Skaff (1990) offers a comprehensive picture of the stress process involved in caregiving. It is composed of four parts: (a) the background and context of stress, (b) primary and secondary stressors, (c) the mediators of stress, and (d) the outcomes or manifestations of stress. Factors under the background or context dimension are:

1. Socio-economic status characteristics, which may explain access to resources or additional sources of stress in one's life.
2. Caregiving history, which includes issues such as history of the problem requiring caregiving, length of caregiving, caregiver and care-receiver past relationship.
3. Family and network composition, which will determine amount of social, emotional and instrumental support available to the caregiver.
4. Program availability, which determines what types of resources, such as information or program, can be accessed by the caregiver.

The types of stressors identified by Pearlin and his associates are grouped into three subgroups: (a) primary stressors, (b) secondary role stressors, and (c) secondary intrapsychic strains. Primary stressors are related to objective indicators (such as behavioral characteristics and dependency level) and subjective indicators (such as overload and relational deprivation). Secondary role strains are conflicts that arise from the time and energy demands placed on the caregiver. They range from family conflicts, to job conflict, to economic problems and reduction of social life. Secondary intrapsychic strains relate to emotional factors such as self-esteem, competence, and identity. Also associated with intrapsychic stressors is role captivity, an interesting concept which refers to a sense of being captive, seeing no alternative, no choice but to engage in such role, a feeling which may result in depression (Pearlin, 1975).

The principal mediators of stress include coping skills and social support. These mediators are believed to limit the proliferation of secondary stressors described earlier, thus buffering outcomes.

According to Pearlin and associates (1990), coping has three functions: (a) management of situation causing stress, (b) management of the meaning of the situation, and (c) management of stress symptoms that result from the situation. Social support is an important resource that may mediate the negative consequences of stressing situations. Caregivers need to vent their feelings, and they also need respite from the demands of their role. Often times, friends and relatives become more distant when the situation leading to caregiving intensifies; this reaction may leave the caregiver with an enormous sense of isolation and abandonment.

The outcomes listed in Pearlin's model are: (a) depression, (b) anxiety, (c) irascibility, (d) cognitive disturbance, (e) physical health, and (f) yielding of role. Another emotional outcome found in the literature is a sense of guilt. The constant stress may take its toll, caregivers may become impatient and resent the care-receiver. Self-blame may follow, and with it a sense of personal failure, which is associated with depression and helplessness.

The role of caregiving is depicted as rather problematic above. Once again, it is necessary to stress that feelings of self-worth and identity may also be attached to this relationship. Some caregivers may derive pleasure from knowing that they are providing a meaningful service to a loved one and see their role almost as a mission. In order to facilitate the adjustment to this role, there are several services that need to be provided to older adults.

At least three major sources of help are needed. The first relates to information regarding what services are available and how to access them. Many individuals are not aware of their rights as senior citizens. Information and referral is available through the local Area Agency on Aging. Another good provider of free information is the American Association of Retired Persons. Publications and audiovisuals may be obtained from these sources. Also, experts on specific topics such as Medicare benefits or in-home services may be asked to deliver informative workshops for those interested in the topics.

The second area of need is that of social support. In this area, the formation of support groups, in which caregivers get together to share their experiences and exchange knowledge, may be very effective in diminishing the feeling of isolation.

Finally the need for respite seems to be clear. Time away from the stresses of caregiving is important not only for the mental health of the caregiver, but also for the quality of the relationship. Placing the care-receiver temporarily in a respite program to give the caregiver the opportunity to take a vacation or simply relax for a while is an option. Another option is to seek a day program, such as adult day care, which keeps the person in need of care for part of the day, allowing the caregiver time to enjoy some normalcy.

A recent report from the AARP (undated c) indicated that caregivers often have to balance the needs of employment with caregiving and as a result personal and family life may suffer. The caregiver must develop coping skills to help deal with the stresses of caregiving. AARP recommends caregivers eat well, find time to get enough sleep, exercise regularly, get regular medical check-ups, maintain social contacts, seek help from family and friends, and use community resources in order to fortify themselves against the strains of caregiving. They specifically suggest that caregivers find time to do things they enjoy, such as reading, walking or listening to music.

As the American population grows older, and caregiving needs increase, so will the need for creative community agencies to assume part of the care for seniors with more severe functional impairments. Such programs may also be called upon to provide supportive services to caregivers, such as seminar and discussion groups. Recreation professionals may be responsible not only for providing meaningful activities to the care recipient, but also for engaging in leisure education for the caregiver, who often times complains of a "leisure-less" life.

The variety of community-based services for the elderly can be confusing and overwhelming. However, they are needed if people are to remain in the community for as long as possible. The leisure service provider has an important role in the range of services. If older individuals are to continue to grow and prosper, it is important they are aware of and use all available programs. At the least, individuals in the leisure field need to be aware of the multitude of programs and services and be able to function in an information and referral role. They must be able to identify needed services and refer their participants to them. In some cases it may be necessary to directly provide some of the services listed above.

For example, it may be appropriate to function as an employment clearinghouse or become involved in the recreation component of a day care program. In many cases it will be necessary to develop a transportation program to provide access to programs. Leisure service providers can best serve their constituents by adopting a broad perspective on service delivery. The leisure service provider working in the age-integrated community should be concerned with the whole person and not solely with the provision of recreation activities. Such a perspective will increase the likelihood of involvement in the entire network of aging services and not only with one small part of it.

SURVIVAL SKILLS

The development of programs to provide older individuals with survival skills needed to function in the community is a role leisure service providers may take. Such programs might include a section on defensive driving, negotiating the government bureaucracy in order to receive benefits to which one is entitled, cooking classes for individuals who either never cooked before or who need tips on cooking for one or two, banking skills such as manipulating a checking account, use of computers, driving classes for individuals who have never driven, accident prevention classes, and classes in recognizing and dealing with con artists. Other programs needed to assist individuals to not only survive, but to actually thrive in their community are needed. Such a broad perspective on programming is needed if people are to continue on the path to Ulyssean lifestyles in the later years.

Harbert and Ginsberg (1990) support the need for supportive services. They stated, "Agencies must sometimes provide supportive services to guarantee that older adults are able to use their programs. The primary service provided by an agency must often be supplemented with support services in order for the agency to respond effectively to the needs of older clients" (p. 203). Personnel involved in leisure services must be involved in this provision of supportive services.

THE COMMUNITY NEEDS ASSESSMENT

One way to determine whether a community has the supports necessary to assist in helping older individuals lead lives marked by growth is to complete a community audit. The National Association of Counties (undated b) indicated that "in order for older persons to 'age in place' communities must be responsive to the safety, physical accessibility, and quality of life concerns of older residents" (p. 1). They recommend the following guidelines be used to determine whether a community is a good place to grow old:

I. Community safety

    a. Are residents encouraged to develop a sense of ownership in their community through programs such as "neighborhood watches" to monitor the community and watch for questionable behavior? (Older individuals are at home more often than other people and may be ideal candidates for block captains.)

    b. Is a "gatekeeper" program in place in which mail carriers and meter readers identify older individuals who appear to be in need of assistance?

    c. Are police, fire, and emergency medical personnel provided instruction in identifying and meeting the needs of the elderly?

    d. Are parking lots, walkways, and bike trails well lit?

    e. Do homebound elderly have an emergency response system available to notify them in case of community emergency?

II. Improving mobility

    a. Are public buildings and other facilities accessible by use of elevators or ramps, as required by the Americans with Disabilities Act?

    b. Are buildings, streets, and signage marked with visible letters and symbols?

    c. Are there pedestrian pathways to connect parks, transportation, shops, and buildings?

    d. Do traffic lights provide sufficient time for crossing?

    e. Are sidewalks kept free of debris, such as ice, snow, and leaves, and smooth of bumps and cracks?

    f. Are the slower reflexes and poorer eyesight of older drivers taken into account when signs and signals are replaced and roadway repairs made?

    g. Has consideration been given to increasing the number of left turn lanes and traffic signals with left turn indicators to reduce accidents?

    h. Are older drivers provided safe driver classes?

    i. Are public transportation services available, and do they provide a variety of routes to accommodate the needs of older users?

    j. Are car pool programs, volunteer services, and home-delivery programs available to those needing them?

Housing

a. Are home-sharing programs, in which two or more unrelated individuals (such as a college student and an older individual) can live together and share responsibility and costs, available?

b. Do zoning laws permit secondary units, such as ECHO cottages?

c. Are home-repair and modification programs, allowing older people to stay safely in their homes, available? Do they include approved contractors and workers?

d. Do local lenders offer programs, such as home equity conversion programs, to allow the elderly to use the equity that is tied up in their homes?

IV. Services

a. Is there a clearly identified agency or organization in the community where the elderly can receive information, help, or a referral on aging issues?

b. Do the aging-related agencies and services exhibit coordination in referrals and services?

c. Are the needs of the elderly taken into account when programs, including transportation, recreation, and public safety, are developed?

d. Is a collaborative decision-making approach used by the public, voluntary, religious, private, civic, and business organizations, and older individuals in the community?

e. Are there special programs targeted at the frail, minority, and isolated elderly?

V. Sense of community

a. Are older individuals' talents used as part of volunteer programs giving opportunities to contribute to the community?

b. Do intergenerational programs provide opportunities for young and old residents to donate their time and talents to the community?

c. Are employment opportunities, including part-time and flexible-hour positions, available?

d. Do community centers and shopping malls offer outreach and community information to residents?

e. Is the development of small home-based businesses, allowing individuals to be employed at home, encouraged by local zoning practices?

f. Are there water fountains, benches, and restrooms that offer rest and rejuvenation in parks, shops, public buildings and supermarkets?

The results of the community audit can be used to target areas for improvement. Trained recreation professionals can take the lead in this process. The National Association of Counties recommends the following steps be taken:

1. Form a broad-based community coalition to solve identified problems.
2. Define a few high-priority problems to work on.
3. Identify strategies and options for addressing the problems.
4. Negotiate agreements among key players in the community, including the government, businesses, churches, and voluntary organizations.
5. Implement and monitor the agreements.

The result of this process will be a community designed for Ulyssean living.

However, some elderly people are not able to find the quality of life they desire in their local communities. As a result, they may seek out special communities more amenable to their lifestyle. The next section of this chapter will examine this living option in greater detail.

AGE-SEGREGATED COMMUNITIES

According to Atchley (1991), retirement may be an opportunity to change living environment. In fact, 35 percent of older individuals stated they plan to move to another home after retirement (Vierck, 1990), and others choose to move into retirement communities with other individuals of their age. The selection of an age-segregated community is not a choice made by many older individuals. According to Streib (1993), individuals choosing retirement communities generally have higher levels of health, educational attainment, and economic status.

Regnier (1975) noted that the older individual's ability to control his or her own destiny in the open neighborhood is less than in the self-contained housing environment. With the losses of aging experienced by many individuals, movement into some type of congregate housing setting may help in retaining independence and control. Such housing units are often designed with older individuals in mind and incorporate many design features, such as handrails and grab bars, which foster independence and control. The move into a more supportive environment may be effective in alleviating many of the losses of old age.

Regardless of personal attitudes toward the appropriateness of retirement communities—old-age ghettos to some and Shangri-La to others—they are a housing alternative that merits consideration. This is especially so for individuals involved in the delivery of leisure services, since retirement communities are often viewed, and sold, as leisure villages.

A recent variation of the age-segregated community is the continuing care retirement community (CCRC). A CCRC provides a range of housing options at one location. They provide comprehensive health care and residential services allowing an individual to move from independent housing to assisted living to long-term care based on health needs. The CCRC typically requires a substantial financial commitment from the resident in exchange for lifetime care.

Data related to retirement communities present a mixed picture. Jacobs (1974) described one he called Fun City. He paints a bleak picture of residents isolated from the rest of society, who felt trapped in a place providing few amenities and little hope for change. On the other hand, Hochschild presented Merrill Court, an apartment for older people, as an effective solution to a bad situation. This congregate living situation assisted in the formation of an effective social group. It is interesting to note that Hochschild observed that a major precipitator of group formation was the presence of a communal coffee pot and, thus, a leisure situation.

Gelfand (1988) provided an example of a successful retirement community, Leisure World in Laguna Hills, California. The community was developed "to provide security, quick accessibility to good health care, good nearby shopping, good transportation, excellent facilities for recreation, and adult education and additional activities to ensure freedom from boredom" (p. 183).

Clearly, recreation is a major factor for immigration to a retirement community. In fact, Gelfand stated, "Retirement communities appear to be growing in popularity, particularly because they offer security, recreation, good housing, and social opportunities with neighborhoods of a similar age" (p. 184).

The opportunities that retirement communities provide to participate in familiar activities and also develop new skills is important (Streib, 1993). Activities are close by and require limited effort to participate. Streib describes the "staggering" number of activity offerings in a community of 2,000 residents:

- social—potlucks, dance, movies, bridge, singles club;
- sports—golf, tennis, swimming, boating, shuffleboard;
- crafts and hobbies—ceramics, lapidary, quilting, stamp collecting;
- arts, music, and dramatics—art classes, concerts, choral groups;
- education—foreign language classes, investment groups, book review club;
- health and fitness—exercise groups, yoga, hiking clubs, Weight Watchers;
- self-governance—committees and groups related to running the community;
- religious—Bible study, religious groups, hymn singing;
- service and philanthropic—money-raising groups for various charities, good neighbor groups.

Clearly, this is a leisure-rich environment for individuals seeking an active lifestyle.

The age-segregated program is inherently neither good nor bad. It is what its residents and the staff make it. This is illustrated in an article by Mary Louise Williams (1972), a retired school teacher who moved into an age-segregated apartment building she calls "the center." Her first reactions to the center are best described by her calling it "Seniliput" where the residents "unlike the diminutive inhabitants of Gulliver's Isle . . . were senile, most of them seemed in their eighties or nineties" (p. 38).

She was unhappy living in an environment one of the other residents described as a snake pit, and the main activities appeared to be bingo and bridge. This was in contrast to the center brochure, which talked about meeting interesting people while participating in numerous activities, discussion groups, and enjoying the advantages of a nearby university and the cultural opportunities of a big city.

She envisioned herself attending plays, symphonies, and operas while growing spiritually, socially, and intellectually. She felt deceived and trapped without the finances to go elsewhere. Rather than giving in and giving up, Williams developed a philosophy of looking for ideas and beauty in her surroundings. She was able to find them, not only in nature, but also in her neighbors. She tells of one woman who started a poetry hour and another who was an author.

She also found salvation in the church, which sponsored the home, and interaction with individuals as part of a research group examining work such as Paul Tournier's "The Strong and The Weak," Carl Jung's "Modern Man in Search of a Soul," and "Becoming" by Gordon Allport. Later they read plays, with assistance from younger church members, such as "Our Town."

The center had changed for the author. The reasons for the change are complex, but she summed them up by stating, "If there is ever to be an ideal retirement center, the leadership, the people, and the program would of course need to be ideal." She goes on to state that a great deal of time and insight are needed to plan and direct activities, people need to be taught how to use their leisure time, and our image of older people must change.

These three components, trained leadership, an educated population, and a more positive image of aging and the elderly can turn any environment into one that is as conducive to Ulyssean living as the one described by Williams in the thought-provoking piece.

CONCLUSION

The vast majority of older individuals live in the community, and the variety of housing and service opportunities available in an increasing number of communities allows the elderly to remain active, contributing members who make contributions to these environments. As a result, they experience many opportunities for Ulyssean living.

Examination of the community in which an individual lives will make it possible to alter the environment in order to facilitate Ulyssean living. Just as earlier chapters discussed designing the micro environment to be prosthetic rather than penalizing, this chapter provided a method of making the macroenvironment more amenable to growth and development by removing obstacles to independence and freedom.

Individuals whose needs are not being met in their local communities may decide to leave and migrate to a retirement community. These facilities are often leisure-rich environments where individuals can select from an array of opportunities for engagement. In some ways, these communities may be models for Ulyssean living. However, they may also be stagnant environments without the tensions and dynamics in age-integrated communities. The option of living solely with other older individuals will therefore be attractive to some and abhorrent to others.

Although there is a clear need to assist in developing prosthetic communities, we must be cautious and not overestimate the need for special services. This may be especially true in the leisure domain. Kelly and Godbey (1992) discussed the concept of leisure in ordinary life. This concept provides an excellent description of leisure in the lives of most older people. They wrote, "Most leisure in ordinary life is woven in the process of the daily round, neither special nor clearly differentiated . . . It is 'ordinary leisure' that consumes the most time for most people" (p. 195).

The implication of ordinary leisure is that many older individuals are able to negotiate their own path to Ulyssean living and need little or no assistance. Our role is to know whether help is needed and how to give it when it is.

REFERENCES

AARP (undated a). *Housing options for older people*. Washington D.C.: AARP. www.aarp.org/confacts/housing/housingoptions.html [August, 2003].

AARP (undated b). *Caregiving: Changing needs*. Washington D.C.: AARP. www.aarp.org/confacts/caregive/planning.html [August, 2003].

AARP (undated c). *Balancing work and caregiving*. Washington D.C.: AARP. www.aarp.org/confacts/caregive/balance.html [August, 2003].

Abra, J. (1989). Changes in creativity with age: Data, explanations and further predictions. International Journal of Aging & Human Development, 28, 105–126.

Administration on Aging (undated a). *Mission*. Washington D.C.: Department of Health and Human Services. www.aoa.gov/about/over/over_mission_pf.asp [August, 2003].

Administration on Aging (undated b). *Volunteer opportunities*. Washington D.C.: Department of Health and Human Services. www.aoa.gov/eldfam/Volunteer_Opps/Volunteer_Opps_pf.asp [August, 2003].

Administration on Aging (undated c). *Behind the wheel safety*. Washington D.C.: Department of Health and Human Services. www.aoa.gov [August, 2003].

Administration on Aging (undated d). *Senior centers*. Washington D.C.: Department of Health and Human Services. www.aoa.gov/naic/Notes/seniorcenters.html [August, 2003].

Administration on Aging (undated e). Decisions about retirement living. Washington, D.C.: Department of Health and Human Services.

Administration on Aging (1997). Profiles of older Americans: 1997. Washington, DC: Administration on Aging.

Administration on Aging (1997b). Projected health conditions among the elderly. Washington D.C.: Department of Health and Human Services. www.aoa.dhha.gov/aoa/stats/aging21/health.htm [March, 1999].

Administration on Aging (2002). *A profile of older Americans: 2002*. Washington, D.C.: Administration on Aging. www.aoa.gov/prof/Statistics/profile/profiles2002.asp [August, 2003].

Administration on Aging (2003). *Celebrate volunteers during National Volunteer Week 2003*. Washington D.C.: Department of Health and Human Services. www.aoa.gov/press/spotlight_on/2003/april_pf.asp [August, 2003].

Agency for Healthcare Research and Quality (2002*). Physical activity and older Americans: Benefits and Strategies*. www.ahrq.gov/ppip/activity.htm [July, 2003].

Aldana, S. & Stone, W. (1991). Changing physical activity preferences of American adults. *Journal of Physical Education, Recreation and Dance,* April, 67–71, 76.

Allen, K. & Chin-Sang, V. (1990). A lifetime of work: The context and meanings of leisure for aging black women. *The Gerontologist*, 30, 734–740.

Allison, M. (1988). Breaking boundaries and barriers: Future directions in cross-cultural research. *Leisure Sciences*, 10, 247–259.

Allison, M. T. & Geiger, G. W. (1993). Nature of leisure activities among the Chinese American elderly. *Leisure Sciences*, 15, 309–319.

Allmer, H. (1992). Incentives for physical activities in older persons. *Physical Activity, Aging and Sports*, (2), 146-149.

Allport, G. W. (1961). Pattern and growth in personality. New York: Holt, Reinhart & Winston.

Altergott, K. (1988). Social action and interaction in later life: Aging in the United States. In K. Altergott (ed.), Daily life in later life: Comparative perspectives. Newbury Park: Sage, 117-146.

Alzheimer's Association (1995). Comparison of general characteristics of Alzheimer's disease and vascular dementia. Chicago, IL: The Alzheimer's Association.

Alzheimer's Association (1998a). Statistics/prevalence. Chicago, IL: The Alzheimer's Association. www.alz.org/facts/rtstats.htm [March, 1999].

Alzheimer's Association (1998b). What are the warning signs? Chicago, IL: The Alzheimer's Association. www.alz.org/facts/rtwrngsns.htm [March, 1999].

Alzheimer's Association. (2003). *Statistics about Alzheimer's Disease.* www.alz.org/AboutAD/Statistics.htm [September, 2003].

Alzheimer's Disease Education & Referral Center (undated*). Challenging behaviors: Special issues for family care.* Washington D.C.: National Institute of Health. www.alzheimer's.org/pubs/challenging.html [September, 2003].

Alzheimer's Disease Education & Referral Center (2003). Alzheimer's Disease fact sheet. Washington D.C.: National Institute of Health. www.alzheimer's.org/pubs/adfact.html [September, 2003].

American Association of Retired Persons (1985). Aging and vision: Making the most of impaired vision. Washington, D.C.: American Association of Retired Persons.

American Association of Retired Persons (1988). National survey of caregivers. Washington, DC: American Association of Retired Persons.

American Association of Retired Persons (1990). Programming techniques: A guide for community crime prevention program planning. Washington, D.C.: American Association of Retired Persons.

American Association of Retired Persons's Educators Community and Dana Alliance for Brain Initiatives (2003). *Staying sharp: Current advances in brain research.* http://assets.aarp.org/www.aarp.org /articles/international/memoryloss_revab.pdf [September, 2003].

American Federation for Aging Research (2003). *The latest research on resistance training and aging.* http://www.infoaging.org/l-exer-9-r-train.html [September, 2003].

American Museum of Natural History (1998). Human aging: Genetic factors. www.amnh.org/enews/aging/a5.html [March, 1999].

American Psychiatric Association (1994) Diagnostic and statistical manual of mental disorders, fourth edition. Washington, D.C.: American Psychiatric Association.

Ananth, M., DeMicco, F., Moreo, P. & Howey, R. (1992). Marketplace lodging needs of mature travelers. *Cornell Hotel and Restaurant Administration Quarterly*, 33(4), 12-24.

Antonucci, T. C. (1990). Social supports and social relationships. In R. H. Binstock & L. K. George (eds.), Handbook of aging and the social sciences. San Diego: Academic Press.

Antonucci, T. C. (2001). Social relations: An examination of social networks, social support, and sense of control. Birren, J. E. & Schaie, K. W. (eds.) *Handbook of the psychology of aging, 5th edition,* San Diego: Academic Press, 427-453.

Atchley, R. C. (1977). *Social forces in later life* (2nd ed.). Belmont, CA: Wadsworth.

Atchley, R. C. (1991). *Social forces in later life* (6th ed.). Belmont, CA: Wadsworth.

Baas, J. M., Ewert, A., & Chavez, D. J. (1993). *Influence of ethnicity on recreation and natural environment use patterns: Managing recreation sites for ethnic and social diversity.* Environmental Management, 17, 523–526.

Backman, K. (1998*). African-American travelers.* The Strom Thurmond Institute of Government and Public Affairs. Clemson University, Clemson, S.C.

Backman, K., Backman, S. & Silverberg, K. (1999). An investigation into the psychographics of senior nature-based travelers. *Tourism Recreation Research*, 24(1), 13-22.

Backman, L., Mantayla, T., & Herlitz, A. (1990). The optimization of episodic remembering in old age. In P. B. Baltes & M. M. Baltes (eds.), *Successful aging: Perspectives from the behavioral sciences*. New York: Cambridge University Press, 118–163.

Backman, L., Small, B. J. & Wahlin, A. (2001). Aging and memory: Cognitive and biological perspectives. Birren, J. E. & Schaie, K. W. (eds*.) Handbook of the psychology of aging, 5th edition,* San Diego: Academic Press, 3349-377.

Baltes, M. M. & Carstensen, L. L. (1996). The process of successful aging. *Aging and Society,* 16, 397-422.

Baltes, M. M. & Carstensen, L. L. (1999). Social-psychological theories and their applications to aging: From individual to collective. Bengston, V. L. & Schaie, K. W. (eds*.). Handbook of theories of aging.* New York: Springer, 209-226.

Baltes, M. M., Wahl, H., & Reichart, M. (1991). Successful aging in long-term care institutions. In K. W. Schaie & M. P. Lawton (eds.), Annual review of gerontology and geriatrics, (11). New York: Springer, 311–337.

Baltes, P. B. & Baltes, M. M. (1990). Selective optimization with compensation. In P. B. Baltes & M. M. Baltes (eds.), *Successful aging: Perspectives from the behavioral sciences*. New York: Cambridge University Press, 1–34.

Baltes, P. B. & Baltes, M. M. (1998). Savior vivre in old age: How to master the shifting balance between gains and losses. *National Forum*, 78(2), 13-18.

Baltes, P. B. & Smith. J. (1999). Multilevel and systemic analyses of old age: Theoretical and empirical evidence for a fourth age. In Bengston, V. L. & Schaie, K. W. (eds.). *Handbook of theories of aging.* New York: Springer, 153-173.

Baltes, P. B., Smith, J., & Staudinger, U. M. (1991) Women and successful aging. In *Nebraska Symposium on Motivation*, (39), 123–162. University of Nebraska, Lincoln NE.

Bandura, A. (1982). Self-efficacy: Toward a unifying theory of behavioral change. *Psychological Review*, 84, 191–215.

Banzinger, G. & Roush, S. (1983). Nursing homes for the birds: A control relevant intervention with bird feeders. *The Gerontologist*, 23, 527–531.

Barba, B., Tesh, A. S., & Courts, N. F. (2002). Promoting thriving in nursing homes: The Eden Alternative. *Journal of Gerontological Nursing*, 28(3), 7-13.

Barbara Krueger & Associates (1996). Aging in place. Delmar, CA: Barbara Krueger & Associates. *www.seniorresource.com/ageinpl.htm* [March, 1999].

Barlow, J. (2003) *Study is first to confirm link between exercise and changes in brain.* News Bureau, University of Illinois at Urbana-Champaign. http://www.news.uiuc.edu/scitips/03/0127exercise.html [September, 2003].

Barrett, C. (1989). The concept of leisure: Idea and ideal. In Winnifrith & Barrett (eds.), *Philosophy of leisure*. New York: St. Martin's Press.

Bartol, M. (1979). Dialogue with dementia: Nonverbal communication in patients with Alzheimer's disease. *Journal of Gerontological Nursing*, 5, 21.

BBC News (2002). *Running protects against arthritis.* http://news.bbc.co.uk/1/low/health/2332409.stm [September, 2003].

Beard, B. B. (1991). In B. B. Beard, N. Wilson, & A. Wilson (eds.), *Centenarians, the new generation.* New York: Greenwood Press.

Beard, G. (1974). Legal responsibility in old age. New York: Russell Sage Foundation.

Becker, M. & Yost, B. (1991). 1990 recreation participation survey: Final report. Harrisburg, PA: Center for Survey Research, Penn State Harrisburg.

Bengston, V. L. (1973). *The social psychology of aging.* Indianapolis: Bobbs-Merrill.

Bengston, V.L., Burgess, E.O., & Parrott, T.M. (1997). Theory, explanation, and a third generation of theoretical development in social gerontology. *Journal of Gerontology: Social Sciences*, 52B, S72-S88.

Bergman, E. & Johnson, E. (1995). Towards accessible human-computer interaction. J. Nielsen (ed.). *Advances in Human-Computer Interaction.* Norwood, NJ: Ablex Publishing Corporation. http://www.sun.com/access/developers/updt.HCI.advance.html [September, 2003].

Bialeschki, D. & Henderson, K. (1991). The provision of leisure services from a feminist perspective. World Leisure and Recreation, 33(3), 30–33.

Bialeschki, D. & Walbert, K. (1998). You have to have some fun to go along with your work: The interplay of race, class, gender and leisure in the industrial new South. *Journal of Leisure Research*, 30(1), 79-100.

Bickson, T. A. & Goodchilds, J. D. (1989). Experiencing the retirement transition: Managerial and professional men before and after. In S. Spacapan and S. Oskamp (eds.), *The social psychology of aging.* Newbury Park: Sage, 81–108.

Birchenall, J. M. & Streight, M. E. (1993). Care of the older adult (3rd ed.). Philadelphia: J. B. Lippincott.

Birren, J. E. & Fisher, L. M. (1991). Aging and slowing of behavior: Consequences for cognition and survival. Nebraska Symposium on Motivation (39), 1–37. University of Nebraska, Lincoln, NE.

Blanding, C. (September, 1993). Have pensions, will travel. *Parks & Recreation*, 72-75.

Blazey, M. (1987). The differences between participants and nonparticipants in a senior travel program. *Journal of Travel Research*, 26, 7–12.

Bloom, M. (2003) "At 52, masters sprinter still faster than a speeding bullet." *The New York Times*, 30 June 2003: D1,D8.

Bocksnick, J. G. & Hall, B. L. (1994). Recreation activity programming for the institutionalized older adult. *Activities, Adaptation & Aging*, 19 (1), 1–25.

Bodger, D. (April, 1998). Leisure, learning and travel. *Journal of Physical Education, Recreation & Dance, Leisure Today*, 2-5.

Bolles, R. (1978). *The three boxes of life*. Berkeley, CA.: Ten Speed Press.

Botwinick, J. (1967). Cognitive processes in maturity and old age. New York: Springer.

Bowlby, G. (1993). Therapeutic activities with persons disabled by Alzheimer's disease and related disorders. Gaithersburg, MD: Aspen Publishers.

Bowles, J. T. (1998). The evolution of aging: A new approach to an old problem of biology. Medical Hypotheses, 51, 179–221.

Boyd, R. & Tedrick, T. (1994). Leisure in the lives of older African American females. Unpublished manuscript.

Braus, P. (1995). Vision in an aging America. *American Demographics Magazine*, June.

Breystpraak, L. M. (1984). The development of self in later life. Boston: Little Brown.

Brock, D. B., Guralink, J. M., & Brody, J. A. (1990). Demography and epiden-dology of aging in the United States. In E. L. Schneider & J. W. Rowe (eds.), *Handbook of the biology of aging*. San Diego: Academic Press, 3–23.

Brooks-Lambing, M. C. (1972). Leisure time pursuits among retired blacks by social status. The *Gerontologist*, 12, 363–367.

Brown, M. & Tedrick, T. (1993). Outdoor leisure involvements of older black Americans: An exploration of ethnicity and marginality. *Activities, Adaptation & Aging*, 17 (3), 55–65.

Bruce, D. G., Devine, A. & Prince, R. L. (2002). Recreational physical activity levels in healthy older women: The importance of fear of falling. *The Journal of the American Geriatrics Society*, 50, 84-89.

Bryen, D. & Goldman, A. (2002). Contexts: Assistive technology at home, school, work, and in the community. D. Olson & F. DeRuyter (eds.). *A clinician guide to assistive technology*, 15-40. St. Louis, Missouri: Mosby.

Buchner, D., Cress, E., deLateur, B., Esselman, P., Margherita, A., Proce, R., & Wagner, E. (1997). The effect of strength and endurance training on gait, balance, fall risk, and health services use in community-living older adults. *Journal of Gerontology: Medical Sciences*, 52A (4), m218-m224.

Buettner, L. & Fitzsimmons, S. (2003). *Dementia practice guideline for recreational therapy: Treatment of disturbing behaviors.* Alexandria, VA: American Therapeutic Recreation Association.

Burch, W. R. & Hamilton-Smith, E. (1991). Mapping a new frontier: Identifying, measuring, and valuing social cohesion benefits related to nonwork opportunities and activities. In B. L. Driver, P. J. Brown. & G. L. Peterson (eds.), *Benefits of leisure.* State College, PA: Venture, 369–382.

Burdge, R. (1969). Levels of occupational prestige and leisure activity. *Journal of Leisure Research*, 1, 262–274.

Burdman, G. M. (1986). Healthful aging. Englewood Cliffs, NJ: Prentice Hall.

burlingame, j., & Skalko, T. K. (1997). Glossary for therapists. Ravensdale, WA: Idyll Arbor.

Calkins, M. (1988). Design for dementia: Planning environments for the elderly and the confused. Owings Mills, MD: National Health.

Calkins, M. P. (2002). The nursing home of the future: Are you ready? *Nursing Homes*, 51(6), 42-47.

Campanelli, L. C. (1990). Theories of aging. In C. B. Lewis (ed.), *Aging: The health care challenge*, 2nd edition. Philadelphia: F. A. Davis, 7–21.

Canadian Division of Aging and Seniors (2003). *Freedom to move.* www.hc-sc.gc.ca/seniors-aines/pubs/expression/16-1_2e.htm [August, 2003].

Carder, P. C. (2002). The social world of assisted living. *Journal of Aging Studies*, 16,1-18.

Carr, D. & Williams, D. (1993). Understanding the role of ethnicity in outdoor recreation experiences. *Journal of Leisure Research*, 25, 22–38.

Carson, J., Battisto, D., & Voelkl, J. (2003). *Activity spaces or therapeutic places?* Presentation at the American Therapeutic Recreation Association Annual Conference, Atlanta, Georgia.

Carstensen, L. L. (1993). Motivation for social contact across the life span: A theory of socioemotional selectivity. In Jacobs, J. E., (ed.). *Developmental perspectives on motivation: Nebraska Symposium on Motivation*, 40. Lincoln: University of Nebraska Press, 209-254.

Caudron, S. (1997) Boomers rock the system. Workforce, 76 (12),42.

Cavanaugh, G. & Emeran, J. (2003). *ASA Study: Aging agencies must do more on assistive tech.* American Society on Aging. http://www.asaging.org/at/at-185/atech-aaa.html [September, 2003].

Centers for Disease Control (1999). *Physical activity and health: A report of the Surgeon General—Older adults.* www.cdc.gov/nccdphp/sgr/olderad.htm [July, 2003].

Chacko, H. & Nebel, E. (1993). The group tour industry: An analysis of motorcoach tour operators. *Journal of Travel & Tourism Marketing,* 2(1), 69-83.

Chambre, S. M. (1993). Volunteerism by elders: Past trends and future prospects. *The Gerontologist,* 33, 221–228.

Charness, N. & Bosman, E. A. (1990). Human factors and design for older adults. In J. E. Birren & K. W. Schaie (eds.), *The handbook of the psychology of aging,* (3rd edition). San Diego: Academic Press, 446–463.

Chasteen, A. L., Schwarz, N., and Park, D. C. (2002). The activation of aging stereotypes in younger and older adults. *The Journal of Gerontology: Psychological Sciences,* 57, 540-547.

Cheek, N., Field, D., & Burdge, R. (1976). Leisure and recreation places. Ann Arbor: Science Publishers.

Cheng, E. (1978). The elder Chinese. San Diego: Center for Aging, San Diego University.

Chon, K.S. & Singh, A. (1995). Marketing resorts to 2000: Review of trends in the USA. *Tourism Management,* 16(6), 463-469.

CIGNA HealthCare of Colorado (1995). Aging, exercise, and depression: Separating myths from realities. *The Medical Reporter.* www.ihr.com/medrept/articles/agingexr.html [March, 1999].

Clark, E. (1986). *Growing old is not for sissies.* San Francisco: Pomegranate Artbooks.

Clark, E. (1995). *Growing old is not for sissies II.* San Francisco: Pomegranate Artbooks.

Clarke, N. (1956). The use of leisure and its relation to level of occupational prestige. *American Sociological Review,* 21, 301–307.

Cohen, G. D. (1990). Psychopathology and mental health in the mature and elderly adult. In J. E. Birren & K. W. Schaie (eds.), *Handbook of the psychology of aging.* San Diego: Academic Press, 359–371.

Cole, N. (1981). Bias in testing. *American Psychologist,* 36, 1067–1077.

Columbia/HCA (undated). Exploring the "aging process." www.columbia.net/consumer/datafile/boomexpl.html [March, 1999].

Comfort, A. (1976). A good age. New York: Crown.

Cook, A. (1983). Contemporary perspectives on adult development and aging. New York: MacMillan.

Cowgill. D. O. (1974). Aging and modernization: A revision of the theory. In J. F. Gubrium (ed.), *Later life: Communities and environmental policy.* Springfield, IL: C. C. Thomas, 123-246.

Cox, H. G. (1993). Later life: The realities of aging. Englewood Cliffs, NJ: Prentice Hall.

Cox, H. G. (1998) Roles for the aged individual in post-industrial societies. In H. Cox (ed.), *Aging,* (12th edition.) Guilford, CT: Dushkin/McGraw Hill.

Crandall, R. C. (1980). Gerontology: A behavioral science approach. Reading, MA: Addison-Wesley.

Crohan, S. & Antonucci, T. (1989). Friends as a source of social support in old age. In R. Adams & R. Blieszner (eds.), *Older adult friendship: Structure and process*. Newbury Park: Sage, 129–146.

Csikszentimihalyi, M. (1975). Beyond boredom and anxiety. San Francisco: Jossey Bass.

Csikszentmihalyi, M. (1990). Flow: The psychology of optimal experience. New York: Harper and Row.

Csikszentmihalyi, M. & Kleiber, D. (1991). Leisure and self-actualization. In B. L. Driver, P. J. Brown, & G. L. Peterson (eds.), *Benefits of leisure*. State College, PA: Venture, 91-102.

Cuddy, A. J. & Fiske, S. T. (2002) Doddering but dear: Processes, content, and function in stereotyping of older persons. In Nelson, T.D. (ed.)., *Ageism: Stereotyping and prejudice against older people*. Cambridge, MA: The MIT Press, 3-26.

Cumming, E. & Henry, W. E. (1961). Growing old: The process of disengagement. New York: Basic Books.

Dangott, L. R. & Kalish, R. A. (1979). A time to enjoy: The pleasures of aging. Englewood Cliffs, NJ: Prentice Hall.

Dannifer, D. (1988). What's in a name? An account of the neglect of variability in the study of aging. In J.E. Birren, and V.L. Bengston (eds.) *Emergent theories of aging*, 356-384. New York: Springer.

Deci, E. L. & Ryan, R. M. (2000) The "what" and "why" of goal pursuits: Human needs and the self-determination of behavior. *Psychological Inquiry*, 11, 227-268.

Deem, R. (1986). All work and no play? The sociology of women and leisure. Milton Keynes, England: Open University Press.

deGrazia, S. (1962). Of time, work and leisure. New York: Twentieth Century Fund.

Dennis, W. (1966). Creative productivity between the ages of 20 and 80 years. *Journal of Gerontology*, 21, 1–8.

Dinsmoor, R. (1993). Strength training after sixty. Harvard Health Letter, 68.

DiPietro, L. (2001). Physical activity in aging: Changes in patterns and their relationship to health and function. *Journals of Gerontology: Series A: Biological Sciences and Medical Sciences*, 56A(11), p. 13-22.

Division of Aging and Seniors (1997). *What causes smell and taste disorders?* National Advisory Council on Aging. http://www.hc-sc.gc.ca/seniors-aines/pubs/vignette/vig89_e.htm#89b [September, 2003].

Dorsey, V. L. Games show positive side to growing old, athletes say. *USA Today*, 11 June 1993: 12C.

Driver, B. L., Tinsley, H. E. A., & Manfredo, M. J. (1991). The Paragraphs about Leisure and Recreation Experiences Preference Scales: Results from two inventories designed to assess the breadth of the perceived psychological benefits of leisure. In B. L. Driver, P. J. Brown, & G. L. Peterson (eds.), *Benefits of leisure*. State College, PA: Venture Press, 263–286.

Dwyer, J. & Gobster, P. (1992). Recreation opportunity and cultural diversity. Parks and Recreation, 22, 24, 25, 27, 28, 30, 33, 128.

Dwyer, J. & Hutchinson, R. (1990). Outdoor recreation participation and preferences for black and white Chicago households. In J. Vining (ed.), *Social science and natural resource recreation management*. Boulder, CO: Westview Press, 49–67.

Dychtwald, K. & Flower, J. (1989). Age Wave: The challenges and opportunities of an aging America. Los Angeles: Jeremy P. Tarcher.

Dye, L (2003). *Jogging the mind: Evidence proves exercise keeps the mind sharp.* http://abcnews.go.com/sections/scitech/DyeHard/dyehard030130.html [September, 2003].

Ebersole, P. & Hess, P. (1990). Toward healthy aging: Human needs and nursing response. 3rd edition. St. Louis: C. V. Mosby.

Ebersole, P. & Hess, P. (1998). Toward healthy aging: Human needs and nursing response. 5th edition. St. Louis: C. V. Mosby.

Ebersol P. & Hess, P. (2001). *Geriatric nursing & healthy aging.* St. Louis: Mosby.

Eden Alternative (1999). *Ten principles: The heart of the Eden Alternative.* Sherburne, NY: The Eden Alternative. www.edenalt.com/about_eden/tenprinciples.htm [March, 1999].

Ehrenreich, B. (2001). *Nickel and dimed: On (not) getting by in America.* New York: Metropolitan Books.

Ekerdt, D.J. (1986). The busy ethic: Moral continuity between work and retirement. *The Gerontologist, 26*(3), 239-244.

Elder, G.H., Jr. (1985). *Life course dynamics: Trajectories and transitions, 1968-1980.* New York: Siminar Press.

Elderhostel: *Adventures in lifelong learning.* www.elderhotel.org [August, 2003].

Ellis, M. (1973). *Why people play.* Englewood Cliffs, NJ: Prentice Hall.

Erikson, E. H. (1950). *Childhood and society.* New York: Norton.

Everard, K. M., Lach, H. W., Fisher, E. B., & Baum, M.C. (2000). Relationship of activity and social support to the functional health of older adults. *Journal of Gerontology: Social Sciences, 55B,* 208-212.

Ewert, A., Chavez, D. J., & Magill, A. W. (1993). *Culture, conflict, and the wildlifeurban interface.* Boulder, CO: Westview Press.

Facts of Life (1998). Getting old: A lot of it is in your head. Washington, DC: Center for the Advancement of Health.

Federal Interagency Forum on Aging Related Statistics (2000*). Older Americans 2000: Key indicators of well-being.* Washington, D.C.: U.S. Government Printing Office. www.agingstats.gov/default.htm [August, 2003].

Feil, N. (1993). The validation breakthrough. Baltimore: Health Professions Press.

Fergunson, K. (1989). Qualitative research with older adults. In E. Thomas (ed.), *Adulthood and aging: The human science approach.* Albany, NY: State University of New York.

Fleisher, A. and Pizam, A. (2002). Tourism constraints among Israel seniors. *Annals of Tourism Research, 29,* 106-123.

Floyd, M. & Gramann, J. (1993). Effects of acculturation and structural assimilation in resource-based recreation: The case of Mexican Americans. *Journal of Leisure Research*, 25, 6-21.

Floyd, M., Shinew, K., McGuire, F., & Noe, F. (1994). Race, class and leisure activity preferences: Marginality and ethnicity revisited. *Journal of Leisure Research*, 26, 158–173.

Floyd, M. (1998). Getting beyond marginality and ethnicity: The challenge for race and ethnic studies in leisure research. *Journal of Leisure Research*. 30(1), 3-22.

Freund, A. M. and Baltes, P. B. (1998). Selection, optimization, and compensation as strategies of life management: Correlations with subjective indicators of successful aging. *Psychology and Aging*, 13, 531–543.

Freund, A. M. and Baltes, P. B. (2002). Life-management strategies of selection, optimization and compensation: Measurement by self-report and construct validity. *Journal of Personality and Social Psychology*, 82, 642 – 662.

Freysinger, V., Alessio, H., & Mehdizadeh, S. (1993). Re-examining the morale-physical health-activity relationship: A longitudinal study of time changes and gender differences. *Activities, Adaptation & Aging*, 17(4), 25-41.

Fried, L. P, Freedman, M., Endres, T. E., & Wasik, B. (1997). Building communities that promote successful aging. *Western Journal of Medicine*, 167, 216–219.

Fried, S., Van Booven, D., & MacQuarrie, C. (1993). Older adulthood: Learning activities for understanding aging. Baltimore: Health Professions Press.

Fung, L. & Ha, A. (1994). Changes in track and field performance with chronological aging. *International Journal of Aging and Human Development*, 38(2), 171-180.

Gagnon, D. (1996) A review of reality orientation (RO), validation therapy (VT), and reminiscence therapy (RT) with the Alzheimer's client. *Physical and Occupational Therapy in Geriatrics*, 14 (2), 61–77.

Gallup, G. (1986). T.V. remains our favorite pastime, but other diversions grow. The Gallup Report, May (248), 7–9.

Gatz, M., Kasl-Godley, J. E. & Karel, M. J. (1996). Aging and mental disorders. In J. E. Birren & K. W. Schaie (eds.), *Handbook of the psychology of aging* (4th edition) San Diego: Academic Press.

Gatz, M. & Smyer, M. A. (2001). Mental health and aging at the outset of the twentyfirst century. In Birren, J. E. & Schaie, K. W. (eds.) *Handbook of the psychology of aging, 5th edition*. San Diego: Academic Press.

Gauthier, A. & Smeeding, T. (2000). Patterns of time use of people age 55 to 64 years old: Some cross-national comparisons. Center of Policy Research, Maxwell School of Citizenship and Public Affairs, Syracuse University. www cpr.maxwell.syr.edu [April, 2003].

Gelfand, D. E. (1988). The aging network: Programs and services, 3rd edition. New York: Springer.

Gendell, M. & Siegel, J. (July, 1992). Trends in retirement age. *Monthly Labor Review*, 22-29.

Gendell, M. & Siegel, J. (1996). Trends in retirement age in the United States, 1955-1993, by sex and race. *Journal of Gerontology: Social Sciences*, 51B(3), S132-S139.

George, L. K. (1996). Missing links: The case for a social psychology of the life course. *The Gerontologist, 36*, 248-255.

George, L. K. (1990). Social structure, social processes, and social-psychological states. In R. H. Binstock & L. K. George (eds.), *Handbook of aging and the social sciences*. San Diego: Academic Press, 186–204.

Gibson, H. (April, 1998). The educational tourist. *Journal of Physical Education, Recreation & Dance, Leisure Today*, 6-8.

Gibson, H., Ashton-Shaeffer, C. & Sanders, G. (2000). It's all fun and sun... or is it? Leisure and retirement in Florida: Women's experiences. Abstracts of the 2000 Leisure Research Symposium, National Recreation and Park Association, 19.

Goldberg, A. & Hagberg, J. M. (1990). Physical exercise in the elderly. In E. L. Schneider & J. W. Rowe (eds.), *Handbook of the biology of aging*. San Diego: Academic Press.

Golub, S. A., Filipowicz, A. and Langer, E. J. (2002). Acting your age. In Nelson, T.D. (ed.), *Ageism: Stereotyping and prejudice against older people*. Cambridge, MA: The MIT Press, 277-294.

Gordon, C. & Gaitz, C. (1976). Leisure and lives: Expressivity across the life span. In R. Binstock & E. Shanas (eds.), *Handbook of aging and the social sciences*. New York: Van Nostrand Reinhold.

Gottesman, L. & Bourestom, N. (1974). Why nursing homes do what they do. *The Gerontologist*, 14, 501-506.

Gottlieb, D. (1957). The neighborhood tavern and the cocktail lounge: A study of class differences. *American Journal of Sociology*, 62, 559–562.

Gramann, J., Floyd, M., & Saenz, R. (1993). Outdoor recreation and Mexican American ethnicity: A benefits perspective. In A. Ewert, D. Chavez, & A. Magill (eds.), *Culture conflict and communication: The wildland-urban interface*. Boulder, CO: Westview Press, 69–84.

Grant, B. C. (2001). You're never too old: Beliefs about physical activity ad playing sport in later life. *Aging & Society*, 21, 777-798.

Green, D. (April, 2003). Personal communication.

Greenblatt, F. S. (1988). Therapeutic recreation for long-term care facilities. New York: Human Sciences Press.

Haberkost, M., Dellman-Jenkins, M., & Bennett, J. M. (1996). Importance of quality recreation activities for older adults residing in nursing homes: Considerations for gerontologists. *Educational Gerontology*, 22, 735–745.

Haggard, L. M. & Williams, D. R. (1991). Self-identity benefits of leisure activities. In B. L. Driver, P. J. Brown, & G. L. Peterson (eds.), *Benefits of leisure*. State College, PA: Venture Press, 103–119.

Haight, B. K. (1991). Psychological illness in aging. In E. M. Baines (ed.), *Perspectives on gerontological nursing*. Newbury Park: Sage, 296–322.

Harbert, A. S. & Ginsberg, L. H. (1990). *Human services for older adults: Concepts and skills*, 2nd edition. Columbia, SC: University of South Carolina Press.

Harris, C. (1978). Fact book on aging. Washington, DC: National Council on Aging.

Harris, J. (1984). Methods of improving memory. In B. A. Wilson & N. Moffat (eds.), *Clinical management of memory problems*. Rockville, Maryland: Aspen, 46–62.

Havighurst, R. J. (1961). The nature and value of meaningful free time activities. In R. W. Kleemier (ed.), *Aging and leisure*. New York: Oxford University Press, 309–344.

Havighurst, R. J. & Albrecht, R. (1953). Older people. New York: Longmans Green.

Hawes, D. (1988). Travel-related lifestyle profiles of older women. *Journal of Travel Research*, 27, 22–32.

Hawkins, H., Kramer, A. and Capaldi, D. (1992). Aging, exercise and attention. *Psychology & Aging*, 7(4), 643-653.

Hayflick, L. (1985). The aging process: Current theories. New York: A. R. Liss.

Hazan, H. (2000a). The cultural trap: The language of images. In Gubrium, J. F. and Holstein, J. A. (eds.). *Aging and everyday life*. Malden MA: Blackwell Publishers, 15-18.

Hazan, H. (2000b). The personal trap: The language of self-presentation. In Gubrium, J. F. and Holstein, J. A. (eds.), *Aging and everyday life*. Malden MA: Blackwell Publishers, 19-24.

HealthAnswers (1997a). Aging changes in the bones, muscles, and joints. Applied Medical Infomatics Inc. and Orbis-AHCN, L.L.C. www.healthanswers.com/database/ami/converted/004015.html [March, 1999].

HealthAnswers (1997b). Aging changes in the heart and blood vessels. Applied Medical Infomatics Inc. and Orbis-AHCN, L.L.C. www.healthanswers.com/database/ami/converted/004006.html (March 1999).

HealthAnswers (1997c). Aging changes in the senses. Applied Medical Infomatics Inc. and Orbis-AHCN, L.L.C. www.healthanswers.com/database/ami/converted/004013.html [March, 1999].

Heckheimer, E. F. (1989). Health promotion of the elderly in the community. Philadelphia: W. B. Saunders.

Heitman, H. (1986). Motives of older adults for participating in physical activity programs. *The 1984 Olympic Scientific Congress Proceedings: Sport and Aging*, (5), 199-203.

Helender, J. (1978). The richness and poorness of being old in Sweden. Paper presented at a seminar on facing an aging society.

Hellen, C. (1993). Alzheimer's disease: Finding purposeful activities. The Council Close-up: Illinois Council on long-term care. www.nursinghome.org/closeup/cupdocument/cu023.htm [March, 1999].

Henderson, K. (1990a). An oral history perspective on the containers in which American farm women experience leisure. *Leisure Studies*, 9 (2), 27–38.

Henderson, K. (1990b). The meaning of leisure for women: An integrative review of the research. *Journal of Leisure Research*, 22, 228–243.

Henderson, K. (1991). The contribution of feminism to an understanding of leisure constraints. *Journal of Leisure Research*, 23, 363–377.

Henderson, K. (1992). Broadening an understanding of the gendered meanings of leisure for women. Paper presented at the NRPA Leisure Research Symposium, Cincinnati, Ohio.

Henderson, K., Bialeschki, D., Shaw, S., & Freysinger, V. (1989). A leisure of one's own: A feminist perspective on women's leisure. State College, PA: Venture Publishing.

Henderson, K. & Rannells, J. (1988). Farm women and the meaning of work and leisure: An oral history perspective. *Leisure Sciences*, 10, 41–50.

Hess, B. (1974). Stereotypes of the aged. *Journal of Communications*, 24, 76–85.

Hochschild, A. R. (1973). The unexpected community. Englewood Cliffs, NJ: Prentice Hall.

Hochschild, A. R. (1989). The second shift: Working parents and the revolution at home. New York: Viking.

Hooyman, N. R. & Kiyak, N. R. (1993). *Social gerontology: A multidisciplinary perspective,* 3rd edition, Boston: Allyn and Bacon.

Hooyman, N. R. & Kiyak, N. R. (2002). *Social gerontology: A multidisciplinary perspective 6th edition*. Boston: Allyn and Bacon.

Horna, J. (1991). The family and leisure domains: Women's involvement and perceptions. World Leisure and Recreation, 33 (3), 11–14.

Howard, D. (1992). Participation rates in selected sport and fitness activities. *Journal of Sport Management*. (6), 191-205.

Howard, D. V. (1992). Implicit memory: An expanding picture of cognitive aging. In K. W. Schaie & M. P. Lawton (eds.), *Annual review of gerontology and geriatrics*, (11). New York: Springer, 1–22.

Howe, D. A. (1992). Creating vital communities: Planning for our aging society. *Planning Commissioners Journal*, 7 (Nov/Dec), 1.

Hultsch, D. F. & Dixon, R. A. (1990). Learning and memory in aging. In J. E. Birren & K. W. Schaie (eds.), *Handbook of the psychology of aging*. San Diego: Academic Press, 258–274.

Iso-Ahola, S. (1980). Social psychological perspectives on leisure and recreation. Springfield, IL: Charles C. Thomas.

Iso-Ahola, S. E. (1989). Motivation for leisure. In E. L. Jackson & T. L. Burton (eds.), *Understanding leisure and recreation: Mapping the past, charting the future*. State College, PA: Venture, 247–279.

Iso-Ahola, S., Jackson, E., & Dunn, E. (1994). Starting, ceasing, and replacing leisure activities over the life-span. *Journal of Leisure Research*, 26(3), 227-249.

Jackson, J. J. (1972). Black women in a racist society. In C. Willie, B. Krouer, & B. Brown (eds.), *Racism and mental health*. Pittsburgh, PA: University of Pittsburgh Press, 185–268.

Jackson, M., Kolody, B., & Wood, J. (1982). To be old and black: The case for double jeopardy on income and health. In R. Manuel (ed.), *Minority aging: Social and social psychological issues*. Westport, CT: Greenwood Press, 77–82.

Jacobs, J. (1974). Older persons and retirement communities. Springfield, IL: C. C. Thomas.

Javalgi, R., Thomas, E., & Rao, S. (1992). Consumer behavior in the U.S. pleasure travel marketplace: An analysis of senior and non-senior travelers. *Journal of Travel Research*, (30), 14-19.

Johnson, C., Bowker, J., English, D., & Worthen, D. (1998). Wildland recreation in the rural South: An examination of marginality and ethnicity theory. *Journal of Leisure Research* 30(1). 101-120.

Johnson, F. B., Marciniak, R., & Guarente, L. (1998). Telomeres, the nucleolus and aging. Current Opinion in Cell Biology, 10, 332–338.

Jones, A. (2002). The National Nursing Home Survey: 1999 Summary. National Center for Health Statistics. *Vital Health, Stat,* 13(152).

Jones, C., Jessie, U., Robinchaux, J., Williams, P., & Rikli, R. (1992). The effects of a 16-week exercise program on the dynamic balance of older adults. *Journal of Clinical and Experimental Gerontology*, 14(2), P 165-182.

Jones, E. B. (November, 1963). New estimates of hours of work per week and hourly earnings, 1900-1957. *Review of Economics and Statistics*, 45(4), 374-385.

Jones, M. (1999*). Gentlecare: Changing the experience of Alzheimer's Disease in a positive way*. Hartley & Marks Publishers.

Jonson, H. and Magnusson, J. A. (2001). A new age of old age? Gerotranscendence and the re-enhancement of aging.
Journal of Aging Studies, 15, 317-331.

Juniu, S. (1997). Effects of ethnicity on leisure behavior and its meaning in the life of a selected group of South American immigrants. Unpublished doctoral dissertation, Temple University, Philadelphia, PA.

Kalish, R. A. (1975). Late adulthood: Perspectives on human development. Monterey, CA: Brooks Cole.

Kalish, R. A. (1979). The new ageism and the failure model: A new polemic. *The Gerontologist*, 19, 398–402.

Kalish, R. A. (1982). *Late adulthood: Perspectives on human development,* 2nd edition. Monterey, CA: Brooks Cole.

Kamptner, N. L. (1989). Personal possessions and their meaning in old age. In S. Spacapan & S. Oskamp (eds.), *The social psychology of aging*. Newbury Park: Sage, 165–196.

Kane, R. (2003). Definition, measurement, and correlates of quality of life in nursing homes: Toward a reasonable practice, research, and policy agenda. *The Gerontologist*, 43 (SPI/2), 28-36.

Kane, R. A., Kane, R. L., & Ladd, R. C. (1998). *The heart of long-term care*. New York, NY: Oxford University Press.

Kaplan, M. (1975). Leisure: Theory and policy. New York: John Wiley.

Kaplan, M. (1979). Leisure: Lifestyle and lifespan perspectives for gerontology. Philadelphia: W. B. Saunders.

Kastenbaum, R. (1987). Prevention of age-related problems. In L. L. Carstensen & B. A. Edelstein (eds.), *Handbook of clinical gerontology*. New York: Pergammon, 322–334.

Kausler, D. H. (1990). Motivation, human aging, and cognitive performance. In J. E. Birren & K. W. Schaie (eds.), *Handbook of the psychology of aging*, 3rd edition. San Diego: Academic Press, 171–182.

Kelly, J. R. (undated). Life-in-between: Continuity and construction. Unpublished paper.

Kelly, J. R. (1982). Leisure. Englewood Cliffs, NJ: Prentice Hall.

Kelly, J.R. (1983). Leisure identities and interactions. London: Allen & Unwin.

Kelly, J. R. (1987a). Freedom to be: A new sociology of leisure. New York: MacMillan.

Kelly, J. R. (1987). Peoria winter. Lexington, MA: Lexington Books.

Kelly, J. R. (1991). Sociological perspectives on recreation benefits. In B. L. Driver, P. J. Brown, & G. L. Peterson (eds.), *Benefits of leisure*. State College, PA: Venture, 419–422.

Kelly, J. R. (1996). Leisure. Englewood Cliffs, NJ: Prentice Hall.

Kelly, J. R. & Godbey, G. (1992). The sociology of leisure. State College, PA: Venture.

Kelly, J. R. & Westcott, G. (1991). Ordinary retirement: Commonalities and continuity. *International Journal of Aging and Human Development*, 32, 81–89.

Kemper, S. & Mitzner, T. L. (2001). Language production and comprehension. In Birren, J. E. & Schaie, K. W. (Eds.). *Handbook of the psychology of aging, 5th edition*. San Diego: Academic Press, 378-398.

Kidder, T. (1994). *Old friends*. Houghton Mifflin Company.

Kliegl, R. & Baltes, P. (1987). Theory-guided analysis of mechanisms of development and aging through testing the limits and research on expertise. In C. Schooler & K. W. Schaie (eds.), *Cognitive functioning and social structure over the life course*. Norwood, NJ: Ablex.

Kogan, N. (1990). Personality and aging. In J. E. Birren & K. W. Schaie (eds.), *Handbook of the psychology of aging*. San Diego: Academic Press, 330–346.

Kovacevic, M. (1995). *Of vital importance*. http://www.paweekly.com/PAW/morgue/monthly/1995 Mar 22.AGING22.html [September, 2003].

Lakatta, E. G. (1990). Heart and circulation. In E. L. Schneider & J. W. Rowe (eds.), *Handbook of the biology of aging*. San Diego: Academic Press, 181–216.

Lang, F. R., Rieckmann, N., & Baltes, M. M. (2002). Adapting to aging losses: Do resources facilitate strategies of selection, compensation, and optimization in everyday functioning. *Journal of Gerontology: Psychological Sciences,* 57B, 501-509.

Langer, E. & Rodin, J. (1976). The effects of choice and enhanced personal responsibility for aged: A field experiment in an institutional setting. *Journal of Personality and Social Psychology,* 34, 191–198.

Langley, D.J. & Knight, S.M. (1999). Continuity in sport participation as an adaptive strategy in the aging process: A lifespan narrative. *Journal of Aging and Physical Activity,* (7), 32-54.

Lawton, M. P. (1989). Environmental proactivity and affect in older people. In S. Spacapan & S. Oskamp (eds.), *The social psychology of aging.* Newbury Park: Sage.

Lawton, M. P. (1986). *Environment and aging.* Albany, NY: Center for the Study of Aging.

Lawton, M. P. (1993). Meanings of activity. In J. R. Kelly (ed.), *Activity and aging: Staying involved in later life.* Newbury Park: Sage, 25–41.

Lawton, M. P., Weisman, G. D., Sloane, P., Norris-Baker, C., Calkins, M., & Zimmerman, S. (2000). Professional Environmental Assessment Procedure for special care units for elders with dementing illness. *Alzheimer's Disease and Related Disorders,* 14, 28-38.

Lehman, H. C. (1953). Age and achievement. Princeton: Princeton University Press.

Leitner, M. & Leitner, S. (1985). Leisure in later years: A source book for the provision of recreational services for elders. New York: Haworth.

Lemon, B. W., Bengston, V. L., & Peterson, J. A. (1972). An exploration of the activity theory of aging: Activity types and life satisfaction among inmovers to a retirement community. *Journal of Gerontology,* 27, 511–523.

Lennartsson, C. & Silverstein, M. (2001). Does engagement with life enhance survival of elderly people in Sweden? The role of social and leisure activities. *Journal of Gerontology: Social Sciences,* 56B, 335-342.

Levinson, D.J. (1978). *The seasons of a man's life.* New York: Alfred A. Knopf.

Levinson, D. J. (1986). A conception of adult development. *American Psychologist,* 41, 3–13.

Levy, B. R. (2001) Eradication of ageism requires addressing the enemy within. *The Gerontologist,* 41, 578-579.

Levy, B. R. and Banaji, M. R. (2002) Implicit ageism. In Nelson, T.D. (ed.), *Ageism: Stereotyping and prejudice against older people.* Cambridge, MA: The MIT Press, 49-76.

Levy, B. R., Slade, M. D., Kunkel, S. R., & Kasl, S.V. (2002). Longevity increased by positive self-perceptions of aging. *Journal of Personality and Social Psychology,* 83, 261-270.

Lewin, F. A. (2001). Gerotranscendence and different cultural settings. *Aging and Society,* 21, 395-415.

Lewis, C. B. (1990). Aging: The health care challenge. Philadelphia: F. A. Davis.

Lieberman, S. (1991). Sports poll 1991: A national survey commissioned by *Sports Illustrated.* New York: Lieberman Research.

Lieux, E., Weaver, P., & McCleary, K. (1994). Lodging preferences of the senior tourism market. *Annals of Tourism Research*, 21(4), 712-728.

Lindeman, L. (1991). Beating time. Modern Maturity, June–July, 27–35.

Loevinger, J. (1976). Ego development: Conception and theory. San Francisco: Jossey Bass.

Longino, C. F. & Kart, C. S. (1982). Explicating activity theory: A formal replication. *Journal of Gerontology*, 37, 713–722.

Losier, G. F., Bourque, P. E., Vallerand, R. J. (1993) A motivational model of leisure participation in the elderly. *Journal of Psychology*, 127, 153–170.

Mace, R. (1997). *What is universal design?* North Carolina State University, The Center for Universal Design. http://www.design.ncsu.edu/cud/univ_design/ud.htm [September, 2003].

MacKenzie, S. (1980). Aging and old age. Glenview, IL: Scott, Foresman and Co.

MacNeil, R. (February, 1998). Leisure, lifelong learning, and older adults: A conceptual overview. *Journal of Physical Education, Recreation & Dance, Leisure Today,* 2-4.

MacNeil, R.D. & Teague, M. L. (1992). *Leisure and aging: Vitality in later life, 2nd edition.* Dubuque, IA: Brown and Benchmark.

MacNeil, R.D. & Teague, M. L. (1987). Leisure and aging: Vitality in later life. Englewood Cliffs, NJ: Prentice-Hall.

Mannell, R. & Kleiber, D. (1997). A social psychology of leisure. State College, PA: Venture Publishing Inc.

Marsden, J. P., Calkins, M. P., & Briller, S. H. (2003). Educating LTC staff about therapeutic environments. *Journal of Architectural and Planning Research*, 20 (1), 68-74.

Marshall, V. W. (1986). Dominant and emerging paradigms in the social psychology of aging. In V. W. Marshall (ed.), Later life: The social psychology of aging. Beverly Hills: Sage, 9–31.

Marshall, V.W. (1979). No Exit: A symbolic interactionist perspective on aging. *International Journal of Aging and Human Development*, 80, 1124-1144.

Marshall, V.W. (1995). Social models of aging. *Canadian Journal on Aging*, 14, 12-34.

Martin, S. & Smith, R.W. (1993) OBRA legislation and recreational activities: Enhancing personal control in nursing homes. *Activities, Adaptation & Aging*, 17 (3), 1–13.

Marvel, M. (1999). Competing in hotel services for seniors. *International Journal of Hospitality Management,* 18(3), 235-243.

Mayo Clinic (1999) Delirium: *Clinical features and course.* www.mayo.edu/geriatrics-rst/DelClin.html [September, 1999].

Mayo Clinic Health Letter (1998) Sexuality and aging: What it means to be sixty or seventy or eighty in the '90s. In H. Cox (ed.), *Aging, 12th edition.* Guilford, CT: Dushkin/McGraw Hill.

Mazzeo, R., Cavanagh, P., Evans, W., Fiatarone, M., Hagberg, J., McAuley, E. & Starzell, J. (1999). Exercise and physical activity for older adults: American College of Sports Medicine Position Stand. *The Physician and Sportsmedicine*, 27(11), 115-118, 122-124, 129-130, 133-136, 141-142.

Mazzeo R., Cavanaugh P., Evans W. J., Fiatarone Singh M., Hagberg J., McAuley E., Startzell J. (1998). Exercise and physical activity for older adults. *Medical Sciences, Sports and Exercise*, 30(6), 992-1008.

McAndrew, F. T. (1993). Environmental psychology. Pacific Grove, CA: Brooks Cole.

McCall, G. J. & Simmons, J. L. (1966). Identities and interactions. New York: Free Press.

McCormick, B. (1993). Same place, different worlds: Leisure styles and community life of older residents of rural retirement and village communities. Doctoral Dissertation. Clemson University.

McDowell, C. F. (1978). So you think you know how to leisure? A guide to leisure well-being in your lifestyle. Eugene, OR: Leisure Lifestyle Consultants.

McGuire, F. A. & Dottavio, F. D. (1986–87). Outdoor recreation participation across the lifespan: Abandonment, continuity or liberation? *International Journal of Aging and Human Development*, 24, 87-100.

McGuire, F. A., and Hawkins, M. O. (1999) Introduction to intergenerational programs. In M. O. Hawkins, F. A. McGuire, and K. E. Backman (eds.). *Preparing participants for intergenerational interaction: Training for success*. New York: Haworth Press.

McGuire, F. A. & Norman, W. (forthcoming). The Role of Constraints in Successful Aging: Inhibiting or Enabling? In Jackson, E. (ed.), *Constraints to leisure*. State College, PA: Venture.

McGuire, F. A., O'Leary, J., Alexander, P., & Dottavio, D. (1987). A comparison of outdoor recreation preferences and constraints of black and white elderly. *Activities, Adaptation & Aging*, 9(4), 95–104.

McLeish, J. (1976). The Ulyssean adult: Creativity in middle and later years. Toronto: McGraw-Hill Ryerson.

McMullin, J. A. (2000). Diversity and the state of sociological aging theory. *The Gerontologist*, 40, 517–530.

McPherson, B. D. (1991). Aging and leisure benefits: A life cycle perspective. In B. L. Driver, P. J. Brown, & G. L. Peterson (eds.), *Benefits of leisure*. State College, PA: Venture, 423–430.

Melamed, L. (1991). Leisure, what leisure? Questioning old theories. *World Leisure and Recreation*, 33 (3), 34–36.

Menec, V. H. (2003). The relation between everyday activities and successful aging: A 6-year longitudinal study. *Journal of Gerontology: Social Sciences*, 58B, 74-82.

Miller, J. (April, 1996). On design: Golden opportunities: Seniors travel frequently and accommodating their needs can quickly produce profits. *Hotel & Motel Management*, 45-46.

Miller, S. J. (1965). The social dilemma of the aging leisure participant. In A. M. Rose & W. A. Peterson (eds.), *Older people and their social world*. Philadelphia: Davis.

Millett, M. (1984). Voices of experience: 1,500 retired people talk about retirement. New York: TIAA–CREF.

Mobily, K. E., Lemke, J. H. and Gisin, G. J. (1991). The idea of leisure repertoire. *The Journal of Applied Gerontology*, 10, 208–223.

Mullins, L. & Mushel, M. (1992). The existence and emotional closeness of relationships with children, friends and spouses: The effect on loneliness among older persons. *Research on Aging*, 14, 448–470.

Murphy, S. L., Williams, C. S. and Gill, T. M. (2002). Characteristics associated with fear of falling and activity restriction in community-living older persons. *Journal of the American Geriatrics Society*, 50, 516-520.

Myers, G. C. (1990). Demography of aging. In R. H. Binstock & L. K. George (eds.), *Handbook of aging and the social sciences, 3rd. edition*. San Diego: Academic Press, 1944.

National Academy on an Aging Society (2000a). *Arthritis: A leading cause of disability in the United States*. Washington D.C.: National Academy on an Aging Society.

National Academy on an Aging Society (2000b). *Hypertension: A common condition for older Americans*. Washington D.C.: National Academy on an Aging Society.

National Association of Counties (undated a). *Aging in place: Options for home and community-based care*. Washington, DC: National Association of Counties.

National Association of Counties (undated b). *Is your community a good place to grow old: A community needs assessment*. Washington, D.C.: National Association of Counties.

National Center on Assisted Living, (2003). www.ncal.org [December, 2003].

National Council on Aging (undated). Healthy aging: A good investment. *Exemplary programs for senior centers and other facilities*. Washington D.C.: National Council on Aging.

National Institute of Mental Health (1994). Alzheimer's disease. Washington, DC: National Institutes of Health.

National Institute on Aging (2000a). *Skin care and aging*. Washington D.C.: National Institutes of Health.

National Institute on Aging (2000b). *Foot care*. Washington D.C.: National Institutes of Health.

National Institute on Aging (2000c). *Dealing with diabetes*. Washington D.C.: National Institutes of Health.

National Institute on Aging (2002a). *Aging Under the Microscope*. Washington D.C.: National Institutes of Health.

National Institute on Aging (2002b). *Osteoporosis: The bone thief*. Washington D.C.: National Institutes of Health.

National Institute on Aging (2002c). *Arthritis advice*. Washington D.C.: National Institutes of Health.

National Institute on Aging (2002d). *High blood pressure: Tips for keeping it under control*. Washington D.C.: National Institutes of Health.

National Institute on Aging (2002e). *Good nutrition: It's a way of life*. Washington D.C.: National Institutes of Health.

National Institute on Aging (2002f). *Taking care of your teeth and mouth.* Washington D.C.: National Institutes of Health.

National Institute on Aging (2002g). *Urinary incontinence.* Washington D.C.: National Institutes of Health.

National Institute on Aging (2002h). *Sexuality in later life.* Washington D.C.: National Institutes of Health.

National Institute on Aging (2002i). *Aging and your eyes.* Washington D.C.: National Institutes of Health.

National Institute on Aging (2002j). *Hearing loss.* Washington D.C.: National Institutes of Health.

National Institute on Aging (2002k). *Exercise: Feeling fit for life.* www.nia.nih.gov/health/agepages/exercise.htm [July, 2003].

National Institute on Aging (2002l). *Depression: Don't let the blues hang around.* Washington D.C.: National Institutes of Health. www.nia.nih.gov/health/agepages/depression.htm [September, 2003].

National Institute on Aging (2002m). *Alcohol use and abuse.* Washington D.C.: National Institutes of Health. www.nia.nih.gov/health/agepages/alcohol.htm [September, 2003].

National Institute on Aging Age Page (1991). *Dealing with diabetes.* Washington DC: U.S. Department of Health and Human Services.

National Institute on Aging Age Page (1995a). *Hearing and older people.* Washington D.C.: U.S. Department of Health and Human Services.

National Institute on Aging Age Page (1995b). *Don't take it easy exercise.* Washington D.C.: U.S. Department of Health and Human Services.

National Institute on Aging Age Page (1995c). *Aging and your eyes.* Washington DC: U.S. Department of Health and Human Services.

National Institute on Aging Age Page (1995d). *Sexuality in later life.* Washington DC: U.S. Department of Health and Human Services.

National Institute on Aging Age Page (1996a) *Urinary incontinence.* Washington DC: U.S. Department of Health and Human Services.

National Institute on Aging Age Page (1996b). *Arthritis advice.* Washington DC: U.S. Department of Health and Human Services

National Institute on Aging Age Page (1996c). *Osteoporosis: The silent bone thinner.* Washington D.C.: U.S. Department of Health and Human Services.

National Institute on Aging (1998). *Preventing falls and fractures.* Washington D.C.: National Institutes of Health.

National Institutes of Health (1997). *Disability rates among older Americans decline dramatically.* Washington, D.C.: National Institutes of Health.

National Institutes of Health (2001). *Dramatic decline in disability continues for older Americans.* National Institutes of Health: Washington D.C. www.nia.nih.gov/news/pr/2001/0507.htm [September, 2003].

National Institute of Health (2001). *Exercise: A guide from the National Institute on Aging.* Washington, D.C.: U.S. Department of Health and Human Services. NIH Publication No. 01-4258.

National Institute of Mental Health (2003*). Older adults: Depression and suicide facts.* www.nimh.nih.gov/publical/elderlydepsuicide.cfm [September, 2003].

National Mental Health Association (1996). Depression and later life. Alexandria, VA: National Mental Health Association. www.nmha.org/infoctr/factsheets/22.cfm [March, 1999].

National Mental Health Association (2003). *Depression in later life.* www.nmha.org/infoctr/factsheets/22.cfm [September, 2003].

National Senior Games Association. (2003). www.nsga.com [July, 2003].

National Sporting Goods Association. (2003). Fitness equipment purchases by age and gender. www.nsga.org/public/pages/index.cfm?pageid=166 [January, 2003].

National Sporting Goods Association. (2003). Golf equipment purchases by age and gender. www.nsga.org/public/pages/index.cfm? [January, 2003].

Neugarten, B. L. (1964). Personality in middle and later life. New York: Atherton Press.

Neugarten, B. (1968). Adult personality: Toward a psychology of the life cycle. In B. Neugarten (ed.), *Middle age and aging: A reader in social psychology.* Chicago: University of Chicago Press.

Neugarten, B. L. (1977). Personality and aging. In J. E. Birren & K. W. Schaie (eds.), *Handbook of the psychology of aging.* New York: Van Nostrand Reinhold, 626–649.

Neugarten, B. L., Havighurst, R. J., & Tobin, S. S. (1961). The measurement of life satisfaction. *The Gerontologist,* 16, 134–143.

Neugarten, B. L., Havighurst, R. J., & Tobin, S. S. (1968). Personality and patterns of aging. In B. L. Neugarten (ed.), *Middle age and aging.* Chicago: University of Chicago, 77–102.

Neulinger, J. (1981). To leisure: An introduction. Boston: Allyn and Bacon.

Newman, S., Ward, C. R., Smith, T. B., Wilsson, J. O., McCrea, J. M., Calhoun, G., & Kingson, E. (1997). Intergenerational programs: Past, present, and future. Washington, D.C.: Taylor & Francis.

New York Hospital Cornell Medical Center (1996). Fact sheet: Dementia. White Plains, NY: New York Hospital—Cornell Medical Center. noah.cuny.edu/illness/mentalhealth/cornell/conditions/dementia.html [March, 1999].

Nied, R. J. & Franklin, B. (2002). Promoting and prescribing exercise for the elderly. *American Family Physician,* 65, 419-26, 427-8.

North Carolina Division of Aging (2003). Residents' rights. www.dhhs.state.nc.us/aging/rights.htm [September, 2003].

O'Brien-Cousins, S. & Burgess, A. (1992). Perspectives on older adults in physical activity and sports. *Educational Gerontology,* (18), 461-481.

O'Neill, W. (1991). Women: The unleisured majority. *World Leisure and Recreation*, 33 (3), 6–10.

Ostroff, J. (1989). An aging market. American Demographics, May, 26–28, 33, 58–59.

Over, R. & Thomas, P. (1995). Age and skilled psychomotor performance: A comparison of younger and older golfers. *International Journal of Aging and Human Development*, 41(1), 1-12.

Paffenberg, R. S., Hyde, R. T., & Dow, A. (1991). Health benefits of physical activity. In B. L. Driver, P. J. Brown & G. L. Peterson (eds.), *Benefits of leisure*. State College, PA: Venture Publishing, 49–57.

Palmore, E. (1990). Ageism: Negative and positive. New York: Springer.

Palmore, E. (2001) The ageism survey: First findings. *The Gerontologist*, 41, 572-575.

Parmelee, L. S. & Lawton, M. P. (1990). The design of special environments for the aged. In J. E. Birren & K. W. Schaie (eds.), *Handbook of the psychology of aging, 3rd edition*. San Diego: Academic Press, 465–488.

Parks, J. (May, 2003). Article of the month: Stress Matters. www.usms.org/fitness/articleofthemonth.php?a=16 [July, 2003].

Pasupathi, M. and Lockenhoff, C. E. (2002). Ageist behavior. In Nelson, T.D. (ed.). *Ageism: Stereotyping and prejudice against older people*. Cambridge, MA: The MIT Press, 201-246.

Pasuth, P. M. & Bengston, V. L. (1988). Sociological theories of aging: Current perspectives and future directions. In J. E. Birren & V. L. Bengston (eds.), *Emergent theories of aging*. New York: Springer, 333–355.

Patterson, I. (1996). Participation in leisure activities by older adults after a stressful life event: The loss of a spouse. *International Journal of Aging and Human Development*, 42, 123–142.

Patterson, I. & Carpenter, G. (1994). Participation in leisure activities after the death of a spouse. *Leisure Sciences*, 16, 105–117.

Payne, L., Mowen, A., & Oserga-Smith, E. (2002). An examination of the preferences and behaviors among urban residents: The role of residential location, race, and age. *Leisure Sciences*, 24(2), 181-198.

Pearlin, L. (1975) Sex roles and depression. In N. Patan & L. Gensburg (eds.), *Life-span Development Psychology: Normative Life Crises*. New York: Academic Press.

Pearlin, L. I., Mullan, J. T., Semple, S., & Skaff, M. M. (1990). Caregiving and the stress process: An overview of concepts and their measures. *The Gerontologist*, 30, 583–594.

Penalta, L., & Uysal, M. (September, 1992). Aging and the future travel market. *Parks & Recreation*, 96-99.

Pennsylvania Department on Aging (undated). Caregivers: Practical health.

Peterson, C. A. & Gunn, S. L. (1984). Therapeutic recreation program design: Principles and procedures. Englewood Cliffs, NJ: Prentice Hall.

Pfister, R. E. (1993). Ethnic identity: A new avenue for understanding leisure and recreation preferences. In A. Ewert, D. Chavez, & A. Magill (eds.), *Culture, conflict and the wildland-urban interface*. Boulder, CO: Westview Press, 53–65.

Plog, S.C. (2004). *Leisure travel: A marketing handbook.* Upper Saddle River, NJ: Pearson Education, Inc.

Prado, C. G. (1986). Rethinking how we age: A new view of the aging mind. Westport, CT: Greenwood Press.

Pynoos, J. & Golant, S. (1996). Housing and living arrangements for the elderly. In R. H. Binstock and L. K. George (eds.), *Handbook of aging and the social sciences.* San Diego: Academic Press, pp. 303–324.

Quadagno, J. & Reid, J. (1999). The political economy perspective in aging. In Bengston, V. L. & Schaie, K. W. (eds.), *Handbook of theories of aging.* New York: Springer, 344-356.

Quinn, J. F. & Burkhauser, R. V. (1990). Work and retirement. In R. H. Binstock & L. K. George (eds.), *Handbook of aging and the social sciences.* San Diego: Academic Press.

Ragan, A. M. & Bowen, A. M. (2001). Improving attitudes regarding the elderly population: The effects of information and reinforcement for change. *The Gerontologist,* 41, 511-515.

Regnier, V. (1975). Neighborhood planning for the urban elderly. In D. Woodruff & J. E. Birren (eds.), *Aging: Scientific perspectives and social issues.* New York: D. Van Nostrand, 295–312.

Reker, G. T., & Wong, P. T. (1988). Aging as an individual process: Toward a theory of personal meaning. In J. E. Birren & V. L. Bengston (eds.), *Emergent theories of aging.* New York: Springer, 214–216.

Riley, M. W. (1971). Social gerontology and the age stratification of society. *The Gerontologist,* 11, 19–87.

Riley, M. W. (1985). Age strata in social systems. In R. H. Binstock & E. Shanas (eds.), *Handbook of aging the social sciences,* 2nd edition. New York: Van Nostrand Reinhold, 369–411.

Robertson, C. & Welcher, D. (1978). Light shed on lives of visually impaired. *Perspectives on Aging,* 7, 17–21.

Robinson, J. (1989a). Time's up. American Demographics, July, 33–35.

Robinson, J. (1989b). Who's doing the housework? American Demographics. December, 24–28.

Robinson, J. (1991). Quitting time. American Demographics, May, 34–36.

Robinson, J. & Godbey, G. (1997). *Time for life: The surprising way Americans use their time.* University Park, PA: Penn State Press.

Robinson, J.P. & Godbey, G. (September, 1993). Has fitness peaked? *American Demographics,* 36-42.

Robinson, J.P. & Godbey, G. (1993). Sport, fitness and the gender gap. *Leisure Sciences,* 15, 291-307.

Robinson, J.P. & Godbey, G. (June, 1996). The great American slowdown. *American Demographics,* 42-48.

Robinson, J.P. & Godbey, G. (1998). Trend, gender and status differences in Americans' perceived stress. *Society and Leisure,* 21(2), 473-489.

Robinson, J.P., Werner, P. & Godbey, G. (October, 1997). Freeing up the golden years. *American Demographics*, 20-24.

Rockstein, M. & Sussman, M. (1979). Biology of aging. Belmont, CA: Wadsworth.

Rogers, W. A., Meyer, B., Walker, N. & Fisk, A. D. (1998). Functional limitations to daily living tasks in the aged: a focus group analysis. *Human Factors*, 40, 111-126.

Rosenberg, J. H. (1993). As you age: 10 keys to a longer, healthier, more vital life. *Nestle Worldview*, 5 (2), 2–3.

Rosow, J. (1974). Socialization to old age. Berkeley: University of California Press.

Rowe, J. W. & Kahn, R. L. (1998). Successful aging. New York: Random House.

Rudman, W.J. (1986). Sport as a part of successful aging. *American Behavioral Scientist (Special Issue: Developmental tasks in later life)*, 29(4), 453-470.

Ruth, J. & Coleman, P. (1996) Personality and aging: Coping and management of the self in later life. In J. E. Birren, & K. W. Schaie (eds.), *Handbook of the psychology of aging, 4th edition*. San Diego: Academic Press

Ryan, J. E. (1993). Building theory for gerontological nursing. In E. M Baines (ed.), *Perspectives on gerontological nursing*. Newbury Park, CA: Sage, 29–40.

Ryan, R. M. & Deci, E. L. (2000). Intrinsic and extrinsic motivations: Classic definitions and new directions. *Contemporary Educational Psychology*, 25, 54-67.

Ryan, R. M. & LaGuardia, J. G. (2000). What is being optimized?: Self-determination theory and basic psychological needs. Qualls, S. H. & Abeles, N., (eds.), *Psychology and the aging revolution: How we adapt to longer life* (145-172). Washington, D.C.: American Psychological Association.

Ryff, C. D., Kwan, C. M. L., & Singer, B. H. (2001). Personality and aging: Flourishing Agendas and future challenges. In Birren, J. E. & Schaie, K.W. (eds.), *Handbook of the psychology of aging*. San Diego, Academic Press, 477-499.

Sabin, E. (1993). Social relationships and mortality among the elderly. *Journal of Applied Gerontology*, 12 (1), 44–60.

Samdahl, D. (1987). A symbolic interactionist model of leisure: Theory and empirical support. *Leisure Sciences*, 10, 27–39.

Saul, S. (1993). Meaningful life activities for elderly residents of residential health care facilities. *Activities, Adaptation and Aging*, 79–86.

Saxon, S. & Ettel, M. (1987). Physical change and aging. New York: The Theresias Press.

Scanland, S. G. & Emershaw, L. E. (1993). Reality orientation and validation therapy: Dementia, depression, and functional status. *Journal of Gerontological Nursing*, 19(6), 7–11.

Scannell, T., & Roberts, A. (1994). Young and old serving together: Meeting community needs through intergenerational partnerships. Washington, D.C.: Generations United.

Schaie (1990). Intellectual development in adulthood. In J. E. Birren & K. W. Schaie (eds.), *Handbook of the psychology of aging, 3rd edition*. San Diego: Academic Press, 291–309.

Schaie, K.W. (1994). *Longitudinal studies in cognitive aging*. Cognitive Aging Conference, Atlanta, GA. http://geron.psu.edu/reprints/300/RP-350.pdf.

Schaie, K. W. (1996). Intellectual development in adulthood. In J. E. Birren & K. W. Schaie (eds.), *Handbook of the psychology of aging, 4th edition*. San Diego: Academic Press, 266-286.

Schaie, K. W. & Hertzog, C. C. (1986). Toward a comprehensive model of adult intellectual development: Contributions of the Seattle Longitudinal study. In R. J. Sternberg (ed.), *Advances in human intelligence* (3). Hillsdale, NJ: Erlbaum.

Schaie, K.W. & Willis, S. L. (1999). Theories of everyday life and aging. In Bengston, V. L. & Schaie, K. W. (eds.), *Handbook of theories of aging*. New York: Springer Publishing.

Scherer, M. (2002). Matching consumers and appropriate assistive technologies. D. Olson & F. DeRuyter (eds.), *A clinician guide to assistive technology*, 3-14. St Louis, Missouri: Mosby.

Schlicht, J., Camaione, D., & Owen, S. (2001). Effect of intense strength training on standing balance, walking speed, and sit-to-stand performance in older adults. *Journal of Gerontology: Medical Sciences*, 56A(5), M281-M286.

Schneider, E. L. & Rowe, J. W. (1990). *Handbook of the biology of aging, 3rd edition*. San Diego: Academic Press.

Schonfield, D. (1982). Who is stereotyping whom and why? *The Gerontologist*, 2, 267–272.

Schooler, C. (1990). Psychosocial factors and effective cognitive functioning in adulthood. In J. E. Birren & K. W. Schaie (eds.), *Handbook of the psychology of aging*. San Diego: Academic, 347–358.

Schor, J.B. (1991). *The overworked American: The unexpected decline of leisure*. New York: Basic Books.

Schroots, J.J.F. (1995a). Gerodynamics: Toward a branching theory of aging. *Canadian Journal on Aging*, 14 (1), 74-81.

Schroots, J.J.F. (1995b). Psychological models of aging. *Canadian Journal on Aging*, 14, 46-66

Schroots, J. J. F. (1996) Theoretical developments in the psychology of aging. *The Gerontologist*, 36, 742–748.

Schultz, R. & Ewen, R. (1993). Adult development and aging myths and emerging realities. New York: Macmillan.

Schwartz, A. N. (1975). Planning macro-environments for the aged. In D. Woodruff and J. E. Birren (eds.), *Aging: Scientific perspectives and social issues*. New York: D. Van Nostrand, 279–294.

Searle, M. S., Mahon, M. J., Iso-Ahola, S. E., Sdrolia, H. A., & van Dyck, J. (1995). Enhancing a sense of independence and psychological well-being among the elderly: A field experiment. *Journal of Leisure Research*, 27, 107–124.

Senior women's travel: For the 50+ woman with a passion for travel. www.poshnosh.com [July, 2003].

Shary, J. M., & Iso-Ahola, S. E. (1989). Effects of a control-relevant intervention on nursing home residents' perceived competence and self-esteem. *Therapeutic Recreation Journal*, 7-16.

Shaull, S. & Gramann, J. (1998). The effect of cultural assimilation on the importance of family-related and nature-related recreation among Hispanic Americans. *Journal of Leisure Research*, 30(1), 47-63.

Shoemaker, S. (1989). Segmentation of the senior pleasure travel market. *Journal of Travel Research*, 27, 14–21.

Shore, B. A., Lerman, D. C., Smith, R. G., Iwata, B. A., & DeLeon, I. G. (1995). Direct assessment of quality of care in a geriatric nursing home. *Journal of Applied Behavior Analysis*, 28, 435-448.

Shore, H. (1976). Designing a training program for understanding sensory losses in aging. *The Gerontologist*, 16, 157–165.

Sibley, B. (2002). *Nuns' Gift to Alzheimer's Research: the Nun Study Reveals Clues about Alzheimer's*. http://www.suite101.com/article.cfm/15157/90363 [September, 2003].

Siegenhaler, K. (1999). Sweating with the oldies: Activity and successful aging. *Parks and Recreation*, 34(8), 1-5.

Siegenthaler, K. (August, 1999). Sweating with the oldies: Physical activity and successful aging. *Parks & Recreation*, 26-29.

Siengenthaler, K. & Thomas, E. (2001). Golf's contribution to successful aging: Perceptions of older golfers. *Abstracts of the 2001 Leisure Research Symposium*, National Recreation and Park Association, Ashburn, VA, 31.

Silverstein, M. & Parker, M. G. (2002). Leisure activities and quality of life among the oldest old in Sweden *Research on Aging*, 24, 528-547.

Simoneau, G. G. & Leibowitz, H. W. (1996). Posture, gait, and falls. In J. E. Birren & K. W. Schaie (eds.), *Handbook of the psychology of aging*. San Diego: Academic Press.

Simonton, D. K. (1988). Age and outstanding achievement: What do we know after a century of research? *Psychological Bulletin*, 104, 251–267.

Simonton, D. K. (1990). Creativity and wisdom in aging. In J. E. Birren & K. W. Schaie (eds.), *Handbook of the psychology of aging*. San Diego: Academic Press, 320–329.

Singleton, J., Forbes, W. & Agwani, N. (1993). Stability of activity across the lifespan. *Activities, Adaptation & Aging*, 18(1), 19-27.

Sloane, P., Mitchell, C. M., Weisman, G., Zimmerman, S., Foley, K., Lynn, M., Calkins, M., Lawton, M.P., Teresi, J., Grant, L., Lindeman, D., & Montgomery, R. (2002). The Therapeutic Environment Screening Survey for Nursing Homes (TESS-NH): An observational instrument for assessing the physical environment of institutional settings for persons with dementia. *Journal of Gerontology: Social Science*, 57B(2), 69-78

Smale, B. & Dupuis, S.L. (1993). The relationship between leisure activity participation and psychological well being across the lifespan. *Journal of Applied Recreation Research,* 18(4), 281-300.

Small, G.W., LaRue, A., Komo, S., & Kaplan, A. (1997). Mnemonics usage and cognitive decline in age-associated memory impairment. *International Psychogeriatrics,* 9(1), 47–56.

Smith, C.L. & Stourandt, M. (1997). Physical activity participation in older adults: A comparison of competitors, noncompetitors, and nonexercisers. *Journal of Aging and Physical Activity,* (5), 98-110.

Smith, I. (1999). *Sight, hearing loss changes life. University of Iowa Hospital and Clinics,* Department of Internal Medicine. http://www.vh.org/adult/patient/internalmedicine/aba30/1999/sensoryloss.html [September, 2003].

Snowdon, D (2001). *Aging with Grace: What the Nun Study Teaches Us about Leading Longer, Healthier, and More Meaningful Lives.* New York, NY: Doubleday.

Spacapan S., & Oskamp, S. (1989). Introduction to the social psychology of aging. In S. Spacapan & S. Oskamp (eds.), *The social psychology of aging.* Newbury Park, CA: Sage, 9–24.

Stamps, S. & Stamps, M. (1985). Race, class, and leisure activities of urban residents. *Journal of Leisure Research,* 17, 40–56.

Stanley, D. & Freysinger, V.J. (1995). The impact of age, health and sex on the frequency of older adults' leisure activity participation: A longitudinal study. *Activities, Adaptation & Aging,* 19(3), 31-42.

Starkes, J.L, Weir, P.J., Singh, P., Hodges, N.J. & Kerr, T. (1999). Aging and retention of sport expertise. *International Journal of Sport Psychology,* (30), 283-301.

Stebbins, R.A.. (1992). *Amateurs, professionals and serious leisure.* Montreal: McGill-Queen's University Press.

Stebbins, R. A. (2000*). World Leisure International position statement on educating for serious leisure.* World Leisure Commission on Education. http;//www.wordleisure.org/Commissions/Education/edcompospaper%25seriousleisure.pdf [July 1, 2003].

Stebbins, R. A. (2001). Serious leisure. *Society,* 38(4), 53-58.

Steinfeld, E. & Shea, S. M. (undated). Enabling home environments: Strategies for aging in place. Buffalo, NY: IDEA—Center for Inclusive Design & Environmental Access, SUNY Buffalo.

Stemberg, R. & Wagner R. (1986). Practical intelligence. Cambridge: Cambridge University Press.

Sternberg, R. J. & Lubart, T. I. (2001). Wisdom and creativity. In Birren, J. E. & Schaie, K. W. (eds.), *Handbook of the psychology of aging ,* 5, San Diego: Academic Press, 500-522.

Stodolska, M. & Jackson, E. (1998). Discrimation in leisure and work experienced by a white ethnic minority group. *Journal of Leisure Research,* 30(1), 23-46.

Strain, L. A., Grabusic, C. C., Searle, M. S., & Dunn, N. J. (2002). Continuing and ceasing leisure activities in later life: A longitudinal study. *The Gerontologist.* 42, 217-223.

Streib, G. F. (1985). Social stratification and aging. In R. H. Binstock & E. Shanas (eds.), *Handbook of aging and the social sciences 2nd edition*. New York: Van Nostrand Reinhold, 339–368.

Streib, G. F. (1993). The life course of activities and retirement communities. In J. R. Kelly (ed.), *Activity and aging: Staying involved in later life*. Newbury Park: Sage, 246–263.

Sturnbo, N. & Thompson, S. (1988). Leisure education: A manual of activities and resources. Peoria: Center for Independent Living and Easter Seals Center.

Taylor, D. (1992). Identity in ethnic leisure pursuits. San Francisco: Meders Research University Press.

Taylor, H. (July 8, 1998) The Harris Poll #35: The increasing popularity of gardening – which displaces fishing as America's favorite leisure time activity discounting reading and watching tv. Retrieved from www.harrisinteractive.com/harris_poll/index.asp?PID=173 2003[March, 2003].

Taylor, R. & Chatters, L. (1986). Church based informal support among elderly blacks. *The Gerontologist*, 26, 637–642.

Teaff, J. (1991). Leisure and life satisfaction of older Catholic women religious. World *Leisure and Recreation*, 33 (3), 27–29. 9

Teaff, J. & Turpin, T. (June, 1996). Travel and the elderly. *Parks & Recreation*, 16, 18, 20, 22.

Teague, M. L. (1987). Health promotion: Achieving high-level wellness in the later years. Indianapolis: Benchmark Press.

Tedrick, T. (1982). Leisure competency: A goal for aging Americans in the 1980s. In N. Osgood (ed.), *Life after work: Retirement, leisure, recreation and the elderly*. New York: Praeger, 315–318.

Tedrick, T. (1989). Images of aging through leisure: From pluralistic ignorance to master status trait? *Journal of Leisurability*, 16(3), 15–19.

Tedrick, T. & Boyd, R. (1992). Leisure in the lives of older Black women. Leisure Research Symposium, National Recreation and Parks Association Annual Conference, Cincinnati, OH.

Tedrick, T. & Boyd, R. (1999, October). Older African American men and leisure. Proceedings of the Leisure Research Symposium, National Recreation and Park Association Congress, Nashville, TN.

Tedrick, R. & Green, E. R. (1995). Activity experiences and programming within long-term care facilities. State College, PA: Venture.

Tedrick, T. & MacNeil, R. (1991). Sociodemographics of older adults: Implications for leisure programming. *Activities, Adaptation & Aging*, 15(3), 73–91.

Texas Agricultural Extension Service (1995a). Fact sheet on aging: Changes in taste. College Station, TX: Texas Agricultural Extension Service, Texas A & M University.

Texas Agricultural Extension Service (1995b). Fact sheet on aging: Changes in hearing. College Station, TX: Texas Agricultural Extension Service, Texas A&M University.

Texas Agricultural Extension Service (1995c). Fact sheet on aging: Changes in vision. College Station, TX: Texas Agricultural Extension Service, Texas A&M University.

Thomas, D. & Butts, F. (1998). Assessing leisure motivations and satisfactions of international Elderhostel participants. *Journal of Travel and Tourism Marketing*, 7(1), 31-38.

Timiras, P. S. & Hudson, D. B. (1993). Physiology of aging: Current and future. In B. Vellas, J. L. Albarede, & P. J. Garry (eds.), *Facts and research in gerontology*. New York: Springer Publishing, 31–39.

Tinsley, H. E. A. & Teaff, J. D. (1983). The psychological benefits of leisure activities for the elderly: A manual and final report of an investigation. Carbondale, IL: Southern Illinois University Department of Psychology.

Tinsley, H. E. A., Teaff, J. D., Colbs, S. L., & Kaufman, N. (1985). A system of classifying leisure activities in terms of the psychological benefits of participation reported by older persons. *Journal of Gerontology*, 49, 172–178.

Tinsley, H., Tinsley, D. & Croskeys, C. (2002). Park usage, social milieu, and psychosocial benefits of park use reported by older urban park users from four ethnic groups. *Leisure Sciences*, 24(2), 199-218.

Tornstam, L. (1992). The quo vadis of gerontology: On the scientific paradigm in gerontology. *The Gerontologist*, 32, 318-325.

Toseland, R. W., Diehl, M., Freeman, K., Manzanares, T., Naleppa, M., & McCallion, P. (1997) The impact of validation group therapy on nursing home residents with dementia. *Journal of Applied Gerontology*, 16(1), 31–50.

Transitions Abroad (2003). www.transitionsabroad.com/listings/travel/senior/resources.shtml [July, 2003].

Trappe, S., Costill D., Vukovich, M., Jones, J., & Melham, T. (1996). Aging among elite distance runners—a 22 year longitudinal study. *Journal of Applied Physiology*, 80(1), 285-290.

Troll, L. (1982). Continuations: Adult development. Philadelphia: W. B. Saunders.

Tsutsumi, T., Don, B., Zaichkowsky, L. Takenaka, K. & Oka, K. (1998). Comparison of high and moderate intensity of strength training on mood and anxiety on older adults. *Perceptual and Motor Skills*, (87), 1003-1011.

United Media Enterprises (1983). Where does time go? New York: Newspaper Enterprise Association.

U.S. Census Bureau (1997). Sixty-five plus in the United States. Washington, D.C.: U.S. Census Bureau. www.census.gov/socdemo/www/agebrief.html [March, 1999].

U.S. Census Bureau, *Statistical Abstract of the United States: 2002*. (2002). Washington, D.C.: U.S. Government Printing Office (1955-2001 editions used in material in chapter eight).

U.S. Congress. (1987). *Omnibus Budget Reconciliation Act of 1987*. Washington, D.C.: 100th Congress, 1st Session, Pub. Law, 100-203.

U.S. Department of Health and Human Services (1999*). Mental health: A report of the Surgeon General.* Rockville, MD: U.S. Department of Health and Human Services, Center for Mental Health Services, National Institutes of Health, National Institute of Mental Health.

U.S. Department of Health and Human Services. (November, 2000). *Healthy People 2010, 2nd edition.* With understanding and improving health and objectives for improving health (2 volumes). Washington, D.C.: U.S. Government Printing Office.

U. S. Department of Health and Human Services (2002a). *Alzheimer's disease: Unraveling the mystery.* Rockville, MD: U. S. Department of Health and Human Services, Center for Mental Health Services, National Institutes of Health, National Institute of Mental Health.

U. S. Department of Health and Human Services (2002b). *Alzheimer's disease medication fact sheet.* Rockville, MD: U.S. Department of Health and Human Services, Center for Mental Health Services, National Institutes of Health, National Institute of Mental Health. www.alzheimers.org/pubs/medications.htm [September, 2003].

U. S. Department of Health and Human Services (2002c). *Caregiver guide: Tips for caregivers of people with Alzheimer's Disease.* Washington D.C.: National Institute of Health.

U.S. Senate. (2002). *Assisted Living Reexamined: Developing policy and practices to ensure quality care.* Washington, D.C.: 107th Congress, 2nd Session, Serial No. 107-24.

U.S. Senate Special Committee on Aging (1987). Developments in aging: Volume 3. Washington, D.C.: U.S. Government Printing Office.

U.S. Senate Special Committee on Aging, American Association of Retired Persons, Federal Council on Aging, U.S. Administration on Aging (1991). Aging America: Trends and predictions. Washington, D.C.: U.S. Department of Health and Human Services.

U.S. State Department, Bureau of Consular Affairs (2003). Travel tips for older Americans. http://travel.state.gov/olderamericans.html [July, 2003].

United States Masters Swimming Top Ten (2003). www.usms.org/comp/tt/toptenlist.php [July, 2003].

Vaillant, G. E. (2002). *Aging well: Surprising guideposts to a happier life from the landmark Harvard Study of Adult Development.* Boston: Little, Brown and Company.

Validation Training Institute (1997). What is validation? Cleveland, OH: The Validation Training Institute. www.vfvalidation.org/whatis.html [March, 1999].

Vallerand, R., O'Connor, B., & Blais, M. (1989). Life satisfaction of elderly individuals in regular community housing, and high and low selfdetermination nursing homes. *International Journal of Aging and Human Development, 28,* 277–283.

Verbrugge, L. M., Gruber-Baldini, A.L. & Fozard, J. L. (1996). Age differences and age changes in activities: Baltimore Longitudinal Study of Aging. *Journal of Gerontology: Social Sciences,* 51B (1), S30-S41.

Vertinsky, P. (2000). Externally wounded women? Feminist perspectives on physical activity and aging or a woman's p(l)ace in the marathon of life. *Journal of Aging and Physical Activity,* (8), 386-406.

Vierck, E. (1990). Fact book on aging. Santa Barbara: ABC-Clio.

Voelkl, J. (1986). Effects of institutionalization upon residents of extended care facilities. *Activities, Adaptation & Aging,* 8(3/4), 37–46.

Voelkl, J. E. (1993). Activity among older adults in institutional settings. In J. R. Kelly (ed.), *Activity and aging: Staying involved in later life*. Newbury Park: Sage, 231–245.

Voelkl, J., Battisto, D., Carson, J., & Green, D. (2003). Efficacy of a family model in long term care: integrating meaningful activities into the organizational culture and physical space. Clemson University, Clemson, SC: Unpublished manuscript.

Voelkl, J. E., Fries, B. T., & Galecki, A. T. (1995). Predictors of nursing home residents' participation in activity programs. *The Gerontologist*, 35, 44–51.

Voelkl, J. E., Winkelhake, K., Jeffries, J., & Yoshioka, N. (in press). Nursing home residents' use of public areas: A case study. *Therapeutic Recreation Journal*.

Wahl, H. W. (2001). Environmental influences on aging and behavior. In Birren, J. E. & Schaie, K. W. (eds.), *Handbook of the Psychology of Aging*. San Diego: Academic Press, 215–237.

Wall, G. (1989). Perspectives on recreation and the environment. In E. L. Jackson & T. L. Burton (eds.), *Understanding leisure and recreation: Mapping the past, charting the future*. State College, PA: Venture, 453–480.

Wallace, J., Flippo, K., Barcus, M., & Behrmann, M. (1995) Legislative foundation of assistive technology policy in the United States . K. Flippo; K.; Inge; & M. Barcus (eds.), *Assistive technology: A resource for school, work and community*. Baltimore, MD. Paul H. Brooks.

Ward, R. (1984). The aging experience: An introduction to social gerontology. New York: Harper and Row.

Washburne, R. (1978). Black underparticipation in wildland recreation: Alternative explanations. *Leisure Sciences*, 1, 175–189.

Weaverdyck, S. E. (1991). Developing an encouraging environment for residents with dementia. *Long-term Care*, 1 (2), 19–20.

Weiner, M. B., Brok, A. J. & Snadowsky, A. M. (1987). *Working with the aged: Practical approaches in the institution and community, 2nd edition*. Norwalk: Appleton-Century-Crofts.

Wells, L. & Singer, C. (1988). Quality of life in institutions for the elderly: Maximizing well-being. *The Gerontologist*, 28, 266–269.

West, M. & Grafman, J. (1998). Cognitive neuroscience section: Memory exercises. Washington D.C.: National Institutes of Health. www.intra.ninds.nih.gov/mnb/cns/memory.html [March, 1999].

West, R., Wincour, G., Ergis, A, & Saint-Cyr, J. (1998) The contribution of impaired working memory monitoring to performance of the self-ordered pointing task in normal aging and Parkinson's disease. *Neuropsychology*, 12, 546-554.

Whitbourne, S. K. (2002) *The aging individual: Physical and psychological perspectives*, 2. New York: Springer Publishing Company.

White J. (1975). The relative importance of education and income as predictors in outdoor recreation. *Journal of Leisure Research*, 7, 191–199.

Williams, M. L. (1972). One of the best retirement centers as seen by one of the residents. *The Gerontologist*, 12, 39–42.

Willis, S. L. (1987). Cognitive training and everyday performance. In K. W. Schaie (ed.), *Annual review of gerontology and geriatrics* (7). New York: Springer, 159–188.

Willis, S. L. (1992). Cognition and everyday competence. In K. W. Schaie & M. P. Lawton (eds.), *Annual review of gerontology and geriatrics*, (11). New York: Springer, 80–109.

Willis, S. L. (1996). Everyday problem solving. In J. E. Birren & K. W. Schaie (eds.), *Handbook of the psychology of aging.* San Diego: Academic Press.

Willis, S. L. & Schaie, K. W. (1986). Training the elderly on the ability factors of spatial orientation and inductive reasoning. *Psychology and Aging*, 1, 239–247.

Wills, A. (2003). Transitions abroad: Senior travel resources. Retrieved from www.transitionsabroad.com/listings/travel/senior/resources.stml [July, 2003].

Wold, G. (1993). Basic geriatric nursing. St. Louis: Mosby.

Women and Aging Newsletter (1996). Memory loss: Is it inevitable? Waltham, MA: The National Policy and Resource Center on Women and Aging, Brandeis University.

Woodard, M. D. (1988). Class, regionality, and leisure among urban black Americans. *Journal of Leisure Research*, 20, 87–105.

World Association of Veteran Athletics. (2003). www.wava.org [July, 2003].

Zimmer, Z., Brayley, R. & Searle, M. (1995). Whether to go and where to go: Identification of important influences on seniors' decisions to travel. *Journal of Travel Research*, (33), 3-10.

Zimmerman, S., Scott, A. C., Park, N. S., Hall, S. A., Wetherby, M. M., Gruber-Baldini, A. L., & Morgan, L. A. (2003). Social engagement and its relationship to service provision in residential care and assisted living. *Social Work Research*, 27(1), 6-18.

Zuzanek, J., Robinson, J.P. & Iwasaki, Y. (1998). The relationships between stress, health and physically active leisure as a function of life-cycle. *Leisure Sciences*, 20(4), 253-275.

Zuzanek, J. & Smale, B. (1997). More work–less leisure? Changing allocations of time in Canada, 1981 to 1992. *Society and Leisure*, 20(1), 73-106.

INDEX

housing options for, 264–65
leisure life in, 265–66
needs assessments for, 275–77
profile of residents, 263–64
programs and services in, 268–74
companionship, 134
compensation, 38–39, 134
competence, 7, 140–43, 152
constraints, 159–61
constricted pattern, 27
continuing care retirement community
(CCRC), 277–79
continuity theory, 25–28, 175–76, 185–86
control, 249–50
coping, 142, 272–73
creativity, 3, 89–93, 139
crime, 225, 234
critical distance, 234
crosslinking theory, 48
cross sectional studies, 77
cueing, 255
custodial care, 245
day care programs, 269
deleteriousness, 43–44
delirium, 103–4
dementia, 104, 250–51, 255–56
demographics, of aging, 14–19
depersonalization, 272
depression, 101–2, 273
Depth Hypothesis, 159
developmental tasks, 97–98
diabetes, 17–18, 44, 60–61
diabetic retinopathy, 64–65
diet and nutrition, 54, 56, 59, 61, 121, 271
differential access model, 211–12
differential aging, 36–37
discrimination, 8–9, 11–14, 186
disengaged pattern, 26
disengagement theory, 22–24
disorganized pattern, 27
Division of Aging and Seniors, 67
double jeopardy, 207

economic characteristics, 17
economic concerns, 133, 267
economic production, modernization
theory and, 33
Eden Alternative, 243, 258–59
educational travel, 198–200
Eldercare Locator, 269
Elderhostel, 152–53, 199–200
embolisms, 56
emotional exhaustion, 272
endocrine system, 60–61

endocrine theory, 48
enthusiasm, 90
entropy, 37
environment
for Alzheimer's disease, 113
See also living environments
environmental cues, 229
environmental design, 251–53
environmental press model, 226
environmental psychology, 224
environmental stimulation, 229–30
environmental support, 230
episodic memory, 81
equilibrium, 37
error theories, 48–49
escape, 155–56
escort services, 270
ethnicity, 15–16
quality of research knowledge and, 203–6
theories explaining leisure participation
and, 206–12
See also race
ethnicity theory, 207–9
everyday competence, 223
exercise, 53–54
aging and, 123–24, 176–78
as leisure for aging persons, 178–79
motivation for, 182–83
preventing aging, 47, 159
research findings of, 179–89
See also sports
explicit memory, 80–81
expressive leisure, 149–51
external aids, 84–85
extrinsic motivation, 119

falls, 54–55
false memory, 82
family making, 259–61
family rooms, 252
family ties, 29–30
fear, 130
feet, 52
feminist theory, 186
FFIGs, 129–30
financial security, 133, 267
flow experience, 131, 155
focused pattern, 26
freedom, 119, 225, 234
free radical theory, 48
friendship, 132
frustration, 130

gait, 52, 53

factors influencing, 226–28
macro environments, 233–36
micro environments, 228–33
Logon, Victor, 145–47
longitudinal studies, 78
long-term care
bill of rights for residents, 246–49
defined, 239–40
facility types, 243–46
program models for, 255–62
program strategies, 249–53
promoting quality of life with leisure,
241–43

MacArthur Foundation Study of Successful
Aging, 4, 47
macular degeneration, 64–65
maintenance, 254–55
marginality theory, 206–7
marital status, 16–17
mass education, 34
masters events, 191–92
maturity, 97
McLeish, John, 3–4, 92–93
meaningful activity, 125–32
median income, 17
medication
for Alzheimer's disease, 108
memory and, 83
meditation, 56
memory and memory improvement, 79–89
memory clinics, 85
men
African-American, 218–19
disengagement theory and, 23
hearing of, 65–66
leisure activities and, 174–75
life expectancy and, 16
marital status of, 16–17
personality and, 96
reproductive system of, 62
See also gender
mental health, 98–102, 124–25
Mexican Americans, 210
Mild Cognitive Impairment (MCI), 108
mindfulness, 11
mnemonics, 84
mobility, 234, 275
modernization theory, 32–35, 135
motivation
leisure and, 147–59
socialization and, 30
muscle elasticity, 51
muscle mass, 51

musculoskeletal system changes, 51–55
mutual satisfaction, 23
myths, 9–10

nail care, 50
National Association of Counties, 276–77
National Mental Health Association, 101
needs assessment, 275–77
nervous system, 62–63
nonwork opportunities, 136
nursing homes, 16, 239, 244–46
nutrition, 54, 56, 59, 61, 121, 271

occupations, 34
odor, 224
Omnibus Budget Reconciliation Act of
1987, 241
optimization, 38–39
optimum arousal, 156–57
oral health, 59
organ reserve capacity, 44
orienting, 255
osteoporosis, 51

pancreas, 60
Paragraphs About Leisure (PAL), 134
passive dependent personality, 27
passive mastery, 96
Pennsylvania Outdoor Recreation Survey,
208
people effect, 227
perceived control, 249–50
perceived freedom, 119
persistence, 91
personal accomplishments, 272
personal experience theories, 21–28
personal growth, 126–27
Personal Growth Model of Aging, 18
personality and personality styles
aging and, 95–97
continuity theory and, 26–27
personalization, 255
personal meaning, 157–59
philosophical concerns, 267
physical activity. See exercise
physical appearance, 50–51
physical concerns, 267
physical fitness, 88. See also exercise
play, 139
pneumonia, 58
political economy, 32
positive feedback, 30
posture, 52
poverty, 17